China Ethnic Statistical Yearbook 2016

Rongxing Guo

China Ethnic Statistical Yearbook 2016

palgrave
macmillan

Rongxing Guo
Regional Science Association of China
Peking University
Peking, China

ISBN 978-3-319-49198-1 ISBN 978-3-319-49199-8 (eBook)
DOI 10.1007/978-3-319-49199-8

Printed on acid-free paper

This Palgrave Macmillan imprint is published by Springer Nature
The registered company is Springer International Publishing AG
The registered company address is: Gewerbestrasse 11, 6330 Cham, Switzerland

Preface

The objective of this book is to collect and estimate a set of data on the socioeconomic situations of China's 56 ethnic groups.

Although the majority of China's population is of the Han nationality (which accounts for more than 90 % of China's population), the non-Han ethnic groups have a population of more than 100 million. China has officially identified, except for other unknown ethnic groups and foreigners with Chinese citizenship, 55 ethnic minorities. In addition, ethnic minorities vary greatly in size. With a population of more than 15 million, the Zhuang are the largest ethnic minority, and the Lhoba, with a population of only about 3000, the smallest.

China's ethnic diversity has resulted in a special socioeconomic landscape for China itself. However, till present, a complete socioeconomic picture of China's ethnic groups – especially of its smallest ethnic minorities – still remains unclear. How different have been China's ethnic groups in every sphere of daily life and economic development during China's fast transition period? In order to answer these questions, we need a detailed and comparable set of data for each of China's ethnic groups.

There has not been any official statement of China's socioeconomic development from a multi-ethnic dimension. The only official data released can be found in *China Ethnic Statistical Yearbook* (released by the State Ethnic Affairs Commission of the People's Republic of China since 1994). However, as the above Yearbook has only reported the socioeconomic statistics for the minority-based autonomous areas, a complete set of China's multi-ethnic data cannot be derived from it. For instance, only five provincial level minority-based autonomous regions (i.e., Inner Mongolia, Tibet, the Zhuang-based Guangxi, the Hui-based Ningxia, and the Uygur-based Xinjiang) and 30 ethnic minority autonomous divisions at prefecture-level and 120 ethnic minority autonomous divisions at county-level – all of the latter cover China's 16 provinces, three autonomous regions and one municipality directly under the central government – are included in this Yearbook. The entire minority-based autonomous areas, however, account for only less than a half of their total population of the ethnic minorities (see Appendix 3 for details). This means that the Han Chinese has now become the majority of many, if not all of the above minority-based autonomous areas. In addition, still quite a few of non-Han minority people are found in the Han-based administrative areas (see Appendix 2 for details) – the breakdowns of their socioeconomic data have never been mentioned in China's existing statistical reports.

Another reason why the data of an ethnic minority autonomous area should not represent as those of that ethnic people stems from two facts in China: first, there usually exist two or more ethnic peoples in each ethnic minority autonomous area; second, each ethnic group is usually included geographically in at least two administrative divisions (provinces, prefectures, counties and others). For instance, according to the composition of population, the Mongol people have now become a true minority in Inner Mongolia, hometown of the ethnic Mongols, as a result of the large-scale Han immigration during the 20th century.

Rongxing Guo

Members of International Editorial Committee

Project Coordinator

A List of 56 Ethnic Groups in China

Name	Chinese name	Name in Pinyin	Other name(s)	Population share (%)
Achang	阿昌族	Āchāng Zú		0.0030
Bai	白族	Bái Zú		0.1451
Baonan	保安族	Bǎo'ān Zú	Bao'an, Bonan	0.0015
Blang	布朗族	Bùlǎng Zú	Bulang	0.0090
Bouyei	布依族	Bùyī Zú	Buyi, Buoyei, Buoyi	0.2153
Dai	傣族	Dǎi Zú		0.0946
Daur	达斡尔族	Dáwò'ěr Zú		0.0099
Deang	德昂族	Dé'áng Zú	Benglong	0.0015
Derung	独龙族	Dúlóng Zú	Drung, Dulong	0.0005
Dong	侗族	Dòng Zú		0.2161
Dongxiang	东乡族	Dōngxiāng Zú		0.0466
Ewenki	鄂温克族	Èwēnkè Zú		0.0023
Gaoshan	高山族	Gāoshān Zú	Taiwan aborigines	0.0003
Gelao	仡佬族	Gēlǎo Zú	Gelo	0.0413
Han	汉族	Hàn Zú		91.6474
Hani	哈尼族	Hāní Zú	Akha	0.1246
Hezhen	赫哲族	Hèzhé Zú	Hezhe	0.0004
Hui	回族	Huí Zú		0.7943
Jing	京族	Jīng Zú	Gin	0.0021
Jingpo	景颇族	Jǐngpō Zú		0.0111
Jino	基诺族	Jīnuò Zú	Juno	0.0017
Kazak	哈萨克族	Hāsàkè Zú	Kazakh	0.1097
Kirgiz	柯尔克孜族	Kē'ěrkèzī Zú		0.0140
Korean	朝鲜族	Cháoxiǎn Zú		0.1374

(continued)

Continued

Name	Chinese name	Name in Pinyin	Other name(s)	Population share (%)
Lahu	拉祜族	Lāhù Zú		0.0365
Lhoba	珞巴族	Luòbā Zú	Luoba	0.0003
Li	黎族	Lí Zú		0.1098
Lisu	傈僳族	Lìsù Zú		0.0527
Manchu	满族	Mǎn Zú	Man	0.7794
Maonan	毛南族	Máonán Zú		0.0076
Miao	苗族	Miáo Zú	Hmong, Xiong, Hmu	0.7072
Monba	门巴族	Ménbā Zú	Menba	0.0008
Mongol	蒙古族	Měnggǔ Zú	Mongolian	0.4488
Mulao	仫佬族	Mùlǎo Zú	Mulam	0.0162
Naxi	纳西族	Nàxī Zú	Nakhi	0.0245
Nu	怒族	Nù Zú		0.0028
Oroqen	鄂伦春族	Èlúnchūn Zú	Oroqin	0.0006
Pumi	普米族	Pǔmǐ Zú	Primi	0.0032
Qiang	羌族	Qiāng Zú		0.0232
Russian	俄罗斯族	Éluósī Zú		0.0012
Salar	撒拉族	Sālā Zú		0.0098
She	畲族	Shē Zú	Shanha	0.0532
Shui	水族	Shuǐ Zú		0.0309
Tajik	塔吉克族	Tǎjíkè Zú		0.0038
Tatar	塔塔尔族	Tǎtǎ'ěr Zú	Dada	0.0003
Tibetan	藏族	Zàng Zú	Zang	0.4713
Tu	土族	Tǔ Zú	Monguor	0.0217
Tujia	土家族	Tǔjiā Zú		0.6268
Uyghur	维吾尔族	Wéiwú'ěr Zú	Uigur	0.7555
Uzbek	乌孜别克族	Wūzībiékè Zú	Ozbek	0.0008
Va	佤族	Wǎ Zú	Wa	0.0322
Xibe	锡伯族	Xībó Zú	Sibe	0.0143
Yao	瑶族	Yáo Zú		0.2098
Yi	彝族	Yí Zú		0.6538
Yugur	裕固族	Yùgù Zú	Yugu	0.0011
Zhuang	壮族	Zhuàng Zú		1.2700

Notes: (1) Population shares are based on the Sixth National Population Census of the People's Republic of China that was conducted on November 1, 2010. (2) See Appendix 1 for a historical and geographical description of each of the 56 ethnic groups

Maps

Maps

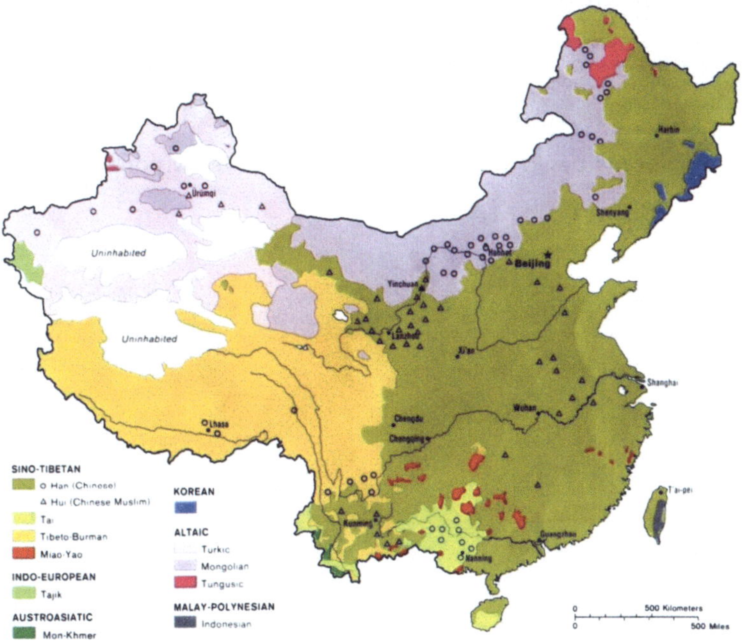

Map 1 The spatial distribution of China's ethno-linguistic groups (*Source*: Courtesy of the University of Texas Libraries, University of Texas at Austin)

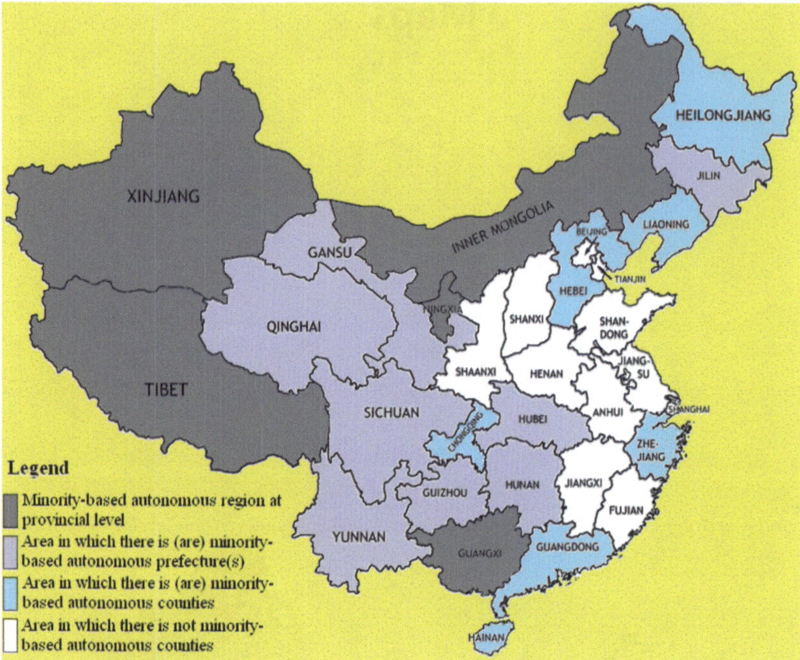

Map 2 The minority-based autonomous administrative divisions in China

Acknowledgments

It is a challenging task for us to prepare the statistical data that cover various fields of all ethnic groups in China. The major obstacle is that China has not established any ethnically-oriented statistical reporting or surveying system. During the process when this research was conducted, we have received generous help from the following organizations:

- Association of Power Generation Enterprises of China (APGE)
- China Mobile Corp. Ltd.
- China Telecom Corp. Ltd.
- China Unicom Corp. Ltd.
- Department of Financial Management, Ministry of Culture (MOC)
- Department of Financial Management, State Administration of Broadcasting, Film and Television (SABFT)
- Department of Financial Management, General Administration of Press and Publication (GAPP)
- Department of Planning and Development, Ministry of Education (MOE)
- Department of Population and Employment Statistics of the National Bureau of Statistics (NBS)
- Department of Urban Socio-economic Survey, National Bureau of Statistics (NBS)
- Finance Department, General Administration of Sport (GAS)

- Information Center, Ministry of Health (MOH)
- Inspection and Quarantine and State Intellectual Property Office (IQSIPO)
- Ministry of Health (MOH)
- Rural Socio-economic Survey Organization, National Bureau of Statistics (NBS)
- State Administration for Industry and Commerce (SAIC)
- General Administration of Press and Publication (GAPP)

This book has also benefited from the skilful assistance from many individuals. They are (in alphabetical order by family name): Ba Yunhong, Bian Lihua, Chang Wenli, Cui Ruchun, Deng Weiping, Ding Yong, Du Weiqun, Du Yan, Guan Xiaojing, Guo Dong, Guo Dong, Guo Dong, Hao Shenglong, Hou Rui, Ju Chuanling, Li Jiao, Li Junbo, Li Suoqiang, Liang Erwei, Liu Huiping, Long Ling, Lu Shan, Luan Jinhui, Luo Weihua Fan Xiaoyu, Qian Chunlin, Que Xiaoqing, Sheng Laiyun, Shi Faqi, Shi Yihua, Song Shaoying, Tan Xiaomei, Tang Ping, Wan Zhongbing, Wang Ping, Wang Qi, Wang Yixuan, Wu You, Xiao Li, Xu Lan, Yan Xianpu, Yang Hongjun, Ye Liqi, Yin Yi, Yu Hongwen, Zhang Huiying, Zhang Lei, Zhang Peng, Zhang Xin, Zhang Yanhua, Zhong Shouyang, and Zhu Hong

We have enjoyed the friendly spirit, encouragement and helpfulness of our first editor, Rachel Sangster (Publisher of Economics and Global Head of Economics and Finance, Palgrave Macmillan, London) and appreciate the continuing efforts and helpfulness of Laura Pacey, Commissioning Editor at Palgrave Macmillan, London, who has managed the final stages of the book's preparation with Rachel on maternity leave.

Last but not least, we are grateful to various anonymous reviewers whose comments and suggestions have helped us refine many parts of this research. However, all views in this book are those of the respective author only and not necessarily those of the book's editors and of the organizations and individuals who provided the original data.

Rongxing Guo
Lake Yanqi, Huairou, Beijing, China

Organization of this Book

This book sets out to present, in an easy-to-use format, a broad collection of social and economic indicators on China's 56 ethnic groups. It is a resource book that profiles the general social and economic situations for each of these ethnic groups.

In this book, data are presented on an ethnic group-by-ethnic group basis, and the ethnic groups are ordered alphabetically, from the Achang to the Zhuang. Though most of the data are as of 2012 – the latest year when our research was conducted, we have also provided some historical data for a few of the indicators and have spent the past years developing these data sets and indicators for analysis. This is intended to help readers to conduct time-series comparisons and analyses.

This book is organized as follows.

This book focuses on the following topics: population growth and structural changes (Chap. 1); economic growth and expenditure (Chap. 2); employment and income distribution (Chap. 3); living conditions and the means of livelihood (Chap. 4); agricultural production and other rural activities (Chap. 5); education, science and technological progress (Chap. 6); health care and social security (Chap. 7); and entertainment and other cultural activities (Chap. 8).

There are four appendices in this book. Appendix 1 presents a short introduction to each of China's 56 ethnic groups. Appendix 2 provides ethnic populations of 31 provinces, autonomous regions and municipalities and of China as a whole, which are derived from China's two recent national population censuses (2000 and 2010). In Appendix 3 the administrative and demographic statistics of the minority-based administrative divisions at different levels (including autonomous regions as the first-class administrative divisions; cities, prefectures and autonomous prefectures as the second-class administrative divisions; and cities, counties, autonomous counties and banners (*Qi*) as the third-class administrative divisions) are presented. At last, Appendix 4 provides selected indicators on the social and economic development of ethnic minority autonomous areas.

At the end of this book, some notes on the data as well as the main statistical indicators are provided.

Contents

List of Tables

1

Population Growth and Structural Change

Data in this chapter are prepared by the Department of Population and Employment Statistics of the National Bureau of Statistics. In Table 1.1 figures for the years of 2000 and 2010 are the census year estimates; and the rest of the figures covered in those tables are estimates from the annual national sample survey on population changes and data for selected years have been revised according to the census results. In Table 1.2 data are estimates from the national sample survey on population changes. In Table 1.3 data are calculated by using the results of the 2000 and 2010 censuses.

The statistical surveys on population, which are conducted by Department of Population and Employment Statistics of the NBS, are as follows: The national population censuses are conducted in the years ending with 0; the 1 percent nation-wide population sample surveys are conducted in the years ending with 5; and the sample surveys on population changes are conducted in the rest of the years which cover about 1 per thousand of the total population of the country.

The sample survey on population change takes the whole nation as the population and each province, autonomous Ethnic group or municipality as sub-populations, and the stratified multi-stage systematic probability

R. Guo, *China Ethnic Statistical Yearbook 2016*,
DOI 10.1007/978-3-319-49199-8_1

proportional to size (PPS) cluster sampling scheme is used. The PPS is a sampling procedure under which the probability of a unit being selected is proportional to the size of the ultimate unit, giving larger clusters a greater probability of selection and smaller clusters a lower probability. It is most useful when the sampling units vary considerably in size because it assures that those in larger sites have the same probability of getting into the sample as those in smaller sites, and vice verse.

Table 1.1 Population at year-end (10,000 persons)

Ethnic group	2000	2006	2007	2008	2009	2010	2011	2012
National total	126,743	131,448	132,129	132,802	133,450	134,091	134,735	135,404
Achang	3.4	3.6	3.6	3.6	3.7	3.9	3.9	3.7
Bai	187.7	195.6	196.5	197.4	198.2	199.4	200.4	201.6
Baonan	1.7	1.7	1.7	1.7	1.7	1.7	1.7	1.7
Blang	9.2	9.7	9.8	9.8	9.9	10.0	10.0	10.1
Buyi	315.8	311.4	307.0	304.3	299.8	295.3	294.6	296.0
Dai	116.1	122.6	123.4	124.2	125.0	125.8	126.6	127.4
Daur	13.6	13.9	13.9	14.0	14.1	14.1	14.2	14.2
Deang	1.8	1.9	1.9	1.9	1.9	1.9	2.0	2.0
Derung	0.7	0.8	0.8	0.8	0.8	0.8	0.8	0.8
Dong	312.1	306.9	304.9	304.2	302.3	300.4	300.7	302.3
Dongxiang	51.5	52.7	52.8	53.0	53.2	53.4	53.5	53.8
Ewenki	3.1	3.2	3.2	3.2	3.2	3.2	3.3	3.3
Gaoshan	0.5	0.5	0.5	0.5	0.5	0.5	0.5	0.5
Gelao	61.6	60.7	59.8	59.3	58.4	57.5	57.3	57.6
Han	115,190.4	118,425.7	119,210.6	120,150.2	121,075.9	122,156.0	122,751.9	123,423.8
Hani	144.2	152.3	153.4	154.4	155.3	156.4	157.4	158.3
Hezhe	0.5	0.5	0.5	0.5	0.5	0.5	0.5	0.5
Hui	997.5	1045.1	1053.2	1062.9	1071.7	1083.2	1091.0	1100.2
Jing	2.4	2.4	2.4	2.5	2.5	2.4	2.4	2.4
Jingpo	13.2	14.0	14.1	14.2	14.3	14.4	14.4	14.5
Jino	2.1	2.2	2.2	2.2	2.3	2.3	2.3	2.3
Kazak	125.3	138.8	141.9	144.3	146.2	148.0	149.6	151.2
Kirgiz	16.1	17.8	18.2	18.5	18.8	19.0	19.2	19.4
Korean	194.6	197.9	198.6	199.1	199.8	200.9	201.3	201.6
Lahu	45.4	48.0	48.3	48.6	48.9	49.3	49.6	49.9

(*continued*)

Table 1.1 Continued

Ethnic group	2000	2006	2007	2008	2009	2010	2011	2012
Lhoba	0.3	0.3	0.3	0.3	0.3	0.3	0.3	0.3
Li	130.3	137.6	138.9	140.3	141.8	142.4	143.8	145.3
Lisu	63.6	67.1	67.5	67.9	68.3	68.8	69.2	69.6
Manchu	1075.6	1102.4	1109.3	1115.2	1122.2	1136.8	1141.2	1145.1
Maonan	11.5	11.4	11.5	11.5	11.6	11.1	11.1	11.2
Miao	929.7	922.4	917.7	916.3	912.0	909.2	910.7	915.9
Monba	0.9	1.0	1.0	1.0	1.0	1.0	1.0	1.0
Mongol	590.5	603.6	607.2	611.1	614.7	619.1	621.6	623.9
Mulao	22.4	22.2	22.4	22.6	22.7	21.7	21.9	22.0
Naxi	30.9	32.6	32.8	33.1	33.3	33.5	33.7	33.9
Nu	2.9	3.0	3.1	3.1	3.1	3.1	3.1	3.2
Oroqen	0.8	0.9	0.9	0.9	0.9	0.9	0.9	0.9
Pumi	3.4	3.6	3.6	3.6	3.6	3.6	3.7	3.7
Qiang	31.0	30.4	30.2	30.3	30.5	30.0	30.0	30.1
Russian	1.6	1.7	1.7	1.7	1.8	1.8	1.8	1.8
Salar	11.1	11.7	11.8	11.8	11.9	12.0	12.1	12.2
She	71.8	75.8	76.5	77.1	77.7	78.7	79.2	79.6
Shui	43.3	42.7	42.1	41.8	41.2	40.5	40.4	40.6
Tajik	4.1	4.5	4.6	4.7	4.8	4.8	4.9	4.9
Tatar	0.5	0.5	0.6	0.6	0.6	0.6	0.6	0.6
Tibetan	547.7	576.9	581.1	586.6	592.9	595.9	599.6	605.6
Tu	25.5	26.9	27.1	27.2	27.3	27.6	27.8	28.0
Tujia	801.9	792.2	791.6	793.4	793.9	800.8	804.4	809.1

Uygur	841.4	932.4	952.8	969.2	981.7	993.8	1004.5	1015.4
Uzbek	1.2	1.4	1.4	1.4	1.4	1.5	1.5	1.5
Va	39.7	41.9	42.2	42.5	42.7	43.0	43.3	43.6
Xibe	19.0	19.7	19.8	20.0	20.1	20.3	20.4	20.5
Yao	279.3	278.8	281.2	283.7	286.0	280.4	282.2	284.3
Yi	784.9	806.4	807.5	810.2	813.2	811.7	814.9	819.1
Yugur	1.4	1.4	1.4	1.4	1.4	1.4	1.4	1.4
Zhuang	1738.0	1740.3	1758.6	1776.6	1792.1	1715.6	1728.3	1741.9

Notes: Data of 2000 and 2010 are the census year estimates; the rest are the estimates from the annual national sample survey on population changes. Since 2005, all data are of usual resident population

Table 1.2 Total population, birth rate, death rate, and natural growth rate

Ethnic group	Total population (year-end) (10,000 persons)	Urban population (%)	Rural population (%)	Birth rate (‰)	Death rate (‰)	Natural growth rate (‰)
National total	135,404	52.57	47.43	12.10	7.15	4.95
Achang	3.73	39.48	60.52	12.62	6.41	6.21
Bai	201.62	39.86	60.14	12.72	6.50	6.22
Baonan	1.72	39.34	60.66	12.30	5.99	6.31
Blang	10.10	39.54	60.46	12.61	6.41	6.20
Buyi	295.98	37.25	62.75	13.19	6.91	6.28
Dai	127.40	39.47	60.53	12.61	6.41	6.19
Daur	14.23	57.05	42.95	8.84	5.67	3.17
Deang	1.97	39.39	60.61	12.63	6.41	6.22
Derung	0.81	42.35	57.65	12.26	6.36	5.89
Dong	302.33	41.50	58.50	13.32	6.83	6.49
Dongxiang	53.82	39.44	60.56	12.47	5.87	6.60
Ewenki	3.27	57.83	42.17	9.08	5.58	3.50
Gaoshan	0.48	51.33	48.67	11.58	6.26	5.32
Gelao	57.57	37.08	62.92	13.22	6.92	6.30
Han	123,423.78	53.04	46.96	11.19	6.24	4.95
Hani	158.32	39.46	60.54	12.62	6.41	6.21
Hezhe	0.50	57.08	42.92	7.61	5.98	1.62
Hui	1100.15	48.83	51.17	12.27	5.74	6.54
Jing	2.41	43.94	56.06	14.02	6.30	7.71
Jingpo	14.53	39.48	60.52	12.62	6.41	6.21
Jino	2.30	39.47	60.53	12.61	6.41	6.20
Kazak	151.19	43.99	56.01	15.30	4.49	10.82
Kirgiz	19.43	44.15	55.85	15.23	4.50	10.73
Korean	201.58	56.41	43.59	6.49	5.69	0.80
Lahu	49.88	39.48	60.52	12.61	6.41	6.20
Lhoba	0.35	25.27	74.73	15.17	5.30	9.87
Li	145.26	51.01	48.99	14.55	5.86	8.69
Lisu	69.60	39.58	60.42	12.54	6.43	6.11
Manchu	1145.12	59.62	40.38	7.97	6.24	1.73
Maonan	11.22	41.85	58.15	13.87	6.48	7.39
Miao	915.87	41.95	58.05	13.01	6.79	6.22
Monba	1.05	24.53	75.47	15.24	5.25	9.99
Mongol	623.90	57.21	42.79	9.19	5.71	3.49
Mulao	22.02	43.33	56.67	13.96	6.36	7.60
Naxi	33.88	39.56	60.44	12.55	6.42	6.13
Nu	3.17	39.38	60.62	12.65	6.39	6.26

(continued)

Table 1.2 Continued

Ethnic group	Total population (year-end) (10,000 persons)	Urban population (%)	Rural population (%)	Birth rate (‰)	Death rate (‰)	Natural growth rate (‰)
Oroqen	0.88	57.49	42.51	8.31	5.80	2.51
Pumi	3.69	39.55	60.45	12.60	6.41	6.19
Qiang	30.07	43.63	56.37	9.93	6.91	3.02
Russian	1.81	50.09	49.91	12.76	4.97	7.79
Salar	12.24	46.48	53.52	14.04	6.00	8.04
She	79.61	57.89	42.11	12.16	5.77	6.39
Shui	40.62	37.31	62.69	13.23	6.90	6.34
Tajik	4.94	44.30	55.70	15.18	4.55	10.63
Tatar	0.59	44.42	55.58	15.02	4.60	10.41
Tibetan	605.55	34.65	65.35	13.54	5.89	7.66
Tu	28.04	46.73	53.27	13.83	6.03	7.80
Tujia	809.15	49.14	50.86	12.24	6.66	5.57
Uygur	1015.43	44.05	55.95	15.29	4.49	10.80
Uzbek	1.49	44.24	55.76	15.25	4.51	10.74
Va	43.57	39.73	60.27	12.59	6.42	6.17
Xibe	20.48	60.77	39.23	8.09	6.08	2.02
Yao	284.29	45.88	54.12	13.69	6.38	7.30
Yi	819.12	40.33	59.67	11.94	6.61	5.33
Yugur	1.42	39.38	60.62	12.18	6.00	6.18
Zhuang	1741.88	44.19	55.81	13.97	6.26	7.71

Notes: Data in the table are estimates from the 2012 national sample survey on population changes. The national total population was adjusted on the basis of sampling errors and survey errors. The military personnel were included in the national total population, but were not included in the ethnic group

Table 1.3 Population life expectancy

Ethnic group	Life expectancy in 2000	Male	Female	Life expectancy in 2010	Male	Female
National total	71.40	69.63	73.33	74.83	72.38	77.37
Achang	65.57	64.31	66.98	69.62	67.13	72.51
Bai	66.03	64.72	67.50	70.18	67.68	73.07
Baonan	67.43	66.67	68.30	72.16	70.50	74.02
Blang	65.60	64.34	67.01	69.64	67.16	72.53
Buyi	66.22	64.77	67.85	71.27	68.61	74.27

(*continued*)

Table 1.3 Continued

Ethnic group	Life expectancy in 2000	Male	Female	Life expectancy in 2010	Male	Female
Dai	65.58	64.32	67.00	69.63	67.14	72.52
Daur	70.74	69.02	72.77	74.95	72.55	77.75
Deang	65.53	64.28	66.93	69.58	67.09	72.47
Derung	66.73	65.37	68.25	70.70	68.24	73.55
Dong	68.24	66.65	70.04	72.83	70.19	75.84
Dongxiang	67.47	66.69	68.38	72.24	70.56	74.15
Ewenki	70.25	68.61	72.21	74.67	72.27	77.49
Gaoshan	71.58	69.73	73.58	75.07	72.55	77.92
Gelao	66.16	64.72	67.79	71.24	68.58	74.25
Han	71.89	70.05	73.89	75.34	72.98	77.99
Hani	65.56	64.30	66.97	69.60	67.12	72.50
Hezhe	72.38	70.44	74.62	75.97	73.55	78.74
Hui	69.97	68.44	71.66	73.65	71.49	76.09
Jing	71.04	68.89	73.42	74.90	71.65	78.73
Jingpo	65.57	64.31	66.98	69.62	67.13	72.51
Jino	65.56	64.30	66.97	69.60	67.12	72.50
Kazak	67.42	65.99	69.14	72.35	70.31	74.86
Kirgiz	67.47	66.03	69.21	72.39	70.34	74.91
Korean	72.97	71.17	74.99	76.18	74.00	78.60
Lahu	65.58	64.32	66.99	69.62	67.14	72.51
Lhoba	64.89	63.06	66.69	68.72	66.83	70.69
Li	72.59	70.37	74.90	76.06	72.98	79.72
Lisu	65.73	64.45	67.16	69.76	67.27	72.65
Manchu	72.89	71.07	74.92	75.99	73.73	78.50
Maonan	69.76	67.78	71.97	73.96	70.83	77.60
Miao	68.01	66.45	69.76	72.52	69.92	75.48
Monba	64.78	62.93	66.57	68.56	66.70	70.48
Mongol	70.48	68.84	72.41	74.67	72.32	77.41
Mulao	70.62	68.51	72.96	74.60	71.39	78.37
Naxi	65.72	64.44	67.16	69.75	67.27	72.64
Nu	65.62	64.34	67.04	69.65	67.18	72.53
Oroqen	71.34	69.55	73.44	75.33	72.92	78.13
Pumi	65.62	64.36	67.03	69.66	67.17	72.55
Qiang	71.17	69.23	73.36	74.73	72.23	77.57
Russian	68.75	67.23	70.56	73.41	71.24	76.02
Salar	66.34	64.95	67.92	70.40	68.56	72.50
She	72.27	70.27	74.49	75.80	73.40	78.58
Shui	66.31	64.85	67.96	71.32	68.64	74.35
Tajik	67.57	66.12	69.31	72.45	70.40	74.98

(continued)

Table 1.3 Continued

Ethnic group	Life expectancy in 2000	Male	Female	Life expectancy in 2010	Male	Female
Tatar	67.61	66.19	69.32	72.49	70.45	74.98
Tibetan	66.67	64.98	68.43	70.52	68.52	72.71
Tu	66.60	65.19	68.19	70.63	68.76	72.77
Tujia	70.22	68.53	72.12	74.35	71.93	77.11
Uygur	67.44	66.01	69.17	72.37	70.32	74.88
Uzbek	67.51	66.07	69.25	72.42	70.37	74.94
Va	65.73	64.45	67.15	69.75	67.27	72.64
Xibe	72.12	70.37	74.10	75.58	73.36	78.08
Yao	70.78	68.79	72.98	74.65	71.70	78.09
Yi	67.18	65.71	68.83	71.21	68.70	74.10
Yugur	67.56	66.81	68.40	72.29	70.63	74.15
Zhuang	70.95	68.79	73.33	74.76	71.53	78.57

Note: Data in this table are calculated according to the 2000 and 2010 national population censuses

Table 1.4 Household, population, and sex ratio

Ethnic group	Number of households (household)	Family household	Collective household	Population (person)	Male	Female	Sex ratio (female = 100)
National total	367,304	356,954	10,350	1,124,661	576,354	548,307	105.12
Achang	9	9	0	31	16	15	105.88
Bai	514	503	12	1682	865	817	105.91
Baonan	4	4	0	14	7	7	105.94
Blang	26	25	1	84	43	41	105.85
Buyi	789	779	10	2470	1269	1201	105.70
Dai	322	314	8	1063	547	516	105.90
Daur	42	41	1	119	61	58	104.13
Deang	5	5	0	16	8	8	105.87
Derung	2	2	0	7	3	3	105.58
Dong	805	794	11	2523	1299	1223	106.17
Dongxiang	138	137	1	449	231	218	105.78
Ewenki	10	9	0	27	14	13	104.41
Gaoshan	1	1	0	4	2	2	104.46
Gelao	153	152	2	480	247	234	105.71
Han	337,201	327,467	9734	1,029,830	527,715	502,118	105.10
Hani	400	390	10	1321	679	642	105.87
Hezhe	1	1	0	4	2	2	103.74
Hui	2889	2822	68	9179	4691	4488	104.55
Jing	6	6	0	20	10	10	107.61
Jingpo	37	36	1	121	62	59	105.88
Jino	6	6	0	19	10	9	105.88
Kazak	400	394	5	1261	643	618	103.98
Kirgiz	51	51	1	162	83	79	103.97
Korean	590	578	12	1682	854	828	103.22
Lahu	126	123	3	416	214	202	105.85

Lhoba	1	1	0	3	1	1	99.25
Li	331	316	15	1212	643	569	113.15
Lisu	176	172	4	581	299	282	105.97
Manchu	3306	3213	93	9555	4833	4722	102.34
Maonan	29	28	0	94	48	45	107.14
Miao	2448	2409	38	7642	3931	3711	105.87
Monba	2	2	0	9	4	4	99.13
Mongol	1822	1770	51	5206	2654	2552	104.02
Mulao	56	55	1	184	95	89	107.49
Naxi	86	84	2	283	145	137	105.95
Nu	8	8	0	26	14	13	105.76
Oroqen	3	3	0	7	4	4	104.00
Pumi	9	9	0	31	16	15	105.87
Qiang	85	83	2	251	131	120	109.88
Russian	5	5	0	15	8	7	104.16
Salar	30	30	1	102	53	50	106.20
She	227	215	12	664	338	326	103.87
Shui	108	107	1	339	174	165	105.72
Tajik	13	13	0	41	21	20	104.02
Tatar	2	2	0	5	3	2	104.10
Tibetan	1426	1405	21	5053	2568	2485	103.72
Tu	70	68	2	234	121	113	106.29
Tujia	2230	2194	36	6751	3455	3296	104.79
Uygur	2684	2649	34	8473	4319	4154	103.98
Uzbek	4	4	0	12	6	6	104.05
Va	110	107	3	364	187	177	105.82
Xibe	60	58	2	171	86	85	101.58
Yao	729	714	15	2372	1230	1143	107.56
Yi	2145	2096	49	6835	3531	3304	106.96
Yugur	4	4	0	12	6	6	105.95
Zhuang	4375	4292	83	14,534	7538	6996	107.72

Notes: Data in this table are obtained from the 2012 national sample survey on population changes. The sampling fraction is 0.831 ‰

Table 1.5 Household size and population by gender

Ethnic group	Family household population (person)	Male	Female	Collective household population (person)	Male	Female	Average family size (person/household)
National total	1,077,355	547,201	530,155	47,306	29,153	18,153	3.02
Achang	30	15	14	1	1	1	3.26
Bai	1620	835	785	62	30	32	3.23
Baonan	14	7	7	0	0	0	3.22
Blang	81	42	39	3	2	2	3.26
Buyi	2415	1227	1188	55	42	12	3.10
Dai	1020	527	493	43	20	23	3.26
Daur	115	59	56	3	1	2	2.80
Deang	16	8	8	1	0	0	3.26
Derung	7	3	3	0	0	0	3.19
Dong	2471	1261	1209	52	38	14	3.11
Dongxiang	440	224	215	9	6	3	3.21
Ewenki	26	13	13	1	0	1	2.79
Gaoshan	4	2	2	0	0	0	3.09
Gelao	470	239	231	10	8	2	3.10
Han	985,383	500,220	485,157	44,455	27,493	16,963	3.03
Hani	1268	655	613	54	25	29	3.26
Hezhe	4	2	2	0	0	0	2.79
Hui	8876	4513	4363	303	177	126	3.17
Jing	20	10	10	0	0	0	3.30
Jingpo	116	60	56	5	2	3	3.26
Jino	18	10	9	1	0	0	3.26
Kazak	1246	634	612	15	9	6	3.16
Kirgiz	160	81	79	2	1	1	3.16

Korean	1635	830	805	47	24	22	2.84
Lahu	399	206	193	17	8	9	3.26
Lhoba	3	1	1	0	0	0	3.97
Li	1141	610	531	71	34	38	3.61
Lisu	557	288	270	24	11	12	3.25
Manchu	9092	4593	4499	463	241	222	2.84
Maonan	92	47	45	2	1	1	3.25
Miao	7453	3805	3647	189	125	64	3.10
Monba	9	4	4	0	0	0	4.01
Mongol	4987	2553	2434	219	102	117	2.83
Mulao	180	93	87	4	2	1	3.28
Naxi	271	140	131	12	5	6	3.25
Nu	25	13	12	1	0	1	3.27
Oroqen	7	4	3	0	0	0	2.79
Pumi	30	15	14	1	1	1	3.25
Qiang	238	120	118	13	11	2	2.85
Russian	15	8	7	0	0	0	3.01
Salar	100	51	49	2	2	1	3.37
She	619	314	304	46	24	22	2.89
Shui	332	169	163	7	6	2	3.11
Tajik	41	21	20	1	0	0	3.16
Tatar	5	2	2	0	0	0	3.15
Tibetan	4943	2487	2456	110	81	29	3.55
Tu	228	116	112	6	5	2	3.35
Tujia	6554	3333	3221	198	123	75	2.99
Uygur	8369	4256	4113	103	63	40	3.16
Uzbek	12	6	6	0	0	0	3.16
Va	349	180	169	15	7	8	3.25

(continued)

Table 1.5 Continued

Ethnic group	Family household population (person)	Male	Female	Collective household population (person)	Male	Female	Average family size (person/household)
Xibe	161	81	80	10	5	5	2.79
Yao	2313	1192	1121	59	37	22	3.24
Yi	6551	3358	3193	284	173	111	3.13
Yugur	12	6	6	0	0	0	3.22
Zhuang	14,222	7346	6876	313	192	121	3.31

Notes: Data in this table are obtained from the 2012 national sample survey on population changes. The sampling fraction is 0.831 ‰

Table 1.6 Population residing in the townships, towns and street communities by sex (person)

Ethnic group	With permanent household registration			With permanent household registration elsewhere having been away from that places for more than 6 months		
	Sub-total	Male	Female	Sub-total	Male	Female
National total	898,059	457,256	440,803	215,952	113,637	102,315
Achang	26	13	13	5	2	2
Bai	1410	726	684	255	131	125
Baonan	13	6	6	2	1	1
Blang	70	36	34	13	7	6
Buyi	2069	1063	1006	366	189	177
Dai	886	456	430	167	85	82
Daur	89	46	43	29	15	15
Deang	14	7	7	3	1	1
Derung	6	3	3	1	1	1
Dong	2166	1116	1050	324	168	157
Dongxiang	393	201	193	54	29	24
Ewenki	19	10	9	8	4	4
Gaoshan	3	2	2	1	0	0
Gelao	403	207	196	71	37	34
Han	819,869	417,099	402,767	200,301	105,632	94,662
Hani	1101	567	534	207	106	102
Hezhe	3	2	2	1	0	0
Hui	7408	3776	3632	1701	880	821
Jing	17	9	8	2	1	1
Jingpo	101	52	49	19	10	9
Jino	16	8	8	3	2	1
Kazak	995	507	488	251	128	123
Kirgiz	128	65	63	32	16	16
Korean	1353	693	660	317	155	161
Lahu	347	179	168	65	33	32
Lhoba	3	1	1	0	0	0
Li	966	522	444	233	115	118
Lisu	484	249	235	91	47	44
Manchu	7505	3822	3683	2003	989	1014
Maonan	81	42	39	11	6	6
Miao	6491	3339	3152	1062	547	514
Monba	9	4	4	0	0	0
Mongol	3734	1917	1816	1443	722	722
Mulao	159	83	76	22	11	11
Naxi	236	121	114	44	23	22

(*continued*)

Table 1.6 Continued

Ethnic group	With permanent household registration			With permanent household registration elsewhere having been away from that places for more than 6 months		
	Sub-total	Male	Female	Sub-total	Male	Female
Nu	22	11	11	4	2	2
Oroqen	6	3	3	2	1	1
Pumi	26	13	12	5	2	2
Qiang	204	103	100	45	27	18
Russian	11	6	6	4	2	2
Salar	85	43	41	17	9	8
She	443	223	219	208	108	100
Shui	285	146	138	49	25	24
Tajik	33	17	16	8	4	4
Tatar	4	2	2	1	1	0
Tibetan	4566	2300	2266	449	251	198
Tu	194	99	95	39	21	18
Tujia	5717	2927	2790	975	498	477
Uygur	6680	3406	3274	1686	862	823
Uzbek	10	5	5	2	1	1
Va	303	156	147	57	29	28
Xibe	129	65	64	41	20	20
Yao	2041	1060	981	299	154	144
Yi	5666	2906	2760	1103	591	512
Yugur	10	5	5	1	1	1
Zhuang	12,540	6543	5997	1764	889	875

Notes: Data in this table are obtained from the 2012 national sample survey on population changes. The sampling fraction is 0.831 ‰

Table 1.7 Age composition and dependency ratio of population

Ethnic group	Population (person)	Aged 0–14	Aged 15–64	Aged 65 and over	Gross dependency ratio (%)	Children dependency ratio	Old dependency ratio
National total	1,124,661	185,135	833,822	105,704	34.88	22.20	12.68
Achang	31	6	23	2	37.56	26.87	10.70
Bai	1682	332	1214	137	38.80	27.45	11.35
Baonan	14	2	11	1	34.98	22.75	12.23
Blang	84	16	61	7	37.56	26.84	10.73
Buyi	2470	558	1686	225	46.66	33.27	13.39
Dai	1063	207	773	83	37.57	26.85	10.72
Daur	119	16	93	10	27.89	17.39	10.49
Deang	16	3	12	1	37.57	26.89	10.69
Derung	7	1	5	1	36.91	25.82	11.10
Dong	2523	533	1744	246	44.90	30.81	14.09
Dongxiang	449	77	332	40	35.09	23.01	12.08
Ewenki	27	4	21	2	27.85	17.60	10.25
Gaoshan	4	1	3	0	36.92	24.41	12.51
Gelao	480	109	327	44	46.92	33.48	13.43
Han	1,029,830	167,270	765,144	97,423	35.18	22.27	12.91
Hani	1321	258	960	103	37.55	26.86	10.70
Hezhe	4	1	3	0	27.04	15.83	11.21
Hui	9179	1669	6749	761	36.37	25.00	11.38
Jing	20	4	14	2	46.02	32.51	13.51
Jingpo	121	24	88	9	37.57	26.88	10.70
Jino	19	4	14	1	37.55	26.85	10.70
Kazak	1261	258	917	86	37.52	28.16	9.35
Kirgiz	162	33	118	11	37.41	28.04	9.36
Korean	1682	205	1337	141	25.89	15.37	10.52

(*continued*)

Table 1.7 Continued

Ethnic group	Population (person)	Aged 0–14	Aged 15–64	Aged 65 and over	Gross dependency ratio (%)	Children dependency ratio	Old dependency ratio
Lahu	416	81	303	32	37.57	26.86	10.71
Lhoba	3	1	2	0	38.00	30.01	7.98
Li	1212	233	890	89	36.32	26.24	10.08
Lisu	581	113	422	46	37.59	26.73	10.87
Manchu	9555	1207	7460	888	28.26	16.33	11.92
Maonan	94	21	64	9	46.68	33.11	13.57
Miao	7642	1574	5331	737	43.69	29.79	13.90
Monba	9	2	6	0	37.72	29.96	7.77
Mongol	5206	731	4046	428	28.76	18.15	10.61
Mulao	184	41	126	17	46.31	32.76	13.55
Naxi	283	55	206	22	37.57	26.74	10.84
Nu	26	5	19	2	37.54	26.87	10.68
Oroqen	7	1	6	1	27.43	16.66	10.76
Pumi	31	6	22	2	37.53	26.81	10.73
Qiang	251	41	181	30	38.96	22.61	16.35
Russian	15	3	11	1	33.65	23.80	9.85
Salar	102	21	74	7	37.69	27.65	10.03
She	664	109	498	57	33.80	22.33	11.47
Shui	339	77	231	31	46.67	33.28	13.39
Tajik	41	8	30	3	37.49	28.01	9.49
Tatar	5	1	4	0	37.24	27.65	9.58
Tibetan	5053	1012	3663	376	37.94	27.38	10.56
Tu	234	47	170	17	37.55	27.33	10.21
Tujia	6751	1193	4827	732	40.10	24.88	15.22

Uygur	8473	1734	6161	577	37.51	28.15	9.36
Uzbek	12	3	9	1	37.48	28.09	9.40
Va	364	71	264	28	37.57	26.79	10.79
Xibe	171	22	133	16	28.01	16.27	11.74
Yao	2372	492	1656	224	43.62	29.95	13.67
Yi	6835	1300	4923	612	38.99	26.42	12.57
Yugur	12	2	9	1	34.82	22.48	12.33
Zhuang	14,534	3202	10,007	1325	45.48	32.18	13.30

Notes: Data in this table are obtained from the 2012 national sample survey on population changes. The sampling fraction is 0.831 ‰

Table 1.8 Population by marital status (I)

Ethnic group	Population aged 15 and over	Male	Female	Never married	Male	Female
National total	939,526	476,037	463,489	191,753	111,298	80,455
Achang	25	13	12	5	3	2
Bai	1351	690	660	277	166	112
Baonan	12	6	6	3	2	1
Blang	68	35	33	14	8	6
Buyi	1911	968	943	405	236	169
Dai	856	438	417	177	106	71
Daur	103	52	50	18	10	8
Deang	13	7	6	3	2	1
Derung	6	3	3	1	1	0
Dong	1990	1010	980	404	240	164
Dongxiang	372	190	182	81	48	33
Ewenki	24	12	12	4	2	2
Gaoshan	3	2	2	1	0	0
Gelao	371	188	183	79	46	33
Han	862,567	436,898	425,669	175,611	101,848	73,765
Hani	1063	544	519	220	131	89
Hezhe	4	2	2	1	0	0
Hui	7511	3798	3712	1527	880	647
Jing	16	8	8	4	2	1
Jingpo	98	50	48	20	12	8
Jino	15	8	8	3	2	1
Kazak	1003	511	493	193	115	78
Kirgiz	129	66	63	25	15	10
Korean	1477	747	730	292	165	126
Lahu	335	171	163	69	41	28
Lhoba	2	1	1	1	0	0
Li	979	514	465	285	173	112
Lisu	468	240	228	96	58	39
Manchu	8348	4205	4143	1749	976	774
Maonan	73	37	36	16	10	7
Miao	6068	3080	2988	1226	726	500
Monba	7	3	3	2	1	1
Mongol	4475	2276	2199	862	484	377
Mulao	143	73	70	32	20	13
Naxi	228	117	111	47	28	19
Nu	21	11	10	4	3	2
Oroqen	6	3	3	1	1	0
Pumi	25	13	12	5	3	2
Qiang	210	110	100	38	23	15

(continued)

Table 1.8 Continued

Ethnic group	Population aged 15 and over	Male	Female	Never married	Male	Female
Russian	12	6	6	2	1	1
Salar	82	42	40	18	10	7
She	555	279	276	115	65	50
Shui	262	133	129	56	32	23
Tajik	33	17	16	6	4	3
Tatar	4	2	2	1	0	0
Tibetan	4041	2040	2000	1038	573	464
Tu	187	96	91	41	24	17
Tujia	5558	2807	2752	1058	626	432
Uygur	6739	3429	3309	1298	774	524
Uzbek	10	5	5	2	1	1
Va	293	150	143	60	36	24
Xibe	149	75	74	33	18	15
Yao	1880	962	918	409	248	161
Yi	5535	2847	2688	1112	663	449
Yugur	10	5	5	2	1	1
Zhuang	11,332	5806	5526	2599	1575	1024

Notes: Data in this table are obtained from the 2012 national sample survey on population changes. The sampling fraction is 0.831 ‰

Table 1.9 Population by marital status (II)

Ethnic group	First married	Male	Female	Re-married	Male	Female
National total	669,629	334,786	334,843	14,647	7005	7642
Achang	18	9	9	0	0	0
Bai	959	480	479	23	12	11
Baonan	8	4	4	0	0	0
Blang	48	24	24	1	1	1
Buyi	1319	657	662	36	18	18
Dai	608	305	304	15	8	7
Daur	75	38	37	2	1	1
Deang	9	5	5	0	0	0
Derung	4	2	2	0	0	0
Dong	1394	694	700	34	17	17
Dongxiang	260	129	130	6	3	3
Ewenki	17	9	8	0	0	0
Gaoshan	2	1	1	0	0	0
Gelao	256	127	128	7	4	3

(continued)

Table 1.9 Continued

Ethnic group	First married	Male	Female	Re-married	Male	Female
Han	615,995	307,925	308,070	13,107	6237	6870
Hani	756	378	377	18	9	9
Hezhe	3	1	1	0	0	0
Hui	5348	2668	2680	139	69	70
Jing	11	5	5	0	0	0
Jingpo	69	35	35	2	1	1
Jino	11	5	5	0	0	0
Kazak	678	340	338	50	26	24
Kirgiz	87	44	44	6	3	3
Korean	1050	525	525	26	12	13
Lahu	238	119	119	6	3	3
Lhoba	1	1	1	0	0	0
Li	636	321	315	9	5	4
Lisu	333	167	166	8	4	4
Manchu	5837	2922	2915	145	69	76
Maonan	50	25	25	1	1	1
Miao	4263	2124	2138	108	54	54
Monba	4	2	2	0	0	0
Mongol	3236	1639	1597	90	41	49
Mulao	98	49	49	2	1	1
Naxi	162	81	81	4	2	2
Nu	15	8	8	0	0	0
Oroqen	5	2	2	0	0	0
Pumi	18	9	9	0	0	0
Qiang	151	79	72	4	2	2
Russian	9	4	4	0	0	0
Salar	56	28	27	2	1	1
She	398	200	198	8	4	4
Shui	181	90	91	5	2	2
Tajik	22	11	11	2	1	1
Tatar	3	1	1	0	0	0
Tibetan	2628	1330	1298	55	27	29
Tu	129	65	63	4	2	2
Tujia	3957	1965	1992	100	48	51
Uygur	4556	2285	2271	335	174	161
Uzbek	7	3	3	0	0	0
Va	208	104	104	5	3	2
Xibe	101	50	50	3	2	2
Yao	1309	654	655	25	12	13
Yi	3932	1990	1942	100	50	50
Yugur	7	3	3	0	0	0
Zhuang	7770	3881	3889	142	71	71

Notes: Data in this table are obtained from the 2012 national sample survey on population changes. The sampling fraction is 0.831 ‰

Table 1.10 Population by marital status (III)

Ethnic group	Divorced	Male	Female	Widowed	Male	Female
National total	12,915	7391	5523	52,223	16,128	36,095
Achang	0	0	0	1	0	1
Bai	18	10	8	73	23	50
Baonan	0	0	0	1	0	0
Blang	1	0	0	4	1	2
Buyi	32	19	13	119	38	82
Dai	11	6	5	45	14	31
Daur	2	1	1	5	2	3
Deang	0	0	0	1	0	0
Derung	0	0	0	0	0	0
Dong	31	19	12	126	39	86
Dongxiang	6	3	3	20	7	14
Ewenki	0	0	0	1	0	1
Gaoshan	0	0	0	0	0	0
Gelao	6	4	3	23	7	16
Han	11,825	6826	5002	46,023	14,063	31,962
Hani	14	8	6	56	17	38
Hezhe	0	0	0	0	0	0
Hui	128	70	59	368	112	256
Jing	0	0	0	1	0	1
Jingpo	1	1	1	5	2	4
Jino	0	0	0	1	0	1
Kazak	40	19	21	42	11	31
Kirgiz	5	2	3	5	1	4
Korean	40	22	18	70	22	48
Lahu	4	2	2	18	5	12
Lhoba	0	0	0	0	0	0
Li	8	5	3	42	11	31
Lisu	6	3	3	25	8	17
Manchu	187	102	85	430	137	293
Maonan	1	1	0	4	1	3
Miao	95	57	38	376	119	257
Monba	0	0	0	0	0	0
Mongol	81	47	34	207	64	143
Mulao	2	1	1	9	3	6
Naxi	3	2	1	12	4	8
Nu	0	0	0	1	0	1
Oroqen	0	0	0	0	0	0
Pumi	0	0	0	1	0	1
Qiang	4	2	2	13	4	9
Russian	0	0	0	1	0	0
Salar	2	1	1	4	1	3
She	6	4	3	28	7	21

(*continued*)

Table 1.10 Continued

Ethnic group	Divorced	Male	Female	Widowed	Male	Female
Shui	4	3	2	16	5	11
Tajik	1	1	1	1	0	1
Tatar	0	0	0	0	0	0
Tibetan	82	35	46	239	75	164
Tu	5	2	2	10	3	7
Tujia	86	51	35	359	117	242
Uygur	267	126	142	283	71	211
Uzbek	0	0	0	0	0	0
Va	4	2	2	15	5	11
Xibe	4	2	2	8	2	5
Yao	24	15	9	113	33	80
Yi	79	46	34	312	98	214
Yugur	0	0	0	1	0	0
Zhuang	142	84	57	679	194	485

Notes: Data in this table are obtained from the 2012 national sample survey on population changes. The sampling fraction is 0.831 ‰

Table 1.11 Population by educational attainment (person) (I)

Ethnic group	Population aged 6 and over	Male	Female	No schooling	Male	Female
National total	1,047,865	534,803	513,062	55,454	16,753	38,701
Achang	29	15	14	2	1	2
Bai	1557	799	758	130	43	86
Baonan	13	7	6	1	0	1
Blang	78	40	38	7	2	4
Buyi	2265	1157	1108	250	75	175
Dai	985	506	479	82	28	54
Daur	112	57	55	4	2	3
Deang	15	8	7	1	0	1
Derung	6	3	3	0	0	0
Dong	2315	1185	1130	189	58	131
Dongxiang	418	215	204	34	12	23
Ewenki	26	13	13	1	0	1
Gaoshan	4	2	2	0	0	0
Gelao	440	225	215	49	15	34
Han	960,333	490,047	470,287	49,583	14,746	34,837
Hani	1224	629	595	102	35	67
Hezhe	4	2	2	0	0	0
Hui	8506	4334	4172	574	193	380

(*continued*)

Table 1.11 Continued

Ethnic group	Population aged 6 and over	Male	Female	No schooling	Male	Female
Jing	18	9	9	1	0	1
Jingpo	112	58	55	9	3	6
Jino	18	9	9	1	1	1
Kazak	1145	584	561	43	19	24
Kirgiz	147	75	72	5	2	3
Korean	1601	811	789	41	14	27
Lahu	386	198	188	32	11	21
Lhoba	3	1	1	1	0	0
Li	1110	587	523	54	16	38
Lisu	538	277	262	45	15	30
Manchu	9070	4579	4491	278	90	188
Maonan	85	44	41	5	2	4
Miao	7036	3600	3436	583	180	403
Monba	8	4	4	3	1	1
Mongol	4908	2499	2410	213	73	140
Mulao	166	86	81	8	2	6
Naxi	262	135	127	22	7	15
Nu	24	13	12	2	1	1
Oroqen	7	4	3	0	0	0
Pumi	29	15	14	2	1	2
Qiang	235	123	112	16	5	11
Russian	14	7	7	1	0	0
Salar	94	49	46	13	5	8
She	617	313	304	34	9	25
Shui	311	159	152	34	10	24
Tajik	37	19	18	1	1	1
Tatar	4	2	2	0	0	0
Tibetan	4649	2361	2288	996	410	586
Tu	216	111	105	28	11	17
Tujia	6265	3190	3075	392	119	272
Uygur	7692	3923	3769	287	126	160
Uzbek	11	6	6	0	0	0
Va	337	173	164	28	9	18
Xibe	162	82	81	5	2	3
Yao	2162	1115	1047	98	30	68
Yi	6343	3271	3072	523	171	352
Yugur	11	6	5	1	0	1
Zhuang	13,141	6781	6360	575	174	401

Notes: Data in this table are obtained from the 2012 national sample survey on population changes. The sampling fraction is 0.831 ‰

Table 1.12 Population by educational attainment (person) (II)

Ethnic group	Primary school	Male	Female	Junior secondary school	Male	Female
National total	281,681	133,547	148,134	430,799	230,637	200,162
Achang	12	6	6	9	5	4
Bai	620	312	308	506	285	221
Baonan	5	2	2	4	2	2
Blang	32	16	16	25	14	11
Buyi	829	416	412	794	443	351
Dai	405	204	201	310	176	134
Daur	28	13	15	48	26	22
Deang	6	3	3	5	3	2
Derung	2	1	1	2	1	1
Dong	780	386	394	878	477	402
Dongxiang	140	68	72	141	76	65
Ewenki	6	3	3	11	6	5
Gaoshan	1	0	1	2	1	1
Gelao	161	81	80	154	86	68
Han	253,643	119,853	133,790	397,382	212,496	184,887
Hani	504	254	250	385	219	166
Hezhe	1	0	1	2	1	1
Hui	2527	1217	1310	3259	1755	1505
Jing	6	3	3	8	4	3
Jingpo	46	23	23	35	20	15
Jino	7	4	4	6	3	2
Kazak	363	176	187	434	231	203
Kirgiz	47	23	24	56	30	26
Korean	379	177	202	721	381	340
Lahu	159	80	79	121	69	52
Lhoba	1	1	1	0	0	0
Li	256	122	134	500	274	226
Lisu	220	111	109	170	97	73
Manchu	1987	927	1060	4087	2149	1939
Maonan	30	14	15	34	19	15
Miao	2439	1214	1225	2584	1409	1175
Monba	3	2	2	1	1	1
Mongol	1203	566	637	2065	1107	958
Mulao	57	27	30	69	38	31
Naxi	107	54	53	83	47	36
Nu	10	5	5	8	4	3
Oroqen	2	1	1	3	2	1
Pumi	12	6	6	9	5	4
Qiang	77	39	38	87	49	38
Russian	4	2	2	5	3	3

(continued)

Table 1.12 Continued

Ethnic group	Primary school	Male	Female	Junior secondary school	Male	Female
Salar	34	17	17	27	15	12
She	186	86	100	238	132	106
Shui	114	57	57	109	61	48
Tajik	12	6	6	14	8	7
Tatar	1	1	1	2	1	1
Tibetan	1791	920	872	1104	621	483
Tu	77	39	38	64	36	28
Tujia	1872	916	957	2409	1272	1137
Uygur	2436	1181	1255	2920	1553	1367
Uzbek	4	2	2	4	2	2
Va	138	69	68	107	61	46
Xibe	37	17	20	70	36	33
Yao	704	339	366	896	486	411
Yi	2445	1232	1213	2112	1197	915
Yugur	4	2	2	4	2	2
Zhuang	4503	2147	2356	5519	3034	2486

Notes: Data in this table are obtained from the 2012 national sample survey on population changes. The sampling fraction is 0.831 ‰

Table 1.13 Population by educational attainment (person) (III)

Ethnic group	Senior secondary school	Male	Female	College and higher level	Male	Female
National total	168,941	94,487	74,454	110,990	59,380	51,610
Achang	4	2	2	2	1	1
Bai	194	100	94	108	59	48
Baonan	2	1	1	1	1	1
Blang	10	5	5	5	3	2
Buyi	239	138	101	153	84	69
Dai	121	60	60	67	37	30
Daur	19	10	9	13	7	6
Deang	2	1	1	1	1	0
Derung	1	0	0	0	0	0
Dong	302	173	129	165	92	74
Dongxiang	63	36	28	40	23	16
Ewenki	4	2	2	3	2	2
Gaoshan	1	0	0	0	0	0
Gelao	46	27	19	30	16	13
Han	157,034	87,996	69,038	102,695	54,952	47,736

(*continued*)

Table 1.13 Continued

Ethnic group	Senior secondary school	Male	Female	College and higher level	Male	Female
Hani	150	75	75	83	46	37
Hezhe	1	0	0	0	0	0
Hui	1230	677	553	917	491	425
Jing	2	1	1	1	1	1
Jingpo	14	7	7	8	4	3
Jino	2	1	1	1	1	1
Kazak	151	79	72	154	79	75
Kirgiz	19	10	9	20	10	10
Korean	282	148	134	177	91	87
Lahu	47	24	24	26	15	12
Lhoba	0	0	0	0	0	0
Li	188	111	77	112	64	48
Lisu	66	33	33	37	20	17
Manchu	1408	744	665	1310	670	640
Maonan	10	6	4	6	3	3
Miao	912	512	401	518	286	232
Monba	0	0	0	0	0	0
Mongol	812	441	371	616	312	303
Mulao	20	12	9	11	6	5
Naxi	32	16	16	18	10	8
Nu	3	2	1	2	1	1
Oroqen	1	1	1	1	0	0
Pumi	4	2	2	2	1	1
Qiang	31	17	14	23	13	11
Russian	2	1	1	2	1	1
Salar	11	6	5	9	5	4
She	98	57	41	61	29	32
Shui	33	19	14	21	11	9
Tajik	5	3	2	5	3	2
Tatar	1	0	0	1	0	0
Tibetan	428	229	198	329	180	149
Tu	26	15	12	21	12	9
Tujia	1017	561	455	576	322	254
Uygur	1016	534	482	1033	528	505
Uzbek	2	1	1	2	1	1
Va	42	21	21	23	13	10
Xibe	24	12	11	27	14	13
Yao	309	175	134	153	85	68
Yi	780	406	374	483	265	218
Yugur	2	1	1	1	1	0
Zhuang	1662	941	720	883	485	397

Notes: Data in this table are obtained from the 2012 national sample survey on population changes. The sampling fraction is 0.831 ‰

Table 1.14 Illiterate population aged 15 and over by sex

Ethnic group	Population aged 15 and over (person)	Male	Female	Percentage of illiterate population to total aged 15 and over (%)	Male	Female
National total	939,526	476,037	463,489	4.96	2.67	7.32
Achang	25	13	12	8.30	5.12	11.64
Bai	1351	690	660	8.36	5.07	11.79
Baonan	12	6	6	8.65	5.36	12.10
Blang	68	35	33	8.30	5.12	11.63
Buyi	1911	968	943	11.60	6.47	16.85
Dai	856	438	417	8.30	5.12	11.64
Daur	103	52	50	3.45	2.17	4.79
Deang	13	7	6	8.32	5.14	11.65
Derung	6	3	3	7.63	4.66	10.73
Dong	1990	1010	980	8.41	4.64	12.28
Dongxiang	372	190	182	8.12	5.06	11.32
Ewenki	24	12	12	3.86	2.34	5.43
Gaoshan	3	2	2	4.86	2.58	7.17
Gelao	371	188	183	11.71	6.53	17.01
Han	862,567	436,898	425,669	4.96	2.64	7.35
Hani	1063	544	519	8.31	5.13	11.64
Hezhe	4	2	2	2.64	1.71	3.60
Hui	7511	3798	3712	6.51	3.94	9.14
Jing	16	8	8	4.10	1.96	6.35
Jingpo	98	50	48	8.31	5.12	11.64
Jino	15	8	8	8.31	5.13	11.64
Kazak	1003	511	493	3.44	2.76	4.14
Kirgiz	129	66	63	3.42	2.74	4.11
Korean	1477	747	730	2.20	1.37	3.05
Lahu	335	171	163	8.30	5.12	11.63
Lhoba	2	1	1	32.18	26.87	37.33
Li	979	514	465	4.78	2.24	7.58
Lisu	468	240	228	8.26	5.09	11.59
Manchu	8348	4205	4143	2.71	1.58	3.86
Maonan	73	37	36	6.15	3.18	9.23
Miao	6068	3080	2988	8.50	4.78	12.32
Monba	7	3	3	33.33	27.93	38.56
Mongol	4475	2276	2199	3.95	2.40	5.55
Mulao	143	73	70	4.87	2.41	7.45
Naxi	228	117	111	8.37	5.18	11.70
Nu	21	11	10	8.65	5.44	12.00

(*continued*)

Table 1.14 Continued

Ethnic group	Population aged 15 and over (person)	Male	Female	Percentage of illiterate population to total aged 15 and over (%)	Male	Female
Oroqen	6	3	3	3.22	2.00	4.47
Pumi	25	13	12	8.29	5.12	11.62
Qiang	210	110	100	6.85	3.94	10.05
Russian	12	6	6	3.71	2.63	4.83
Salar	82	42	40	11.44	7.41	15.67
She	555	279	276	5.04	2.19	7.93
Shui	262	133	129	11.38	6.34	16.53
Tajik	33	17	16	3.48	2.75	4.23
Tatar	4	2	2	3.67	2.84	4.53
Tibetan	4041	2040	2000	20.62	16.20	25.07
Tu	187	96	91	11.19	7.17	15.40
Tujia	5558	2807	2752	6.17	3.39	9.01
Uygur	6739	3429	3309	3.43	2.75	4.13
Uzbek	10	5	5	3.44	2.74	4.16
Va	293	150	143	8.24	5.08	11.56
Xibe	149	75	74	2.56	1.65	3.49
Yao	1880	962	918	4.23	2.15	6.40
Yi	5535	2847	2688	8.28	4.95	11.80
Yugur	10	5	5	8.50	5.24	11.93
Zhuang	11,332	5806	5526	4.08	1.97	6.29

Notes: Illiterate population in this table refers to the population aged 15 and over who are unable or have difficulty in reading. Data in this table are obtained from the 2012 national sample survey on population changes. The sampling fraction is 0.831 ‰

Table 1.15 Family households by size (household)

Ethnic group	Number of family households	One person	Two persons	Three persons	Four persons	Five persons
National total	356,954	50,261	94,323	98,432	59,938	32,830
Achang	9	1	2	2	2	1
Bai	503	69	109	125	103	56
Baonan	4	1	1	1	1	0
Blang	25	3	5	6	5	3
Buyi	779	111	201	187	143	83
Dai	314	42	66	78	66	36

(*continued*)

Table 1.15 Continued

Ethnic group	Number of family households	One person	Two persons	Three persons	Four persons	Five persons
Daur	41	5	13	15	5	2
Deang	5	1	1	1	1	1
Derung	2	0	0	1	0	0
Dong	794	117	196	193	148	83
Dongxiang	137	21	29	34	24	15
Ewenki	9	1	3	3	1	0
Gaoshan	1	0	0	0	0	0
Gelao	152	22	39	36	28	16
Han	327,467	46,272	87,041	90,467	54,695	29,903
Hani	390	52	81	97	82	44
Hezhe	1	0	0	1	0	0
Hui	2822	346	692	786	513	286
Jing	6	1	1	1	1	1
Jingpo	36	5	7	9	7	4
Jino	6	1	1	1	1	1
Kazak	394	49	94	111	72	42
Kirgiz	51	6	12	14	9	5
Korean	578	71	182	189	72	45
Lahu	123	16	26	31	26	14
Lhoba	1	0	0	0	0	0
Li	316	35	55	73	69	43
Lisu	172	23	36	43	36	19
Manchu	3213	408	984	1047	424	235
Maonan	28	4	6	7	6	3
Miao	2409	360	595	591	448	248
Monba	2	0	0	0	0	0
Mongol	1770	203	549	627	246	104
Mulao	55	7	12	13	11	6
Naxi	84	11	18	21	17	9
Nu	8	1	2	2	2	1
Oroqen	3	0	1	1	0	0
Pumi	9	1	2	2	2	1
Qiang	83	15	23	22	13	7
Russian	5	1	1	2	1	0
Salar	30	4	6	8	6	3
She	215	39	60	54	32	17
Shui	107	15	27	26	20	11
Tajik	13	2	3	4	2	1
Tatar	2	0	0	0	0	0
Tibetan	1405	197	284	324	248	155
Tu	68	9	14	17	13	8
Tujia	2194	346	562	576	381	203

(*continued*)

Table 1.15 Continued

Ethnic group	Number of family households	One person	Two persons	Three persons	Four persons	Five persons
Uygur	2649	330	632	746	483	284
Uzbek	4	0	1	1	1	0
Va	107	14	23	27	22	12
Xibe	58	8	18	19	7	4
Yao	714	103	156	173	141	79
Yi	2096	308	491	527	404	218
Yugur	4	1	1	1	1	0
Zhuang	4292	577	907	1039	861	493

Notes: Data in this table are obtained from the 2012 national sample survey on population changes. The sampling fraction is 0.831 ‰

2

Macroeconomic Growth and Structural Change

Data on Gross Domestic Product (GDP) are computed by the Department of National Accounts of the National Bureau of Statistics (NBS) based on different approaches in the light of the different features of various sectors, various expenditure structures and different data sources. GDP is a measurement of value which changes depending on changes of price and production. GDP at constant prices converts the gross domestic product based on the current price into a value based on the price of the base period. When adjusted for price changes, the values of two different periods can be compared to reflect changes of both products and production activities.

GDP index is derived from the constant-price GDPs of the two periods. As economy grows, changes will take place in the price structures of various industries, and the base period for the measurement of constant-price GDP thus needs to be adjusted every few years in order to better reflect the impact of price change on the economy. Since China started GDP calculation, eight constant-price base periods have been used, i.e., 1952, 1957, 1970, 1980, 1990, 2000, 2005, and 2010 and the current base period is 2010. That is to say, the 2011 GDP is calculated on the basis of the 2010 prices. As the calculation of constant-

R. Guo, *China Ethnic Statistical Yearbook 2016*,
DOI 10.1007/978-3-319-49199-8_2

price GDP is based on different base periods, the constant-price GDP data shall also be announced in accordance with various periods.

The coefficient for the conversion of electric power into standard coal equivalent (SCE) is calculated on the basis of the heat value equivalent. One kilowatt is equal to 0.1229 kg SCE.

Data on investments in fixed assets by individuals in rural areas are provided by the Department of Rural Social and Economic Survey of the NBS through its rural social and economic survey. Other data on investments in fixed assets are from surveys conducted by the Department of Investment and Construction Statistics of the NBS. All data on investments in fixed assets are collected by the system of reporting form with complete enumeration, except data on individual investments in fixed assets in rural areas, which are collected through sample surveys.

Data for compilation of the consumer price indices and the retail price indices in China are collected by the Department of Urban Social and Economic Survey, NBS and the Department of Rural Social and Economic Survey, NBS through a combination of sample surveys and surveys of key units. Areas distributed in different economic regions are selected as the sample areas and representative commodities are selected as the sample commodities. Regular surveys are conducted to collect data on their market prices. Population parameters are inferred on the basis of the sample data. At present, 500 cities and counties of all provinces, autonomous regions and municipalities directly under the central government have been selected for this purpose.

Table 2.1 Gross domestic product (GDP), 2007–2011 (100 million yuan) and per capita GDP (yuan)

Ethnic group	2008	2009	2010	2011	2012	Per capita GDP
Achang	4.63	5.02	5.88	7.23	8.37	22,474
Bai	256.09	279.08	328.64	403.89	467.16	23,203
Baonan	2.21	2.36	2.88	3.51	3.95	22,953
Blang	12.57	13.63	15.97	19.63	22.73	22,564
Buyi	328.12	359.96	424.15	522.56	621.04	20,837
Dai	157.72	171.03	200.36	246.41	285.32	22,455
Daur	41.73	46.43	55.80	68.27	75.30	52,912
Deang	2.43	2.63	3.08	3.79	4.39	22,328
Derung	1.21	1.32	1.56	1.90	2.17	26,729
Dong	426.63	473.67	570.32	698.58	802.72	26,259
Dongxiang	71.02	75.41	92.46	112.62	126.94	23,433
Ewenki	10.77	12.25	14.68	18.00	19.89	60,812
Gaoshan	1.16	1.28	1.53	1.82	2.02	40,896
Gelao	62.69	68.79	81.00	99.89	119.01	20,552
Han	312,399.25	342,370.85	409,254.77	487,614.46	538,440.14	42,778
Hani	196.01	212.52	248.91	306.12	354.47	22,449
Hezhe	1.15	1.20	1.45	1.75	1.91	38,064
Hui	2347.98	2565.61	3107.43	3753.42	4188.98	37,337
Jing	3.72	4.11	5.04	6.16	6.86	28,462
Jingpo	18.01	19.53	22.87	28.12	32.56	22,461
Jino	2.84	3.08	3.61	4.44	5.14	22,417
Kazak	283.34	289.77	368.29	447.69	508.28	33,792
Kirgiz	36.52	37.36	47.46	57.68	65.46	33,883
Korean	505.18	559.76	669.40	810.85	906.34	44,640
Lahu	61.86	67.08	78.57	96.61	111.85	22,490
Lhoba	0.47	0.53	0.61	0.73	0.84	24,359
Li	245.09	269.64	335.65	409.92	464.26	32,026
Lisu	86.84	94.25	110.53	135.90	157.24	22,679

(*continued*)

Table 2.1 Continued

Ethnic group	2008	2009	2010	2011	2012	Per capita GDP
Manchu	3253.69	3588.50	4314.31	5193.93	5764.78	50,057
Maonan	15.81	17.43	21.25	26.03	29.36	26,039
Miao	1286.87	1426.44	1711.74	2103.11	2422.42	26,297
Monba	1.45	1.61	1.86	2.21	2.54	24,235
Mongol	1961.51	2222.38	2667.95	3264.06	3616.68	58,023
Mulao	33.45	36.86	45.09	55.03	61.47	27,787
Naxi	42.40	46.02	53.97	66.34	76.74	22,707
Nu	3.98	4.31	5.05	6.21	7.18	22,719
Oroqen	2.45	2.70	3.24	3.95	4.35	49,448
Pumi	4.61	4.99	5.85	7.20	8.33	22,601
Qiang	47.28	53.05	64.40	78.76	89.38	29,730
Russian	4.46	4.83	5.93	7.22	8.07	45,244
Salar	21.41	22.73	28.31	34.90	39.52	32,214
She	232.64	256.91	309.30	366.47	404.51	50,478
Shui	45.01	49.41	58.33	71.93	85.37	20,908
Tajik	9.34	9.57	12.14	14.75	16.73	34,019
Tatar	1.12	1.15	1.45	1.76	2.00	34,063
Tibetan	882.52	970.76	1159.74	1407.97	1608.95	26,722
Tu	49.76	53.00	65.68	80.75	91.23	32,422
Tujia	1445.91	1628.15	1982.60	2439.72	2768.89	34,180
Uygur	1907.30	1951.30	2479.29	3013.36	3420.74	33,863
Uzbek	2.83	2.90	3.68	4.47	5.07	34,038
Va	55.20	59.88	70.16	86.13	99.54	22,921
Xibe	57.78	63.43	77.28	93.16	104.20	51,266
Yao	489.01	540.19	656.86	797.30	887.26	31,034
Yi	1069.81	1173.81	1391.52	1708.99	1971.47	24,229
Yugur	1.84	1.97	2.40	2.91	3.28	22,949
Zhuang	2738.99	3015.27	3688.57	4495.62	4997.31	28,642

Table 2.2 Gross domestic product – indices (preceding year = 100)

Ethnic group	2008	2009	2010	2011	2012
Achang	110.61	112.10	112.31	113.68	112.93
Bai	110.92	112.14	112.53	113.74	112.85
Baonan	110.28	110.23	111.91	112.54	112.51
Blang	110.63	112.11	112.33	113.68	112.93
Buyi	111.30	111.42	112.81	114.83	113.41
Dai	110.61	112.11	112.32	113.69	112.93
Daur	115.28	114.49	113.97	113.43	110.95
Deang	110.61	112.10	112.31	113.69	112.95
Derung	111.04	112.14	112.64	113.55	112.56
Dong	112.23	112.32	113.50	113.90	112.44
Dongxiang	110.23	110.07	111.70	112.47	112.48
Ewenki	116.95	116.13	114.70	113.98	111.26
Gaoshan	112.38	112.08	113.35	112.30	110.72
Gelao	111.31	111.41	112.81	114.88	113.45
Han	112.17	111.97	113.43	112.32	110.70
Hani	110.62	112.10	112.31	113.68	112.94
Hezhe	112.00	111.55	112.77	112.30	110.12
Hui	112.02	111.32	112.97	112.42	111.40
Jing	112.66	113.67	114.08	112.38	111.30
Jingpo	110.62	112.09	112.31	113.68	112.93
Jino	110.62	112.11	112.32	113.69	112.94
Kazak	111.00	108.11	110.61	112.00	111.96
Kirgiz	111.02	108.15	110.63	112.00	111.94
Korean	114.56	113.00	113.57	113.14	111.14
Lahu	110.62	112.10	112.31	113.68	112.93
Lhoba	110.29	112.32	112.38	112.74	111.78
Li	110.37	111.68	115.81	112.13	109.34
Lisu	110.62	112.16	112.39	113.72	112.92
Manchu	112.91	112.44	113.55	112.21	109.95
Maonan	112.32	113.10	113.76	113.06	111.89
Miao	112.07	112.37	113.54	114.12	112.63
Monba	110.16	112.36	112.34	112.67	111.73
Mongol	116.18	115.33	114.49	113.70	111.16
Mulao	112.52	113.42	113.95	112.61	111.49
Naxi	110.62	112.16	112.39	113.71	112.91
Nu	110.62	112.10	112.32	113.65	112.89
Oroqen	114.48	113.86	113.73	113.13	110.67
Pumi	110.63	112.11	112.33	113.68	112.92
Qiang	111.01	114.45	115.07	114.97	112.54
Russian	113.28	111.31	112.26	112.72	111.62
Salar	112.99	110.09	114.69	113.30	112.24
She	112.10	111.41	113.30	111.61	110.55
Shui	111.34	111.51	112.84	114.77	113.37

(continued)

Table 2.2 Continued

Ethnic group	2008	2009	2010	2011	2012
Tajik	111.05	108.25	110.73	112.03	111.93
Tatar	111.01	108.35	110.76	112.02	111.92
Tibetan	111.03	112.24	113.53	113.40	112.13
Tu	112.88	110.23	114.61	113.26	112.17
Tujia	113.28	113.32	114.70	114.02	112.00
Uygur	111.01	108.13	110.62	112.00	111.95
Uzbek	111.02	108.18	110.66	111.99	111.92
Va	110.66	112.11	112.34	113.65	112.88
Xibe	112.93	112.11	113.42	112.20	110.11
Yao	112.71	113.33	114.01	112.40	111.17
Yi	110.80	112.68	113.13	114.18	112.88
Yugur	110.20	110.29	111.84	112.50	112.49
Zhuang	112.54	113.59	113.99	112.32	111.27

Table 2.3 Gross domestic product (GDP) by three strata of industry (100 million yuan)

Ethnic group	GDP	Primary industry	Secondary industry	Industry	Construction	Tertiary industry
Achang	8.37	1.33	3.60	2.82	0.78	3.44
Bai	467.16	71.11	201.74	160.97	40.77	194.31
Baonan	3.95	0.54	1.85	1.48	0.37	1.56
Blang	22.73	3.59	9.79	7.68	2.11	9.34
Buyi	621.04	77.88	249.47	208.05	41.41	293.69
Dai	285.32	45.30	122.73	96.16	26.57	117.30
Daur	75.30	7.97	39.16	34.27	4.89	28.17
Deang	4.39	0.70	1.89	1.47	0.41	1.81
Derung	2.17	0.30	0.99	0.81	0.18	0.88
Dong	802.72	103.92	356.07	304.62	51.45	342.73
Dongxiang	126.94	18.26	58.62	46.93	11.70	50.06
Ewenki	19.89	1.85	10.79	9.48	1.31	7.25
Gaoshan	2.02	0.20	0.99	0.86	0.13	0.83
Gelao	119.01	14.95	47.40	39.53	7.87	56.67
Han	538,440.14	47,556.08	26,7415.79	23,4639.84	32,775.95	223,468.28
Hani	354.47	56.26	152.40	119.37	33.03	145.81
Hezhe	1.91	0.26	0.84	0.73	0.11	0.81
Hui	4188.98	405.98	2037.13	1707.83	329.30	1745.87
Jing	6.86	1.09	3.27	2.76	0.50	2.50
Jingpo	32.56	5.16	14.00	10.97	3.03	13.40
Jino	5.14	0.82	2.21	1.73	0.48	2.11
Kazak	508.28	89.25	235.69	192.95	42.74	183.35
Kirgiz	65.46	11.47	30.36	24.87	5.49	23.64
Korean	906.34	101.22	459.93	402.51	57.41	345.19
Lahu	111.85	17.74	48.18	37.77	10.41	45.94
Lhoba	0.84	0.09	0.30	0.10	0.20	0.44
Li	464.26	112.55	134.09	88.88	45.22	217.62
Lisu	157.24	24.85	68.15	53.60	14.55	64.25

(continued)

Table 2.3 Continued

Ethnic group	GDP	Primary industry	Secondary industry	Industry	Construction	Tertiary industry
Manchu	5764.78	540.21	2930.68	2572.13	358.55	2293.89
Maonan	29.36	4.52	13.54	11.44	2.10	11.30
Miao	2422.42	312.09	1078.95	910.82	168.13	1031.39
Monba	2.54	0.28	0.90	0.28	0.62	1.36
Mongol	3616.68	337.10	1957.03	1716.01	241.02	1322.55
Mulao	61.47	9.48	28.95	24.58	4.36	23.05
Naxi	76.74	12.06	33.14	25.99	7.14	31.54
Nu	7.18	1.12	3.09	2.41	0.68	2.97
Oroqen	4.35	0.48	2.20	1.92	0.27	1.67
Pumi	8.33	1.31	3.59	2.82	0.77	3.42
Qiang	89.38	12.24	46.04	39.39	6.65	31.10
Russian	8.07	1.02	4.00	3.41	0.59	3.05
Salar	39.52	3.89	22.06	18.07	4.00	13.56
She	404.51	31.29	205.21	176.02	29.20	168.00
Shui	85.37	11.00	34.46	28.68	5.78	39.91
Tajik	16.73	2.89	7.78	6.38	1.39	6.07
Tatar	2.00	0.34	0.92	0.76	0.17	0.74
Tibetan	1608.95	186.65	736.22	476.34	259.88	686.08
Tu	91.23	8.80	50.65	41.71	8.94	31.79
Tujia	2768.89	323.62	1340.71	1154.07	186.64	1104.56
Uygur	3420.74	599.18	1586.60	1299.46	287.13	1234.97
Uzbek	5.07	0.88	2.34	1.92	0.42	1.85
Va	99.54	15.54	43.18	34.04	9.15	40.82
Xibe	104.20	10.39	53.58	46.58	7.00	40.23
Yao	887.26	123.02	420.98	362.98	58.00	343.26
Yi	1971.47	293.96	895.76	728.41	167.35	781.75
Yugur	3.28	0.44	1.50	1.20	0.30	1.33
Zhuang	4997.31	780.16	2378.03	2017.91	360.13	1839.11

Table 2.4 Gross domestic product of tertiary industry (100 million yuan)

Ethnic group	Transport, storage and post	Wholesale and retail trade	Hotels and catering services	Financial intermediation	Real estate	Others
Achang	0.21	0.84	0.27	0.44	0.20	1.48
Bai	15.47	45.35	14.53	23.63	11.69	83.65
Baonan	0.22	0.27	0.09	0.14	0.10	0.74
Blang	0.56	2.29	0.72	1.20	0.55	4.02
Buyi	57.68	48.52	22.95	33.63	17.63	113.28
Dai	6.99	28.72	9.08	15.03	6.88	50.61
Daur	4.95	6.86	1.99	2.66	2.15	9.54
Deang	0.11	0.44	0.14	0.23	0.10	0.78
Derung	0.07	0.21	0.06	0.11	0.06	0.36
Dong	54.72	65.22	23.16	34.37	24.27	140.98
Dongxiang	6.98	8.64	2.92	4.57	3.30	23.64
Ewenki	1.43	1.80	0.54	0.68	0.52	2.29
Gaoshan	0.10	0.18	0.05	0.11	0.09	0.31
Gelao	11.34	9.21	4.46	6.45	3.35	21.86
Han	25,563.97	51,826.23	11,578.60	28,694.87	23,422.48	82,382.12
Hani	8.68	35.79	11.28	18.65	8.54	62.87
Hezhe	0.09	0.19	0.05	0.08	0.08	0.33
Hui	234.31	344.68	84.74	240.25	151.84	690.04
Jing	0.33	0.53	0.19	0.31	0.26	0.87
Jingpo	0.81	3.28	1.04	1.71	0.79	5.78
Jino	0.13	0.52	0.16	0.27	0.12	0.91
Kazak	24.24	28.97	7.36	24.45	13.20	85.13
Kirgiz	3.12	3.76	0.96	3.14	1.71	10.95
Korean	39.23	81.25	19.26	29.38	26.95	149.12
Lahu	2.75	11.28	3.56	5.87	2.70	19.79

(*continued*)

Table 2.4 Continued

Ethnic group	Transport, storage and post	Wholesale and retail trade	Hotels and catering services	Financial intermediation	Real estate	Others
Lhoba	0.03	0.05	0.03	0.04	0.03	0.26
Li	22.24	48.49	16.01	21.46	37.75	71.66
Lisu	3.91	15.63	4.97	8.26	3.81	27.68
Manchu	322.96	515.48	115.21	247.67	229.78	862.80
Maonan	1.72	2.26	0.88	1.37	1.06	4.02
Miao	151.69	199.88	69.29	115.28	76.53	418.72
Monba	0.10	0.17	0.08	0.13	0.08	0.80
Mongol	248.60	320.44	92.16	127.07	100.65	433.63
Mulao	3.21	4.80	1.75	2.85	2.35	8.09
Naxi	1.91	7.62	2.42	4.07	1.88	13.64
Nu	0.18	0.72	0.23	0.38	0.18	1.28
Oroqen	0.27	0.41	0.11	0.16	0.14	0.59
Pumi	0.21	0.84	0.26	0.44	0.20	1.48
Qiang	2.70	5.11	2.32	4.90	2.67	13.41
Russian	0.48	0.62	0.17	0.36	0.23	1.19
Salar	1.57	2.37	0.50	1.78	0.74	6.60
She	19.91	37.28	7.65	24.18	21.13	57.85
Shui	7.76	6.66	3.14	4.56	2.42	15.38
Tajik	0.80	0.98	0.25	0.81	0.45	2.79
Tatar	0.10	0.12	0.03	0.10	0.05	0.34
Tibetan	59.44	98.49	40.65	75.67	42.02	369.80
Tu	3.69	5.77	1.25	4.11	1.89	15.07
Tujia	140.53	222.18	62.26	127.95	97.35	454.28

Uygur	163.13	195.68	49.59	164.73	89.12	572.71
Uzbek	0.24	0.30	0.07	0.25	0.14	0.85
Va	2.53	10.06	3.13	5.20	2.46	17.44
Xibe	5.36	8.88	2.02	4.39	4.14	15.44
Yao	41.19	75.22	22.58	36.97	33.43	133.87
Yi	64.39	167.06	60.12	105.20	51.57	333.41
Yugur	0.18	0.23	0.08	0.12	0.09	0.63
Zhuang	231.29	399.80	138.45	228.42	195.19	645.96

Table 2.5 Composition of gross domestic product (GDP) (%)

Ethnic group	Primary industry	Secondary industry	Tertiary industry
Achang	15.99	42.92	41.09
Bai	15.44	42.92	41.63
Baonan	13.75	46.48	39.78
Blang	15.95	42.98	41.07
Buyi	12.94	39.56	47.51
Dai	15.98	42.96	41.06
Daur	11.52	50.93	37.55
Deang	16.01	42.91	41.07
Derung	14.82	44.50	40.67
Dong	13.29	43.00	43.71
Dongxiang	14.17	46.12	39.71
Ewenki	9.66	53.95	36.39
Gaoshan	11.45	50.18	38.37
Gelao	12.91	39.39	47.70
Han	10.38	50.47	39.16
Hani	15.98	42.93	41.09
Hezhe	14.53	44.72	40.74
Hui	11.25	49.63	39.12
Jing	16.21	47.57	36.22
Jingpo	15.97	42.93	41.10
Jino	15.98	42.94	41.08
Kazak	17.57	46.38	36.05
Kirgiz	17.55	46.37	36.08
Korean	11.84	51.04	37.13
Lahu	15.97	42.98	41.05
Lhoba	11.46	35.76	52.78
Li	24.14	28.98	46.88
Lisu	15.91	43.21	40.88
Manchu	10.16	51.55	38.29
Maonan	15.40	45.36	39.24
Miao	13.29	43.25	43.46
Monba	11.34	35.28	53.38
Mongol	9.71	53.96	36.33
Mulao	15.77	46.72	37.51
Naxi	15.89	43.14	40.98
Nu	15.85	42.90	41.25
Oroqen	12.11	49.44	38.45
Pumi	15.94	43.01	41.05
Qiang	13.77	51.56	34.68
Russian	13.99	49.21	36.80
Salar	10.14	55.67	34.19
She	8.44	50.49	41.07
Shui	13.13	39.76	47.11

(*continued*)

Table 2.5 Continued

Ethnic group	Primary industry	Secondary industry	Tertiary industry
Tajik	17.35	46.51	36.15
Tatar	17.11	46.33	36.56
Tibetan	11.87	44.54	43.58
Tu	10.08	55.13	34.79
Tujia	12.06	47.66	40.29
Uygur	17.55	46.40	36.05
Uzbek	17.46	46.35	36.19
Va	15.84	43.16	41.00
Xibe	10.65	51.29	38.06
Yao	14.81	47.28	37.91
Yi	15.04	44.94	40.02
Yugur	13.75	46.13	40.12
Zhuang	16.16	47.51	36.33

Table 2.6 Indices of gross domestic product (GDP) (preceding year = 100)

Ethnic group	GDP	Primary sector	Secondary sector	Tertiary sector
Achang	112.93	106.63	116.62	110.87
Bai	112.85	106.55	116.32	111.08
Baonan	112.51	106.77	114.18	112.40
Blang	112.93	106.62	116.61	110.88
Buyi	113.41	108.40	116.54	112.00
Dai	112.93	106.62	116.63	110.88
Daur	110.95	105.92	112.21	110.37
Deang	112.95	106.64	116.65	110.88
Derung	112.56	106.37	115.79	110.82
Dong	112.44	106.43	115.00	111.78
Dongxiang	112.48	106.84	114.15	112.43
Ewenki	111.26	105.66	112.89	110.09
Gaoshan	110.72	104.84	112.35	110.20
Gelao	113.45	108.48	116.59	112.04
Han	110.70	104.71	112.02	110.39
Hani	112.94	106.63	116.63	110.88
Hezhe	110.12	106.20	110.55	110.70
Hui	111.40	105.54	113.18	110.67
Jing	111.30	105.61	114.16	109.91
Jingpo	112.93	106.63	116.62	110.88
Jino	112.94	106.63	116.64	110.88
Kazak	111.96	107.02	113.65	112.32
Kirgiz	111.94	107.01	113.62	112.30
Korean	111.14	105.44	112.52	110.94
Lahu	112.93	106.62	116.61	110.88
Lhoba	111.78	103.59	114.37	111.96

(continued)

Table 2.6 Continued

Ethnic group	GDP	Primary sector	Secondary sector	Tertiary sector
Li	109.34	106.37	111.29	109.61
Lisu	112.92	106.56	116.58	110.89
Manchu	109.95	105.03	110.82	109.98
Maonan	111.89	106.42	114.85	110.49
Miao	112.63	106.50	115.32	111.72
Monba	111.73	103.39	114.29	111.98
Mongol	111.16	105.53	112.75	110.17
Mulao	111.49	105.90	114.34	110.13
Naxi	112.91	106.55	116.57	110.90
Nu	112.89	106.56	116.54	110.88
Oroqen	110.67	105.94	111.69	110.38
Pumi	112.92	106.61	116.60	110.88
Qiang	112.54	104.53	115.12	111.60
Russian	111.62	106.34	113.26	111.37
Salar	112.24	105.43	114.04	111.26
She	110.55	104.00	112.35	109.46
Shui	113.37	108.34	116.53	111.93
Tajik	111.93	106.95	113.61	112.26
Tatar	111.92	106.91	113.59	112.25
Tibetan	112.13	104.38	114.54	111.74
Tu	112.17	105.42	113.96	111.21
Tujia	112.00	104.92	113.99	111.67
Uygur	111.95	107.01	113.64	112.31
Uzbek	111.92	106.97	113.61	112.28
Va	112.88	106.58	116.52	110.87
Xibe	110.11	105.54	110.72	110.58
Yao	111.17	104.87	113.50	110.55
Yi	112.88	106.25	116.21	111.21
Yugur	112.49	106.78	114.14	112.39
Zhuang	111.27	105.57	114.11	109.89

Table 2.7 Government expenditure in selected sectors (100 million yuan)

Ethnic group	Expenditure for public security	Expenditure for education	Expenditure for science and technology	Expenditure for culture, sport and media	Expenditure for social safety and employment effort	Expenditure for medical and health care
Achang	0.27	0.54	0.03	0.05	0.35	0.21
Bai	15.81	28.92	1.50	2.66	18.30	11.39
Baonan	0.16	0.26	0.01	0.04	0.21	0.10
Blang	0.74	1.46	0.07	0.13	0.95	0.58
Buyi	35.76	42.59	2.62	4.24	20.25	17.02
Dai	9.26	18.45	0.91	1.70	11.99	7.29
Daur	1.62	2.39	0.17	0.38	2.15	0.89
Deang	0.14	0.29	0.01	0.03	0.19	0.11
Derung	0.06	0.12	0.01	0.01	0.08	0.05
Dong	31.64	40.94	2.69	3.64	21.42	16.00
Dongxiang	5.13	8.21	0.40	1.12	6.13	3.17
Ewenki	0.42	0.57	0.04	0.11	0.54	0.22
Gaoshan	0.04	0.07	0.01	0.01	0.04	0.03
Gelao	7.02	8.28	0.51	0.82	3.91	3.31
Han	10,470.34	18,324.42	2107.25	1861.73	10,823.93	6498.01
Hani	11.52	22.94	1.13	2.11	14.90	9.06
Hezhe	0.04	0.07	0.01	0.01	0.06	0.02
Hui	107.60	190.56	17.70	23.22	138.30	70.85
Jing	0.20	0.31	0.02	0.02	0.15	0.13
Jingpo	1.06	2.11	0.10	0.19	1.37	0.83
Jino	0.17	0.33	0.02	0.03	0.22	0.13
Kazak	20.54	32.07	2.24	4.62	15.44	9.88
Kirgiz	2.63	4.11	0.29	0.59	1.99	1.27
Korean	18.14	32.68	2.68	3.48	24.22	11.08

(*continued*)

Table 2.7 Continued

Ethnic group	Expenditure for public security	Expenditure for education	Expenditure for science and technology	Expenditure for culture, sport and media	Expenditure for social safety and employment effort	Expenditure for medical and health care
Lahu	3.63	7.22	0.36	0.66	4.69	2.85
Lhoba	0.16	0.10	0.01	0.03	0.07	0.04
Li	16.16	25.75	1.96	3.19	17.01	9.72
Lisu	5.05	10.04	0.50	0.93	6.53	3.97
Manchu	111.58	182.55	21.75	20.47	154.77	58.14
Maonan	1.05	1.47	0.10	0.12	0.70	0.62
Miao	92.25	127.23	8.03	11.45	71.47	49.49
Monba	0.49	0.32	0.02	0.08	0.22	0.12
Mongol	78.51	108.95	8.33	18.70	100.89	41.39
Mulao	1.94	2.85	0.21	0.23	1.36	1.20
Naxi	2.52	4.92	0.25	0.46	3.20	1.95
Nu	0.25	0.47	0.02	0.05	0.30	0.18
Oroqen	0.09	0.14	0.01	0.02	0.13	0.05
Pumi	0.27	0.54	0.03	0.05	0.35	0.21
Qiang	2.08	3.72	0.23	0.45	2.54	1.58
Russian	0.24	0.36	0.03	0.06	0.23	0.12
Salar	1.70	3.42	0.15	0.39	3.46	1.20
She	6.66	12.01	1.36	1.08	4.81	4.11
Shui	4.85	5.82	0.36	0.58	2.78	2.33
Tajik	0.66	1.04	0.07	0.15	0.50	0.32
Tatar	0.08	0.12	0.01	0.02	0.06	0.04
Tibetan	172.40	151.39	7.80	29.77	118.95	57.42
Tu	3.76	7.55	0.35	0.85	7.57	2.67
Tujia	72.95	109.40	7.60	8.85	71.83	40.34

Uygur	137.87	215.22	15.07	30.96	103.62	66.31
Uzbek	0.20	0.32	0.02	0.05	0.15	0.10
Va	3.17	6.30	0.32	0.58	4.09	2.48
Xibe	2.33	3.60	0.43	0.43	3.04	1.05
Yao	23.55	36.48	2.81	2.86	19.34	14.60
Yi	63.05	114.09	6.06	11.36	72.83	45.95
Yugur	0.13	0.21	0.01	0.03	0.17	0.08
Zhuang	143.12	223.75	16.92	17.86	110.08	94.29

Table 2.8 Final consumption expenditure (100 million yuan)

Ethnic group	Final consumption expenditures	Household consumption	Rural household	Urban household	Government consumption
Achang	5.09	3.66	1.30	2.36	1.42
Bai	275.21	199.44	69.03	130.41	75.77
Baonan	2.30	1.50	0.49	1.01	0.81
Blang	13.79	9.94	3.52	6.41	3.86
Buyi	352.33	259.68	85.87	173.82	92.65
Dai	173.57	125.09	44.44	80.65	48.48
Daur	32.61	19.87	4.17	15.69	12.74
Deang	2.68	1.93	0.69	1.24	0.75
Derung	1.21	0.87	0.28	0.59	0.34
Dong	411.50	307.93	93.18	214.75	103.57
Dongxiang	74.09	47.52	15.35	32.16	26.57
Ewenki	8.06	4.92	0.98	3.94	3.14
Gaoshan	0.93	0.67	0.16	0.51	0.26
Gelao	67.83	50.05	16.55	33.50	17.79
Han	250,440.59	180,659.64	41,477.50	139,182.14	69,780.96
Hani	215.70	155.41	55.20	100.20	60.29
Hezhe	0.99	0.62	0.14	0.48	0.37
Hui	2067.48	1368.98	339.02	1029.95	698.51
Jing	3.44	2.58	0.74	1.84	0.86
Jingpo	19.80	14.27	5.06	9.20	5.53
Jino	3.13	2.25	0.80	1.45	0.88
Kazak	288.63	160.63	45.74	114.89	127.99
Kirgiz	37.12	20.68	5.88	14.80	16.44
Korean	397.59	270.79	62.53	208.26	126.80
Lahu	67.96	48.97	17.40	31.57	18.99
Lhoba	0.52	0.21	0.08	0.12	0.32
Li	226.43	153.95	42.66	111.28	72.48
Lisu	94.99	68.53	24.37	44.15	26.46
Manchu	2467.47	1779.81	344.59	1435.22	687.67
Maonan	15.14	11.34	3.37	7.97	3.80
Miao	1263.72	938.50	284.59	653.91	325.22
Monba	1.61	0.63	0.25	0.38	0.98
Mongol	1475.43	933.44	188.88	744.56	541.99
Mulao	31.16	23.42	6.69	16.72	7.75
Naxi	46.42	33.40	11.84	21.56	13.02
Nu	4.35	3.11	1.10	2.01	1.24
Oroqen	1.95	1.20	0.25	0.95	0.75
Pumi	5.05	3.64	1.29	2.35	1.41
Qiang	44.67	34.00	12.07	21.93	10.68
Russian	3.92	2.30	0.54	1.76	1.62
Salar	21.05	12.50	3.89	8.61	8.55

(continued)

Table 2.8 Continued

Ethnic group	Final consumption expenditures	Household consumption	Rural household	Urban household	Government consumption
She	178.11	135.47	32.32	103.14	42.64
Shui	48.33	35.58	11.81	23.76	12.75
Tajik	9.44	5.30	1.50	3.81	4.14
Tatar	1.13	0.64	0.18	0.46	0.49
Tibetan	922.34	487.40	179.72	307.69	434.93
Tu	48.27	29.37	8.94	20.42	18.90
Tujia	1309.53	968.74	251.93	716.81	340.79
Uygur	1940.48	1081.13	307.33	773.80	859.35
Uzbek	2.87	1.61	0.45	1.15	1.26
Va	59.86	43.14	15.19	27.94	16.72
Xibe	45.45	32.97	6.18	26.79	12.48
Yao	440.87	334.12	90.36	243.77	106.74
Yi	1124.56	824.60	291.48	533.12	299.95
Yugur	1.91	1.25	0.40	0.85	0.66
Zhuang	2532.49	1904.42	537.81	1366.61	628.07

Table 2.9 Composition of final consumption expenditure

	Final consumption expenditures = 100		Household consumption expenditures = 100	
Ethnic group	Household consumption	Government consumption	Rural household	Urban household
Achang	72.04	27.96	35.62	64.38
Bai	72.51	27.49	34.93	65.07
Baonan	65.34	34.66	32.89	67.11
Blang	72.05	27.95	35.57	64.43
Buyi	73.68	26.32	33.78	66.22
Dai	72.07	27.93	35.64	64.36
Daur	61.01	38.99	21.62	78.38
Deang	72.02	27.98	35.69	64.31
Derung	71.85	28.15	33.36	66.64
Dong	74.62	25.38	31.51	68.49
Dongxiang	64.83	35.17	32.58	67.42
Ewenki	61.11	38.89	20.22	79.78
Gaoshan	72.70	27.30	26.55	73.45
Gelao	73.72	26.28	33.79	66.21
Han	72.49	27.51	25.79	74.21
Hani	72.05	27.95	35.64	64.36
Hezhe	62.40	37.60	23.84	76.16
Hui	67.26	32.74	27.50	72.50

(*continued*)

Table 2.9 Continued

Ethnic group	Final consumption expenditures = 100		Household consumption expenditures = 100	
	Household consumption	Government consumption	Rural household	Urban household
Jing	75.05	24.95	29.20	70.80
Jingpo	72.06	27.94	35.61	64.39
Jino	72.05	27.95	35.64	64.36
Kazak	55.67	44.33	28.50	71.50
Kirgiz	55.71	44.29	28.44	71.56
Korean	68.14	31.86	24.29	75.71
Lahu	72.05	27.95	35.62	64.38
Lhoba	39.25	60.75	43.17	56.83
Li	68.04	31.96	27.94	72.06
Lisu	72.16	27.84	35.64	64.36
Manchu	72.59	27.41	21.05	78.95
Maonan	74.80	25.20	30.42	69.58
Miao	74.16	25.84	31.50	68.50
Monba	37.83	62.17	43.78	56.22
Mongol	63.78	36.22	20.96	79.04
Mulao	75.07	24.93	29.43	70.57
Naxi	72.01	27.99	35.65	64.35
Nu	71.54	28.46	35.67	64.33
Oroqen	61.83	38.17	22.00	78.00
Pumi	72.03	27.97	35.58	64.42
Qiang	76.17	23.83	35.65	64.35
Russian	58.49	41.51	25.00	75.00
Salar	59.68	40.32	31.54	68.46
She	75.99	24.01	25.02	74.98
Shui	73.66	26.34	33.75	66.25
Tajik	56.24	43.76	28.38	71.62
Tatar	56.57	43.43	28.41	71.59
Tibetan	53.73	46.27	38.64	61.36
Tu	60.94	39.06	31.26	68.74
Tujia	73.98	26.02	26.98	73.02
Uygur	55.72	44.28	28.48	71.52
Uzbek	55.97	44.03	28.39	71.61
Va	72.07	27.93	35.43	64.57
Xibe	72.59	27.41	19.71	80.29
Yao	75.53	24.47	28.57	71.43
Yi	73.38	26.62	35.45	64.55
Yugur	65.71	34.29	32.78	67.22
Zhuang	75.09	24.91	29.07	70.93

Table 2.10 Household consumption expenditure

Ethnic group	Level (yuan)			Urban/rural consumption ratio (rural household = 1)	Index (preceding year = 100)		
	All households	Rural household	Urban household		All households	Rural household	Urban household
Achang	9843.24	5673.00	16,564.31	2.92	113.65	114.41	108.83
Bai	9897.72	5630.36	16,608.66	2.97	112.86	113.83	108.26
Baonan	8714.72	4668.42	15,156.00	3.26	112.07	113.20	108.89
Blang	9863.60	5680.78	16,581.53	2.92	113.65	114.42	108.83
Buyi	8726.97	4641.07	15,739.60	3.43	109.26	110.95	105.59
Dai	9843.71	5676.24	16,560.30	2.92	113.66	114.42	108.82
Daur	13,930.26	6858.88	19,297.33	2.81	109.80	111.53	108.16
Deang	9806.92	5655.51	16,532.71	2.92	113.68	114.43	108.85
Derung	10,660.66	5958.55	17,158.93	2.90	113.00	114.12	108.58
Dong	10,093.30	5348.17	16,836.10	3.22	109.31	110.94	105.83
Dongxiang	8812.59	4675.89	15,334.53	3.28	112.25	113.18	109.28
Ewenki	15,005.67	7071.59	20,875.61	2.96	111.03	113.16	109.11
Gaoshan	13,515.55	7179.41	19,301.51	2.80	109.76	111.58	106.86
Gelao	8652.03	4576.91	15,687.57	3.45	109.20	110.89	105.53
Han	14,294.22	7629.66	19,882.28	2.70	110.03	112.32	107.09
Hani	9841.37	5673.14	16,563.32	2.92	113.66	114.41	108.84
Hezhe	12,286.46	6733.09	16,394.65	2.45	106.47	107.40	105.38
Hui	12,220.45	6431.28	18,106.47	2.90	111.02	113.75	107.86
Jing	10,712.94	5481.60	17,558.33	3.22	110.31	109.72	107.47
Jingpo	9841.53	5667.08	16,565.15	2.93	113.64	114.40	108.82
Jino	9835.57	5668.55	16,554.39	2.92	113.67	114.42	108.83
Kazak	10,679.91	5413.29	17,442.45	3.22	115.84	116.18	114.79
Kirgiz	10,703.16	5429.63	17,439.22	3.21	115.75	116.09	114.71

(continued)

Table 2.10 Continued

Ethnic group	Level (yuan)			Urban/rural consumption ratio (rural household = 1)	Index (preceding year = 100)		
	All households	Rural household	Urban household		All households	Rural household	Urban household
Korean	13,300.83	7245.41	17,866.85	2.47	109.57	109.51	109.06
Lahu	9844.07	5673.57	16,566.60	2.92	113.65	114.41	108.83
Lhoba	6054.42	3449.39	13,512.79	4.07	108.74	107.72	109.35
Li	10,631.02	5983.70	15,208.41	2.55	109.28	111.75	106.96
Lisu	9877.69	5714.41	16,560.38	2.91	113.62	114.49	108.74
Manchu	15,430.81	7735.09	20,496.61	2.67	109.49	112.41	107.07
Maonan	10,074.39	5165.00	17,028.39	3.31	109.95	109.89	106.91
Miao	10,193.22	5405.64	16,866.95	3.19	109.98	111.88	106.23
Monba	5982.47	3425.63	13,463.69	4.10	108.66	107.50	109.42
Mongol	14,947.76	7143.17	20,799.08	2.93	111.28	113.61	109.12
Mulao	10,590.72	5380.06	17,505.79	3.27	110.09	109.66	107.22
Naxi	9881.93	5713.04	16,565.31	2.91	113.59	114.44	108.75
Nu	9836.57	5669.01	16,559.15	2.94	113.55	114.29	108.82
Oroqen	13,627.22	6892.52	18,614.22	2.70	108.71	110.27	107.18
Pumi	9867.18	5687.86	16,575.28	2.92	113.64	114.41	108.82
Qiang	11,309.97	7139.75	16,689.95	2.34	112.16	116.82	105.91
Russian	12,775.87	6280.05	19,117.44	3.10	113.79	114.93	112.32
Salar	10,215.24	5956.17	15,235.76	2.59	114.74	119.83	110.49
She	16,857.94	9859.00	21,900.29	2.29	107.36	110.28	105.06
Shui	8726.88	4644.52	15,742.57	3.42	109.38	110.97	105.71
Tajik	10,781.93	5467.97	17,504.93	3.21	115.64	116.05	114.54
Tatar	10,851.19	5514.24	17,531.17	3.20	115.45	115.88	114.27
Tibetan	8206.21	4885.65	14,584.59	3.28	111.17	112.97	108.79
Tu	10,461.11	6030.30	15,556.50	2.61	114.34	119.21	110.13

Tujia	11,941.48	6147.19	17,993.14	2.98	109.82	113.24	106.08
Uygur	10,702.34	5425.06	17,460.81	3.22	115.82	116.16	114.77
Uzbek	10,785.02	5464.26	17,525.13	3.22	115.72	116.07	114.65
Va	9928.33	5706.58	16,638.56	2.92	113.59	114.41	108.79
Xibe	16,213.41	7916.95	21,539.57	2.76	111.16	114.09	108.91
Yao	11,663.36	5932.79	18,366.79	3.11	110.09	110.25	107.12
Yi	10,103.17	5953.45	16,486.26	2.82	112.75	114.69	107.65
Yugur	8775.68	4676.20	15,241.60	3.28	111.88	112.89	108.73
Zhuang	10,907.23	5530.63	17,790.00	3.22	110.46	109.78	107.60

Table 2.11 Total investment in fixed assets by status of registration (100 million yuan)

Ethnic group	Total	State-owned firms	Private firms	Self-employed individuals	Others
Achang	6.32	2.30	1.20	0.29	0.17
Bai	348.93	124.70	66.58	15.58	9.54
Baonan	3.58	1.57	0.54	0.10	0.23
Blang	17.16	6.23	3.27	0.78	0.46
Buyi	498.77	188.43	70.10	18.62	6.48
Dai	215.58	78.51	40.87	9.82	5.75
Daur	55.21	17.85	8.77	1.11	1.44
Deang	3.33	1.22	0.63	0.15	0.09
Derung	1.61	0.54	0.33	0.06	0.05
Dong	577.16	184.93	116.96	24.48	17.92
Dongxiang	113.39	49.03	17.43	3.47	6.77
Ewenki	14.64	4.71	2.20	0.22	0.31
Gaoshan	1.34	0.31	0.34	0.04	0.06
Gelao	95.99	36.62	13.11	3.58	1.17
Han	33,9610.03	81,203.21	85,002.48	10,501.36	14,673.87
Hani	267.92	97.54	50.93	12.21	7.11
Hezhe	1.32	0.40	0.26	0.05	0.06
Hui	3162.55	921.35	775.67	102.27	110.72
Jing	5.05	1.24	1.43	0.29	0.24
Jingpo	24.59	8.95	4.66	1.12	0.65
Jino	3.89	1.42	0.74	0.18	0.10
Kazak	416.82	169.39	65.06	21.60	6.00
Kirgiz	53.59	21.73	8.39	2.77	0.78
Korean	693.96	159.12	163.86	23.22	32.78
Lahu	84.55	30.70	16.10	3.85	2.27
Lhoba	0.77	0.47	0.06	0.04	0.06
Li	347.17	88.65	36.06	13.79	9.63
Lisu	118.76	42.95	22.55	5.36	3.28

Manchu	4573.67	948.69	1437.81	103.31	162.81
Maonan	22.16	6.08	5.60	1.19	0.91
Miao	1770.27	587.31	348.88	70.68	50.54
Monba	2.30	1.45	0.15	0.11	0.20
Mongol	2735.51	828.37	495.47	45.73	64.66
Mulao	44.97	11.46	12.19	2.51	2.06
Naxi	57.85	21.06	10.89	2.61	1.60
Nu	5.42	1.99	1.02	0.25	0.15
Oroqen	3.14	0.99	0.53	0.07	0.10
Pumi	6.29	2.28	1.20	0.29	0.17
Qiang	63.64	20.00	10.56	2.14	3.57
Russian	6.12	2.20	0.96	0.20	0.11
Salar	38.27	17.46	4.38	1.51	1.13
She	240.41	64.01	57.53	6.93	6.19
Shui	68.82	25.69	10.16	2.63	0.99
Tajik	13.62	5.48	2.16	0.70	0.21
Tatar	1.61	0.65	0.25	0.08	0.03
Tibetan	1443.21	737.44	147.92	59.38	89.87
Tu	85.68	38.43	10.21	3.32	2.61
Tujia	1920.21	562.88	454.12	66.10	75.21
Uygur	2800.83	1136.21	438.28	145.04	40.44
Uzbek	4.12	1.66	0.65	0.21	0.06
Va	74.84	26.78	14.40	3.38	2.10
Xibe	88.11	20.08	28.39	2.09	2.71
Yao	585.54	150.63	154.92	30.87	27.21
Yi	1474.28	517.03	261.91	60.67	50.35
Yugur	2.92	1.26	0.45	0.08	0.19
Zhuang	3588.69	885.28	1004.30	205.63	172.90

Table 2.12 Indicators of energy consumption

Ethnic group	Energy consumption per 10,000 yuan of GDP (equivalent value)		Energy consumption per 10,000 yuan of Industrial value-added change (above designated size, equivalent weight) (±%)	Electricity consumption per 10,000 yuan of GDP change (±%)
	Index (ton of SCE/10,000 yuan)	Change (±%)		
Achang	1.16	−3.21	−9.86	5.40
Bai	1.19	−3.29	−9.56	4.09
Baonan	1.43	−1.72	−1.14	2.66
Blang	1.16	−3.22	−9.85	5.37
Buyi	1.67	−3.50	−7.94	−1.51
Dai	1.16	−3.23	−9.88	5.37
Daur	1.27	−2.50	−4.22	1.61
Deang	1.16	−3.21	−9.88	5.44
Derung	1.15	−3.18	−8.96	4.35
Dong	1.33	−3.55	−7.84	−1.67
Dongxiang	1.43	−1.40	−0.63	3.52
Ewenki	1.35	−2.63	−4.53	3.31
Gaoshan	0.94	−3.24	−5.97	0.18
Gelao	1.68	−3.51	−7.94	−1.63
Han	0.92	−3.49	−6.27	−0.45
Hani	1.16	−3.22	−9.89	5.41
Hezhe	1.03	−3.45	−5.27	−3.93
Hui	1.42	−0.07	−0.06	5.43
Jing	0.83	−3.32	−6.15	−0.15
Jingpo	1.16	−3.22	−9.87	5.38
Jino	1.16	−3.23	−9.88	5.40
Kazak	1.63	6.92	9.22	14.63
Kirgiz	1.62	6.83	9.09	14.47
Korean	0.97	−3.57	−4.76	−3.68
Lahu	1.16	−3.23	−9.88	5.39
Lhoba	0.11	−0.20	−0.41	0.08

Li	0.74	4.70	11.32	3.62
Lisu	1.16	−3.25	−9.82	5.20
Manchu	1.11	−3.49	−5.56	−2.36
Maonan	1.06	−3.40	−6.65	−0.70
Miao	1.31	−3.47	−7.83	−0.84
Monba	0.05	−0.17	−0.30	−0.04
Mongol	1.33	−2.38	−4.25	2.85
Mulao	0.92	−3.39	−6.36	−0.50
Naxi	1.15	−3.24	−9.78	5.17
Nu	1.14	−3.17	−9.68	5.28
Oroqen	1.19	−3.08	−4.94	−0.34
Pumi	1.16	−3.22	−9.84	5.35
Qiang	1.00	−4.20	−7.74	−1.83
Russian	1.48	2.81	3.19	9.61
Salar	1.96	7.77	7.98	5.93
She	0.70	−3.25	−2.78	1.84
Shui	1.64	−3.49	−7.93	−1.38
Tajik	1.61	6.58	8.72	14.12
Tatar	1.59	6.19	8.20	13.56
Tibetan	0.80	0.59	−0.35	1.12
Tu	1.89	6.82	6.80	5.30
Tujia	1.05	−3.68	−7.26	−2.41
Uygur	1.63	6.89	9.18	14.59
Uzbek	1.61	6.75	8.97	14.36
Va	1.15	−3.23	−9.82	5.26
Xibe	1.19	−1.51	−2.49	0.23
Yao	0.85	−3.45	−6.97	−0.45
Yi	1.17	−3.53	−9.08	2.62
Yugur	1.41	−2.19	−1.67	2.38
Zhuang	0.82	−3.34	−6.31	0.09

Notes: GDP (gross domestic product) and industrial value-added are at 2010 constant prices. SCE denotes standard coal equivalent

Table 2.13 Consumer price indices and retail price indices (preceding year = 100)

Ethnic group	Consumer price index			Retail price index		
	General	Urban household	Rural household	General	Urban household	Rural household
National average	102.96	102.99	101.63	102.38	104.7	105.5
Achang	102.73	103.00	102.22	102.35	104.9	105.2
Bai	102.68	102.91	102.10	102.27	105.0	105.2
Baonan	102.75	102.53	103.03	102.60	105.6	104.9
Blang	102.73	102.99	101.96	102.35	104.9	105.0
Buyi	102.71	102.68	102.61	102.00	105.4	105.7
Dai	102.73	103.00	102.18	102.35	104.9	105.2
Daur	103.14	103.27	101.59	102.39	104.7	104.0
Deang	102.73	103.00	102.22	102.35	104.9	105.2
Derung	102.73	102.94	99.96	102.30	104.9	102.9
Dong	102.57	102.59	102.28	101.97	105.4	105.6
Dongxiang	102.82	102.57	103.18	102.66	105.5	105.1
Ewenki	103.09	103.27	101.47	102.42	104.9	103.8
Gaoshan	102.69	102.72	96.90	102.09	105.0	99.9
Gelao	102.72	102.68	102.48	101.99	105.4	105.6
Han	102.60	102.63	96.44	102.03	104.9	99.3
Hani	102.73	103.00	102.17	102.35	104.9	105.2
Hezhe	103.11	103.20	100.26	102.15	104.3	103.1
Hui	102.65	102.65	97.65	102.03	105.0	100.9
Jing	103.18	103.16	102.97	102.28	105.6	106.2
Jingpo	102.73	103.00	102.23	102.35	104.9	105.2
Jino	102.73	103.00	102.04	102.35	104.9	105.0
Kazak	103.82	103.37	104.64	103.27	104.5	106.5
Kirgiz	103.82	103.37	104.63	103.26	104.5	106.5
Korean	102.69	102.74	100.52	101.86	104.7	103.5
Lahu	102.73	102.99	102.16	102.35	104.9	105.2
Lhoba	103.44	103.53	102.26	102.81	104.0	102.4

Li	103.18	103.19	103.09	102.63	105.2	106.6
Lisu	102.73	102.99	102.22	102.33	104.9	105.2
Manchu	102.81	102.89	99.45	102.12	104.8	102.4
Maonan	103.07	103.04	103.04	102.21	105.6	106.3
Miao	102.59	102.64	96.59	101.99	105.3	99.7
Monba	103.47	103.57	101.96	102.83	103.9	102.0
Mongol	103.02	103.16	101.43	102.38	104.9	103.8
Mulao	103.14	103.11	102.98	102.25	105.6	106.2
Naxi	102.73	102.99	102.09	102.33	104.9	105.1
Nu	102.74	103.00	102.21	102.35	104.9	105.2
Oroqen	103.10	103.23	101.27	102.29	104.6	103.9
Pumi	102.73	103.00	102.18	102.35	104.9	105.2
Qiang	102.54	102.83	101.77	101.63	104.4	105.0
Russian	103.49	103.29	101.36	102.87	104.7	103.4
Salar	103.04	102.98	102.66	102.17	105.4	104.7
She	102.44	102.42	102.26	101.90	104.9	105.1
Shui	102.73	102.70	102.70	102.01	105.4	105.8
Tajik	103.78	103.35	103.98	103.23	104.6	105.9
Tatar	103.74	103.32	103.45	103.19	104.6	105.3
Tibetan	103.10	103.20	102.78	102.38	104.5	104.2
Tu	102.99	102.94	102.65	102.15	105.4	104.8
Tujia	102.51	102.55	84.01	101.99	105.2	86.9
Uygur	103.82	103.37	104.59	103.26	104.5	106.5
Uzbek	103.80	103.36	104.36	103.25	104.5	106.2
Va	102.72	102.98	101.86	102.34	104.9	104.9
Xibe	103.03	103.02	101.76	102.38	104.8	104.4
Yao	102.83	102.88	102.63	102.14	105.5	106.0
Yi	102.68	102.91	102.14	102.11	104.8	105.2
Yugur	102.73	102.51	102.62	102.59	105.6	104.5
Zhuang	103.18	103.17	103.09	102.30	105.6	106.3

3

Employment and Income Distribution

Data on basic conditions of employment, total wage bills of staff and workers are collected and compiled through *The Reporting Form System on Labor Statistics*, *The Sample Survey System on Labor Force*, and *The System of Rural Social and Economic Surveys* by the Department of Population and Employment Statistics, the NBS. *The Reporting Form System on Labor Statistics* covers corporate units (does not include township enterprises, private units or self-employed individuals). The scope of survey and estimate of *The Sample Survey System on Labor Force* are the whole country. The scope of statistics in the chapter is the population aged 16 and over of the whole country. *The System of Rural Social and Economic Surveys* covers all rural areas below township level in China.

Data on the number of registered unemployed persons in urban areas are collected through *The Reporting Form System on Training and Employment Statistics,* which provided by the Ministry of Human Resources and Social Security. *The Reporting Form System* covers all agencies and units providing employment services. Data on the number of employed persons in private enterprises and self-employed individuals are provided by the State Administration for Industry and Commerce.

R. Guo, *China Ethnic Statistical Yearbook 2016*,
DOI 10.1007/978-3-319-49199-8_3

The scope of statistics on private enterprises and self-employed individuals covers the whole country.

A complete reporting form system from lower-level statistical bureaus to higher level statistical bureaus is used in the labor statistics. *The Sample Survey on Labor Force* is conducted by using sampling methods. Statistics on training, employment, private enterprises and self-employed individuals are collected and compiled on basis of administrative registering records.

Table 3.1 Number of employed persons in urban units at year-end (10,000 persons) (I)

Ethnic group	Total	Agriculture, forestry, animal husbandry and fishery	Mining	Manufacturing	Production and distribution of electricity, gas and water
National total	15,236.37	338.85	631.02	4262.19	297.57
Achang	0.32	0.01	0.02	0.06	0.01
Bai	17.06	0.35	0.93	3.17	0.43
Baonan	0.15	0.01	0.01	0.02	0.00
Blang	0.86	0.02	0.05	0.16	0.02
Buyi	23.58	0.16	1.50	4.42	0.71
Dai	10.78	0.25	0.61	1.96	0.27
Daur	1.67	0.21	0.13	0.26	0.06
Deang	0.17	0.00	0.01	0.03	0.00
Derung	0.07	0.00	0.00	0.01	0.00
Dong	25.08	0.21	1.11	5.28	0.72
Dongxiang	4.75	0.27	0.24	0.72	0.16
Ewenki	0.37	0.04	0.03	0.06	0.02
Gaoshan	0.06	0.00	0.00	0.02	0.00
Gelao	4.55	0.03	0.29	0.84	0.14
Han	14,106.24	276.34	577.63	4042.74	312.61
Hani	13.40	0.31	0.76	2.43	0.33
Hezhe	0.06	0.01	0.00	0.01	0.00
Hui	124.45	5.11	7.17	25.76	3.93
Jing	0.19	0.01	0.00	0.04	0.01
Jingpo	1.23	0.03	0.07	0.22	0.03
Jino	0.19	0.00	0.01	0.04	0.00
Kazak	19.55	3.79	1.27	2.08	0.51
Kirgiz	2.51	0.49	0.16	0.27	0.07
Korean	23.59	1.86	1.43	5.16	0.70
Lahu	4.22	0.10	0.24	0.77	0.10
Lhoba	0.03	0.00	0.00	0.00	0.00
Li	14.67	1.85	0.19	1.64	0.35
Lisu	5.88	0.13	0.33	1.07	0.15
Manchu	145.56	7.36	7.75	35.16	4.12
Maonan	0.88	0.02	0.03	0.18	0.02
Miao	78.29	0.82	3.61	16.23	2.16
Monba	0.09	0.00	0.00	0.00	0.00
Mongol	70.95	5.69	4.97	13.00	2.71
Mulao	1.74	0.04	0.04	0.36	0.05
Naxi	2.88	0.07	0.16	0.52	0.07

(*continued*)

Table 3.1 (continued)

Ethnic group	Total	Agriculture, forestry, animal husbandry and fishery	Mining	Manufacturing	Production and distribution of electricity, gas and water
Nu	0.27	0.01	0.01	0.05	0.01
Oroqen	0.10	0.01	0.01	0.02	0.00
Pumi	0.31	0.01	0.02	0.06	0.01
Qiang	2.41	0.02	0.09	0.54	0.07
Russian	0.23	0.03	0.01	0.03	0.01
Salar	1.31	0.04	0.06	0.24	0.04
She	12.69	0.09	0.11	5.08	0.20
Shui	3.21	0.03	0.20	0.59	0.10
Tajik	0.64	0.12	0.04	0.07	0.02
Tatar	0.08	0.01	0.00	0.01	0.00
Tibetan	52.98	1.10	1.42	6.52	1.61
Tu	2.97	0.08	0.12	0.58	0.09
Tujia	78.85	0.67	2.37	19.02	2.11
Uygur	131.33	25.42	8.55	14.03	3.45
Uzbek	0.19	0.04	0.01	0.02	0.01
Va	3.71	0.08	0.21	0.69	0.09
Xibe	2.77	0.21	0.16	0.65	0.08
Yao	23.91	0.44	0.49	5.59	0.61
Yi	67.81	1.19	3.58	13.05	1.76
Yugur	0.12	0.00	0.01	0.02	0.00
Zhuang	138.69	3.64	2.43	29.61	3.66

Table 3.2 Number of employed persons in urban units at year-end (10,000 persons) (II)

Ethnic group	Construction	Transport, storage and post	Information transmission, computer service and software	Wholesale and retail trades	Hotels and catering services
National total	2010.26	667.52	222.80	711.85	265.05
Achang	0.05	0.01	0.00	0.02	0.01
Bai	2.81	0.60	0.19	0.97	0.35
Baonan	0.02	0.01	0.00	0.00	0.00
Blang	0.14	0.03	0.01	0.05	0.02
Buyi	3.12	0.81	0.23	1.15	0.35
Dai	1.82	0.37	0.12	0.64	0.23
Daur	0.12	0.10	0.03	0.06	0.02

(continued)

Table 3.2 (continued)

Ethnic group	Construction	Transport, storage and post	Information transmission, computer service and software	Wholesale and retail trades	Hotels and catering services
Deang	0.03	0.01	0.00	0.01	0.00
Derung	0.01	0.00	0.00	0.00	0.00
Dong	3.54	0.97	0.28	1.08	0.39
Dongxiang	0.49	0.23	0.05	0.14	0.04
Ewenki	0.03	0.02	0.01	0.01	0.00
Gaoshan	0.01	0.00	0.00	0.00	0.00
Gelao	0.59	0.16	0.04	0.22	0.07
Han	1878.19	616.00	207.79	665.09	247.53
Hani	2.26	0.46	0.15	0.80	0.29
Hezhe	0.00	0.00	0.00	0.00	0.00
Hui	12.69	6.17	2.11	5.83	1.96
Jing	0.02	0.01	0.00	0.01	0.00
Jingpo	0.21	0.04	0.01	0.07	0.03
Jino	0.03	0.01	0.00	0.01	0.00
Kazak	1.52	0.85	0.18	0.56	0.19
Kirgiz	0.19	0.11	0.02	0.07	0.02
Korean	1.75	1.31	0.42	0.89	0.30
Lahu	0.71	0.15	0.05	0.25	0.09
Lhoba	0.00	0.00	0.00	0.00	0.00
Li	1.01	0.73	0.16	0.87	0.98
Lisu	0.99	0.20	0.06	0.35	0.13
Manchu	13.95	8.00	2.84	6.09	2.15
Maonan	0.11	0.04	0.01	0.03	0.01
Miao	11.92	2.99	0.85	3.64	1.35
Monba	0.00	0.00	0.00	0.00	0.00
Mongol	5.57	4.19	1.20	2.40	0.86
Mulao	0.21	0.09	0.02	0.07	0.02
Naxi	0.48	0.10	0.03	0.17	0.06
Nu	0.04	0.01	0.00	0.02	0.01
Oroqen	0.01	0.01	0.00	0.00	0.00
Pumi	0.05	0.01	0.00	0.02	0.01
Qiang	0.43	0.09	0.02	0.07	0.03
Russian	0.02	0.01	0.00	0.01	0.00
Salar	0.15	0.07	0.02	0.05	0.02
She	2.66	0.38	0.13	0.49	0.19
Shui	0.42	0.11	0.03	0.16	0.05
Tajik	0.05	0.03	0.01	0.02	0.01
Tatar	0.01	0.00	0.00	0.00	0.00
Tibetan	4.62	1.96	0.66	1.53	0.64

(*continued*)

Table 3.2 (continued)

Ethnic group	Construction	Transport, storage and post	Information transmission, computer service and software	Wholesale and retail trades	Hotels and catering services
Tu	0.35	0.16	0.04	0.11	0.03
Tujia	13.72	3.24	0.89	3.63	1.35
Uygur	10.21	5.74	1.21	3.76	1.28
Uzbek	0.02	0.01	0.00	0.01	0.00
Va	0.62	0.13	0.04	0.22	0.08
Xibe	0.26	0.15	0.04	0.10	0.03
Yao	3.12	1.12	0.30	0.94	0.40
Yi	11.37	2.39	0.71	3.46	1.26
Yugur	0.01	0.01	0.00	0.00	0.00
Zhuang	16.74	6.92	1.74	5.41	2.08

Table 3.3 Number of employed persons in urban units at year-end (10,000 persons) (III)

Ethnic group	Financial intermediation	Real estate	Leasing and business services	Scientific research, technical services, and geological prospecting	Management of water conservancy, environment and public facilities
National total	527.77	273.71	292.29	330.68	243.78
Achang	0.01	0.01	0.01	0.01	0.00
Bai	0.45	0.32	0.27	0.34	0.25
Baonan	0.00	0.00	0.00	0.00	0.00
Blang	0.02	0.02	0.01	0.02	0.01
Buyi	0.66	0.47	0.28	0.47	0.36
Dai	0.27	0.20	0.17	0.21	0.16
Daur	0.06	0.02	0.02	0.04	0.04
Deang	0.00	0.00	0.00	0.00	0.00
Derung	0.00	0.00	0.00	0.00	0.00
Dong	0.79	0.48	0.37	0.49	0.42
Dongxiang	0.16	0.04	0.05	0.12	0.11
Ewenki	0.01	0.00	0.01	0.01	0.01
Gaoshan	0.00	0.00	0.00	0.00	0.00
Gelao	0.13	0.09	0.05	0.09	0.07
Han	490.74	254.80	271.67	303.53	221.91
Hani	0.34	0.25	0.21	0.27	0.20

(continued)

Table 3.3 (continued)

Ethnic group	Financial intermediation	Real estate	Leasing and business services	Scientific research, technical services, and geological prospecting	Management of water conservancy, environment and public facilities
Hezhe	0.00	0.00	0.00	0.00	0.00
Hui	4.53	2.27	2.88	3.43	2.43
Jing	0.01	0.00	0.00	0.00	0.00
Jingpo	0.03	0.02	0.02	0.02	0.02
Jino	0.00	0.00	0.00	0.00	0.00
Kazak	0.55	0.22	0.36	0.41	0.37
Kirgiz	0.07	0.03	0.05	0.05	0.05
Korean	0.89	0.44	0.44	0.66	0.59
Lahu	0.11	0.08	0.07	0.08	0.06
Lhoba	0.00	0.00	0.00	0.00	0.00
Li	0.45	0.67	0.32	0.28	0.41
Lisu	0.15	0.11	0.09	0.12	0.09
Manchu	5.65	2.99	3.10	4.28	3.38
Maonan	0.03	0.01	0.02	0.02	0.02
Miao	2.41	1.52	1.15	1.52	1.25
Monba	0.00	0.00	0.00	0.00	0.00
Mongol	2.75	0.80	1.06	1.55	1.86
Mulao	0.06	0.03	0.04	0.04	0.04
Naxi	0.07	0.05	0.05	0.06	0.04
Nu	0.01	0.00	0.00	0.01	0.00
Oroqen	0.00	0.00	0.00	0.00	0.00
Pumi	0.01	0.01	0.00	0.01	0.00
Qiang	0.09	0.03	0.02	0.06	0.04
Russian	0.01	0.00	0.00	0.01	0.00
Salar	0.05	0.02	0.02	0.06	0.02
She	0.35	0.21	0.20	0.17	0.13
Shui	0.09	0.06	0.04	0.07	0.05
Tajik	0.02	0.01	0.01	0.01	0.01
Tatar	0.00	0.00	0.00	0.00	0.00
Tibetan	1.80	0.37	0.52	2.04	0.73
Tu	0.10	0.04	0.04	0.12	0.05
Tujia	2.58	1.50	1.16	1.50	1.22
Uygur	3.70	1.46	2.44	2.77	2.46
Uzbek	0.01	0.00	0.00	0.00	0.00
Va	0.09	0.07	0.06	0.07	0.05
Xibe	0.10	0.05	0.05	0.07	0.07
Yao	0.80	0.42	0.53	0.52	0.48
Yi	1.91	1.13	0.92	1.44	1.03
Yugur	0.00	0.00	0.00	0.00	0.00
Zhuang	4.48	2.27	3.39	3.47	3.17

Table 3.4 Number of employed persons in urban units at year-end (10,000 persons) (IV)

Ethnic group	Services to households and other services	Education	Health, social securities and social welfare	Culture, sports and entertainment	Public management and social organization
National total	62.13	1653.38	719.28	137.74	1541.51
Achang	0.00	0.04	0.02	0.00	0.04
Bai	0.04	2.38	0.86	0.14	2.20
Baonan	0.00	0.02	0.01	0.00	0.03
Blang	0.00	0.12	0.04	0.01	0.11
Buyi	0.08	3.74	1.26	0.15	3.65
Dai	0.02	1.50	0.53	0.09	1.35
Daur	0.01	0.19	0.08	0.02	0.20
Deang	0.00	0.02	0.01	0.00	0.02
Derung	0.00	0.01	0.00	0.00	0.01
Dong	0.08	3.67	1.44	0.19	3.59
Dongxiang	0.01	0.78	0.26	0.06	0.84
Ewenki	0.00	0.05	0.02	0.00	0.05
Gaoshan	0.00	0.01	0.00	0.00	0.01
Gelao	0.02	0.73	0.24	0.03	0.71
Han	58.39	1505.02	657.82	126.64	1391.79
Hani	0.03	1.87	0.66	0.11	1.68
Hezhe	0.00	0.01	0.00	0.00	0.01
Hui	0.59	14.69	6.29	1.38	15.20
Jing	0.00	0.03	0.01	0.00	0.02
Jingpo	0.00	0.17	0.06	0.01	0.15
Jino	0.00	0.03	0.01	0.00	0.02
Kazak	0.04	2.44	1.07	0.20	2.94
Kirgiz	0.01	0.31	0.14	0.03	0.38
Korean	0.13	2.67	1.21	0.27	2.46
Lahu	0.01	0.59	0.21	0.04	0.53
Lhoba	0.00	0.00	0.00	0.00	0.01
Li	0.04	2.00	0.79	0.18	1.77
Lisu	0.01	0.82	0.29	0.05	0.74
Manchu	0.82	15.14	7.09	1.50	14.18
Maonan	0.00	0.14	0.06	0.01	0.11
Miao	0.24	11.10	4.24	0.59	10.70
Monba	0.00	0.01	0.01	0.00	0.04
Mongol	0.25	8.59	3.43	0.82	9.25
Mulao	0.00	0.28	0.12	0.02	0.21

(continued)

Table 3.4 (continued)

Ethnic group	Services to households and other services	Education	Health, social securities and social welfare	Culture, sports and entertainment	Public management and social organization
Naxi	0.01	0.40	0.14	0.02	0.36
Nu	0.00	0.04	0.01	0.00	0.03
Oroqen	0.00	0.01	0.00	0.00	0.01
Pumi	0.00	0.04	0.02	0.00	0.04
Qiang	0.00	0.33	0.15	0.02	0.31
Russian	0.00	0.03	0.01	0.00	0.03
Salar	0.01	0.16	0.08	0.02	0.20
She	0.03	0.96	0.42	0.08	0.81
Shui	0.01	0.51	0.17	0.02	0.50
Tajik	0.00	0.08	0.03	0.01	0.09
Tatar	0.00	0.01	0.00	0.00	0.01
Tibetan	0.11	8.08	3.25	0.87	15.15
Tu	0.01	0.37	0.17	0.04	0.44
Tujia	0.23	9.66	4.17	0.68	9.17
Uygur	0.28	16.34	7.17	1.34	19.71
Uzbek	0.00	0.02	0.01	0.00	0.03
Va	0.01	0.51	0.18	0.03	0.46
Xibe	0.01	0.28	0.14	0.03	0.28
Yao	0.06	3.46	1.52	0.21	2.90
Yi	0.15	9.59	3.57	0.54	8.76
Yugur	0.00	0.02	0.01	0.00	0.02
Zhuang	0.32	22.35	9.48	1.25	16.30

Table 3.5 Number of engaged persons in private enterprises and self-employed individuals at year-end (10,000 persons) (I)

Ethnic group	Total	Manufacturing	Construction	Transport, storage and post
National total	19,924.44	4467.85	840.15	837.65
Achang	0.45	0.06	0.03	0.01
Bai	23.65	3.03	1.42	0.48
Baonan	0.15	0.02	0.01	0.00
Blang	1.23	0.16	0.08	0.02
Buyi	25.02	3.19	0.77	0.62
Dai	15.44	1.96	1.00	0.31
Daur	1.99	0.22	0.07	0.12

(*continued*)

Table 3.5 (continued)

Ethnic group	Total	Manufacturing	Construction	Transport, storage and post
Deang	0.24	0.03	0.02	0.00
Derung	0.10	0.01	0.01	0.00
Dong	29.42	4.03	0.82	0.97
Dongxiang	4.80	0.54	0.22	0.09
Ewenki	0.47	0.05	0.02	0.03
Gaoshan	0.07	0.01	0.00	0.00
Gelao	4.77	0.58	0.14	0.12
Han	18,557.05	4274.45	782.10	773.40
Hani	19.21	2.45	1.25	0.38
Hezhe	0.07	0.01	0.00	0.00
Hui	141.81	22.07	6.31	4.57
Jing	0.25	0.04	0.01	0.02
Jingpo	1.76	0.22	0.11	0.04
Jino	0.28	0.04	0.02	0.01
Kazak	14.35	1.92	0.34	0.42
Kirgiz	1.85	0.25	0.04	0.06
Korean	30.46	4.27	1.45	1.40
Lahu	6.05	0.77	0.39	0.12
Lhoba	0.06	0.00	0.01	0.00
Li	18.92	1.11	1.52	1.56
Lisu	8.42	1.08	0.54	0.17
Manchu	178.25	30.70	8.25	13.47
Maonan	1.09	0.15	0.02	0.09
Miao	96.05	12.93	3.37	2.67
Monba	0.18	0.01	0.02	0.00
Mongol	90.81	11.01	3.50	6.10
Mulao	2.26	0.32	0.05	0.21
Naxi	4.12	0.53	0.27	0.08
Nu	0.39	0.05	0.03	0.01
Oroqen	0.12	0.01	0.00	0.01
Pumi	0.45	0.06	0.03	0.01
Qiang	3.31	0.50	0.09	0.09
Russian	0.21	0.03	0.01	0.01
Salar	1.45	0.23	0.12	0.03
She	15.38	4.66	0.50	0.28
Shui	3.45	0.44	0.11	0.10
Tajik	0.48	0.06	0.01	0.01
Tatar	0.06	0.01	0.00	0.00
Tibetan	83.75	8.14	8.14	1.68
Tu	3.37	0.56	0.28	0.06
Tujia	107.95	16.14	3.46	2.74

(continued)

Table 3.5 (continued)

Ethnic group	Total	Manufacturing	Construction	Transport, storage and post
Uygur	96.62	12.97	2.30	2.87
Uzbek	0.14	0.02	0.00	0.00
Va	5.30	0.69	0.34	0.11
Xibe	3.32	0.58	0.16	0.24
Yao	31.70	4.71	0.82	2.07
Yi	93.59	12.41	4.98	2.06
Yugur	0.13	0.01	0.01	0.00
Zhuang	186.10	26.64	4.41	17.55

Table 3.6 Number of engaged persons in private enterprises and self-employed individuals at year-end (10,000 persons) (II)

Ethnic group	Wholesale and retail trades	Hotels and catering services	Leasing and business services	Services to households and other services
National total	7721.03	1161.94	1119.55	1149.12
Achang	0.19	0.04	0.02	0.03
Bai	10.09	1.86	1.14	1.38
Baonan	0.08	0.02	0.00	0.01
Blang	0.52	0.10	0.05	0.07
Buyi	11.69	2.08	1.11	1.56
Dai	6.53	1.24	0.64	0.90
Daur	0.81	0.25	0.08	0.17
Deang	0.10	0.02	0.01	0.01
Derung	0.04	0.01	0.00	0.01
Dong	13.31	1.97	2.33	1.65
Dongxiang	2.31	0.53	0.15	0.34
Ewenki	0.19	0.07	0.02	0.04
Gaoshan	0.03	0.00	0.00	0.00
Gelao	2.25	0.40	0.21	0.30
Han	7149.63	1056.41	1047.62	1062.50
Hani	8.12	1.54	0.79	1.12
Hezhe	0.03	0.01	0.00	0.01
Hui	59.61	10.97	7.27	9.89
Jing	0.11	0.01	0.01	0.01
Jingpo	0.74	0.14	0.07	0.10
Jino	0.12	0.02	0.01	0.02
Kazak	5.16	1.28	0.67	0.97
Kirgiz	0.67	0.17	0.09	0.13

(*continued*)

Table 3.6 (continued)

Ethnic group	Wholesale and retail trades	Hotels and catering services	Leasing and business services	Services to households and other services
Korean	12.05	2.25	1.21	2.53
Lahu	2.56	0.49	0.25	0.35
Lhoba	0.02	0.01	0.00	0.00
Li	6.42	1.26	1.71	1.42
Lisu	3.57	0.68	0.35	0.49
Manchu	67.46	10.37	8.55	12.46
Maonan	0.50	0.07	0.05	0.05
Miao	42.74	6.76	7.01	5.53
Monba	0.07	0.02	0.01	0.01
Mongol	35.70	11.08	3.70	6.95
Mulao	1.02	0.13	0.11	0.11
Naxi	1.74	0.33	0.17	0.24
Nu	0.16	0.03	0.02	0.02
Oroqen	0.05	0.01	0.01	0.01
Pumi	0.19	0.04	0.02	0.03
Qiang	1.58	0.29	0.14	0.22
Russian	0.08	0.02	0.01	0.02
Salar	0.59	0.16	0.04	0.09
She	5.94	0.76	0.88	0.84
Shui	1.61	0.28	0.15	0.21
Tajik	0.17	0.04	0.02	0.03
Tatar	0.02	0.01	0.00	0.00
Tibetan	35.99	10.28	3.19	6.24
Tu	1.37	0.35	0.10	0.21
Tujia	47.48	7.22	9.08	6.34
Uygur	34.76	8.62	4.54	6.55
Uzbek	0.05	0.01	0.01	0.01
Va	2.24	0.42	0.22	0.31
Xibe	1.25	0.19	0.16	0.23
Yao	14.01	1.75	2.38	1.55
Yi	41.22	7.69	3.90	5.69
Yugur	0.06	0.01	0.00	0.01
Zhuang	83.15	10.64	8.99	8.76

Table 3.7 Number of engaged persons in urban private enterprises and self-employed individuals at year-end (10,000 persons) (I)

Ethnic group	Total	Manufacturing	Construction	Transport, storage and post
National total	13,200.10	2357.86	599.81	573.93
Achang	0.30	0.04	0.03	0.01
Bai	15.75	1.93	1.24	0.34
Baonan	0.10	0.01	0.01	0.00
Blang	0.82	0.10	0.07	0.02
Buyi	13.97	1.57	0.59	0.33
Dai	10.33	1.29	0.88	0.23
Daur	1.55	0.16	0.06	0.10
Deang	0.16	0.02	0.01	0.00
Derung	0.07	0.01	0.01	0.00
Dong	18.66	2.12	0.67	0.56
Dongxiang	3.21	0.29	0.17	0.06
Ewenki	0.38	0.04	0.02	0.03
Gaoshan	0.04	0.01	0.00	0.00
Gelao	2.65	0.29	0.11	0.06
Han	12,248.10	2240.75	552.79	530.33
Hani	12.85	1.61	1.10	0.28
Hezhe	0.05	0.01	0.00	0.00
Hui	96.16	12.42	4.61	3.17
Jing	0.15	0.02	0.00	0.01
Jingpo	1.18	0.15	0.10	0.03
Jino	0.19	0.02	0.02	0.00
Kazak	12.44	1.54	0.33	0.41
Kirgiz	1.60	0.20	0.04	0.05
Korean	22.87	3.05	1.23	1.07
Lahu	4.05	0.51	0.34	0.09
Lhoba	0.05	0.00	0.00	0.00
Li	16.13	0.80	1.34	1.27
Lisu	5.61	0.70	0.47	0.12
Manchu	128.25	18.89	6.44	9.86
Maonan	0.63	0.08	0.02	0.05
Miao	62.67	7.11	2.82	1.67
Monba	0.14	0.01	0.02	0.00
Mongol	70.69	7.63	3.06	4.82
Mulao	1.33	0.17	0.04	0.11
Naxi	2.75	0.34	0.23	0.06
Nu	0.26	0.03	0.02	0.01
Oroqen	0.09	0.01	0.00	0.01
Pumi	0.30	0.04	0.03	0.01
Qiang	1.88	0.24	0.07	0.06
Russian	0.17	0.02	0.01	0.01

(continued)

Table 3.7 (continued)

Ethnic group	Total	Manufacturing	Construction	Transport, storage and post
Salar	0.99	0.09	0.09	0.02
She	10.39	2.34	0.38	0.21
Shui	1.93	0.22	0.08	0.05
Tajik	0.41	0.05	0.01	0.01
Tatar	0.05	0.01	0.00	0.00
Tibetan	61.80	4.68	5.77	1.32
Tu	2.28	0.23	0.19	0.05
Tujia	77.39	9.53	2.97	1.87
Uygur	83.70	10.36	2.24	2.77
Uzbek	0.12	0.02	0.00	0.00
Va	3.54	0.44	0.30	0.08
Xibe	2.53	0.36	0.13	0.19
Yao	21.00	2.72	0.69	1.16
Yi	59.47	7.39	4.28	1.45
Yugur	0.08	0.01	0.00	0.00
Zhuang	112.47	14.85	3.54	9.43

Table 3.8 Number of engaged persons in urban private enterprises and self-employed individuals at year-end (10,000 persons) (II)

Ethnic group	Wholesale and retail trades	Hotels and catering services	Leasing and business services	Services to households and other services
National total	5407.21	838.21	923.17	807.10
Achang	0.12	0.02	0.02	0.02
Bai	6.51	1.22	1.01	0.95
Baonan	0.05	0.01	0.00	0.01
Blang	0.34	0.06	0.05	0.05
Buyi	6.48	1.26	0.83	0.97
Dai	4.22	0.81	0.57	0.62
Daur	0.66	0.16	0.07	0.13
Deang	0.07	0.01	0.01	0.01
Derung	0.03	0.01	0.00	0.00
Dong	8.33	1.34	1.97	1.18
Dongxiang	1.57	0.37	0.12	0.24
Ewenki	0.16	0.04	0.02	0.03
Gaoshan	0.02	0.00	0.00	0.00
Gelao	1.24	0.24	0.16	0.19
Han	5008.09	762.89	860.87	742.43
Hani	5.24	1.01	0.71	0.77

(continued)

Table 3.8 (continued)

Ethnic group	Wholesale and retail trades	Hotels and catering services	Leasing and business services	Services to households and other services
Hezhe	0.02	0.00	0.00	0.00
Hui	42.27	8.16	5.72	6.68
Jing	0.07	0.01	0.01	0.01
Jingpo	0.48	0.09	0.07	0.07
Jino	0.08	0.01	0.01	0.01
Kazak	4.40	0.99	0.64	0.77
Kirgiz	0.57	0.13	0.08	0.10
Korean	9.38	1.73	1.02	2.08
Lahu	1.65	0.32	0.22	0.24
Lhoba	0.02	0.01	0.00	0.00
Li	5.43	1.08	1.62	1.23
Lisu	2.29	0.44	0.31	0.34
Manchu	51.27	7.81	7.23	9.98
Maonan	0.28	0.04	0.04	0.04
Miao	27.64	4.66	6.02	3.97
Monba	0.06	0.02	0.01	0.01
Mongol	29.27	7.31	3.30	5.77
Mulao	0.59	0.09	0.09	0.08
Naxi	1.12	0.22	0.15	0.16
Nu	0.11	0.02	0.01	0.02
Oroqen	0.04	0.01	0.00	0.01
Pumi	0.12	0.02	0.02	0.02
Qiang	0.86	0.18	0.11	0.14
Russian	0.07	0.02	0.01	0.01
Salar	0.45	0.13	0.03	0.07
She	4.48	0.55	0.79	0.57
Shui	0.89	0.17	0.11	0.13
Tajik	0.15	0.03	0.02	0.03
Tatar	0.02	0.00	0.00	0.00
Tibetan	26.99	8.13	2.83	4.89
Tu	1.05	0.29	0.08	0.15
Tujia	34.95	5.35	8.00	4.85
Uygur	29.60	6.65	4.33	5.17
Uzbek	0.04	0.01	0.01	0.01
Va	1.45	0.28	0.20	0.21
Xibe	1.00	0.15	0.14	0.19
Yao	9.11	1.27	2.11	1.19
Yi	25.14	4.94	3.35	3.77
Yugur	0.04	0.01	0.00	0.01
Zhuang	49.08	7.09	7.84	6.31

Table 3.9 Number of engaged persons in private enterprises at year-end (10,000 persons)

Ethnic group	Number of engaged persons	Employers	Number of engaged persons in urban area	Employers	Number of Engaged persons in rural area	Employers
National total	11,296.12	2200.10	7557.44	1646.04	3738.68	554.06
Achang	0.24	0.03	0.19	0.03	0.05	0.00
Bai	12.35	1.76	9.61	1.50	2.74	0.27
Baonan	0.07	0.01	0.05	0.01	0.02	0.00
Blang	0.65	0.09	0.52	0.08	0.13	0.01
Buyi	11.62	2.61	6.56	1.61	5.06	1.01
Dai	8.10	1.09	6.47	0.97	1.62	0.12
Daur	0.88	0.19	0.72	0.16	0.16	0.03
Deang	0.13	0.02	0.10	0.01	0.02	0.00
Derung	0.05	0.01	0.04	0.01	0.01	0.00
Dong	14.82	2.92	9.31	1.98	5.51	0.94
Dongxiang	2.19	0.44	1.53	0.32	0.66	0.11
Ewenki	0.21	0.04	0.18	0.04	0.03	0.01
Gaoshan	0.04	0.01	0.03	0.01	0.01	0.00
Gelao	2.20	0.50	1.23	0.31	0.97	0.20
Han	10,596.29	2068.08	7050.48	1540.86	3545.81	527.22
Hani	10.09	1.36	8.07	1.20	2.02	0.15
Hezhe	0.03	0.01	0.02	0.01	0.01	0.00
Hui	73.81	15.37	50.88	11.79	22.93	3.58
Jing	0.13	0.03	0.08	0.02	0.06	0.01
Jingpo	0.92	0.12	0.74	0.11	0.18	0.01
Jino	0.15	0.02	0.12	0.02	0.03	0.00
Kazak	7.76	1.64	7.43	1.59	0.33	0.05
Kirgiz	1.00	0.21	0.96	0.20	0.04	0.01
Korean	13.82	2.71	10.82	2.25	3.00	0.46
Lahu	3.17	0.43	2.54	0.38	0.64	0.05
Lhoba	0.03	0.00	0.02	0.00	0.00	0.00
Li	11.28	3.49	9.89	3.34	1.39	0.15
Lisu	4.40	0.60	3.50	0.53	0.90	0.07
Manchu	90.17	17.21	65.98	13.71	24.19	3.50
Maonan	0.55	0.11	0.31	0.08	0.24	0.04
Miao	49.87	9.20	33.53	6.59	16.34	2.60
Monba	0.08	0.01	0.07	0.01	0.02	0.00
Mongol	41.36	8.41	33.75	7.27	7.60	1.13
Mulao	1.17	0.24	0.67	0.17	0.50	0.07
Naxi	2.15	0.29	1.71	0.26	0.44	0.03
Nu	0.20	0.03	0.16	0.02	0.04	0.00

(*continued*)

Table 3.9 (continued)

Ethnic group	Number of engaged persons	Employers	Number of engaged persons in urban area	Employers	Number of Engaged persons in rural area	Employers
Oroqen	0.06	0.01	0.04	0.01	0.01	0.00
Pumi	0.24	0.03	0.19	0.03	0.05	0.00
Qiang	1.52	0.36	0.82	0.28	0.70	0.07
Russian	0.11	0.02	0.10	0.02	0.01	0.00
Salar	0.78	0.10	0.43	0.07	0.34	0.04
She	9.30	1.72	6.55	1.35	2.75	0.37
Shui	1.62	0.36	0.92	0.22	0.70	0.14
Tajik	0.26	0.05	0.24	0.05	0.01	0.00
Tatar	0.03	0.01	0.03	0.01	0.00	0.00
Tibetan	40.30	5.31	28.73	4.28	11.57	1.02
Tu	1.80	0.24	1.02	0.16	0.78	0.09
Tujia	56.11	10.03	40.47	7.66	15.64	2.37
Uygur	52.32	11.02	50.02	10.70	2.30	0.32
Uzbek	0.08	0.02	0.07	0.02	0.00	0.00
Va	2.78	0.38	2.21	0.33	0.57	0.04
Xibe	1.74	0.30	1.35	0.25	0.39	0.05
Yao	17.13	3.20	11.35	2.41	5.78	0.79
Yi	47.08	7.72	34.12	6.41	12.96	1.31
Yugur	0.06	0.01	0.04	0.01	0.02	0.00
Zhuang	98.04	19.30	58.91	13.96	39.13	5.34

Table 3.10 Number of self-employed individuals at year-end (10,000 households, 10,000 persons)

Ethnic group	Number of households	Number of engaged persons	Urban area	Rural area
National total	4059.27	8628.31	5642.67	2985.64
Achang	0.11	0.22	0.04	0.10
Bai	5.91	11.30	2.56	5.16
Baonan	0.04	0.08	0.06	0.03
Blang	0.30	0.58	0.12	0.28
Buyi	7.73	13.40	3.06	5.99
Dai	3.82	7.34	1.46	3.49
Daur	0.50	1.11	0.77	0.27
Deang	0.06	0.11	0.02	0.05
Derung	0.02	0.05	0.02	0.02
Dong	7.90	14.60	5.35	5.25
Dongxiang	1.39	2.61	1.36	0.93
Ewenki	0.12	0.27	0.23	0.06

(continued)

Table 3.10 (continued)

Ethnic group	Number of households	Number of engaged persons	Urban area	Rural area
Gaoshan	0.01	0.03	0.02	0.01
Gelao	1.49	2.57	0.56	1.15
Han	3729.87	7960.76	4852.08	2763.14
Hani	4.75	9.13	1.77	4.34
Hezhe	0.02	0.04	0.01	0.01
Hui	31.34	68.01	160.21	22.72
Jing	0.06	0.12	0.06	0.05
Jingpo	0.44	0.84	0.16	0.40
Jino	0.07	0.13	0.03	0.06
Kazak	3.90	6.59	9.72	1.58
Kirgiz	0.50	0.85	1.24	0.20
Korean	7.01	16.64	14.29	4.59
Lahu	1.49	2.88	0.56	1.37
Lhoba	0.01	0.03	0.18	0.01
Li	4.55	7.64	46.93	1.40
Lisu	2.09	4.02	0.88	1.90
Manchu	38.06	88.08	74.34	25.82
Maonan	0.29	0.54	0.22	0.22
Miao	24.96	46.17	18.31	17.04
Monba	0.04	0.09	0.56	0.02
Mongol	22.81	49.46	48.70	12.52
Mulao	0.56	1.08	0.49	0.43
Naxi	1.02	1.96	0.51	0.93
Nu	0.10	0.18	0.06	0.09
Oroqen	0.03	0.07	0.04	0.02
Pumi	0.11	0.21	0.04	0.10
Qiang	0.94	1.79	1.98	0.73
Russian	0.05	0.10	0.12	0.03
Salar	0.30	0.68	3.95	0.12
She	2.49	6.08	1.81	2.24
Shui	1.06	1.84	0.42	0.82
Tajik	0.13	0.22	0.31	0.05
Tatar	0.02	0.03	0.04	0.01
Tibetan	18.72	43.44	216.54	10.37
Tu	0.70	1.57	8.52	0.31
Tujia	24.18	51.84	24.30	14.93
Uygur	26.21	44.30	65.22	10.63
Uzbek	0.04	0.07	0.10	0.02
Va	1.30	2.51	0.50	1.19
Xibe	0.72	1.57	1.61	0.40
Yao	7.49	14.57	6.94	4.92
Yi	24.47	46.51	20.59	21.16
Yugur	0.04	0.07	0.03	0.03
Zhuang	45.04	88.06	41.74	34.50

Table 3.11 Total wage bill of employed persons in urban units

Ethnic group	Total	State-owned units	Urban collective-owned units	Units of other types of ownership
	(100 million yuan)			
National total	70,914.21	32,950.01	1990.40	35,973.80
Achang	1.17	0.68	0.04	0.46
Bai	64.68	37.32	1.96	25.40
Baonan	0.58	0.44	0.02	0.13
Blang	3.19	1.83	0.10	1.26
Buyi	96.72	64.31	2.30	30.10
Dai	40.12	23.09	1.24	15.80
Daur	7.54	4.88	0.21	2.45
Deang	0.62	0.36	0.02	0.24
Derung	0.29	0.16	0.01	0.12
Dong	100.97	60.61	2.87	37.49
Dongxiang	19.19	14.02	0.54	4.63
Ewenki	1.77	1.13	0.05	0.58
Gaoshan	0.26	0.12	0.01	0.14
Gelao	18.69	12.53	0.44	5.72
Han	66,014.46	30,087.19	1864.33	34,062.94
Hani	49.82	28.66	1.54	19.63
Hezhe	0.26	0.16	0.01	0.09
Hui	616.42	322.85	13.39	280.18
Jing	0.70	0.43	0.02	0.25
Jingpo	4.58	2.63	0.14	1.80
Jino	0.72	0.42	0.02	0.29
Kazak	94.01	58.50	1.21	34.31
Kirgiz	12.06	7.51	0.16	4.40
Korean	98.78	55.99	2.66	40.13
Lahu	15.69	9.02	0.48	6.18
Lhoba	0.15	0.14	0.00	0.01
Li	57.93	35.57	1.78	20.57
Lisu	21.91	12.65	0.68	8.58
Manchu	662.76	335.84	20.62	306.30
Maonan	3.30	2.08	0.10	1.11
Miao	315.67	184.85	8.72	122.10
Monba	0.46	0.42	0.00	0.04
Mongol	336.61	207.98	9.82	118.81
Mulao	6.55	3.98	0.21	2.36
Naxi	10.81	6.22	0.33	4.25
Nu	1.01	0.59	0.03	0.39
Oroqen	0.46	0.29	0.01	0.15
Pumi	1.17	0.67	0.04	0.46

(continued)

Table 3.11 (continued)

	(100 million yuan)			
Ethnic group	Total	State-owned units	Urban collective-owned units	Units of other types of ownership
Qiang	10.20	6.39	0.41	3.40
Russian	1.14	0.68	0.02	0.44
Salar	6.12	4.54	0.10	1.48
She	57.60	19.63	1.33	36.64
Shui	13.04	8.72	0.32	4.00
Tajik	3.06	1.89	0.04	1.13
Tatar	0.37	0.22	0.00	0.14
Tibetan	249.36	207.27	4.49	37.60
Tu	13.70	10.04	0.24	3.42
Tujia	323.92	165.03	8.76	150.14
Uygur	631.80	392.58	8.12	231.10
Uzbek	0.93	0.58	0.01	0.35
Va	13.84	7.92	0.43	5.49
Xibe	12.40	6.71	0.40	5.29
Yao	92.77	51.05	3.09	38.63
Yi	263.28	157.97	8.61	96.70
Yugur	0.49	0.35	0.01	0.12
Zhuang	514.57	306.37	17.36	190.84

Table 3.12 Indices of total wage bill of employed persons in urban units (preceding year = 100)

Ethnic group	Total	State-owned units	Urban collective-owned units	Units of other types of ownership
National average	118.3	113.8	114.6	122.9
Achang	123.53	113.60	130.00	141.19
Bai	123.42	114.47	126.74	140.39
Baonan	125.43	126.17	124.77	122.65
Blang	123.50	113.60	129.90	141.08
Buyi	127.14	119.87	111.14	150.29
Dai	123.52	113.62	129.96	141.14
Daur	116.77	115.20	115.90	120.23
Deang	123.56	113.62	130.09	141.26
Derung	122.53	113.79	127.01	137.78
Dong	122.59	117.66	111.02	137.49
Dongxiang	125.67	126.27	125.27	123.22
Ewenki	116.42	114.40	116.47	120.78
Gaoshan	118.33	114.41	113.49	124.22

(continued)

Table 3.12 (continued)

Ethnic group	Total	State-owned units	Urban collective-owned units	Units of other types of ownership
Gelao	127.28	120.02	110.85	150.70
Han	118.36	114.38	114.90	123.34
Hani	123.54	113.60	130.02	141.21
Hezhe	116.82	115.92	113.55	118.66
Hui	122.09	119.50	115.48	125.97
Jing	115.77	110.86	105.85	127.33
Jingpo	123.54	113.62	129.96	141.21
Jino	123.55	113.61	130.01	141.21
Kazak	123.40	121.80	122.79	126.39
Kirgiz	123.32	121.72	122.69	126.31
Korean	117.07	114.62	113.06	121.21
Lahu	123.52	113.60	129.97	141.13
Lhoba	113.04	113.43	178.60	78.76
Li	116.17	109.84	125.02	128.53
Lisu	123.41	113.72	129.62	140.65
Manchu	116.34	112.78	115.38	121.42
Maonan	118.75	113.21	106.53	133.75
Miao	122.81	117.21	112.91	137.82
Monba	112.54	113.15	181.77	75.98
Mongol	116.60	114.26	116.44	121.22
Mulao	116.86	111.68	105.69	129.80
Naxi	123.37	113.71	129.82	140.40
Nu	123.33	113.61	130.61	140.07
Oroqen	116.58	115.17	115.04	119.63
Pumi	123.48	113.62	129.92	140.98
Qiang	119.04	117.77	116.37	121.88
Russian	120.54	118.55	120.12	124.15
Salar	116.51	116.32	105.14	118.09
She	122.24	116.71	113.73	126.71
Shui	126.78	119.54	111.19	149.66
Tajik	123.21	121.53	122.44	126.28
Tatar	123.27	121.64	122.53	126.12
Tibetan	115.81	115.68	145.26	99.76
Tu	116.84	116.29	105.87	118.91
Tujia	118.13	114.77	114.64	124.51
Uygur	123.37	121.75	122.75	126.37
Uzbek	123.28	121.62	122.61	126.34
Va	123.39	113.61	129.63	140.72
Xibe	115.92	113.87	118.98	118.42
Yao	116.60	112.48	109.08	125.35
Yi	122.71	115.47	124.11	136.90
Yugur	125.67	126.40	125.21	122.85
Zhuang	115.78	110.57	106.73	127.45

Table 3.13 Average wage of employed persons in urban units (yuan)

Ethnic group	Total	Staff and workers	State-owned units	Urban collective-owned units	Units of other types of ownership
National average	46,769.00	47,593.00	48,357.00	33,784.00	46,360.00
Achang	37,706.27	38,979.00	43,492.91	37,178.95	31,574.06
Bai	38,257.58	39,542.79	43,428.00	36,809.32	32,651.03
Baonan	38,329.22	39,080.97	39,105.68	32,946.33	36,614.62
Blang	37,740.21	39,012.18	43,534.22	37,158.33	31,615.64
Buyi	41,257.58	42,797.14	44,090.64	38,701.06	36,370.24
Dai	37,726.43	38,998.60	43,511.81	37,168.51	31,584.16
Daur	43,270.71	44,345.04	45,049.57	39,377.27	40,488.16
Deang	37,674.65	38,950.25	43,443.32	37,186.79	31,534.42
Derung	38,939.65	40,135.73	44,139.98	36,693.11	33,730.84
Dong	40,329.15	41,669.30	42,718.28	34,953.39	37,125.39
Dongxiang	38,539.30	39,293.58	38,977.51	34,132.59	37,514.17
Ewenki	45,804.98	46,462.58	48,392.12	43,283.87	41,469.18
Gaoshan	42,358.92	43,189.08	45,990.87	32,781.88	40,469.92
Gelao	41,290.20	42,840.13	44,014.01	38,718.86	36,407.59
Han	43,624.31	44,496.77	48,174.55	33,762.00	41,297.83
Hani	37,707.94	38,982.47	43,500.31	37,193.16	31,567.61
Hezhe	38,120.26	40,082.34	38,915.37	29,599.37	37,862.55
Hui	43,937.34	44,884.53	45,816.93	36,255.57	42,430.83
Jing	37,004.31	38,218.08	38,677.26	29,533.43	35,440.39
Jingpo	37,717.03	38,990.40	43,484.14	37,170.57	31,596.03
Jino	37,712.38	38,986.50	43,493.96	37,175.54	31,571.94
Kazak	44,571.48	45,239.15	42,492.47	46,395.84	48,576.51
Kirgiz	44,512.38	45,193.58	42,463.06	46,260.04	48,481.72
Korean	39,459.85	40,446.67	40,613.78	29,768.04	38,899.49
Lahu	37,705.24	38,977.41	43,491.06	37,162.38	31,578.29
Lhoba	51,024.99	57,146.03	51,831.53	26,961.30	49,019.70
Li	39,653.47	40,267.46	40,572.18	32,068.23	38,996.18
Lisu	37,828.35	39,087.22	43,601.71	37,071.97	31,682.43
Manchu	41,740.48	42,586.27	42,966.63	29,768.52	41,590.75
Maonan	38,029.94	39,344.61	39,857.69	31,857.76	35,623.87
Miao	40,451.58	41,759.79	43,537.89	35,322.91	36,731.98
Monba	51,709.41	58,066.05	52,497.83	26,568.01	49,655.42
Mongol	45,210.34	45,813.73	47,578.14	40,972.72	41,602.45
Mulao	37,541.85	38,789.34	39,325.28	30,387.78	35,662.52
Naxi	37,930.27	39,211.32	43,696.94	37,051.85	31,805.01
Nu	37,977.41	39,322.07	43,713.90	37,025.86	31,930.45
Oroqen	41,804.21	43,124.66	43,451.10	36,359.70	39,538.41
Pumi	37,766.24	39,038.33	43,534.99	37,148.25	31,653.90
Qiang	42,375.01	43,151.08	47,733.81	33,460.27	35,848.94

(continued)

Table 3.13 (continued)

Ethnic group	Total	Staff and workers	State-owned units	Urban collective-owned units	Units of other types of ownership
Russian	45,716.39	46,374.00	45,751.03	44,754.74	46,254.29
Salar	45,540.35	45,964.63	49,145.03	30,405.07	37,669.30
She	45,273.43	45,917.20	56,683.26	39,201.45	41,486.85
Shui	41,031.29	42,565.03	43,791.57	38,431.39	36,223.80
Tajik	44,527.41	45,204.87	42,627.46	45,926.36	48,351.39
Tatar	44,555.81	45,234.67	42,822.15	45,435.95	48,110.46
Tibetan	46,921.03	50,249.47	49,501.47	29,299.02	42,319.82
Tu	45,228.14	45,683.17	49,103.99	30,456.24	37,480.57
Tujia	41,008.78	42,102.49	43,996.28	32,489.84	38,755.05
Uygur	44,583.40	45,252.23	42,523.15	46,368.56	48,578.56
Uzbek	44,621.89	45,292.16	42,662.48	46,164.84	48,523.90
Va	37,801.74	39,063.02	43,565.27	37,066.10	31,740.29
Xibe	42,538.09	43,264.56	43,284.39	32,098.71	43,367.54
Yao	38,395.41	39,511.84	40,716.49	30,041.24	36,699.61
Yi	39,384.19	40,551.73	44,701.26	36,318.68	33,282.68
Yugur	38,200.47	38,963.53	38,935.47	32,927.89	36,647.29
Zhuang	37,079.27	38,273.54	39,034.94	29,593.48	35,338.83

Table 3.14 Indices of average wage of employed persons in urban units (preceding year = 100)

Ethnic group	Total	Staff and workers	State-owned units	Urban collective-owned units	Units of other types of ownership
National average	111.90	112.10	111.20	117.30	112.20
Achang	110.71	111.11	112.19	115.93	112.59
Bai	111.19	111.57	112.73	116.84	112.16
Baonan	117.13	117.13	118.08	117.51	113.66
Blang	110.72	111.12	112.19	115.90	112.60
Buyi	113.84	114.33	116.64	125.46	108.93
Dai	110.72	111.12	112.20	115.93	112.60
Daur	114.27	114.03	113.81	119.41	115.09
Deang	110.72	111.11	112.20	115.91	112.61
Derung	111.07	111.42	112.23	116.33	112.55
Dong	113.06	113.36	114.58	122.54	110.11
Dongxiang	117.24	117.31	118.33	117.40	113.44
Ewenki	113.38	113.47	112.73	120.70	114.54
Gaoshan	111.95	112.07	111.58	118.07	112.15
Gelao	113.91	114.40	116.77	125.68	108.83

(continued)

Table 3.14 (continued)

Ethnic group	Total	Staff and workers	State-owned units	Urban collective-owned units	Units of other types of ownership
Han	112.14	112.30	111.58	117.45	112.54
Hani	110.71	111.11	112.19	115.90	112.59
Hezhe	115.67	114.76	115.54	116.61	115.94
Hui	112.66	112.35	112.94	118.00	112.07
Jing	110.46	110.67	108.60	129.25	111.64
Jingpo	110.72	111.12	112.20	115.96	112.59
Jino	110.72	111.12	112.20	115.90	112.60
Kazak	116.59	116.49	116.99	119.30	115.19
Kirgiz	116.58	116.47	116.97	119.27	115.20
Korean	113.92	113.73	114.00	116.93	113.39
Lahu	110.71	111.11	112.19	115.90	112.59
Lhoba	105.32	105.33	103.93	166.35	137.87
Li	109.17	109.38	107.60	127.41	111.02
Lisu	110.79	111.18	112.22	115.96	112.61
Manchu	111.04	111.08	110.20	117.47	111.43
Maonan	111.34	111.63	110.75	128.77	110.71
Miao	112.88	113.21	114.58	120.87	110.44
Monba	104.84	104.85	103.35	168.40	139.05
Mongol	112.80	112.91	112.10	120.25	113.85
Mulao	110.78	111.02	109.42	129.21	111.16
Naxi	110.76	111.16	112.19	116.19	112.72
Nu	110.64	111.03	112.05	116.72	113.00
Oroqen	114.52	114.10	114.12	118.61	115.23
Pumi	110.73	111.13	112.19	115.96	112.62
Qiang	113.39	113.69	113.49	117.94	113.18
Russian	115.03	115.03	114.99	119.77	114.73
Salar	113.09	111.27	109.65	122.72	120.97
She	114.11	114.18	113.17	115.97	115.54
Shui	113.71	114.18	116.37	125.56	109.02
Tajik	116.44	116.35	116.82	119.24	115.10
Tatar	116.43	116.34	116.81	119.14	115.02
Tibetan	109.46	109.11	108.03	142.82	127.26
Tu	113.03	111.35	109.84	122.43	120.31
Tujia	112.29	112.42	112.74	117.53	111.65
Uygur	116.57	116.47	116.97	119.29	115.18
Uzbek	116.49	116.40	116.86	119.34	115.14
Va	110.74	111.14	112.18	115.88	112.59
Xibe	111.48	111.48	110.47	118.33	111.94
Yao	111.08	111.26	110.13	123.97	111.66
Yi	111.81	112.19	113.06	117.56	112.34
Yugur	117.20	117.27	118.30	117.29	113.31
Zhuang	110.31	110.53	108.52	128.79	111.61

Table 3.15 Indices of average real wage of employed persons in urban units (preceding year = 100)

Ethnic group	Total	Staff and workers	State-owned units	Urban collective-owned units	Units of other types of ownership
National average	108.97	109.17	108.29	114.23	109.27
Achang	107.49	107.88	108.92	112.56	109.32
Bai	108.05	108.41	109.55	113.54	108.99
Baonan	114.24	114.25	115.17	114.61	110.85
Blang	107.50	107.89	108.93	112.53	109.33
Buyi	110.87	111.34	113.60	122.19	106.09
Dai	107.50	107.89	108.93	112.56	109.32
Daur	110.66	110.42	110.21	115.63	111.44
Deang	107.49	107.88	108.93	112.54	109.33
Derung	107.90	108.23	109.02	113.01	109.33
Dong	110.21	110.50	111.69	119.42	107.33
Dongxiang	114.30	114.36	115.37	114.45	110.59
Ewenki	109.80	109.88	109.16	116.89	110.92
Gaoshan	108.99	109.11	108.63	114.94	109.18
Gelao	110.94	111.42	113.73	122.40	105.99
Han	109.27	109.43	108.73	114.44	109.66
Hani	107.49	107.88	108.93	112.53	109.32
Hezhe	112.08	111.20	111.95	113.00	112.34
Hui	109.75	109.45	110.04	114.96	109.18
Jing	107.08	107.29	105.28	125.29	108.22
Jingpo	107.50	107.89	108.94	112.58	109.31
Jino	107.50	107.88	108.94	112.53	109.32
Kazak	112.79	112.69	113.18	115.41	111.44
Kirgiz	112.78	112.67	113.16	115.38	111.45
Korean	110.89	110.70	110.97	113.82	110.37
Lahu	107.50	107.88	108.93	112.53	109.32
Lhoba	101.73	101.74	100.39	160.63	133.15
Li	105.80	106.01	104.28	123.47	107.59
Lisu	107.57	107.95	108.96	112.59	109.34
Manchu	107.92	107.96	107.11	114.17	108.31
Maonan	108.06	108.34	107.49	124.97	107.44
Miao	109.98	110.30	111.63	117.75	107.60
Monba	101.23	101.23	99.79	162.57	134.24
Mongol	109.34	109.45	108.67	116.56	110.36
Mulao	107.44	107.68	106.13	125.31	107.80
Naxi	107.54	107.92	108.93	112.81	109.44
Nu	107.42	107.80	108.78	113.32	109.71
Oroqen	110.93	110.53	110.55	114.89	111.62
Pumi	107.51	107.89	108.93	112.59	109.34
Qiang	110.27	110.56	110.37	114.69	110.07

(continued)

Table 3.15 (continued)

Ethnic group	Total	Staff and workers	State-owned units	Urban collective-owned units	Units of other types of ownership
Russian	111.36	111.36	111.32	115.95	111.07
Salar	109.82	108.05	106.49	119.17	117.47
She	111.41	111.48	110.50	113.23	112.81
Shui	110.72	111.18	113.31	122.26	106.15
Tajik	112.67	112.58	113.03	115.38	111.37
Tatar	112.69	112.60	113.06	115.32	111.33
Tibetan	106.09	105.75	104.71	138.30	123.27
Tu	109.81	108.18	106.71	118.92	116.87
Tujia	109.50	109.63	109.94	114.60	108.88
Uygur	112.77	112.68	113.15	115.40	111.43
Uzbek	112.70	112.61	113.06	115.45	111.39
Va	107.54	107.92	108.93	112.52	109.33
Xibe	108.20	108.21	107.23	114.86	108.65
Yao	107.98	108.16	107.06	120.48	108.54
Yi	108.65	109.02	109.86	114.23	109.16
Yugur	114.34	114.40	115.40	114.42	110.54
Zhuang	106.92	107.14	105.19	124.84	108.18

Table 3.16 Average wage of employed persons in urban units by status of registration (yuan) (I)

Ethnic group	Total	State-owned units	Urban collective-owned units	Cooperative units	Joint ownership units
National average	46,769.00	48,357.00	33,784.00	43,433.00	42,083.00
Achang	37,706.27	43,492.91	37,178.95	32,798.80	30,137.94
Bai	38,257.58	43,428.00	36,809.32	35,871.93	30,431.35
Baonan	38,329.22	39,105.68	32,946.33	29,941.33	29,600.35
Blang	37,740.21	43,534.22	37,158.33	32,849.81	30,163.82
Buyi	41,257.58	44,090.64	38,701.06	57,700.72	29,905.38
Dai	37,726.43	43,511.81	37,168.51	32,831.11	30,146.90
Daur	43,270.71	45,049.57	39,377.27	42,569.58	34,512.76
Deang	37,674.65	43,443.32	37,186.79	32,777.13	30,076.08
Derung	38,939.65	44,139.98	36,693.11	34,797.34	31,250.28
Dong	40,329.15	42,718.28	34,953.39	49,952.87	31,817.53
Dongxiang	38,539.30	38,977.51	34,132.59	35,090.17	30,742.09
Ewenki	45,804.98	48,392.12	43,283.87	41,503.26	32,559.62
Gaoshan	42,358.92	45,990.87	32,781.88	41,023.23	36,420.08
Gelao	41,290.20	44,014.01	38,718.86	58,168.84	29,711.65

(continued)

Table 3.16 (continued)

Ethnic group	Total	State-owned units	Urban collective-owned units	Cooperative units	Joint ownership units
Han	43,624.31	48,174.55	33,762.00	41,236.54	38,768.91
Hani	37,707.94	43,500.31	37,193.16	32,807.41	30,127.48
Hezhe	38,120.26	38,915.37	29,599.37	37,694.52	37,854.27
Hui	43,937.34	45,816.93	36,255.57	43,344.91	34,954.73
Jing	37,004.31	38,677.26	29,533.43	40,678.50	33,477.23
Jingpo	37,717.03	43,484.14	37,170.57	32,861.36	30,140.24
Jino	37,712.38	43,493.96	37,175.54	32,798.13	30,107.54
Kazak	44,571.48	42,492.47	46,395.84	96,954.83	43,847.81
Kirgiz	44,512.38	42,463.06	46,260.04	96,483.92	43,821.07
Korean	39,459.85	40,613.78	29,768.04	33,578.34	31,501.09
Lahu	37,705.24	43,491.06	37,162.38	32,809.34	30,147.36
Lhoba	51,024.99	51,831.53	26,961.30	4869.07	25,203.34
Li	39,653.47	40,572.18	32,068.23	31,369.19	26,273.60
Lisu	37,828.35	43,601.71	37,071.97	33,002.27	30,278.05
Manchu	41,740.48	42,966.63	29,768.52	36,243.92	32,834.81
Maonan	38,029.94	39,857.69	31,857.76	45,767.44	32,407.60
Miao	40,451.58	43,537.89	35,322.91	48,367.43	31,571.79
Monba	51,709.41	52,497.83	26,568.01	2594.45	24,901.27
Mongol	45,210.34	47,578.14	40,972.72	41,584.62	32,273.57
Mulao	37,541.85	39,325.28	30,387.78	42,988.02	33,341.95
Naxi	37,930.27	43,696.94	37,051.85	32,926.65	30,318.89
Nu	37,977.41	43,713.90	37,025.86	32,491.34	30,209.48
Oroqen	41,804.21	43,451.10	36,359.70	39,493.55	35,120.36
Pumi	37,766.24	43,534.99	37,148.25	32,838.34	30,182.42
Qiang	42,375.01	47,733.81	33,460.27	39,818.45	35,227.16
Russian	45,716.39	45,751.03	44,754.74	73,388.79	39,571.06
Salar	45,540.35	49,145.03	30,405.07	32,648.70	28,696.83
She	45,273.43	56,683.26	39,201.45	47,271.26	50,049.46
Shui	41,031.29	43,791.57	38,431.39	56,947.79	29,781.83
Tajik	44,527.41	42,627.46	45,926.36	95,096.46	43,597.44
Tatar	44,555.81	42,822.15	45,435.95	92,208.88	43,163.38
Tibetan	46,921.03	49,501.47	29,299.02	18,973.79	28,113.93
Tu	45,228.14	49,103.99	30,456.24	31,898.20	29,068.25
Tujia	41,008.78	43,996.28	32,489.84	43,997.71	33,905.19
Uygur	44,583.40	42,523.15	46,368.56	96,869.18	43,855.81
Uzbek	44,621.89	42,662.48	46,164.84	95,944.44	43,800.04
Va	37,801.74	43,565.27	37,066.10	32,977.77	30,300.65
Xibe	42,538.09	43,284.39	32,098.71	44,211.07	33,661.08
Yao	38,395.41	40,716.49	30,041.24	39,493.02	34,263.54
Yi	39,384.19	44,701.26	36,318.68	37,549.06	31,475.26
Yugur	38,200.47	38,935.47	32,927.89	29,223.71	29,687.89
Zhuang	37,079.27	39,034.94	29,593.48	39,903.30	33,678.07

Table 3.17 Average wage of employed persons in urban units by status of registration (yuan) (II)

Ethnic group	Limited liability corporations	Share-holding corporations	Others	Units with funds from Hong Kong, Macau & Taiwan	Foreign funded units
National average	41,860.00	56,254.00	34,694.00	44,103.00	55,888.00
Achang	31,703.12	44,943.98	27,046.46	33,265.42	38,324.90
Bai	32,344.47	45,163.27	27,579.54	33,636.91	38,131.14
Baonan	35,442.32	42,984.46	23,830.23	29,526.05	45,403.87
Blang	31,738.68	44,962.16	27,088.19	33,287.63	38,343.60
Buyi	33,570.79	45,938.39	26,958.96	36,179.92	35,551.31
Dai	31,707.97	44,926.34	27,073.57	33,232.99	38,330.55
Daur	38,246.57	45,989.58	28,563.68	41,088.73	46,339.65
Deang	31,674.03	44,909.99	26,994.59	33,249.06	38,303.70
Derung	33,490.62	45,981.34	28,259.30	34,396.69	39,361.07
Dong	34,978.30	45,128.42	29,790.83	35,247.45	37,722.33
Dongxiang	35,989.89	44,646.23	24,185.54	30,429.76	45,204.81
Ewenki	40,072.58	44,884.68	28,749.87	42,750.40	49,977.12
Gaoshan	38,584.14	48,010.95	33,394.73	38,544.27	43,808.26
Gelao	33,557.06	45,972.10	26,887.48	36,225.72	35,468.87
Han	39,492.34	49,510.77	34,685.44	37,936.60	43,885.97
Hani	31,699.11	44,938.37	27,042.53	33,263.96	38,326.66
Hezhe	34,015.52	47,010.74	28,598.37	36,846.97	40,337.87
Hui	41,066.90	48,042.32	30,058.01	38,999.88	43,869.43
Jing	34,860.54	36,991.98	30,526.83	33,028.92	44,157.18
Jingpo	31,720.01	44,948.92	27,052.60	33,275.80	38,330.43
Jino	31,695.82	44,946.40	27,040.67	33,259.52	38,354.96
Kazak	42,705.46	65,750.40	29,398.96	47,530.69	40,313.68
Kirgiz	42,627.55	65,590.74	29,404.86	47,451.99	40,285.64
Korean	34,074.08	46,703.67	27,990.69	35,244.62	50,514.69
Lahu	31,711.84	44,911.99	27,060.71	33,268.22	38,310.79
Lhoba	56,472.71	45,357.50	8095.42	3743.53	49,014.30
Li	35,621.02	57,475.42	28,391.73	34,916.84	40,969.86
Lisu	31,765.34	44,831.88	27,239.35	33,091.48	38,293.45
Manchu	38,226.90	50,124.52	29,997.59	40,189.64	46,700.58
Maonan	34,429.82	38,958.01	29,429.64	33,820.20	41,859.76
Miao	34,690.46	45,938.86	29,724.36	35,528.57	37,942.36
Monba	57,501.05	45,374.88	7194.63	2082.72	49,821.43
Mongol	39,864.96	46,121.48	29,008.74	42,302.38	49,219.27
Mulao	34,804.93	37,941.47	30,252.03	33,442.12	43,414.75
Naxi	31,900.51	44,917.89	27,176.48	33,025.24	38,414.43
Nu	32,159.85	44,983.20	26,838.18	32,843.01	38,534.76
Oroqen	36,974.54	45,710.74	28,645.92	39,672.23	44,880.80
Pumi	31,770.26	44,951.61	27,092.49	33,263.56	38,378.02
Qiang	34,147.87	42,721.36	34,299.98	27,402.76	37,753.84

(*continued*)

Table 3.17 (continued)

Ethnic group	Limited liability corporations	Share-holding corporations	Others	Units with funds from Hong Kong, Macau & Taiwan	Foreign funded units
Russian	42,053.09	57,987.61	29,553.61	46,039.12	45,287.30
Salar	36,332.23	45,084.09	26,215.67	43,206.16	39,829.98
She	39,697.49	53,667.41	41,153.27	38,204.14	42,639.66
Shui	33,534.69	45,537.81	26,947.48	36,026.42	35,795.73
Tajik	42,623.68	65,223.41	29,578.69	47,214.40	40,412.14
Tatar	42,473.14	64,676.33	29,423.81	46,849.57	41,086.57
Tibetan	45,406.54	43,957.46	18,776.93	18,974.72	44,008.95
Tu	36,267.70	45,024.90	26,709.18	42,304.44	40,017.72
Tujia	36,675.02	46,028.99	33,596.52	37,360.94	41,864.62
Uygur	42,713.80	65,738.77	29,437.31	47,529.43	40,321.87
Uzbek	42,703.81	65,609.25	29,533.81	47,440.82	40,514.54
Va	31,833.33	44,947.40	27,218.55	33,353.26	38,358.92
Xibe	39,426.45	55,410.69	30,286.93	41,550.80	45,234.16
Yao	35,928.05	41,875.23	32,165.61	33,532.63	42,655.07
Yi	32,578.47	44,402.14	29,021.92	31,953.75	37,840.96
Yugur	35,470.85	42,874.90	23,866.43	29,192.42	45,909.23
Zhuang	34,862.13	37,557.44	30,646.41	33,019.14	44,275.86

Table 3.18 Total wage bill of employed persons in urban units (100 million yuan) (I)

Ethnic group	Total	Agriculture, forestry, animal husbandry and fishery	Mining	Manufacturing	Production and distribution of electricity, gas and water
National total	70,914.21	760.83	3600.67	17,668.07	1999.62
Achang	1.17	0.02	0.07	0.21	0.04
Bai	64.68	0.75	3.61	11.74	2.28
Baonan	0.58	0.01	0.04	0.10	0.02
Blang	3.19	0.04	0.18	0.57	0.11
Buyi	96.72	0.47	6.35	16.15	4.21
Dai	40.12	0.53	2.32	7.15	1.40
Daur	7.54	0.49	0.74	1.06	0.35
Deang	0.62	0.01	0.04	0.11	0.02
Derung	0.29	0.00	0.02	0.06	0.01
Dong	100.97	0.50	4.58	20.06	3.84
Dongxiang	19.19	0.70	1.51	3.05	0.67
Ewenki	1.77	0.09	0.16	0.26	0.09

(continued)

Table 3.18 (continued)

Ethnic group	Total	Agriculture, forestry, animal husbandry and fishery	Mining	Manufacturing	Production and distribution of electricity, gas and water
Gaoshan	0.26	0.00	0.01	0.06	0.01
Gelao	18.69	0.09	1.24	3.08	0.82
Han	66,014.46	611.68	3305.95	16,797.59	1827.18
Hani	49.82	0.66	2.89	8.89	1.74
Hezhe	0.26	0.02	0.02	0.04	0.01
Hui	616.42	13.15	47.45	111.60	23.91
Jing	0.70	0.01	0.01	0.13	0.02
Jingpo	4.58	0.06	0.27	0.82	0.16
Jino	0.72	0.01	0.04	0.13	0.03
Kazak	94.01	9.91	9.80	9.85	2.74
Kirgiz	12.06	1.27	1.26	1.27	0.35
Korean	98.78	3.71	6.64	21.22	3.23
Lahu	15.69	0.21	0.91	2.80	0.55
Lhoba	0.15	0.00	0.00	0.01	0.00
Li	57.93	3.79	0.75	5.80	1.71
Lisu	21.91	0.29	1.27	3.92	0.77
Manchu	662.76	12.63	42.09	144.48	22.11
Maonan	3.30	0.04	0.10	0.60	0.13
Miao	315.67	1.96	14.86	61.57	11.78
Monba	0.46	0.00	0.00	0.02	0.01
Mongol	336.61	14.30	29.29	54.32	15.53
Mulao	6.55	0.08	0.14	1.26	0.23
Naxi	10.81	0.14	0.62	1.92	0.38
Nu	1.01	0.01	0.06	0.18	0.04
Oroqen	0.46	0.03	0.04	0.07	0.02
Pumi	1.17	0.02	0.07	0.21	0.04
Qiang	10.20	0.05	0.48	2.02	0.34
Russian	1.14	0.09	0.10	0.14	0.04
Salar	6.12	0.12	0.32	1.03	0.24
She	57.60	0.21	0.45	19.81	1.35
Shui	13.04	0.07	0.85	2.16	0.57
Tajik	3.06	0.32	0.32	0.33	0.09
Tatar	0.37	0.04	0.04	0.04	0.01
Tibetan	249.36	2.32	7.52	26.06	8.48
Tu	13.70	0.23	0.69	2.46	0.53
Tujia	323.92	1.66	9.76	75.13	11.06
Uygur	631.80	66.46	65.75	66.51	18.37

(continued)

Table 3.18 (continued)

Ethnic group	Total	Agriculture, forestry, animal husbandry and fishery	Mining	Manufacturing	Production and distribution of electricity, gas and water
Uzbek	0.93	0.10	0.10	0.10	0.03
Va	13.84	0.18	0.81	2.51	0.48
Xibe	12.40	0.43	0.93	2.67	0.39
Yao	92.77	0.88	1.81	20.87	2.99
Yi	263.28	2.67	14.77	47.88	9.32
Yugur	0.49	0.01	0.03	0.08	0.02
Zhuang	514.57	7.22	8.97	102.14	17.74

Table 3.19 Total wage bill of employed persons in urban units (100 million yuan) (II)

Ethnic group	Construction	Transport, storage and post	Information transmission, computer service and software	Wholesale and retail trades	Hotels and catering services
National total	7392.68	3531.51	1769.44	3271.27	824.44
Achang	0.14	0.05	0.02	0.07	0.02
Bai	7.81	2.98	0.98	3.47	0.84
Baonan	0.06	0.03	0.01	0.01	0.00
Blang	0.39	0.15	0.05	0.18	0.04
Buyi	11.01	3.83	1.26	4.81	0.90
Dai	4.87	1.86	0.58	2.24	0.54
Daur	0.58	0.50	0.16	0.22	0.06
Deang	0.08	0.03	0.01	0.03	0.01
Derung	0.03	0.01	0.00	0.01	0.00
Dong	12.01	4.54	1.48	4.29	1.02
Dongxiang	2.08	1.10	0.17	0.42	0.11
Ewenki	0.12	0.12	0.03	0.05	0.01
Gaoshan	0.03	0.01	0.01	0.01	0.00
Gelao	2.10	0.74	0.24	0.94	0.17
Han	6857.13	3266.75	1673.01	3083.50	774.57
Hani	6.05	2.31	0.71	2.79	0.67
Hezhe	0.02	0.02	0.01	0.01	0.00

(continued)

Table 3.19 (continued)

Ethnic group	Construction	Transport, storage and post	Information transmission, computer service and software	Wholesale and retail trades	Hotels and catering services
Hui	61.48	33.68	18.36	27.47	6.35
Jing	0.08	0.04	0.01	0.03	0.01
Jingpo	0.55	0.21	0.07	0.26	0.06
Jino	0.09	0.03	0.01	0.04	0.01
Kazak	13.32	5.20	0.98	2.51	0.63
Kirgiz	1.71	0.67	0.13	0.32	0.08
Korean	6.97	6.28	2.74	3.57	0.91
Lahu	1.91	0.73	0.22	0.87	0.21
Lhoba	0.00	0.00	0.00	0.00	0.00
Li	3.58	3.74	1.10	3.01	2.68
Lisu	2.67	1.02	0.31	1.20	0.29
Manchu	56.38	41.36	23.49	26.61	7.03
Maonan	0.37	0.18	0.05	0.13	0.03
Miao	39.42	14.17	4.71	14.25	3.45
Monba	0.01	0.01	0.01	0.01	0.00
Mongol	25.94	22.10	7.05	9.76	2.72
Mulao	0.71	0.38	0.11	0.24	0.06
Naxi	1.30	0.50	0.16	0.60	0.14
Nu	0.12	0.05	0.01	0.06	0.01
Oroqen	0.03	0.03	0.01	0.02	0.00
Pumi	0.14	0.05	0.02	0.07	0.02
Qiang	1.32	0.47	0.14	0.27	0.09
Russian	0.13	0.07	0.02	0.04	0.01
Salar	0.64	0.41	0.11	0.18	0.04
She	10.06	2.02	1.04	2.24	0.60
Shui	1.47	0.52	0.17	0.64	0.12
Tajik	0.43	0.17	0.03	0.08	0.02
Tatar	0.05	0.02	0.01	0.01	0.00
Tibetan	15.76	10.73	3.02	5.80	1.99
Tu	1.43	0.90	0.24	0.40	0.10
Tujia	47.04	15.50	5.07	13.53	3.60
Uygur	89.44	34.97	6.64	16.94	4.22
Uzbek	0.13	0.05	0.01	0.03	0.01
Va	1.68	0.64	0.20	0.77	0.19
Xibe	1.27	0.78	0.30	0.40	0.11
Yao	10.12	5.15	1.59	3.43	1.05
Yi	32.32	12.02	3.63	12.46	3.07
Yugur	0.05	0.03	0.01	0.01	0.00
Zhuang	55.39	30.65	8.63	18.79	5.35

Table 3.20 Total wage bill of employed persons in urban units (100 million yuan) (III)

Ethnic group	Financial intermediation	Real estate	Leasing and business services	Scientific research, technical services, and geological prospecting	Management of water conservancy, environment and public facilities
National total	4668.98	1271.26	1531.16	2259.38	784.56
Achang	0.07	0.02	0.02	0.03	0.01
Bai	3.89	1.08	0.93	1.52	0.68
Baonan	0.02	0.00	0.00	0.02	0.01
Blang	0.19	0.05	0.05	0.07	0.03
Buyi	5.37	1.58	0.92	1.95	1.00
Dai	2.41	0.66	0.58	0.94	0.42
Daur	0.41	0.07	0.11	0.21	0.14
Deang	0.04	0.01	0.01	0.01	0.01
Derung	0.02	0.00	0.00	0.01	0.00
Dong	5.91	1.69	1.25	2.17	1.11
Dongxiang	0.76	0.15	0.15	0.53	0.32
Ewenki	0.10	0.01	0.02	0.04	0.04
Gaoshan	0.02	0.01	0.01	0.01	0.00
Gelao	1.03	0.31	0.18	0.38	0.19
Han	4383.96	1197.59	1445.95	2111.29	720.91
Hani	3.00	0.82	0.71	1.16	0.52
Hezhe	0.02	0.00	0.01	0.01	0.00
Hui	38.47	10.75	16.40	23.75	8.10
Jing	0.04	0.01	0.01	0.02	0.01
Jingpo	0.28	0.08	0.07	0.11	0.05
Jino	0.04	0.01	0.01	0.02	0.01
Kazak	3.73	0.82	1.27	2.08	1.16
Kirgiz	0.48	0.11	0.16	0.27	0.15
Korean	6.20	1.70	2.09	3.95	1.46
Lahu	0.94	0.26	0.22	0.36	0.16
Lhoba	0.01	0.00	0.00	0.01	0.00
Li	3.15	2.59	0.91	1.19	1.07
Lisu	1.31	0.36	0.31	0.52	0.23
Manchu	45.13	12.81	16.47	28.53	9.73
Maonan	0.20	0.05	0.05	0.09	0.05
Miao	18.78	5.49	3.91	7.02	3.36
Monba	0.04	0.00	0.01	0.02	0.00
Mongol	19.09	3.34	4.99	8.72	6.60
Mulao	0.41	0.10	0.13	0.19	0.10
Naxi	0.66	0.18	0.16	0.26	0.11

(continued)

Table 3.20 (continued)

Ethnic group	Financial intermediation	Real estate	Leasing and business services	Scientific research, technical services, and geological prospecting	Management of water conservancy, environment and public facilities
Nu	0.06	0.02	0.01	0.02	0.01
Oroqen	0.03	0.01	0.01	0.02	0.01
Pumi	0.07	0.02	0.02	0.03	0.01
Qiang	0.60	0.11	0.10	0.41	0.11
Russian	0.06	0.01	0.02	0.03	0.02
Salar	0.28	0.06	0.11	0.35	0.07
She	3.46	1.02	0.88	1.00	0.47
Shui	0.72	0.21	0.12	0.26	0.14
Tajik	0.12	0.03	0.04	0.07	0.04
Tatar	0.02	0.00	0.01	0.01	0.00
Tibetan	15.35	1.37	2.79	11.22	2.13
Tu	0.63	0.13	0.23	0.75	0.17
Tujia	19.16	6.05	4.14	8.03	3.38
Uygur	25.12	5.52	8.55	14.02	7.77
Uzbek	0.04	0.01	0.01	0.02	0.01
Va	0.83	0.23	0.20	0.32	0.14
Xibe	0.73	0.21	0.21	0.43	0.19
Yao	5.94	1.57	1.76	2.41	1.22
Yi	15.60	3.91	3.30	7.23	2.81
Yugur	0.02	0.00	0.01	0.02	0.01
Zhuang	32.67	7.70	10.34	14.81	7.87

Table 3.21 Total wage bill of employed persons in urban units (100 million yuan) (IV)

Ethnic group	Services to households and other services	Education	Health, social securities and social welfare	Culture, sports and entertainment	Public management and social organization
National total	217.10	7851.00	3718.46	735.44	7058.33
Achang	0.00	0.18	0.06	0.01	0.15
Bai	0.11	9.57	3.63	0.54	8.27
Baonan	0.00	0.10	0.03	0.01	0.10
Blang	0.00	0.47	0.17	0.03	0.40
Buyi	0.24	15.77	5.54	0.56	14.81
Dai	0.06	5.99	2.18	0.34	5.04

(*continued*)

Table 3.21 (continued)

Ethnic group	Services to households and other services	Education	Health, social securities and social welfare	Culture, sports and entertainment	Public management and social organization
Daur	0.04	0.98	0.37	0.09	0.96
Deang	0.00	0.09	0.03	0.01	0.08
Derung	0.00	0.04	0.02	0.00	0.03
Dong	0.24	14.90	6.61	0.76	14.00
Dongxiang	0.02	3.14	0.97	0.21	3.12
Ewenki	0.01	0.25	0.09	0.02	0.25
Gaoshan	0.00	0.03	0.01	0.00	0.02
Gelao	0.05	3.07	1.07	0.11	2.88
Han	205.13	7202.90	3439.25	684.01	6426.10
Hani	0.07	7.44	2.71	0.42	6.26
Hezhe	0.00	0.03	0.01	0.00	0.02
Hui	2.00	69.25	29.72	7.88	66.66
Jing	0.00	0.11	0.06	0.01	0.08
Jingpo	0.01	0.68	0.25	0.04	0.58
Jino	0.00	0.11	0.04	0.01	0.09
Kazak	0.11	11.35	4.68	0.90	12.97
Kirgiz	0.01	1.45	0.60	0.11	1.66
Korean	0.47	11.57	5.28	1.17	9.64
Lahu	0.02	2.34	0.85	0.13	1.97
Lhoba	0.00	0.03	0.01	0.00	0.06
Li	0.10	9.97	3.90	0.63	8.25
Lisu	0.03	3.27	1.20	0.18	2.76
Manchu	2.97	71.33	32.72	8.17	58.71
Maonan	0.01	0.53	0.25	0.03	0.43
Miao	0.71	45.97	19.62	2.40	42.22
Monba	0.00	0.08	0.03	0.01	0.20
Mongol	0.87	45.81	16.86	4.16	45.15
Mulao	0.01	1.02	0.51	0.06	0.80
Naxi	0.02	1.60	0.59	0.09	1.37
Nu	0.00	0.15	0.06	0.01	0.13
Oroqen	0.00	0.06	0.02	0.01	0.05
Pumi	0.00	0.17	0.06	0.01	0.15
Qiang	0.01	1.48	0.77	0.08	1.36
Russian	0.00	0.14	0.06	0.01	0.15
Salar	0.02	0.82	0.32	0.08	0.91
She	0.10	5.28	2.58	0.43	4.61
Shui	0.03	2.14	0.76	0.08	2.00
Tajik	0.00	0.37	0.15	0.03	0.42
Tatar	0.00	0.04	0.02	0.00	0.05
Tibetan	0.39	41.07	14.82	4.52	74.01

(*continued*)

Table 3.21 (continued)

Ethnic group	Services to households and other services	Education	Health, social securities and social welfare	Culture, sports and entertainment	Public management and social organization
Tu	0.05	1.85	0.73	0.16	2.02
Tujia	0.72	40.48	20.20	2.90	36.51
Uygur	0.75	76.21	31.48	6.03	87.07
Uzbek	0.00	0.11	0.05	0.01	0.13
Va	0.02	2.05	0.75	0.12	1.73
Xibe	0.04	1.35	0.63	0.12	1.19
Yao	0.20	12.98	6.97	0.85	11.01
Yi	0.41	39.45	15.91	2.05	34.47
Yugur	0.00	0.08	0.02	0.01	0.08
Zhuang	0.94	79.40	40.82	4.71	60.45

Table 3.22 Average wage of employed persons in urban units (yuan) (I)

Ethnic group	Total	Agriculture, forestry, animal husbandry and fishery	Mining	Manufacturing	Production and distribution of electricity, gas and water
National average	46,769.00	22,687.00	56,946.00	41,650.00	58,202.00
Achang	37,706.27	21,303.35	38,666.51	36,597.50	53,161.88
Bai	38,257.58	22,287.44	39,123.39	36,833.45	53,216.99
Baonan	38,329.22	25,174.00	59,887.85	42,024.53	42,376.01
Blang	37,740.21	21,353.00	38,711.26	36,618.13	53,205.23
Buyi	41,257.58	30,499.89	43,250.31	36,317.86	59,441.56
Dai	37,726.43	21,343.47	38,693.95	36,602.04	53,154.30
Daur	43,270.71	24,629.88	56,814.55	40,306.33	54,968.37
Deang	37,674.65	21,268.07	38,643.02	36,602.01	53,105.89
Derung	38,939.65	22,062.12	42,013.23	37,238.57	53,995.76
Dong	40,329.15	26,402.82	40,758.45	37,203.43	53,713.36
Dongxiang	38,539.30	25,161.25	61,408.77	42,407.36	42,771.01
Ewenki	45,804.98	26,016.82	58,406.96	41,189.34	58,325.35
Gaoshan	42,358.92	23,867.81	50,313.75	38,400.37	55,592.20
Gelao	41,290.20	30,640.04	43,248.45	36,297.69	59,503.43
Han	43,624.31	25,593.93	52,658.98	39,372.69	58,113.74
Hani	37,707.94	21,304.65	38,666.67	36,609.07	53,176.61
Hezhe	38,120.26	21,514.76	50,387.97	37,783.31	48,414.85
Hui	43,937.34	26,206.08	61,885.34	40,697.78	57,484.89
Jing	37,004.31	20,088.81	35,981.72	33,845.08	48,035.65

(*continued*)

Table 3.22 (continued)

Ethnic group	Total	Agriculture, forestry, animal husbandry and fishery	Mining	Manufacturing	Production and distribution of electricity, gas and water
Jingpo	37,717.03	21,313.38	38,705.38	36,602.69	53,163.35
Jino	37,712.38	21,314.66	38,650.64	36,615.52	53,157.23
Kazak	44,571.48	26,324.68	76,405.38	47,351.00	53,785.46
Kirgiz	44,512.38	26,275.98	76,162.52	47,254.81	53,761.67
Korean	39,459.85	20,640.11	45,608.43	39,771.55	45,977.33
Lahu	37,705.24	21,321.52	38,712.90	36,597.98	53,145.87
Lhoba	51,024.99	14,822.89	41,697.77	37,610.78	51,663.55
Li	39,653.47	20,954.71	39,889.52	34,829.46	49,233.08
Lisu	37,828.35	21,579.34	38,944.84	36,586.80	53,090.12
Manchu	41,740.48	16,082.02	54,958.96	39,480.44	53,292.21
Maonan	38,029.94	22,914.37	37,733.52	34,328.19	50,919.33
Miao	40,451.58	26,748.70	41,015.27	37,342.03	54,644.77
Monba	51,709.41	14,462.14	41,726.17	37,690.55	51,708.07
Mongol	45,210.34	24,383.95	57,992.72	41,072.31	57,294.18
Mulao	37,541.85	21,245.63	36,819.77	34,050.59	49,423.36
Naxi	37,930.27	21,579.97	38,943.53	36,622.45	53,152.71
Nu	37,977.41	21,262.40	38,819.43	36,643.87	53,243.70
Oroqen	41,804.21	23,549.21	54,406.76	39,365.79	53,241.23
Pumi	37,766.24	21,348.65	38,803.49	36,627.44	53,173.18
Qiang	42,375.01	31,356.84	46,869.06	36,305.95	50,661.87
Russian	45,716.39	26,489.15	69,079.51	45,089.01	56,483.35
Salar	45,540.35	28,486.19	56,043.90	42,743.00	56,899.05
She	45,273.43	28,485.07	40,255.49	39,202.07	68,847.61
Shui	41,031.29	30,037.31	42,881.79	36,214.06	58,961.43
Tajik	44,527.41	26,295.27	75,574.29	47,078.85	53,887.31
Tatar	44,555.81	26,357.50	75,038.27	47,026.78	53,758.58
Tibetan	46,921.03	22,104.63	46,616.72	38,532.17	51,766.39
Tu	45,228.14	28,216.77	55,091.31	42,323.68	57,003.08
Tujia	41,008.78	25,809.82	40,712.09	39,226.46	52,483.38
Uygur	44,583.40	26,319.61	76,337.52	47,331.79	53,824.26
Uzbek	44,621.89	26,302.18	75,929.26	47,232.34	53,936.67
Va	37,801.74	21,483.80	39,013.63	36,624.12	53,156.79
Xibe	42,538.09	16,095.35	58,135.49	41,086.30	52,311.04
Yao	38,395.41	20,244.23	37,533.31	36,036.57	48,598.04
Yi	39,384.19	25,116.63	41,453.46	36,482.18	53,145.86
Yugur	38,200.47	25,096.23	59,862.31	41,961.78	42,096.91
Zhuang	37,079.27	19,771.76	36,154.98	33,933.93	48,347.20

Table 3.23 Average wage of employed persons in urban units (yuan) (II)

Ethnic group	Construction	Transport, storage and post	Information transmission, computer service and software	Wholesale and retail trades	Hotels and catering services
National average	36,483.00	53,391.00	80,510.00	46,340.00	31,267.00
Achang	28,442.05	50,077.17	48,534.36	34,206.48	23,365.46
Bai	29,647.85	49,518.99	49,128.51	35,017.39	23,804.37
Baonan	33,771.29	44,863.63	34,836.45	28,187.10	23,434.54
Blang	28,466.02	50,075.93	48,600.90	34,227.39	23,387.99
Buyi	36,402.51	47,309.47	53,907.44	40,261.68	25,490.41
Dai	28,447.99	50,096.86	48,539.23	34,234.29	23,378.01
Daur	33,360.69	50,941.08	48,677.22	36,563.45	30,599.48
Deang	28,408.01	50,078.30	48,403.02	34,181.55	23,336.72
Derung	29,891.67	50,178.60	50,171.48	34,863.92	24,474.16
Dong	35,489.77	46,644.13	51,653.74	38,252.62	25,646.75
Dongxiang	34,225.68	45,773.56	35,736.40	29,281.71	23,972.64
Ewenki	33,295.34	52,767.57	47,463.71	37,356.85	30,532.04
Gaoshan	35,694.97	48,963.80	57,260.88	37,347.28	28,099.06
Gelao	36,534.75	47,241.90	53,883.07	40,379.89	25,485.50
Han	35,439.52	50,097.54	59,526.20	37,639.95	28,293.85
Hani	28,430.32	50,075.29	48,512.27	34,212.40	23,356.96
Hezhe	32,906.01	45,745.74	52,242.37	34,275.36	30,342.46
Hui	36,282.40	50,773.36	54,555.59	36,824.70	27,832.79
Jing	36,265.82	44,194.49	47,129.91	33,555.69	24,897.96
Jingpo	28,462.92	50,073.46	48,511.64	34,224.31	23,370.47
Jino	28,430.91	50,089.44	48,501.18	34,223.55	23,355.03
Kazak	41,210.30	62,365.62	54,839.78	45,686.59	32,440.14
Kirgiz	41,131.77	62,230.59	54,850.71	45,600.55	32,440.58
Korean	32,427.27	46,679.21	50,369.22	33,236.66	27,306.24
Lahu	28,436.75	50,059.32	48,504.81	34,194.23	23,370.28
Lhoba	24,251.15	55,304.17	39,096.47	42,958.01	33,267.00
Li	36,524.06	51,742.05	66,897.38	35,708.37	27,483.55
Lisu	28,522.90	50,174.69	48,717.14	34,292.86	23,502.51
Manchu	33,930.86	49,494.75	60,184.71	34,646.41	29,226.85
Maonan	36,484.24	44,745.73	48,628.90	35,333.78	25,022.44
Miao	34,690.94	47,460.60	52,794.39	38,079.82	25,587.05
Monba	23,683.74	55,704.86	38,724.18	43,475.68	33,613.00
Mongol	33,669.98	52,646.87	49,904.56	37,051.60	30,089.50
Mulao	36,466.85	44,431.93	48,083.33	34,459.65	25,040.92
Naxi	28,539.11	50,220.84	48,771.30	34,404.04	23,556.20
Nu	28,439.01	50,179.79	48,525.04	34,392.73	23,567.84
Oroqen	33,019.94	49,121.28	49,686.95	35,640.73	30,445.79
Pumi	28,487.23	50,089.32	48,576.34	34,238.72	23,411.95

(*continued*)

Table 3.23 (continued)

Ethnic group	Construction	Transport, storage and post	Information transmission, computer service and software	Wholesale and retail trades	Hotels and catering services
Qiang	32,021.10	53,793.31	56,572.81	38,370.20	28,386.50
Russian	38,342.75	58,520.55	53,505.73	42,839.67	31,665.64
Salar	37,626.53	56,208.24	52,671.24	34,955.27	27,323.66
She	39,667.08	53,694.24	71,726.23	44,350.46	30,105.30
Shui	36,318.30	47,143.84	53,449.31	39,926.04	25,399.78
Tajik	41,032.92	61,942.12	54,950.20	45,411.39	32,298.29
Tatar	40,864.01	61,361.56	54,727.15	44,978.00	32,021.22
Tibetan	29,192.18	54,499.20	45,343.23	38,890.68	30,072.47
Tu	37,246.19	55,514.90	52,837.37	34,891.23	27,133.84
Tujia	35,447.00	47,930.32	52,962.16	36,492.15	26,292.54
Uygur	41,201.91	62,351.89	54,904.49	45,697.82	32,444.75
Uzbek	41,164.70	62,197.32	55,105.51	45,650.54	32,390.51
Va	28,557.53	50,058.20	48,721.41	34,227.14	23,481.50
Xibe	35,714.09	53,054.57	63,511.40	37,600.77	30,785.98
Yao	34,879.46	45,781.67	49,401.58	35,113.20	25,459.76
Yi	30,321.73	50,775.30	51,287.90	36,026.76	24,981.99
Yugur	33,677.78	44,346.46	34,552.62	27,996.74	23,295.57
Zhuang	35,886.55	44,547.15	47,497.48	33,659.06	24,901.76

Table 3.24 Average wage of employed persons in urban units (yuan) (III)

Ethnic group	Financial intermediation	Real estate	Leasing and business services	Scientific research, technical services, and geological prospecting	Management of water conservancy, environment and public facilities
National average	89,743.00	46,764.00	53,162.00	69,254.00	32,343.00
Achang	88,592.34	33,663.88	34,006.54	43,899.96	52,390.00
Bai	86,310.68	34,091.18	33,713.84	43,824.51	50,079.36
Baonan	46,223.05	31,733.74	30,391.02	42,981.34	54,243.36
Blang	88,574.70	33,720.92	34,036.48	44,028.50	52,311.85
Buyi	82,007.21	34,033.96	30,627.03	40,146.96	51,314.91
Dai	88,558.51	33,693.65	34,080.65	44,013.66	52,392.38
Daur	62,680.14	36,882.77	39,772.39	52,007.44	30,073.44
Deang	88,588.95	33,608.66	33,993.94	43,825.08	52,495.60
Derung	85,491.29	34,800.71	34,499.38	46,232.67	48,314.00

(*continued*)

Table 3.24 (continued)

Ethnic group	Financial intermediation	Real estate	Leasing and business services	Scientific research, technical services, and geological prospecting	Management of water conservancy, environment and public facilities
Dong	76,004.36	35,397.39	31,480.22	42,639.17	38,983.18
Dongxiang	47,475.97	32,014.02	29,750.67	42,933.78	53,429.13
Ewenki	64,600.58	39,056.62	41,253.38	49,932.40	28,845.87
Gaoshan	74,672.77	39,978.21	36,057.16	53,955.10	31,898.05
Gelao	81,966.14	33,956.38	30,508.82	39,955.05	51,480.57
Han	75,586.27	41,163.68	38,328.00	58,804.71	32,543.68
Hani	88,638.64	33,663.39	34,014.48	43,912.69	52,441.60
Hezhe	60,178.30	32,894.45	37,681.58	57,759.48	32,534.73
Hui	69,247.41	38,545.15	37,075.70	53,187.37	35,070.74
Jing	71,145.31	32,538.15	28,858.89	41,281.32	23,458.67
Jingpo	88,568.79	33,653.64	34,009.89	43,895.06	52,371.56
Jino	88,640.52	33,663.53	34,042.64	43,952.39	52,436.61
Kazak	69,430.91	36,266.66	35,030.45	50,562.85	30,619.74
Kirgiz	69,371.92	36,243.76	35,058.77	50,646.50	30,584.62
Korean	62,922.08	34,376.07	36,476.00	53,488.50	27,184.09
Lahu	88,533.25	33,675.04	34,010.04	43,928.14	52,369.13
Lhoba	115,668.07	45,882.04	52,523.83	51,276.93	35,857.34
Li	70,170.54	38,321.38	28,372.88	41,925.19	32,502.63
Lisu	88,017.99	33,882.49	34,376.93	44,570.19	52,087.75
Manchu	68,158.22	36,357.07	33,085.63	56,838.06	28,964.08
Maonan	73,798.84	32,641.49	28,978.31	40,529.88	30,497.53
Miao	78,473.15	35,948.66	32,163.85	44,707.16	41,377.03
Monba	118,095.89	46,502.05	53,935.74	52,118.04	35,750.85
Mongol	65,652.49	38,635.00	39,653.91	50,591.38	28,969.11
Mulao	72,542.33	32,672.83	29,034.19	41,394.98	25,850.33
Naxi	88,311.18	33,967.38	34,501.53	44,634.77	52,027.60
Nu	88,983.02	33,943.13	34,360.42	44,168.95	51,964.17
Oroqen	61,948.01	35,862.79	39,203.91	53,699.55	30,658.11
Pumi	88,461.13	33,729.54	34,106.87	44,078.50	52,266.00
Qiang	70,082.99	41,777.40	47,342.14	66,892.19	41,061.98
Russian	69,754.89	38,051.26	38,319.04	51,615.48	29,962.36
Salar	59,044.17	33,594.85	54,950.71	58,524.57	27,768.00
She	94,841.85	48,292.59	40,476.85	57,141.04	30,644.65
Shui	81,648.33	33,881.59	30,441.02	39,993.22	50,613.56
Tajik	69,612.85	36,404.89	35,087.02	50,805.47	30,614.86
Tatar	69,455.67	36,443.43	35,307.90	50,942.37	31,572.93
Tibetan	88,389.10	41,176.89	50,924.59	55,920.81	36,666.64

(continued)

Table 3.24 (continued)

Ethnic group	Financial intermediation	Real estate	Leasing and business services	Scientific research, technical services, and geological prospecting	Management of water conservancy, environment and public facilities
Tu	60,237.18	33,997.23	53,695.36	58,351.35	28,967.54
Tujia	72,758.34	39,895.29	33,350.59	51,678.81	31,101.16
Uygur	69,518.91	36,302.77	35,054.31	50,616.54	30,560.23
Uzbek	69,823.35	36,407.94	35,170.02	50,777.82	30,547.78
Va	88,207.13	33,807.65	34,108.00	44,208.89	51,903.19
Xibe	69,635.22	36,237.59	32,489.05	55,004.19	28,839.60
Yao	72,737.91	35,030.76	31,687.02	45,357.48	24,856.11
Yi	82,679.49	35,925.82	37,299.77	49,806.22	49,183.32
Yugur	46,193.18	31,783.00	29,701.73	42,677.78	55,051.46
Zhuang	72,456.93	32,673.84	29,322.26	42,158.25	23,955.43

Table 3.25 Average wage of employed persons in urban units (yuan) (IV)

Ethnic group	Services to households and other services	Education	Health, social securities and social welfare	Culture, sports and entertainment	Public management and social organization
National average	35,135.00	47,734.00	52,564.00	53,558.00	46,074.00
Achang	26,278.10	40,093.56	41,943.69	36,138.63	37,720.56
Bai	27,184.34	40,345.67	42,904.31	36,783.58	37,984.78
Baonan	25,307.38	38,583.10	36,451.75	36,289.63	35,446.06
Blang	26,324.96	40,129.93	42,009.48	36,200.58	37,770.16
Buyi	28,496.05	42,726.80	44,786.04	36,511.24	41,010.29
Dai	26,280.54	40,094.36	41,984.65	36,159.45	37,730.22
Daur	36,046.31	50,367.69	47,260.30	45,181.75	46,173.25
Deang	26,214.34	40,030.87	41,857.04	36,073.34	37,632.91
Derung	27,624.53	41,513.84	43,291.71	37,755.23	39,128.16
Dong	30,758.82	40,960.07	46,509.17	38,916.25	39,260.07
Dongxiang	25,050.10	38,809.26	36,847.04	36,655.25	35,778.22
Ewenki	33,849.16	54,644.26	50,351.73	48,660.42	50,203.69
Gaoshan	32,860.61	45,661.08	48,342.85	43,288.84	43,408.90
Gelao	28,424.35	42,667.47	44,737.02	36,395.26	40,947.58
Han	34,953.77	47,008.90	50,406.04	45,274.66	46,231.24
Hani	26,271.17	40,084.09	41,937.34	36,135.08	37,712.13
Hezhe	41,549.47	41,702.91	41,799.54	38,213.26	38,083.26

(*continued*)

Table 3.25 (continued)

Ethnic group	Services to households and other services	Education	Health, social securities and social welfare	Culture, sports and entertainment	Public management and social organization
Hui	33,251.23	45,802.99	45,185.53	43,956.85	42,805.55
Jing	28,792.21	35,533.87	43,401.91	36,961.38	36,791.67
Jingpo	26,272.37	40,078.69	41,932.89	36,133.92	37,700.78
Jino	26,237.31	40,076.88	41,947.20	36,122.81	37,692.98
Kazak	27,383.63	47,176.53	44,864.82	45,043.28	45,054.60
Kirgiz	27,541.70	47,145.44	44,853.90	44,990.63	45,013.75
Korean	34,376.54	42,786.87	42,869.95	37,398.82	38,657.50
Lahu	26,295.46	40,082.84	41,934.16	36,143.97	37,701.88
Lhoba	26,226.53	54,803.88	47,242.70	56,014.37	51,302.50
Li	25,482.90	49,892.57	49,976.64	35,656.41	46,893.77
Lisu	26,489.28	40,198.02	42,228.07	36,333.40	37,869.48
Manchu	35,540.06	45,985.41	44,345.03	41,773.73	40,323.90
Maonan	28,625.46	37,101.10	43,613.74	36,563.70	37,635.19
Miao	30,204.39	41,703.62	46,819.52	38,993.49	39,843.75
Monba	26,069.29	55,541.75	47,690.24	57,043.00	52,014.63
Mongol	33,216.08	53,038.72	49,179.62	47,407.98	48,400.16
Mulao	28,861.14	36,230.66	43,803.43	36,999.43	37,335.98
Naxi	26,450.76	40,317.89	42,328.55	36,479.41	37,983.81
Nu	26,379.43	40,414.39	42,140.47	36,578.16	38,058.05
Oroqen	37,852.07	48,011.12	45,822.21	43,253.00	43,953.02
Pumi	26,345.39	40,142.59	42,007.03	36,220.79	37,780.97
Qiang	32,792.58	44,493.19	53,397.48	43,682.45	44,153.26
Russian	30,092.96	50,693.32	48,025.21	47,343.79	47,608.19
Salar	36,630.15	49,733.30	42,678.38	44,259.76	45,966.57
She	35,302.53	54,765.16	59,931.40	51,091.53	56,436.15
Shui	28,432.88	42,353.86	44,543.95	36,381.28	40,737.28
Tajik	27,584.50	47,123.49	45,037.68	45,011.70	45,033.90
Tatar	27,609.01	47,112.14	45,094.47	45,081.11	44,925.41
Tibetan	29,944.79	50,198.26	46,705.60	49,208.74	47,343.53
Tu	36,333.06	49,353.63	43,134.71	44,041.36	45,958.88
Tujia	32,234.28	41,963.25	49,278.31	41,573.25	40,355.02
Uygur	27,420.01	47,195.03	44,915.49	45,069.61	45,079.01
Uzbek	27,486.44	47,247.94	45,107.12	45,155.12	45,162.94
Va	26,533.79	40,196.83	42,101.40	36,346.16	37,813.30
Xibe	32,289.39	47,748.77	45,233.18	43,916.30	42,274.09
Yao	30,925.17	37,671.71	46,568.83	39,805.92	37,986.03
Yi	28,305.32	41,570.58	45,387.72	38,224.19	39,822.75
Yugur	25,045.52	38,299.56	36,454.44	36,201.26	35,159.13
Zhuang	28,752.86	35,653.15	43,671.55	37,111.82	37,030.63

Table 3.26 Average wage of employed persons in urban private units (yuan) (I)

Ethnic group	Total	Agriculture, forestry, animal husbandry and fishery	Mining	Manufacturing	Production and distribution of electricity, gas and water
National average	28,752.00	21,973.00	29,684.00	28,215.00	25,478.00
Achang	21,038.45	17,193.75	21,193.54	17,969.19	10,274.57
Bai	21,828.14	17,238.05	23,293.79	18,905.42	14,252.95
Baonan	21,308.65	15,827.47	25,013.57	20,081.21	19,238.73
Blang	21,069.45	17,227.83	21,225.66	18,011.86	10,352.81
Buyi	25,978.96	15,740.44	33,931.11	22,450.84	37,469.61
Dai	21,046.38	17,207.78	21,213.34	17,981.65	10,315.15
Daur	27,068.17	23,531.49	32,972.58	27,749.43	27,659.15
Deang	20,993.73	17,160.41	21,150.45	17,912.75	10,179.81
Derung	22,252.41	18,186.98	22,995.26	19,730.42	13,663.27
Dong	25,543.50	17,446.56	32,300.80	23,398.63	32,423.81
Dongxiang	21,898.32	16,315.09	26,271.65	20,645.41	19,833.30
Ewenki	29,031.62	26,141.80	35,639.74	29,946.16	30,392.66
Gaoshan	26,049.39	20,905.96	27,466.93	25,475.12	25,192.20
Gelao	26,041.72	15,640.86	34,168.74	22,477.19	37,964.97
Han	26,685.80	21,757.16	27,998.08	26,220.03	25,459.16
Hani	21,027.31	17,188.98	21,169.69	17,952.00	10,247.83
Hezhe	22,655.14	17,715.17	25,872.21	22,804.67	21,423.64
Hui	25,397.07	20,213.97	28,447.06	25,199.21	23,629.04
Jing	25,164.03	19,451.18	26,234.25	25,191.47	26,347.79
Jingpo	21,047.53	17,185.98	21,222.46	17,976.83	10,334.26
Jino	21,022.03	17,183.31	21,173.31	17,945.17	10,234.91
Kazak	29,462.38	23,658.01	40,518.08	28,849.38	28,163.92
Kirgiz	29,412.09	23,620.63	40,405.02	28,811.05	28,116.14
Korean	23,142.04	18,738.82	26,242.29	22,217.51	20,682.51
Lahu	21,036.20	17,203.12	21,188.36	17,971.68	10,290.61
Lhoba	2554.95	1950.78	2928.95	2428.32	2701.86
Li	24,578.26	16,996.90	28,775.53	24,329.82	19,610.84
Lisu	21,168.99	17,363.42	21,464.16	18,171.72	10,748.23
Manchu	25,837.31	21,042.86	26,685.82	25,601.17	24,481.62
Maonan	25,445.08	18,379.19	28,491.16	24,534.18	29,890.26
Miao	25,354.05	17,756.44	31,338.89	23,066.26	30,120.04
Monba	1372.79	1090.50	1209.41	1325.55	1325.35
Mongol	28,492.32	25,195.77	34,114.94	29,083.18	29,408.64
Mulao	25,415.80	19,074.95	27,233.25	25,090.42	27,953.80
Naxi	21,097.14	17,280.61	21,383.78	18,101.46	10,706.24
Nu	20,814.25	17,020.01	20,970.48	17,811.96	10,297.77

(continued)

Table 3.26 (continued)

Ethnic group	Total	Agriculture, forestry, animal husbandry and fishery	Mining	Manufacturing	Production and distribution of electricity, gas and water
Oroqen	25,808.46	21,941.77	30,702.81	26,377.05	25,925.90
Pumi	21,067.18	17,229.95	21,237.78	18,020.92	10,387.08
Qiang	25,930.72	22,792.60	31,280.96	25,324.70	27,166.08
Russian	29,361.87	24,596.74	38,037.81	29,269.46	29,047.40
Salar	23,113.38	19,163.41	24,488.76	23,920.08	22,486.84
She	30,137.37	24,970.50	30,855.99	28,997.30	26,272.50
Shui	25,875.80	15,825.73	33,563.97	22,449.96	36,909.22
Tajik	29,375.22	23,595.02	40,125.02	28,774.53	28,098.88
Tatar	29,139.78	23,333.15	39,491.96	28,491.30	27,765.28
Tibetan	13,224.77	11,174.78	14,935.26	13,138.69	12,984.64
Tu	23,195.96	19,088.55	24,370.21	23,846.23	22,342.47
Tujia	25,748.08	19,170.40	30,752.78	24,672.62	28,149.70
Uygur	29,467.40	23,666.75	40,497.72	28,856.95	28,171.27
Uzbek	29,450.18	23,631.12	40,307.83	28,839.12	28,108.96
Va	21,177.40	17,346.24	21,379.59	18,173.03	10,691.03
Xibe	26,831.19	21,386.47	28,900.62	26,455.94	25,409.37
Yao	25,161.99	19,645.78	27,421.50	24,878.44	24,479.96
Yi	22,931.35	18,564.25	25,412.19	20,488.25	18,011.49
Yugur	21,300.13	15,731.56	24,949.14	20,002.72	19,178.25
Zhuang	25,063.03	19,466.91	25,762.15	25,032.82	25,085.23

Table 3.27 Average wage of employed persons in urban private units (yuan) (II)

Ethnic group	Construction	Transport, storage and post	Information transmission, computer service and software	Wholesale and retail trades	Hotels and catering services
National average	30,911.00	28,159.00	39,518.00	27,233.00	23,933.00
Achang	25,489.81	21,629.32	16,484.61	21,422.07	18,190.99
Bai	25,483.45	21,708.86	19,280.37	21,200.55	18,431.59
Baonan	22,788.72	23,227.62	23,486.95	22,017.20	18,966.83
Blang	25,506.58	21,658.98	16,548.14	21,447.30	18,218.20
Buyi	23,402.27	21,542.22	32,586.40	20,039.74	18,948.98
Dai	25,483.74	21,641.67	16,520.84	21,424.73	18,205.37
Daur	27,638.45	28,691.67	25,055.94	24,241.97	25,110.21

(continued)

Table 3.27 (continued)

Ethnic group	Construction	Transport, storage and post	Information transmission, computer service and software	Wholesale and retail trades	Hotels and catering services
Deang	25,466.93	21,590.36	16,378.17	21,382.82	18,157.47
Derung	26,138.54	22,705.07	19,051.14	22,113.75	19,159.55
Dong	25,373.74	22,341.65	31,293.96	20,904.70	19,777.65
Dongxiang	23,908.35	23,676.00	23,760.21	22,194.64	19,246.56
Ewenki	28,408.88	31,402.41	26,938.49	26,261.24	25,579.27
Gaoshan	27,752.06	25,890.17	28,791.95	24,203.43	22,386.38
Gelao	23,302.07	21,467.95	32,908.69	19,974.15	18,908.19
Han	28,319.51	26,830.28	31,567.39	24,961.38	23,108.05
Hani	25,484.76	21,623.88	16,460.81	21,411.72	18,184.54
Hezhe	24,801.94	22,804.28	22,274.36	20,254.48	24,071.65
Hui	27,693.43	24,746.65	25,263.22	23,046.33	21,555.48
Jing	26,558.01	24,756.23	21,632.66	25,973.19	22,096.99
Jingpo	25,478.98	21,627.38	16,541.92	21,415.66	18,189.76
Jino	25,475.63	21,618.80	16,465.95	21,410.85	18,179.16
Kazak	37,787.74	28,946.67	25,621.73	24,045.71	23,792.85
Kirgiz	37,687.76	28,901.46	25,583.96	24,012.87	23,810.76
Korean	24,889.89	24,430.71	27,222.22	22,586.80	21,780.39
Lahu	25,487.87	21,629.44	16,476.22	21,416.01	18,196.18
Lhoba	2675.96	2443.80	2997.47	2242.42	2082.64
Li	28,679.05	21,440.61	22,144.10	23,619.69	18,939.66
Lisu	25,509.03	21,775.76	16,828.74	21,494.88	18,350.62
Manchu	27,793.91	26,896.19	28,364.88	24,124.69	23,225.03
Maonan	25,601.54	23,855.58	24,667.42	24,433.07	21,272.20
Miao	25,594.94	22,573.10	30,075.37	21,345.17	19,793.01
Monba	1414.19	1398.75	1834.90	1273.43	1202.79
Mongol	28,546.49	30,491.12	27,265.83	25,911.44	24,841.98
Mulao	26,224.26	24,527.56	23,344.05	25,528.19	21,861.49
Naxi	25,421.16	21,687.99	16,809.45	21,415.18	18,273.32
Nu	25,179.48	21,407.56	16,403.17	21,171.53	17,998.50
Oroqen	26,583.30	27,097.68	24,416.17	23,203.68	24,857.53
Pumi	25,493.96	21,663.48	16,570.11	21,434.48	18,229.24
Qiang	26,413.03	26,489.88	29,819.51	24,240.01	23,619.41
Russian	33,897.90	29,906.26	26,957.66	25,107.20	24,477.93
Salar	24,611.98	23,274.67	20,780.08	21,830.79	21,661.34
She	32,280.29	31,921.61	36,458.70	28,129.26	24,678.51
Shui	23,474.08	21,576.31	31,955.19	20,196.46	19,012.51
Tajik	37,483.56	28,862.26	25,766.44	24,083.27	23,762.51
Tatar	36,922.89	28,708.18	25,941.94	24,083.50	23,635.18
Tibetan	13,817.88	13,543.47	13,663.88	12,625.77	12,176.31

(continued)

Table 3.27 (continued)

Ethnic group	Construction	Transport, storage and post	Information transmission, computer service and software	Wholesale and retail trades	Hotels and catering services
Tu	24,508.32	23,400.11	21,735.28	22,057.27	21,592.93
Tujia	26,969.78	23,127.40	35,604.15	22,379.12	21,079.90
Uygur	37,781.42	28,947.95	25,653.54	24,050.98	23,798.65
Uzbek	37,650.33	28,930.43	25,808.09	24,110.75	23,789.65
Va	25,554.90	21,759.05	16,786.35	21,515.45	18,325.20
Xibe	30,419.79	26,996.65	28,402.98	24,523.74	23,294.77
Yao	27,334.58	24,538.93	25,783.78	24,689.22	21,536.12
Yi	25,490.90	22,945.74	21,948.77	22,022.59	19,766.01
Yugur	22,673.62	23,253.42	23,756.56	22,106.83	18,926.27
Zhuang	26,634.27	24,839.65	21,755.92	26,149.31	22,056.99

Table 3.28 Average wage of employed persons in urban private units (yuan) (III)

Ethnic group	Financial intermediation	Real estate	Leasing and business services	Scientific research, technical services, and geological prospecting	Management of water conservancy, environment and public facilities
National average	32,696.00	30,778.00	31,796.00	36,598.00	26,402.00
Achang	25,528.91	19,299.81	20,382.33	23,683.23	20,841.99
Bai	27,797.72	20,658.67	20,400.15	24,019.32	20,351.78
Baonan	17,464.09	16,606.26	22,340.72	20,329.13	17,271.21
Blang	25,568.50	19,356.49	20,418.25	23,722.41	20,859.32
Buyi	47,793.28	28,256.10	18,450.90	26,522.01	14,612.22
Dai	25,540.47	19,313.56	20,378.64	23,683.23	20,858.07
Daur	29,333.28	26,489.66	24,199.45	27,288.80	23,460.03
Deang	25,469.65	19,229.38	20,325.50	23,616.11	20,799.77
Derung	26,608.55	21,272.40	21,398.37	24,911.93	21,377.34
Dong	37,902.59	27,220.44	20,937.55	26,014.58	17,950.40
Dongxiang	18,233.66	17,597.81	22,395.85	20,925.80	17,702.11
Ewenki	30,916.45	28,070.25	26,725.09	26,852.14	25,994.46
Gaoshan	28,876.10	27,702.48	25,809.72	29,834.78	23,242.13
Gelao	48,282.56	28,397.06	18,349.04	26,549.64	14,408.68
Han	30,331.02	28,620.09	26,422.54	31,467.02	24,197.75
Hani	25,525.19	19,277.31	20,366.66	23,666.88	20,827.25
Hezhe	26,505.80	22,806.95	19,428.83	28,477.02	18,430.97

(*continued*)

Table 3.28 (continued)

Ethnic group	Financial intermediation	Real estate	Leasing and business services	Scientific research, technical services, and geological prospecting	Management of water conservancy, environment and public facilities
Hui	25,888.41	26,085.64	23,876.84	27,315.95	23,330.01
Jing	23,779.77	27,399.11	25,789.42	26,784.84	21,057.15
Jingpo	25,577.97	19,315.83	20,371.68	23,689.28	20,812.15
Jino	25,528.41	19,280.61	20,360.24	23,662.45	20,826.41
Kazak	28,829.06	31,212.32	23,600.16	30,475.99	22,439.97
Kirgiz	28,830.36	31,159.15	23,559.64	30,477.63	22,412.12
Korean	28,555.18	23,629.38	23,221.79	27,972.88	20,460.38
Lahu	25,515.90	19,299.50	20,380.70	23,681.43	20,838.51
Lhoba	3298.38	2768.16	2307.60	2866.37	2024.63
Li	24,013.83	29,676.46	25,894.58	31,411.17	29,315.69
Lisu	25,635.07	19,517.68	20,462.40	23,769.52	21,040.99
Manchu	28,163.92	26,951.31	25,711.23	27,367.85	22,670.77
Maonan	30,410.74	27,749.43	23,786.52	26,648.56	19,065.67
Miao	37,637.80	27,106.66	21,241.60	26,453.66	18,701.04
Monba	1610.43	1410.87	1408.72	1660.24	1288.75
Mongol	30,397.00	27,991.76	26,702.79	26,782.71	25,413.03
Mulao	26,606.23	27,689.45	25,175.57	26,973.03	20,255.56
Naxi	25,596.71	19,461.45	20,392.62	23,696.66	20,957.16
Nu	25,246.03	19,127.62	20,168.91	23,426.21	20,588.88
Oroqen	28,548.86	25,374.39	23,006.53	27,589.22	22,150.15
Pumi	25,533.48	19,347.44	20,403.42	23,710.54	20,868.19
Qiang	29,944.29	27,604.23	23,656.52	27,546.58	28,065.71
Russian	30,018.77	30,177.54	25,263.55	29,302.41	24,193.87
Salar	20,990.86	21,132.42	23,695.67	25,592.71	17,397.83
She	36,526.85	31,761.69	30,150.77	35,648.11	25,252.55
Shui	46,816.46	28,101.03	18,623.81	26,410.84	14,805.71
Tajik	28,870.40	31,168.87	23,685.82	30,505.18	22,491.62
Tatar	28,574.12	30,680.05	23,783.92	30,197.76	22,457.42
Tibetan	13,533.45	12,815.35	12,934.08	14,224.16	12,187.36
Tu	21,611.70	21,276.55	23,862.81	25,905.35	17,612.53
Tujia	34,810.76	29,653.43	23,778.26	28,067.64	21,236.52
Uygur	28,853.85	31,232.79	23,614.38	30,499.32	22,459.42
Uzbek	28,875.51	31,223.46	23,717.79	30,554.83	22,530.19
Va	25,634.69	19,532.99	20,540.26	23,845.80	20,949.53
Xibe	28,131.60	28,274.24	26,192.82	26,990.67	22,866.42
Yao	24,318.89	26,389.73	25,517.41	27,110.70	21,897.90
Yi	29,250.22	22,584.09	21,035.20	25,039.24	22,111.71
Yugur	17,484.87	16,538.41	22,419.41	20,245.51	17,413.58
Zhuang	23,327.53	27,041.56	25,957.89	27,036.72	21,216.62

Table 3.29 Average wage of employed persons in urban private units (yuan) (IV)

Ethnic group	Services to households and other services	Education	Health, social securities and social welfare	Culture, sports and entertainment	Public management and social organization
National Average	24,068.00	26,625.00	29,173.00	26,177.00	10,858.00
Achang	20,382.81	18,803.10	16,609.88	11,950.27	20,136.14
Bai	20,110.28	19,912.23	18,488.55	13,206.82	19,293.15
Baonan	16,900.59	25,242.75	21,502.83	17,443.30	12,599.77
Blang	20,403.84	18,849.57	16,662.29	12,022.39	20,110.59
Buyi	17,484.42	22,983.32	25,138.97	17,350.67	16,903.68
Dai	20,384.85	18,823.64	16,627.45	11,987.99	20,042.67
Daur	22,505.40	24,355.76	25,748.14	24,103.37	21,007.59
Deang	20,352.29	18,755.82	16,519.75	11,871.22	20,160.99
Derung	20,833.62	20,209.21	18,687.00	14,399.73	19,266.50
Dong	19,120.32	24,378.87	26,985.30	18,971.45	14,174.89
Dongxiang	17,168.13	25,347.21	21,890.19	17,398.69	12,082.45
Ewenki	25,260.32	25,734.52	27,547.62	27,315.74	24,520.39
Gaoshan	22,230.32	25,005.75	27,952.41	23,236.02	13,891.87
Gelao	17,392.06	23,001.77	25,217.66	17,353.55	16,961.70
Han	22,945.97	26,225.80	28,339.34	24,075.24	12,303.40
Hani	20,377.94	18,802.06	16,579.76	11,930.61	20,149.34
Hezhe	16,923.29	21,793.68	22,563.66	18,058.38	14,704.09
Hui	20,845.49	24,207.90	24,981.28	20,572.54	14,200.10
Jing	22,065.43	21,670.99	27,188.16	20,542.06	1345.94
Jingpo	20,374.74	18,810.25	16,623.05	11,957.91	20,123.36
Jino	20,370.49	18,795.18	16,582.25	11,931.75	20,120.74
Kazak	21,832.61	23,503.87	26,453.13	18,176.52	58.02
Kirgiz	21,795.65	23,481.56	26,422.60	18,182.67	198.25
Korean	20,958.57	23,405.58	27,707.44	20,701.34	7065.70
Lahu	20,384.97	18,816.29	16,608.91	11,969.12	20,142.95
Lhoba	2023.51	2399.88	2608.46	2087.35	1271.71
Li	18,349.52	19,794.42	31,327.95	19,736.54	15,538.47
Lisu	20,452.59	18,992.54	16,890.76	12,340.41	19,604.32
Manchu	22,439.61	24,620.99	25,637.64	23,751.96	19,384.11
Maonan	20,788.37	21,987.47	26,751.23	19,706.86	5187.25
Miao	19,487.43	24,022.82	26,027.73	18,829.52	15,837.11
Monba	1137.86	1413.42	1503.46	1263.18	346.76
Mongol	24,930.98	25,544.47	27,277.96	26,652.91	22,491.27
Mulao	21,657.19	21,914.04	27,290.05	20,374.41	2618.16
Naxi	20,361.35	18,933.49	16,852.79	12,291.13	19,499.65
Nu	20,136.81	18,625.96	16,506.02	11,915.91	19,722.22
Oroqen	21,073.49	23,733.96	24,909.62	22,693.94	19,881.40

(*continued*)

Table 3.29 (continued)

Ethnic group	Services to households and other services	Education	Health, social securities and social welfare	Culture, sports and entertainment	Public management and social organization
Pumi	20,392.92	18,857.87	16,673.96	12,046.11	20,006.16
Qiang	22,758.32	25,675.40	27,577.58	25,748.77	233.38
Russian	23,333.79	24,711.13	27,185.81	22,106.50	10,000.97
Salar	20,144.43	19,518.06	21,894.32	20,202.79	1796.78
She	25,511.52	29,142.77	34,070.35	28,331.05	11,445.82
Shui	17,628.03	22,849.99	25,012.77	17,305.34	16,483.62
Tajik	21,854.32	23,584.86	26,515.00	18,374.68	492.31
Tatar	21,721.29	23,767.45	26,436.62	18,422.25	1182.00
Tibetan	11,557.50	12,549.86	13,268.69	12,157.69	1728.53
Tu	20,246.17	19,941.37	22,251.47	20,323.59	2683.34
Tujia	21,062.62	25,986.83	28,347.54	22,556.72	17,227.68
Uygur	21,846.76	23,513.34	26,475.48	18,202.67	85.07
Uzbek	21,875.14	23,562.11	26,566.99	18,298.03	230.63
Va	20,480.29	18,983.76	16,862.68	12,267.65	20,107.78
Xibe	22,841.69	25,060.55	25,102.84	23,734.15	15,966.92
Yao	22,083.56	23,586.45	28,047.28	20,517.85	5658.05
Yi	20,692.91	21,164.81	20,570.65	16,354.87	14,271.67
Yugur	16,858.55	25,533.69	21,593.53	17,477.64	13,200.30
Zhuang	22,264.00	21,554.74	26,943.03	20,278.33	1667.24

Table 3.30 Registered unemployed persons and unemployment rate in urban area

	Unemployed persons (10,000 persons)				Unemployment rate (%)			
Ethnic group	1990	2005	2011	2012	1990	2005	2011	2012
National total	383.20	839.00	922.00	917.00	2.50	4.20	4.10	4.10
Achang	0.01	0.01	0.01	0.01	2.50	4.16	4.04	4.02
Bai	0.38	0.63	0.74	0.80	2.67	4.17	4.01	3.95
Baonan	0.01	0.01	0.01	0.01	4.84	3.31	3.14	2.74
Blang	0.02	0.03	0.03	0.04	2.50	4.16	4.04	4.02
Buyi	0.89	1.04	1.08	1.09	4.01	4.18	3.62	3.30
Dai	0.22	0.36	0.44	0.48	2.51	4.17	4.04	4.02
Daur	0.08	0.10	0.12	0.13	3.16	4.28	3.85	3.83
Deang	0.00	0.01	0.01	0.01	2.50	4.17	4.05	4.03
Derung	0.00	0.00	0.00	0.00	2.51	4.13	3.95	3.91
Dong	0.85	1.37	1.41	1.41	3.55	4.18	3.76	3.57
Dongxiang	0.26	0.20	0.23	0.22	4.69	3.34	3.13	2.77
Ewenki	0.02	0.02	0.03	0.03	3.58	4.24	3.79	3.73
Gaoshan	0.00	0.00	0.00	0.00	2.81	3.87	3.46	3.34
Gelao	0.17	0.20	0.21	0.21	4.04	4.18	3.62	3.29
Han	345.49	660.90	691.13	687.37	2.56	3.79	3.50	3.39
Hani	0.27	0.44	0.55	0.60	2.50	4.16	4.04	4.02
Hezhe	0.00	0.00	0.00	0.00	2.22	4.33	3.98	4.01
Hui	4.61	5.94	6.65	6.41	3.65	3.91	3.61	3.47
Jing	0.01	0.01	0.01	0.01	3.79	4.11	3.45	3.40
Jingpo	0.02	0.04	0.05	0.05	2.51	4.16	4.04	4.02
Jino	0.00	0.01	0.01	0.01	2.50	4.17	4.04	4.02
Kazak	0.65	0.75	0.75	0.80	3.00	3.92	3.22	3.39
Kirgiz	0.08	0.10	0.10	0.10	2.99	3.92	3.23	3.40
Korean	0.86	1.96	1.66	1.73	2.04	4.36	3.74	3.70
Lahu	0.08	0.14	0.17	0.19	2.50	4.16	4.04	4.02
Lhoba	0.00	0.00	0.00	0.00	0.26	0.37	3.23	2.66

Li	0.57	0.82	0.47	0.59	3.04	3.58	1.84	2.09
Lisu	0.12	0.20	0.24	0.26	2.53	4.18	4.05	4.02
Manchu	4.79	11.40	8.98	9.03	2.02	4.82	3.68	3.59
Maonan	0.03	0.04	0.04	0.04	3.93	4.14	3.50	3.36
Miao	2.35	3.99	4.09	4.13	3.24	4.18	3.77	3.59
Monba	0.00	0.00	0.00	0.01	0.13	0.16	3.22	2.62
Mongol	3.43	4.75	5.15	5.37	3.38	4.35	3.74	3.66
Mulao	0.06	0.09	0.09	0.09	3.86	4.11	3.46	3.37
Naxi	0.06	0.10	0.12	0.13	2.52	4.16	4.04	4.01
Nu	0.01	0.01	0.01	0.01	2.47	4.10	4.02	3.99
Oroqen	0.00	0.01	0.01	0.01	2.89	4.31	3.90	3.88
Pumi	0.01	0.01	0.01	0.01	2.51	4.16	4.04	4.02
Qiang	0.14	0.13	0.14	0.15	3.68	4.60	4.15	4.01
Russian	0.01	0.01	0.01	0.01	3.18	4.00	3.42	3.48
Salar	0.08	0.07	0.09	0.08	5.36	3.84	3.66	3.29
She	0.18	0.35	0.36	0.37	2.56	3.80	3.42	3.34
Shui	0.12	0.14	0.15	0.15	4.00	4.18	3.63	3.31
Tajik	0.02	0.02	0.02	0.03	2.98	3.91	3.23	3.39
Tatar	0.00	0.00	0.00	0.00	3.05	3.88	3.22	3.35
Tibetan	1.80	1.59	2.79	3.34	2.48	2.28	3.55	3.13
Tu	0.19	0.16	0.19	0.18	5.23	3.82	3.64	3.28
Tujia	1.67	5.14	5.13	4.68	2.19	4.21	3.90	3.74
Uygur	4.36	5.07	5.06	5.39	3.00	3.92	3.22	3.39
Uzbek	0.01	0.01	0.01	0.01	3.00	3.91	3.22	3.38
Va	0.07	0.12	0.15	0.16	2.51	4.15	4.03	4.01
Xibe	0.10	0.23	0.16	0.16	2.37	5.13	3.60	3.53
Yao	0.75	1.26	1.31	1.33	3.34	4.06	3.62	3.60
Yi	2.13	2.67	3.08	3.34	3.00	4.29	4.03	3.94
Yugur	0.01	0.01	0.01	0.01	4.82	3.29	3.12	2.72
Zhuang	4.93	6.72	6.93	7.02	3.72	4.09	3.46	3.42

4

Living Conditions and the Means of Livelihood

Data for compilation of the consumer price indices in China are collected by the Department of Urban Social and Economic Survey and the Department of Rural Social and Economic Survey, the National Bureau of Statistics (NBS) through a combination of sample surveys and surveys of key units. Areas distributed in different economic regions are selected as the sample areas and representative commodities are selected as the sample commodities. Regular surveys are conducted to collect data on their market prices. Population parameters are inferred on the basis of the sample data. At present, 500 cities and counties of all provinces, autonomous regions and municipalities directly under the central government have been selected for this purpose.

Data for compilation of the consumer price indices and the retail price indices in China are collected by the Department of Urban Social and Economic Survey, NBS and the Department of Rural Social and Economic Survey, NBS through a combination of sample surveys and surveys of key units. Areas distributed in different economic regions are selected as the sample areas and representative commodities are selected as the sample commodities. Regular surveys are conducted to collect data on their market prices. Population parameters are inferred on the basis

R. Guo, *China Ethnic Statistical Yearbook 2016*,
DOI 10.1007/978-3-319-49199-8_4

of the sample data. At present, 500 cities and counties of all provinces, autonomous regions and municipalities directly under the central government have been selected for this purpose.

Data on the living condition of urban residents come from the data collected through a sample survey on the urban households conducted by the Office of Household Surveys of the NBS. The NBS survey offices in provinces, autonomous regions and municipalities directly under the central government as well as the survey offices in selected cities and counties are responsible for collecting data in accordance with the survey scheme stipulated by the NBS and submitting the data to the offices at higher levels. The survey had covered only non-farm households until 2001. Starting from 2002, the survey covers the households in district areas of all city and county towns.

Sample cities and towns in urban areas are selected by using stratified random sampling method. The selection of sample households in urban areas is done by two steps: the first step is to have a one-off large sample survey; the second step is to select a small sample from the large sample to be used as regular sample households for diaries. The large sample survey is conducted for every three years; the objective is to provide sample frame for regular surveys and basic information for data evaluation of regular surveys. In the large sample survey, samples in sample cities and towns are selected by systematic sampling method schemes, such as two-phase sampling and stratifying method, two-stage (multi) method and probability proportional to size (PPS) method. In some large cities, three-stage sampling method is used.

The national sample included 66,000 households at the end of 2012.

Data on the living conditions of rural residents come from data collected through the sample survey on rural households, which is organized by the Office of Household Survey of the NBS. Sample survey on rural households is conducted by first selecting sampled villages and then selecting households in the selected villages in each province, with all rural households in the province as the population. A combination of various sampling approaches is used to identify a total of 74,000 households selected from 7100 villages throughout the whole country.

It is required that the sampling error should not exceed ±3 %, with a confidence probability as 95 %. In order to ensure the accuracy of the survey data on the rural households, two accounts are designed for the respondent households by the Office of Household Survey of the NBS: the cash account and the account on goods in kind. In order to overcome the tedium of respondent households and to ensure that the sample is accurately representative over time and reflects the changing rural social and economic situation, a rotation sampling scheme is implemented, and the complete cycle of rotation is five years.

Data on electricity consumption are provided by the Association of Power Generation Enterprises of China.

Table 4.1 Savings deposit of urban and rural households at year-end (100 million yuan)

Ethnic group	2007	2008	2009	2010	2011	2012
National total	172,534.2	217,885.4	260,771.7	303,302.5	343,635.9	399,551.0
Achang	2.5	3.1	3.8	4.6	5.4	6.27
Bai	135.0	167.8	205.7	250.1	291.7	341.09
Baonan	1.3	1.7	2.0	2.4	2.9	3.42
Blang	6.7	8.3	10.3	12.6	14.6	17.00
Buyi	166.3	208.0	248.9	300.4	361.1	437.55
Dai	84.4	104.9	129.3	158.2	184.0	214.17
Daur	15.9	19.9	23.8	27.7	32.0	37.90
Deang	1.3	1.6	2.0	2.4	2.8	3.30
Derung	0.6	0.8	1.0	1.2	1.3	1.56
Dong	208.1	258.0	308.3	365.7	432.2	516.90
Dongxiang	41.3	52.9	64.8	77.3	91.0	108.65
Ewenki	3.6	4.5	5.4	6.4	7.4	8.94
Gaoshan	0.6	0.7	0.9	1.0	1.2	1.37
Gelao	31.8	39.8	47.6	57.4	69.2	83.96
Han	161,224.8	203,873.8	243,098.2	282,215.2	320,675.9	372,678.70
Hani	104.7	130.1	160.4	196.3	228.3	265.66
Hezhe	0.6	0.8	0.9	1.0	1.2	1.34
Hui	1215.9	1550.4	1872.9	2206.3	2536.3	3008.33
Jing	1.7	2.1	2.6	3.1	3.6	4.26
Jingpo	9.6	12.0	14.7	18.0	21.0	24.41
Jino	1.5	1.9	2.3	2.9	3.3	3.86
Kazak	139.3	173.2	206.9	251.8	299.8	358.09
Kirgiz	18.0	22.3	26.7	32.4	38.6	46.05
Korean	265.4	330.2	389.3	439.0	495.5	576.59

(continued)

Table 4.1 Continued

Ethnic group	2007	2008	2009	2010	2011	2012
Lahu	33.0	41.0	50.5	61.8	71.9	83.69
Lhoba	0.2	0.2	0.3	0.3	0.4	0.50
Li	140.2	172.1	208.4	269.7	303.8	352.35
Lisu	46.5	57.9	71.3	87.1	101.4	118.10
Manchu	1851.9	2339.9	2780.2	3177.5	3582.6	4146.77
Maonan	7.4	9.1	11.0	13.3	15.6	18.60
Miao	646.3	802.9	965.5	1151.4	1360.1	1622.50
Monba	0.6	0.7	0.9	1.0	1.2	1.54
Mongol	720.2	909.5	1097.9	1283.0	1487.1	1778.96
Mulao	15.7	19.2	23.2	28.0	32.7	38.72
Naxi	22.8	28.3	34.9	42.6	49.6	57.81
Nu	2.1	2.6	3.2	3.9	4.6	5.35
Oroqen	1.0	1.3	1.5	1.8	2.0	2.36
Pumi	2.5	3.1	3.8	4.6	5.4	6.24
Qiang	27.9	36.1	43.3	51.1	60.4	72.65
Russian	1.9	2.4	2.9	3.5	4.1	4.84
Salar	9.8	12.7	15.6	18.9	22.6	27.53
She	111.5	140.9	170.9	197.3	223.3	256.06
Shui	22.6	28.2	33.8	40.9	49.1	59.52
Tajik	4.6	5.7	6.8	8.3	9.9	11.78
Tatar	0.6	0.7	0.8	1.0	1.2	1.43
Tibetan	416.2	519.5	632.4	753.5	896.0	1098.89
Tu	23.0	29.9	36.4	44.1	52.5	63.60
Tujia	720.0	893.0	1075.6	1270.5	1488.6	1769.61
Uygur	938.0	1165.6	1393.0	1694.7	2017.2	2408.74
Uzbek	1.4	1.7	2.1	2.5	3.0	3.58
Va	29.2	36.3	44.8	54.7	63.6	74.00
Xibe	33.0	41.5	49.3	56.6	64.0	74.41
Yao	239.0	292.5	349.5	415.3	480.4	563.92
Yi	587.5	740.5	902.5	1089.9	1278.1	1509.12
Yugur	1.1	1.4	1.7	2.1	2.4	2.89
Zhuang	1297.8	1578.3	1907.8	2308.1	2677.8	3157.04

Table 4.2 Per capita annual income of urban households by sources (yuan)

Ethnic group	Disposable income	Total income	Income from wages and salaries	Net business income	Income from properties	Income from transfers
National average	24,564.72	26,958.99	17,335.62	2548.29	706.96	6368.12
Achang	21,119.37	23,050.08	14,447.41	2428.86	997.23	5176.58
Bai	20,931.40	22,782.45	14,189.91	2422.65	921.21	5248.69
Baonan	17,236.97	18,649.80	12,616.03	1152.59	251.69	4629.50
Blang	21,131.69	23,063.33	14,456.27	2428.46	995.38	5183.24
Buyi	19,054.30	20,461.59	12,599.42	2032.18	393.33	5436.66
Dai	21,109.46	23,040.62	14,441.00	2425.41	996.01	5178.21
Daur	21,258.95	22,959.05	15,114.63	2313.55	422.22	5108.65
Deang	21,083.90	23,011.19	14,419.97	2423.90	996.78	5170.56
Derung	21,423.27	23,389.03	14,743.36	2403.52	914.19	5327.96
Dong	20,167.23	21,706.88	13,216.82	2349.12	591.75	5549.18
Dongxiang	17,271.57	18,724.22	12,742.06	1190.44	247.20	4544.52
Ewenki	22,810.79	24,506.14	16,503.81	2598.38	537.45	4866.49
Gaoshan	22,963.47	25,033.03	15,825.66	2511.72	683.27	6012.38
Gelao	18,962.60	20,354.41	12,534.41	2016.44	381.05	5422.51
Han	23,601.84	25,818.38	16,546.86	2485.83	674.46	6111.23
Hani	21,117.78	23,048.33	14,443.85	2428.36	997.33	5178.80
Hezhe	18,735.99	20,452.35	12,514.88	1811.68	238.41	5887.39
Hui	20,838.09	22,854.08	14,827.86	2071.29	386.67	5568.26
Jing	21,358.06	23,331.41	14,779.21	2166.74	870.82	5514.64
Jingpo	21,111.05	23,040.82	14,443.88	2426.55	995.84	5174.57
Jino	21,105.06	23,034.70	14,435.01	2424.64	996.77	5178.29
Kazak	17,930.77	20,202.89	14,432.85	1632.68	146.53	3990.83
Kirgiz	17,943.89	20,211.81	14,418.24	1637.29	147.76	4008.51
Korean	20,588.58	22,318.71	13,796.83	2160.52	344.35	6017.00
Lahu	21,118.55	23,048.07	14,445.64	2428.87	995.77	5177.79
Lhoba	18,426.07	20,614.33	17,483.76	729.98	435.54	1965.04
Li	20,902.44	22,784.17	14,633.43	2388.01	706.67	5056.06
Lisu	21,090.11	23,021.44	14,434.77	2415.76	985.56	5185.36
Manchu	22,191.64	24,378.58	14,555.10	2422.76	427.20	6973.51
Maonan	20,645.26	22,455.78	14,128.90	2110.99	735.93	5479.96
Miao	20,342.61	21,937.35	13,432.60	2326.57	615.22	5562.96
Monba	18,438.49	20,659.77	17,749.03	653.64	430.30	1826.80
Mongol	22,672.33	24,486.94	16,163.12	2565.14	518.84	5239.84
Mulao	21,187.29	23,119.14	14,625.19	2159.74	824.23	5509.97
Naxi	21,095.91	23,031.95	14,457.61	2409.29	984.27	5180.80
Nu	21,120.06	23,059.71	14,525.42	2406.34	987.80	5140.16
Oroqen	20,734.61	22,434.40	14,460.13	2209.79	386.71	5377.77
Pumi	21,120.52	23,053.39	14,453.06	2424.44	992.94	5182.96
Qiang	20,345.04	22,367.54	14,274.81	2022.48	633.51	5436.73

(*continued*)

Table 4.2 Continued

Ethnic group	Disposable income	Total income	Income from wages and salaries	Net business income	Income from properties	Income from transfers
Russian	20,303.44	22,399.46	15,539.05	2021.72	319.08	4519.60
Salar	17,674.46	19,772.15	12,777.77	1216.83	124.42	5653.13
She	28,138.08	30,878.88	19,426.51	3419.39	1452.01	6580.97
Shui	19,085.27	20,504.94	12,634.30	2030.91	409.21	5430.52
Tajik	18,097.92	20,365.45	14,487.67	1655.56	163.47	4058.74
Tatar	18,196.09	20,448.41	14,506.60	1639.70	170.35	4131.76
Tibetan	18,539.20	20,617.06	15,351.89	1144.14	406.57	3714.46
Tu	18,111.54	20,211.31	13,041.19	1316.51	183.29	5670.32
Tujia	21,316.15	23,069.50	14,039.46	2456.77	624.00	5949.28
Uygur	17,958.57	20,232.30	14,446.96	1638.02	148.76	3998.56
Uzbek	18,074.57	20,353.70	14,509.26	1651.07	160.84	4032.53
Va	21,170.62	23,103.56	14,503.49	2429.15	988.70	5182.23
Xibe	22,049.94	24,579.00	14,782.38	2432.42	416.46	6947.73
Yao	21,925.30	23,895.49	14,950.89	2500.84	922.36	5521.40
Yi	20,649.80	22,543.87	14,171.95	2268.03	826.95	5276.94
Yugur	17,342.48	18,738.73	12,674.51	1159.71	262.57	4641.93
Zhuang	21,573.54	23,603.63	15,003.10	2209.97	909.01	5481.54

Table 4.3 Per capita annual cash consumption expenditure of urban households (yuan) (I)

Ethnic group	Cash consumption expenditure	Food	Grain	Starches and tubers	Beans and bean products	Oil and fats
National average	16,674.32	6040.85	458.53	54.05	72.68	161.48
Achang	13,915.93	5475.43	409.02	48.85	41.13	155.24
Bai	13,870.67	5438.19	410.02	46.16	46.50	160.24
Baonan	12,881.70	4635.51	411.17	48.90	48.83	160.75
Blang	13,926.99	5479.09	409.21	48.93	41.33	155.53
Buyi	12,822.67	5066.08	398.68	32.24	59.13	166.68
Dai	13,918.56	5478.02	409.18	48.99	41.26	155.46
Daur	15,968.74	5218.19	483.94	51.78	53.21	131.05
Deang	13,894.18	5468.80	409.06	48.87	40.98	155.25
Derung	14,280.28	5514.19	417.77	49.75	46.28	156.35
Dong	13,678.34	5293.22	411.49	33.55	69.38	176.66
Dongxiang	12,971.79	4676.39	414.97	49.41	48.48	163.00
Ewenki	17,294.94	5438.34	486.36	43.36	47.48	121.64
Gaoshan	15,570.23	5650.21	440.12	52.01	67.70	152.40
Gelao	12,776.51	5054.84	398.37	31.73	59.17	167.19

(*continued*)

Table 4.3 Continued

Ethnic group	Cash consumption expenditure	Food	Grain	Starches and tubers	Beans and bean products	Oil and fats
Han	16,007.32	5827.29	449.81	53.29	71.86	161.63
Hani	13,914.12	5474.73	409.17	48.88	41.15	155.28
Hezhe	13,547.38	4835.44	474.93	69.04	68.72	147.93
Hui	14,469.18	5133.65	428.04	53.81	55.29	146.94
Jing	14,339.98	5584.19	392.46	37.80	68.92	146.28
Jingpo	13,913.70	5473.04	409.20	48.81	41.17	155.27
Jino	13,912.55	5475.71	409.23	48.93	41.15	155.43
Kazak	13,894.01	5238.56	494.15	56.34	39.51	177.36
Kirgiz	13,895.37	5236.37	494.17	56.49	39.79	177.05
Korean	14,788.96	4909.37	460.70	62.83	72.73	141.65
Lahu	13,914.97	5472.70	409.08	48.93	41.21	155.26
Lhoba	11,570.79	5543.01	461.62	29.04	15.64	145.61
Li	14,432.53	6488.76	335.39	29.29	37.11	152.37
Lisu	13,938.74	5486.43	409.11	49.62	42.00	156.32
Manchu	15,453.61	5297.00	454.05	62.41	69.49	148.58
Maonan	13,880.09	5426.64	392.40	35.73	66.42	151.10
Miao	13,822.59	5401.72	411.87	37.28	66.07	179.50
Monba	11,527.56	5577.28	464.06	28.69	13.75	144.33
Mongol	16,918.90	5428.61	478.44	46.42	51.06	127.93
Mulao	14,256.19	5550.10	393.36	36.86	68.18	148.23
Naxi	13,942.90	5492.98	409.61	49.50	41.95	156.34
Nu	13,905.46	5481.46	410.31	48.61	41.07	155.11
Oroqen	15,387.74	5123.85	481.01	56.45	58.24	134.46
Pumi	13,925.92	5476.55	409.45	49.01	41.40	155.34
Qiang	15,054.34	6068.58	413.58	73.47	71.91	195.48
Russian	15,422.29	5381.31	488.68	51.25	44.09	155.56
Salar	12,544.08	4708.73	472.19	50.83	39.32	132.66
She	18,392.64	6994.36	513.81	52.97	80.44	153.08
Shui	12,831.76	5070.71	397.79	32.44	59.13	165.66
Tajik	13,954.45	5259.62	492.38	56.18	40.60	177.21
Tatar	13,988.71	5252.84	488.94	55.90	40.98	176.26
Tibetan	12,585.15	5406.75	448.65	45.37	34.89	154.14
Tu	12,812.33	4806.31	469.85	50.38	41.26	134.48
Tujia	14,786.60	5800.78	463.94	39.78	80.50	205.82
Uygur	13,906.81	5242.91	494.16	56.34	39.65	177.36
Uzbek	13,963.25	5263.04	493.21	56.13	40.03	177.08
Va	13,953.10	5476.49	409.24	49.06	41.68	155.62
Xibe	15,948.84	5637.41	475.86	66.03	67.87	156.07
Yao	14,932.17	5721.97	411.20	37.82	71.87	164.97
Yi	14,094.66	5589.02	409.11	53.81	51.68	167.67
Yugur	12,952.44	4644.38	408.29	48.81	49.61	161.30
Zhuang	14,522.99	5647.13	394.97	38.46	67.36	146.19

(continued)

Table 4.4 Per capita annual cash consumption expenditure of urban households (yuan) (II)

Ethnic group	Meat, poultry and processed products	Eggs	Aquatic products	Vegetables	Condiments	Sugar
National average	1183.59	119.00	408.92	591.97	76.10	55.06
Achang	1140.29	70.27	120.94	743.02	65.60	51.72
Bai	1145.85	73.51	132.02	716.09	65.52	52.68
Baonan	736.00	87.75	91.23	509.40	75.76	38.31
Blang	1140.83	70.60	121.08	742.86	65.83	51.80
Buyi	1158.43	80.17	118.13	564.37	67.31	60.81
Dai	1141.83	70.44	119.96	743.33	65.88	51.83
Daur	957.50	95.14	176.11	465.41	67.49	44.62
Deang	1138.50	70.04	117.77	743.52	65.60	51.73
Derung	1133.77	79.14	159.11	706.87	67.65	51.67
Dong	1220.70	86.67	206.35	582.56	62.67	57.64
Dongxiang	762.87	88.11	91.86	508.39	74.78	40.72
Ewenki	992.12	87.77	166.53	464.80	64.82	41.54
Gaoshan	1141.65	115.05	379.39	546.13	70.75	50.48
Gelao	1161.03	79.95	114.41	562.07	67.37	61.13
Han	1149.69	118.15	368.00	582.49	74.34	52.72
Hani	1139.30	70.27	119.68	743.40	65.64	51.76
Hezhe	881.81	112.45	227.95	475.32	75.59	48.72
Hui	940.90	100.90	184.07	504.92	68.80	48.35
Jing	1584.07	84.17	374.16	535.32	48.15	59.71
Jingpo	1139.84	70.32	120.21	742.29	65.60	51.77
Jino	1140.27	70.24	119.09	743.78	65.81	51.80
Kazak	1204.48	91.03	115.58	499.51	57.99	71.80
Kirgiz	1202.31	91.26	117.03	499.24	58.12	71.62
Korean	859.81	108.09	255.17	500.16	79.48	40.06
Lahu	1138.50	70.50	119.78	742.44	65.67	51.72
Lhoba	1204.34	47.23	77.80	673.56	60.79	54.12
Li	1804.19	62.33	917.88	717.33	54.43	34.56
Lisu	1148.13	71.81	121.27	741.56	67.07	52.04
Manchu	915.44	123.20	340.12	520.95	82.57	44.23
Maonan	1481.01	82.58	302.75	535.52	52.62	60.48
Miao	1223.58	87.71	194.95	616.75	68.80	57.87
Monba	1209.81	45.01	71.08	680.81	60.87	54.50
Mongol	989.69	93.83	195.33	481.67	67.96	42.42
Mulao	1555.21	83.74	351.45	533.29	49.86	60.54
Naxi	1149.24	71.59	121.79	741.89	67.06	52.12
Nu	1141.26	70.34	123.00	740.66	65.59	51.80
Oroqen	932.12	100.59	198.31	468.24	70.11	44.97
Pumi	1140.11	70.73	120.96	741.92	65.85	51.77
Qiang	1507.28	120.12	187.22	708.61	115.22	63.97

(*continued*)

Table 4.4 Continued

Ethnic group	Meat, poultry and processed products	Eggs	Aquatic products	Vegetables	Condiments	Sugar
Russian	1119.72	91.69	148.29	492.11	62.30	59.94
Salar	949.62	82.63	113.74	498.15	63.41	42.46
She	1359.92	118.12	949.60	641.66	70.85	52.05
Shui	1170.37	79.87	121.64	564.62	66.49	60.69
Tajik	1205.81	91.92	123.60	502.76	58.60	71.24
Tatar	1185.57	92.08	124.64	503.69	59.64	69.95
Tibetan	1186.41	73.03	103.07	637.29	74.77	52.30
Tu	970.24	83.63	136.32	509.08	64.20	42.91
Tujia	1245.24	106.12	274.58	667.52	78.81	55.28
Uygur	1205.44	91.17	116.79	499.87	58.01	71.80
Uzbek	1209.89	91.29	123.53	501.73	58.18	71.59
Va	1138.29	71.81	124.11	738.38	66.01	51.72
Xibe	1015.54	121.49	381.16	556.47	82.92	49.73
Yao	1489.82	87.79	360.28	584.40	53.05	58.32
Yi	1242.71	85.17	137.21	713.26	79.56	56.14
Yugur	727.82	88.24	93.31	509.77	76.43	38.06
Zhuang	1594.49	83.37	375.77	546.19	48.51	60.05

Table 4.5 Per capita annual cash consumption expenditure of urban households (yuan) (III)

Ethnic group	Tobacco	Liquor and beverages	Dried and fresh melons and fruits	Cake	Milk and processed products	Other food
National average	271.47	294.58	506.30	122.97	253.57	93.64
Achang	453.74	145.54	423.34	155.39	216.26	59.99
Bai	427.05	160.74	425.78	142.92	207.73	67.19
Baonan	274.21	261.70	446.10	75.55	221.71	165.32
Blang	453.37	146.25	423.58	155.17	216.78	60.21
Buyi	309.55	222.70	412.82	78.06	173.88	86.25
Dai	453.65	145.83	423.23	155.17	216.64	59.94
Daur	267.95	307.13	497.38	82.99	219.72	168.36
Deang	454.79	144.86	422.93	155.55	216.17	59.92
Derung	418.29	174.48	436.43	144.99	222.23	70.01
Dong	289.92	222.45	431.22	87.06	170.32	93.34
Dongxiang	263.58	256.23	455.33	77.72	223.19	161.39
Ewenki	316.73	351.54	490.15	78.31	233.45	216.33
Gaoshan	240.83	278.47	478.14	112.11	230.66	92.88
Gelao	307.41	223.19	411.68	76.70	172.50	86.46

(continued)

Table 4.5 Continued

Ethnic group	Tobacco	Liquor and beverages	Dried and fresh melons and fruits	Cake	Milk and processed products	Other food
Han	269.37	288.77	485.28	116.63	245.62	94.41
Hani	454.56	145.50	423.33	155.51	216.45	60.01
Hezhe	178.45	223.36	509.72	93.78	189.69	69.40
Hui	258.01	267.77	482.17	103.60	238.50	113.24
Jing	179.49	172.00	411.51	101.85	192.19	58.75
Jingpo	453.21	145.82	423.40	155.26	216.13	60.07
Jino	454.50	145.23	423.25	155.44	216.47	59.92
Kazak	133.53	199.41	549.57	105.03	237.06	82.58
Kirgiz	133.77	199.54	549.36	104.96	236.59	82.34
Korean	205.20	230.30	540.21	88.48	183.57	92.36
Lahu	453.66	146.06	423.36	155.34	216.51	60.14
Lhoba	475.23	296.37	331.65	40.47	383.25	149.72
Li	165.05	120.44	381.10	83.52	147.37	36.40
Lisu	449.05	148.77	423.38	153.23	217.95	60.28
Manchu	222.58	282.01	560.83	106.40	226.08	100.69
Maonan	207.92	184.84	409.99	93.62	185.10	65.63
Miao	315.24	216.48	430.81	93.97	185.45	89.26
Monba	487.07	299.45	326.45	38.90	393.87	152.80
Mongol	302.79	337.39	502.69	83.66	234.08	193.46
Mulao	186.90	178.50	412.52	98.49	189.19	61.30
Naxi	449.81	149.29	423.33	152.92	218.77	60.58
Nu	452.83	149.13	422.77	153.34	219.35	61.72
Oroqen	246.59	287.77	500.11	85.74	211.51	142.84
Pumi	452.70	146.93	423.64	154.90	216.89	60.28
Qiang	283.96	251.94	426.55	78.80	269.32	66.15
Russian	212.22	266.04	528.82	98.18	240.29	134.33
Salar	262.47	270.61	419.83	78.15	209.34	102.70
She	278.87	284.19	548.89	121.32	256.93	71.02
Shui	307.61	219.64	411.61	79.38	174.34	85.15
Tajik	137.78	201.84	546.88	105.19	237.32	82.85
Tatar	144.67	206.76	545.08	105.25	237.70	86.36
Tibetan	378.47	276.29	375.36	59.93	309.07	120.81
Tu	267.58	270.01	421.43	80.67	209.92	102.95
Tujia	330.15	246.51	438.46	98.63	206.06	92.82
Uygur	133.78	199.66	549.57	105.16	237.11	82.47
Uzbek	135.24	200.68	548.78	105.57	237.08	82.50
Va	448.61	149.54	424.87	154.40	217.34	60.93
Xibe	226.33	269.92	608.93	107.33	239.81	91.27
Yao	223.25	192.57	437.00	107.32	184.62	75.90
Yi	390.88	183.63	422.74	125.39	226.16	64.67
Yugur	275.73	263.01	447.46	76.25	222.57	167.59
Zhuang	186.55	169.96	413.95	106.25	193.78	57.13

Table 4.6 Per capita annual cash consumption expenditure of urban households (yuan) (IV)

Ethnic group	Dining out	Food processing service fees	Clothing	Garments	Clothing materials	Shoes
National average	1315.09	1.85	1823.39	1344.87	10.77	401.71
Achang	1173.78	1.30	1759.73	1269.50	13.01	437.01
Bai	1156.62	1.54	1715.10	1241.21	12.95	419.64
Baonan	981.92	0.89	1641.92	1174.91	12.53	376.32
Blang	1174.39	1.32	1761.87	1271.17	13.01	437.26
Buyi	1074.18	2.67	1416.74	1020.74	14.78	339.86
Dai	1174.06	1.31	1759.64	1269.52	13.00	436.86
Daur	1147.23	1.19	2361.87	1723.26	7.26	523.55
Deang	1171.97	1.30	1760.35	1269.66	13.03	437.50
Derung	1177.96	1.43	1788.89	1294.24	12.56	434.69
Dong	1088.66	2.56	1459.22	1075.24	12.27	327.61
Dongxiang	995.46	0.91	1675.66	1198.08	13.33	383.81
Ewenki	1234.01	1.38	2602.08	1916.76	6.60	556.52
Gaoshan	1199.80	1.65	1750.41	1291.20	9.75	388.56
Gelao	1071.76	2.69	1407.83	1013.81	14.80	338.08
Han	1243.31	1.91	1786.92	1319.27	10.69	392.70
Hani	1173.51	1.30	1761.00	1270.30	13.03	437.43
Hezhe	987.77	0.83	1842.54	1309.16	7.13	452.09
Hui	1137.21	1.14	1831.48	1334.78	11.62	414.90
Jing	1135.30	2.06	1192.61	905.17	6.90	245.61
Jingpo	1173.34	1.30	1759.26	1269.09	13.01	436.92
Jino	1173.84	1.30	1760.85	1270.18	13.01	437.43
Kazak	1122.68	0.96	2029.83	1457.20	20.44	451.56
Kirgiz	1121.78	0.96	2029.31	1456.77	20.32	451.80
Korean	987.77	0.83	1999.00	1440.27	7.32	471.85
Lahu	1173.23	1.31	1761.87	1271.06	13.02	437.46
Lhoba	1093.66	2.89	1397.08	977.30	4.78	390.43
Li	1409.52	0.46	901.52	699.55	1.51	177.74
Lisu	1173.44	1.36	1758.23	1269.45	12.91	435.08
Manchu	1036.42	0.95	1957.31	1386.37	11.50	474.24
Maonan	1116.68	2.26	1231.14	920.46	8.92	265.65
Miao	1123.52	2.61	1544.49	1132.85	12.55	352.45
Monba	1102.87	2.93	1386.09	968.00	4.35	390.87
Mongol	1198.44	1.34	2469.00	1810.45	8.06	536.28
Mulao	1140.32	2.15	1202.70	907.82	7.60	251.89
Naxi	1175.78	1.37	1756.80	1268.32	12.88	434.94
Nu	1173.22	1.33	1755.17	1266.13	12.89	435.95
Oroqen	1103.68	1.10	2222.87	1612.85	6.88	504.79
Pumi	1173.34	1.31	1760.70	1270.32	12.99	436.92
Qiang	1231.47	3.54	1652.27	1234.97	8.55	352.42

(continued)

Table 4.6 Continued

Ethnic group	Dining out	Food processing service fees	Clothing	Garments	Clothing materials	Shoes
Russian	1186.65	1.16	2243.32	1629.34	14.92	491.65
Salar	920.07	0.55	1550.88	1148.07	7.88	331.16
She	1439.10	1.56	1714.49	1318.31	9.20	337.11
Shui	1071.61	2.64	1409.85	1016.79	14.56	337.50
Tajik	1126.43	1.00	2020.03	1451.32	20.09	449.22
Tatar	1128.38	0.99	2009.95	1443.24	19.77	448.27
Tibetan	1074.51	2.38	1496.66	1080.68	6.57	366.78
Tu	950.78	0.63	1547.70	1146.39	7.82	331.16
Tujia	1167.46	3.08	1739.57	1299.54	11.22	370.01
Uygur	1123.62	0.97	2029.75	1457.32	20.42	451.49
Uzbek	1129.57	0.97	2022.06	1452.43	20.21	449.67
Va	1173.54	1.33	1766.40	1274.92	12.98	437.45
Xibe	1119.83	0.84	2036.53	1440.66	14.05	490.59
Yao	1179.73	2.08	1355.40	1023.45	7.64	284.17
Yi	1177.13	2.07	1691.22	1231.67	11.98	402.77
Yugur	989.19	0.91	1645.41	1176.32	12.56	378.18
Zhuang	1162.15	1.99	1209.63	916.34	6.79	251.72

Table 4.7 Per capita annual cash consumption expenditure of urban households (yuan) (V)

Ethnic group	Tailoring and laundering service fees	Residence	Housing	Water, electricity, fuels and others	Household facilities and articles	Durable consumer goods
National average	9.42	1484.26	463.64	900.62	1116.06	431.52
Achang	2.49	980.07	402.77	503.78	639.93	244.37
Bai	3.02	1011.38	376.82	559.27	693.86	258.16
Baonan	9.50	1281.77	321.22	858.04	841.64	356.44
Blang	2.53	980.94	402.50	504.69	642.37	245.32
Buyi	4.09	1034.99	227.60	734.58	859.29	277.19
Dai	2.51	980.20	402.82	503.65	641.43	244.87
Daur	12.45	1483.56	486.84	903.73	1060.20	435.68
Deang	2.47	976.77	402.16	501.43	637.31	243.33
Derung	3.91	1067.75	407.65	579.54	724.02	278.88
Dong	5.26	1171.12	281.25	807.65	951.16	337.55
Dongxiang	10.18	1274.14	325.87	848.09	847.23	350.71
Ewenki	11.48	1562.89	579.17	879.45	1194.18	509.60
Gaoshan	8.74	1405.93	453.63	852.66	1097.15	447.08
Gelao	4.05	1032.57	222.58	737.03	861.10	276.28

(continued)

Table 4.7 Continued

Ethnic group	Tailoring and laundering service fees	Residence	Housing	Water, electricity, fuels and others	Household facilities and articles	Durable consumer goods
Han	8.94	1443.24	447.51	882.16	1079.96	424.87
Hani	2.49	978.73	402.53	502.80	639.31	244.08
Hezhe	13.58	1368.58	300.77	992.08	795.96	291.97
Hui	9.93	1306.59	399.96	813.76	969.90	398.95
Jing	6.09	1367.16	487.15	802.06	1106.74	510.38
Jingpo	2.50	980.67	402.24	504.82	640.76	244.57
Jino	2.49	978.73	402.44	502.77	639.33	243.92
Kazak	18.05	1167.37	402.87	689.59	950.16	303.42
Kirgiz	18.02	1169.31	402.14	692.33	948.92	303.27
Korean	12.55	1524.14	342.57	1094.23	896.92	310.75
Lahu	2.51	979.71	402.56	503.69	640.92	245.06
Lhoba	6.98	889.48	209.23	637.84	526.25	121.05
Li	1.80	1499.92	555.12	836.54	787.15	272.45
Lisu	2.69	988.13	403.50	509.63	652.34	249.21
Manchu	11.87	1471.62	360.11	1026.37	1001.94	371.81
Maonan	5.55	1280.32	415.93	788.57	1048.24	453.39
Miao	5.05	1139.46	292.39	761.84	918.78	322.99
Monba	6.98	877.64	206.78	629.39	513.80	113.89
Mongol	11.45	1526.86	536.35	889.86	1165.96	485.96
Mulao	5.93	1345.36	460.48	805.59	1094.60	491.74
Naxi	2.71	987.49	402.86	509.76	652.11	248.43
Nu	2.63	982.60	400.43	508.85	642.28	244.16
Oroqen	12.55	1463.97	437.92	936.69	993.87	400.89
Pumi	2.56	982.78	403.05	505.95	643.30	245.79
Qiang	9.25	1284.34	433.26	718.11	1096.33	413.75
Russian	15.17	1336.04	478.17	769.43	1059.45	391.76
Salar	8.92	1240.19	358.31	775.59	917.88	403.81
She	7.58	1602.32	551.49	915.18	1180.15	430.78
Shui	4.10	1039.24	236.25	730.98	862.30	283.61
Tajik	17.73	1175.86	403.89	695.72	954.39	307.53
Tatar	17.41	1185.43	404.14	703.69	953.07	311.06
Tibetan	7.84	1072.31	299.73	691.86	751.34	262.66
Tu	8.54	1257.47	361.98	785.95	925.51	403.11
Tujia	6.73	1265.39	336.31	832.85	1025.31	374.06
Uygur	18.03	1168.37	403.24	690.13	951.16	303.88
Uzbek	17.86	1175.35	405.51	693.78	954.52	306.27
Va	2.65	989.48	402.94	512.09	651.17	249.95
Xibe	14.26	1389.73	327.37	978.02	1035.84	360.39
Yao	6.11	1378.31	435.34	846.09	1086.32	457.88
Yi	4.54	1069.00	391.02	588.31	790.15	294.68
Yugur	9.43	1289.09	322.50	863.70	843.42	357.88
Zhuang	5.94	1374.33	493.48	798.52	1100.43	505.73

Table 4.8 Per capita annual cash consumption expenditure of urban households (yuan) (VI)

Ethnic group	Articles for interior decoration	Bed articles	Household articles for daily use	Furniture materials	Household services	Transport and communications
National average	27.37	108.05	460.64	10.94	77.54	2455.47
Achang	12.07	55.34	276.91	1.50	49.74	2267.06
Bai	13.16	62.09	303.27	4.19	52.99	2219.54
Baonan	29.19	62.28	342.70	13.37	37.67	1581.90
Blang	12.15	55.74	277.72	1.59	49.85	2266.02
Buyi	13.98	85.80	402.91	10.52	68.89	1938.67
Dai	12.08	55.57	277.56	1.51	49.84	2265.42
Daur	31.25	110.04	412.58	24.60	46.03	2165.90
Deang	12.04	55.10	275.83	1.46	49.54	2263.21
Derung	15.38	65.93	307.29	4.16	52.37	2253.96
Dong	19.68	92.70	417.16	14.32	69.74	2020.97
Dongxiang	30.08	62.42	352.53	12.61	38.88	1589.33
Ewenki	33.00	127.04	439.70	32.53	52.31	2481.09
Gaoshan	26.92	108.76	436.68	9.95	67.76	2226.46
Gelao	13.92	86.13	404.95	10.69	69.14	1929.31
Han	26.17	104.81	441.82	11.36	70.93	2298.93
Hani	12.05	55.35	276.59	1.49	49.76	2266.74
Hezhe	24.26	78.30	356.51	8.58	36.34	1601.51
Hui	34.12	86.88	391.54	9.26	49.16	2000.63
Jing	36.66	102.96	375.84	2.83	78.06	2113.82
Jingpo	12.10	55.44	277.29	1.51	49.84	2266.70
Jino	12.04	55.38	276.75	1.49	49.76	2265.42
Kazak	54.04	71.15	466.10	5.29	50.16	1661.46
Kirgiz	53.77	71.27	465.24	5.32	50.05	1661.76
Korean	21.82	86.67	414.86	5.71	57.11	1856.89
Lahu	12.10	55.57	276.97	1.53	49.71	2265.26
Lhoba	33.48	93.57	253.61	8.99	15.54	1461.96
Li	13.50	50.47	420.97	8.28	21.48	2015.23
Lisu	12.26	56.79	282.25	1.76	50.06	2255.78
Manchu	28.74	98.86	432.32	9.64	60.56	2114.66
Maonan	31.13	99.09	383.36	4.80	76.47	2059.97
Miao	18.32	90.81	406.40	13.85	66.41	2030.04
Monba	33.87	94.64	248.41	8.84	14.14	1453.74
Mongol	33.20	122.05	442.32	27.65	54.78	2409.91
Mulao	34.78	102.28	382.93	3.66	79.21	2119.93
Naxi	12.35	57.05	282.40	1.78	50.11	2255.84
Nu	12.54	56.39	277.95	1.67	49.58	2257.83
Oroqen	28.61	102.66	397.21	20.55	43.94	2032.68
Pumi	12.20	55.82	278.09	1.57	49.84	2263.97
Qiang	18.77	107.59	481.32	10.62	64.30	1952.01

(continued)

Table 4.8 Continued

Ethnic group	Articles for interior decoration	Bed articles	Household articles for daily use	Furniture materials	Household services	Transport and communications
Russian	45.29	95.23	458.47	15.71	52.98	2031.06
Salar	56.70	73.73	336.28	16.00	31.36	1574.32
She	21.97	105.08	507.01	4.93	110.38	3050.79
Shui	14.65	85.84	399.43	10.15	68.61	1936.05
Tajik	53.16	72.44	464.98	5.56	50.72	1679.06
Tatar	52.21	72.43	460.99	5.85	50.54	1693.13
Tibetan	34.82	89.40	323.04	11.08	30.34	1598.99
Tu	53.70	74.92	342.73	15.70	35.35	1652.88
Tujia	23.16	100.92	440.67	23.13	63.36	1908.24
Uygur	53.97	71.35	466.36	5.31	50.29	1664.65
Uzbek	53.60	71.87	466.57	5.36	50.86	1682.05
Va	12.49	56.69	280.39	1.81	49.84	2264.38
Xibe	36.11	100.91	469.01	6.56	62.86	2166.22
Yao	31.31	100.65	408.57	9.04	78.85	2259.55
Yi	14.11	73.23	347.27	5.03	55.84	2139.42
Yugur	28.03	62.62	343.25	13.31	38.33	1596.98
Zhuang	36.21	101.34	375.31	2.45	79.38	2177.13

Table 4.9 Per capita annual cash consumption expenditure of urban households (yuan) (VII)

Ethnic group	Transport	Communi-cations	Education, culture and recreation	Recreation articles	Education	Recreation services
National average	1628.35	827.12	2033.5	451.88	819.62	762.00
Achang	1478.64	788.43	1440.89	290.66	506.49	643.74
Bai	1442.68	776.86	1464.70	297.55	528.79	638.36
Baonan	819.03	762.87	1375.16	383.49	517.52	474.15
Blang	1477.51	788.50	1442.40	291.16	507.05	644.18
Buyi	1186.22	752.45	1431.44	321.68	517.19	592.57
Dai	1476.47	788.95	1441.11	290.84	506.49	643.78
Daur	1509.63	656.28	1698.84	431.16	728.03	539.66
Deang	1475.48	787.73	1436.51	289.64	504.29	642.58
Derung	1468.45	785.52	1507.79	316.58	550.89	640.33
Dong	1299.79	721.18	1572.53	339.02	626.42	607.10
Dongxiang	830.84	758.48	1376.93	383.57	526.66	466.70
Ewenki	1776.92	704.18	1914.89	492.63	775.63	646.64
Gaoshan	1466.79	759.67	1802.27	424.31	707.34	670.62

(continued)

Table 4.9 Continued

Ethnic group	Transport	Communi-cations	Education, culture and recreation	Recreation articles	Education	Recreation services
Gelao	1177.38	751.93	1425.20	320.87	512.95	591.37
Han	1504.74	794.18	1918.07	430.03	779.05	708.99
Hani	1478.24	788.50	1440.86	290.52	506.26	644.07
Hezhe	1022.02	579.48	1336.86	312.68	659.02	365.15
Hui	1292.26	708.37	1586.20	397.80	628.14	560.26
Jing	1454.90	658.92	1640.84	419.36	677.99	543.49
Jingpo	1478.19	788.51	1440.84	290.72	506.46	643.65
Jino	1476.70	788.72	1439.39	290.21	505.62	643.56
Kazak	1031.35	630.12	1282.47	359.75	600.13	322.58
Kirgiz	1032.48	629.28	1283.12	359.26	601.08	322.78
Korean	1164.64	692.24	1625.51	359.74	819.88	445.89
Lahu	1477.25	788.02	1440.87	290.81	506.44	643.62
Lhoba	658.27	803.68	660.96	163.39	268.21	229.36
Li	1269.26	745.97	1338.34	324.48	574.26	439.59
Lisu	1465.94	789.84	1443.37	292.94	509.09	641.34
Manchu	1377.68	736.98	1686.38	403.15	742.59	540.64
Maonan	1379.65	680.32	1578.38	394.64	633.56	550.17
Miao	1290.38	739.66	1538.91	329.92	595.77	613.23
Monba	641.88	811.85	634.13	158.37	255.42	220.34
Mongol	1692.70	717.22	1872.29	477.08	765.32	629.90
Mulao	1446.79	673.15	1634.01	413.01	668.27	552.75
Naxi	1465.14	790.70	1443.15	292.61	509.31	641.23
Nu	1468.68	789.15	1434.86	290.20	506.13	638.54
Oroqen	1393.73	638.95	1618.31	401.96	714.46	501.90
Pumi	1475.56	788.42	1443.45	291.68	508.19	643.59
Qiang	1094.52	857.49	1590.89	377.28	623.26	590.34
Russian	1357.07	674.00	1583.05	421.07	681.93	480.05
Salar	977.12	597.20	1154.98	338.60	445.96	370.42
She	2064.92	985.87	2238.86	473.05	900.00	865.81
Shui	1189.21	746.84	1433.05	324.12	518.66	590.27
Tajik	1044.14	634.93	1299.35	361.44	604.27	333.63
Tatar	1049.78	643.36	1319.38	365.54	605.88	347.95
Tibetan	831.97	767.02	1009.20	260.25	394.86	354.08
Tu	1030.96	621.92	1216.35	344.49	466.85	405.01
Tujia	1201.35	706.89	1640.14	328.93	673.79	637.42
Uygur	1034.14	630.53	1285.19	360.02	601.18	323.98
Uzbek	1047.48	634.59	1298.96	361.96	604.86	332.14
Va	1476.73	787.65	1445.68	293.51	509.78	642.39
Xibe	1399.84	766.38	1724.71	417.69	769.57	537.45
Yao	1549.38	710.18	1742.44	397.68	724.14	620.63
Yi	1336.42	803.00	1479.30	317.78	539.10	622.42
Yugur	826.57	770.39	1398.40	387.83	524.59	485.98
Zhuang	1501.31	675.82	1661.31	419.15	682.01	560.16

Table 4.10 Per capita annual cash consumption expenditure of urban households (yuan) (VIII)

Ethnic group	Health care and medical services	Others	Other goods	Other services
National average	1063.68	657.10	439.80	217.30
Achang	939.90	412.90	249.93	162.97
Bai	910.75	417.15	256.48	160.67
Baonan	1042.69	481.12	356.57	124.55
Blang	940.26	414.04	250.78	163.26
Buyi	674.78	400.70	272.47	128.23
Dai	938.93	413.80	250.18	163.62
Daur	1277.50	702.68	488.32	214.36
Deang	939.55	411.66	248.95	162.71
Derung	966.72	456.94	285.49	171.45
Dong	778.17	431.94	286.35	145.59
Dongxiang	1046.33	485.78	361.06	124.72
Ewenki	1328.69	772.77	548.48	224.29
Gaoshan	1029.37	608.43	407.22	201.21
Gelao	667.23	398.44	271.58	126.86
Han	1036.41	616.52	411.88	204.64
Hani	939.90	412.85	249.81	163.04
Hezhe	1193.30	573.20	366.65	206.55
Hui	1065.91	574.83	404.27	170.56
Jing	882.61	452.01	300.77	151.23
Jingpo	939.33	413.08	250.11	162.97
Jino	940.06	413.03	249.75	163.28
Kazak	1027.80	536.35	408.72	127.63
Kirgiz	1029.58	536.99	408.49	128.50
Korean	1356.23	620.90	383.94	236.96
Lahu	940.28	413.35	250.25	163.10
Lhoba	511.82	580.25	326.95	253.30
Li	978.74	422.87	288.98	133.89
Lisu	935.42	419.03	252.78	166.25
Manchu	1259.35	665.35	425.67	239.68
Maonan	820.56	434.85	291.45	143.40
Miao	808.23	440.97	289.96	151.00
Monba	493.33	591.56	330.84	260.71
Mongol	1299.20	747.06	522.33	224.73
Mulao	859.51	449.97	300.19	149.77
Naxi	934.27	420.26	253.39	166.87
Nu	933.62	417.63	252.74	164.89
Oroqen	1259.42	672.78	457.35	215.43
Pumi	940.22	414.93	251.17	163.77
Qiang	775.72	634.20	354.34	279.86

(continued)

Table 4.10 Continued

Ethnic group	Health care and medical services	Others	Other goods	Other services
Russian	1148.72	639.33	469.06	170.27
Salar	929.83	467.28	348.41	118.87
She	879.92	731.74	490.45	241.29
Shui	681.36	399.20	271.22	127.98
Tajik	1027.70	538.44	408.48	129.96
Tatar	1034.02	540.88	409.50	131.38
Tibetan	692.82	557.09	334.97	222.12
Tu	930.79	475.31	350.43	124.88
Tujia	939.47	467.72	314.13	153.58
Uygur	1027.84	536.93	408.91	128.02
Uzbek	1028.39	538.86	409.51	129.36
Va	941.55	417.95	254.25	163.69
Xibe	1250.68	707.70	455.98	251.72
Yao	907.20	480.98	312.43	168.55
Yi	864.21	472.33	280.95	191.38
Yugur	1050.13	484.64	358.56	126.08
Zhuang	894.69	458.34	302.93	155.41

Table 4.11 Consumer price indices by category (preceding year = 100) (I)

Ethnic group	General index	Food	Grain	Oil or fat	Meat, poultry and processed products	Eggs	Aquatic products
National average	102.65	104.84	103.95	105.10	102.07	97.14	107.95
Achang	102.73	106.14	103.53	102.96	103.12	100.04	104.91
Bai	102.68	105.79	103.77	103.09	102.61	99.58	105.64
Baonan	102.75	104.35	102.50	104.55	104.38	97.63	105.35
Blang	102.73	106.13	103.54	102.97	103.10	100.04	104.93
Buyi	102.71	104.76	104.49	104.41	101.35	95.84	107.58
Dai	102.73	106.13	103.54	102.96	103.10	100.03	104.94
Daur	103.14	105.74	105.31	104.40	105.26	98.30	106.62
Deang	102.73	106.15	103.53	102.94	103.12	100.06	104.90
Derung	102.73	105.87	103.72	103.40	102.92	99.54	105.47
Dong	102.57	104.39	104.68	104.28	100.73	97.25	108.36
Dongxiang	102.82	104.52	102.84	104.56	104.39	97.91	105.20
Ewenki	103.09	105.73	105.51	105.05	105.21	98.13	107.43
Gaoshan	102.69	104.60	103.93	105.24	101.67	96.77	107.69
Gelao	102.72	104.75	104.52	104.43	101.33	95.78	107.60
Han	102.60	104.61	103.96	105.13	101.63	97.18	108.37
Hani	102.73	106.14	103.53	102.95	103.11	100.04	104.91

(continued)

Table 4.11 Continued

Ethnic group	General index	Food	Grain	Oil or fat	Meat, poultry and processed products	Eggs	Aquatic products
Hezhe	103.11	105.46	104.52	103.03	105.13	98.04	105.15
Hui	102.65	104.96	103.23	104.65	103.47	97.67	107.15
Jing	103.18	105.18	103.83	107.81	102.87	97.37	105.14
Jingpo	102.73	106.13	103.54	102.96	103.11	100.03	104.92
Jino	102.73	106.14	103.54	102.95	103.11	100.05	104.91
Kazak	103.82	107.59	107.25	105.30	105.84	102.11	105.18
Kirgiz	103.82	107.58	107.23	105.27	105.84	102.08	105.18
Korean	102.69	105.05	104.19	104.97	103.87	95.78	107.51
Lahu	102.73	106.13	103.54	102.96	103.10	100.03	104.93
Lhoba	103.44	106.70	103.14	105.43	108.29	101.99	103.26
Li	103.18	105.19	104.15	106.13	103.67	102.28	102.53
Lisu	102.73	106.08	103.57	103.02	103.02	99.97	105.10
Manchu	102.81	104.82	103.72	105.08	102.89	96.47	106.66
Maonan	103.07	105.05	104.02	107.04	102.49	96.86	105.73
Miao	102.59	104.63	104.73	104.16	100.91	97.71	107.93
Monba	103.47	106.77	103.05	105.46	108.59	102.20	103.08
Mongol	103.02	105.57	105.18	105.20	104.60	97.80	107.55
Mulao	103.14	105.12	103.92	107.57	102.75	97.13	105.36
Naxi	102.73	106.09	103.57	103.02	103.05	99.98	105.08
Nu	102.74	106.13	103.53	103.01	103.18	100.05	104.92
Oroqen	103.10	105.57	105.00	104.03	105.15	98.06	106.28
Pumi	102.73	106.12	103.54	102.97	103.10	100.02	104.95
Qiang	102.54	104.22	104.92	105.23	99.92	97.74	111.43
Russian	103.49	106.76	106.37	105.22	105.44	100.35	106.17
Salar	103.04	106.36	102.90	105.47	107.08	99.11	108.85
She	102.44	104.89	103.46	104.77	101.45	97.00	108.56
Shui	102.73	104.79	104.45	104.50	101.43	95.93	107.45
Tajik	103.78	107.49	107.15	105.30	105.70	101.97	105.27
Tatar	103.74	107.37	106.93	105.24	105.68	101.78	105.26
Tibetan	103.10	105.93	103.38	105.31	105.94	100.17	106.50
Tu	102.99	106.21	102.89	105.40	106.73	98.93	108.77
Tujia	102.51	104.45	105.53	104.29	100.14	98.88	109.50
Uygur	103.82	107.59	107.24	105.30	105.83	102.10	105.19
Uzbek	103.80	107.55	107.19	105.30	105.79	102.04	105.21
Va	102.72	106.09	103.55	103.03	103.06	99.97	105.01
Xibe	103.03	105.45	104.38	104.96	103.42	97.45	106.84
Yao	102.83	104.76	104.29	106.03	101.86	98.31	106.73
Yi	102.68	105.45	104.03	103.75	102.03	98.92	107.02
Yugur	102.73	104.25	102.44	104.52	104.26	97.51	105.24
Zhuang	103.18	105.25	103.82	107.71	103.02	97.56	104.99

Table 4.12 Consumer price indices by category (preceding year = 100) (II)

Ethnic group	Vegetables	Fresh vegetables	Dried and fresh melons and fruits	Fresh fruits	Dining out	Tobacco, liquor and articles	Tobacco
National average	113.75	115.87	100.07	98.83	106.72	102.87	100.50
Achang	117.75	121.00	103.49	103.68	108.78	100.66	99.98
Bai	116.38	119.32	102.81	102.84	108.65	100.99	100.31
Baonan	109.06	111.24	98.42	96.92	106.72	103.08	100.19
Blang	117.73	120.97	103.49	103.67	108.77	100.68	99.98
Buyi	109.43	111.25	100.05	99.79	109.47	102.72	102.20
Dai	117.77	121.02	103.48	103.67	108.77	100.67	99.98
Daur	113.58	115.63	104.87	103.49	106.77	103.00	100.85
Deang	117.78	121.03	103.51	103.71	108.80	100.65	99.98
Derung	116.96	119.98	102.92	102.83	108.37	101.18	100.14
Dong	110.64	112.28	99.64	98.99	108.26	102.58	101.69
Dongxiang	109.56	111.69	99.11	97.70	106.78	103.28	100.26
Ewenki	112.64	114.83	105.45	104.00	106.50	102.85	100.42
Gaoshan	114.14	116.53	99.42	97.93	106.79	102.93	100.60
Gelao	109.26	111.05	100.01	99.76	109.52	102.76	102.25
Han	113.72	115.81	99.76	98.44	106.49	102.96	100.56
Hani	117.76	121.01	103.50	103.69	108.79	100.66	99.98
Hezhe	114.94	116.81	102.96	101.66	107.07	102.94	101.69
Hui	112.54	114.68	99.39	98.05	107.68	102.85	100.36
Jing	116.44	118.76	98.99	98.34	108.30	102.96	100.30
Jingpo	117.73	120.98	103.48	103.66	108.79	100.67	99.99
Jino	117.77	121.02	103.51	103.70	108.79	100.66	99.98
Kazak	117.58	119.06	108.09	107.72	109.02	105.56	101.13
Kirgiz	117.57	119.05	108.06	107.69	109.00	105.54	101.13
Korean	112.56	115.17	103.70	103.02	106.36	102.39	101.19
Lahu	117.74	120.99	103.48	103.66	108.78	100.67	99.98
Lhoba	114.44	116.47	107.02	105.63	109.98	101.65	99.88
Li	115.30	117.61	102.20	101.78	105.59	101.27	100.40
Lisu	117.77	121.00	103.39	103.54	108.66	100.72	99.98
Manchu	115.64	118.57	99.27	98.11	106.39	102.90	100.77
Maonan	114.44	116.60	99.11	98.57	108.65	102.96	100.84
Miao	111.49	113.29	100.64	100.11	108.19	102.60	101.42
Monba	114.54	116.58	107.28	105.85	110.05	101.54	99.79
Mongol	113.20	115.56	104.17	102.81	106.57	102.88	100.42
Mulao	115.58	117.82	98.95	98.34	108.42	102.99	100.53
Naxi	117.75	120.98	103.42	103.57	108.68	100.72	99.98
Nu	117.68	120.90	103.52	103.67	108.78	100.70	99.99

(*continued*)

Table 4.12 Continued

Ethnic group	Vegetables	Fresh vegetables	Dried and fresh melons and fruits	Fresh fruits	Dining out	Tobacco, liquor and articles	Tobacco
Oroqen	113.84	115.87	104.14	102.75	106.76	102.90	101.07
Pumi	117.74	120.98	103.46	103.64	108.76	100.68	99.98
Qiang	118.03	120.54	100.15	99.22	104.66	102.72	99.93
Russian	115.47	117.27	106.62	105.80	108.00	104.40	100.79
Salar	112.49	114.75	99.13	97.58	109.87	102.92	100.09
She	115.75	119.40	100.58	99.45	106.01	102.20	100.89
Shui	109.69	111.53	100.04	99.79	109.46	102.71	102.12
Tajik	117.46	118.96	107.83	107.43	108.94	105.49	101.11
Tatar	117.10	118.64	107.41	106.96	108.86	105.36	101.06
Tibetan	114.62	116.86	103.14	101.82	108.57	102.16	99.90
Tu	112.41	114.69	98.98	97.47	109.65	102.82	100.12
Tujia	111.61	112.95	101.20	100.32	107.17	103.35	100.86
Uygur	117.58	119.06	108.07	107.71	109.01	105.55	101.13
Uzbek	117.53	119.03	107.94	107.57	108.99	105.51	101.11
Va	117.64	120.86	103.41	103.56	108.70	100.73	99.99
Xibe	117.09	120.15	100.05	99.11	106.90	102.99	100.68
Yao	114.93	116.99	99.25	98.48	107.59	102.55	100.58
Yi	116.89	119.78	102.18	102.00	107.72	101.46	100.22
Yugur	108.89	111.08	98.29	96.78	106.60	103.05	100.18
Zhuang	116.69	119.08	99.10	98.51	108.27	102.86	100.24

Table 4.13 Consumer price indices by category (preceding year = 100) (III)

Ethnic group	Liquor	Clothing	Garments	Clothing material	Footgear and hats	Clothing manufac-turing service	Household facilities, articles and services
National average	106.32	103.13	103.33	103.52	102.33	107.07	101.94
Achang	103.18	98.80	100.37	101.45	94.15	106.95	101.36
Bai	103.28	99.53	100.80	102.01	95.68	106.76	101.33
Baonan	107.96	102.40	102.54	101.44	101.71	106.24	101.10
Blang	103.24	98.82	100.38	101.44	94.20	106.96	101.36
Buyi	103.58	103.70	103.48	106.89	103.70	104.85	101.12
Dai	103.20	98.85	100.41	101.45	94.20	106.96	101.35
Daur	105.46	103.32	103.48	105.19	102.64	108.71	101.53

(continued)

Table 4.13 Continued

Ethnic group	Liquor	Clothing	Garments	Clothing material	Footgear and hats	Clothing manufac-turing service	Household facilities, articles and services
Deang	103.17	98.78	100.35	101.42	94.11	106.96	101.35
Derung	103.95	99.66	100.93	101.94	95.83	107.05	101.43
Dong	103.89	102.97	102.97	105.09	102.40	106.06	101.24
Dongxiang	108.19	102.49	102.65	101.81	101.67	106.46	101.21
Ewenki	105.67	103.65	103.61	105.18	103.54	108.82	101.43
Gaoshan	105.77	103.18	103.38	103.79	102.38	107.75	102.01
Gelao	103.57	103.77	103.52	106.99	103.85	104.77	101.11
Han	106.43	103.25	103.43	103.54	102.53	107.56	101.84
Hani	103.19	98.79	100.36	101.43	94.13	106.95	101.36
Hezhe	104.43	102.71	103.31	104.90	100.82	108.12	101.69
Hui	106.17	102.41	102.38	103.68	102.21	108.24	101.35
Jing	105.44	103.41	104.46	106.18	99.68	109.15	101.19
Jingpo	103.17	98.81	100.37	101.45	94.17	106.94	101.35
Jino	103.20	98.80	100.37	101.43	94.14	106.96	101.35
Kazak	110.14	101.90	101.77	106.48	101.20	109.36	101.90
Kirgiz	110.08	101.91	101.79	106.47	101.20	109.36	101.90
Korean	104.00	101.80	102.09	103.57	100.76	106.29	101.29
Lahu	103.20	98.81	100.37	101.43	94.17	106.95	101.36
Lhoba	104.18	104.23	104.10	101.48	102.68	111.91	101.54
Li	103.01	102.88	102.93	111.07	101.10	109.00	103.33
Lisu	103.31	99.11	100.64	101.52	94.58	107.04	101.31
Manchu	105.57	102.77	103.33	103.73	101.27	108.92	102.46
Maonan	104.94	103.62	104.33	106.52	100.88	107.99	101.14
Miao	104.83	102.58	102.67	104.57	101.85	106.23	101.22
Monba	104.07	104.35	104.24	101.30	102.71	112.17	101.53
Mongol	105.80	103.36	103.39	104.81	103.12	108.66	101.59
Mulao	105.25	103.57	104.49	106.32	100.25	108.64	101.16
Naxi	103.32	99.12	100.64	101.52	94.59	107.06	101.31
Nu	103.23	98.93	100.45	101.46	94.35	107.04	101.36
Oroqen	105.04	103.21	103.50	105.04	102.18	108.50	101.58
Pumi	103.22	98.86	100.41	101.46	94.24	106.97	101.35
Qiang	107.55	109.60	109.95	104.37	108.99	109.42	99.65
Russian	108.29	102.60	102.50	105.84	102.15	109.09	101.74
Salar	106.22	99.08	97.95	102.34	101.92	106.92	99.65
She	104.59	103.41	103.57	103.81	102.55	106.25	101.86
Shui	103.63	103.63	103.47	106.85	103.45	105.01	101.13
Tajik	110.06	101.94	101.82	106.39	101.25	109.31	101.89
Tatar	109.91	101.95	101.84	106.19	101.26	109.19	101.87
Tibetan	105.51	104.12	103.92	102.18	103.76	109.92	100.60

(*continued*)

Table 4.13 Continued

Ethnic group	Liquor	Clothing	Garments	Clothing material	Footgear and hats	Clothing manufacturing service	Household facilities, articles and services
Tu	106.09	99.35	98.33	102.29	101.88	106.78	99.76
Tujia	108.03	102.30	102.19	102.90	102.19	108.32	101.46
Uygur	110.13	101.91	101.78	106.47	101.21	109.36	101.90
Uzbek	110.05	101.92	101.80	106.45	101.21	109.33	101.91
Va	103.29	98.91	100.44	101.49	94.37	106.93	101.35
Xibe	106.09	102.24	102.88	104.26	100.47	107.67	102.60
Yao	104.77	102.59	103.41	104.25	99.74	108.01	101.28
Yi	104.43	102.35	103.37	102.86	99.33	107.40	100.86
Yugur	107.96	102.53	102.71	101.41	101.70	106.20	101.15
Zhuang	105.35	103.22	104.36	105.85	99.30	109.03	101.19

Table 4.14 Consumer price indices by category (preceding year = 100) (IV)

Ethnic group	Durable consumer goods	Interior decorations	Bed articles	Daily use household articles	Household services and maintenance and renovation	Health care and personal articles	Health care
National average	100.36	100.78	100.43	102.60	109.71	102.00	101.70
Achang	99.44	98.72	101.53	102.45	109.12	101.56	101.13
Bai	99.45	98.98	101.33	102.25	109.43	101.74	101.35
Baonan	100.00	100.78	100.25	101.73	105.66	103.64	104.06
Blang	99.44	98.72	101.52	102.45	109.10	101.57	101.13
Buyi	99.13	99.48	100.41	101.22	111.40	102.44	102.23
Dai	99.42	98.72	101.52	102.44	109.11	101.56	101.13
Daur	100.39	101.62	99.93	101.88	108.66	102.26	101.66
Deang	99.43	98.71	101.54	102.45	109.11	101.56	101.12
Derung	99.60	99.11	101.36	102.46	109.00	101.67	101.26
Dong	99.59	100.16	100.34	101.36	110.53	102.48	102.27
Dongxiang	100.12	100.82	100.17	101.69	106.42	103.68	104.04
Ewenki	100.74	101.47	100.32	101.67	106.73	102.11	101.44
Gaoshan	100.45	101.00	100.89	102.93	110.58	102.05	101.69
Gelao	99.11	99.47	100.38	101.19	111.44	102.46	102.25
Han	100.25	100.88	100.62	102.68	109.57	102.06	101.75
Hani	99.44	98.72	101.54	102.45	109.11	101.56	101.12

(*continued*)

Table 4.14 Continued

Ethnic group	Durable consumer goods	Interior decorations	Bed articles	Daily use household articles	Household services and maintenance and renovation	Health care and personal articles	Health care
Hezhe	99.62	101.96	99.29	102.47	112.02	102.45	102.03
Hui	99.99	100.62	99.62	102.49	108.04	102.13	101.78
Jing	100.39	100.76	99.61	101.73	107.05	101.99	101.62
Jingpo	99.44	98.73	101.53	102.44	109.12	101.57	101.13
Jino	99.43	98.71	101.53	102.44	109.10	101.56	101.12
Kazak	100.44	100.36	98.68	101.21	114.37	102.94	102.58
Kirgiz	100.44	100.38	98.68	101.22	114.36	102.93	102.57
Korean	99.65	100.67	101.50	101.99	108.07	102.21	101.71
Lahu	99.44	98.73	101.54	102.45	109.12	101.56	101.12
Lhoba	101.36	101.52	102.84	100.31	104.86	101.06	100.63
Li	102.19	101.08	100.39	103.61	111.30	102.03	101.85
Lisu	99.36	98.71	101.46	102.43	109.11	101.57	101.14
Manchu	100.65	101.35	102.73	103.68	108.43	102.08	101.57
Maonan	100.05	100.42	99.80	101.53	108.14	102.12	101.80
Miao	99.51	99.80	100.34	101.60	110.15	102.34	102.13
Monba	101.43	101.60	102.93	100.23	104.53	100.98	100.54
Mongol	100.68	101.26	100.87	102.02	106.96	102.07	101.45
Mulao	100.26	100.63	99.66	101.62	107.46	102.05	101.70
Naxi	99.37	98.72	101.46	102.42	109.10	101.57	101.13
Nu	99.48	98.78	101.54	102.41	109.05	101.56	101.12
Oroqen	100.19	101.76	99.84	102.10	109.38	102.29	101.73
Pumi	99.43	98.73	101.52	102.45	109.11	101.57	101.13
Qiang	96.60	98.17	98.78	101.88	109.23	101.71	101.51
Russian	100.57	100.78	99.40	101.50	111.22	102.56	102.09
Salar	97.73	98.90	98.80	101.94	103.10	101.30	101.42
She	99.78	101.02	100.10	102.56	110.65	102.03	102.16
Shui	99.18	99.51	100.42	101.25	111.24	102.42	102.20
Tajik	100.43	100.37	98.72	101.26	114.18	102.90	102.56
Tatar	100.42	100.39	98.78	101.30	113.88	102.92	102.60
Tibetan	99.31	100.06	100.88	101.12	105.29	101.37	101.17
Tu	97.86	99.00	98.94	101.97	103.35	101.36	101.48
Tujia	99.96	100.39	100.01	102.28	108.99	102.52	102.40
Uygur	100.44	100.37	98.68	101.22	114.37	102.93	102.58
Uzbek	100.45	100.38	98.69	101.24	114.29	102.92	102.57
Va	99.45	98.75	101.51	102.45	109.11	101.57	101.14
Xibe	100.58	101.09	102.76	103.52	109.70	102.10	101.67
Yao	100.21	100.73	99.91	101.66	108.15	102.15	101.84
Yi	98.62	98.65	100.65	102.15	109.40	101.70	101.36
Yugur	100.08	100.86	100.29	101.76	105.70	103.71	104.13
Zhuang	100.36	100.67	99.67	101.75	107.00	101.95	101.57

Table 4.15 Consumer price indices by category (preceding year = 100) (V)

Ethnic group	Medical appliances and articles	Traditional Chinese medicine	Western medicine	Health care appliances and articles	Health care services	Personal articles and services	Cosmetics
National average	102.74	105.02	100.30	102.54	100.70	102.63	101.27
Achang	103.63	104.76	98.90	100.51	100.34	103.07	101.62
Bai	103.33	105.21	99.31	100.62	100.40	103.04	101.47
Baonan	101.91	108.32	102.33	100.63	102.64	102.47	103.70
Blang	103.61	104.76	98.91	100.52	100.34	103.07	101.62
Buyi	101.82	108.01	100.82	99.84	100.62	102.79	100.29
Dai	103.62	104.76	98.90	100.51	100.34	103.07	101.62
Daur	99.59	105.53	100.90	101.15	100.33	103.47	101.06
Deang	103.64	104.76	98.90	100.50	100.34	103.08	101.63
Derung	103.21	104.86	99.27	100.77	100.43	102.99	101.58
Dong	101.99	106.94	101.13	100.92	100.70	102.88	100.74
Dongxiang	101.96	108.39	102.41	100.77	102.51	102.59	103.68
Ewenki	99.71	105.01	100.51	101.08	100.58	103.40	101.47
Gaoshan	101.89	104.98	100.81	101.86	100.70	102.86	101.52
Gelao	101.80	108.10	100.86	99.80	100.63	102.79	100.26
Han	102.02	105.07	100.42	102.03	100.76	102.76	101.35
Hani	103.63	104.76	98.90	100.51	100.34	103.07	101.63
Hezhe	99.19	106.39	101.50	101.25	99.80	103.55	100.12
Hui	103.04	105.20	100.37	102.55	100.84	102.92	101.70
Jing	102.36	103.64	100.90	100.56	100.82	102.76	101.05
Jingpo	103.63	104.77	98.91	100.51	100.34	103.07	101.62

(*continued*)

Table 4.15 Continued

Ethnic group	Medical appliances and articles	Traditional Chinese medicine	Western medicine	Health care appliances and articles	Health care services	Personal articles and services	Cosmetics
Jino	103.63	104.77	98.90	100.51	100.34	103.07	101.63
Kazak	102.06	107.31	101.94	102.14	100.40	103.33	101.96
Kirgiz	102.03	107.30	101.93	102.13	100.39	103.33	101.94
Korean	99.93	106.15	100.50	101.39	100.02	103.39	100.97
Lahu	103.63	104.76	98.90	100.52	100.34	103.07	101.63
Lhoba	100.75	103.54	97.97	100.06	102.15	101.65	100.90
Li	101.81	106.50	101.35	103.57	100.39	102.55	100.67
Lisu	103.57	104.78	98.89	100.53	100.37	103.05	101.60
Manchu	102.34	104.97	101.09	101.10	100.21	103.28	101.45
Maonan	102.21	104.82	100.93	100.30	100.78	102.76	100.82
Miao	101.87	106.78	100.78	100.92	100.65	102.82	100.85
Monba	100.73	103.37	97.75	100.05	102.23	101.58	100.88
Mongol	100.40	104.97	100.54	101.12	100.57	103.29	101.54
Mulao	102.31	104.09	100.92	100.45	100.81	102.75	100.95
Naxi	103.55	104.78	98.89	100.54	100.38	103.04	101.59
Nu	103.57	104.74	98.89	100.52	100.38	103.05	101.61
Oroqen	99.46	105.68	101.03	101.15	100.19	103.49	100.79
Pumi	103.61	104.76	98.91	100.52	100.35	103.07	101.62
Qiang	101.12	105.57	98.63	101.25	101.47	102.22	100.59
Russian	101.28	106.31	101.28	101.76	100.49	103.30	101.76
Salar	101.26	104.26	99.55	100.66	101.39	101.01	100.73
She	100.99	104.19	100.42	102.97	101.91	101.93	101.53
Shui	101.86	107.86	100.81	99.84	100.62	102.80	100.32
Tajik	102.04	107.23	101.90	102.13	100.41	103.30	101.94

Teatar	102.06	107.26	101.90	102.08	100.49	103.27	102.00
Tibetan	101.05	104.36	98.62	100.45	101.87	101.66	100.95
Tu	101.33	104.35	99.59	100.67	101.40	101.10	100.81
Tujia	101.15	106.40	101.29	102.37	100.76	102.76	101.18
Uygur	102.06	107.30	101.93	102.14	100.40	103.33	101.95
Uzbek	102.06	107.26	101.91	102.14	100.40	103.31	101.94
Va	103.60	104.76	98.94	100.56	100.36	103.06	101.62
Xibe	102.48	104.90	101.20	101.30	100.28	103.01	101.36
Yao	102.47	104.40	100.95	101.21	100.79	102.85	101.23
Yi	102.73	105.36	99.04	100.64	100.68	102.81	101.19
Yugur	101.95	108.43	102.41	100.64	102.68	102.52	103.78
Zhuang	102.49	103.55	100.79	100.55	100.81	102.77	101.11

Table 4.16 Consumer price indices by category (preceding year = 100) (VI)

Ethnic group	Sanitation articles	Personal ornaments	Personal services	Transportation and communication	Transportation	Transportation facility	Fuels and parts
National average	103.51	100.21	105.33	99.88	101.16	99.21	102.86
Achang	102.08	100.95	106.98	100.22	101.49	98.90	102.38
Bai	102.37	100.89	106.71	100.13	101.39	98.97	102.51
Baonan	102.18	101.45	104.87	100.37	101.95	100.38	102.32
Blang	102.09	100.94	106.96	100.21	101.49	98.90	102.39
Buyi	104.45	100.08	105.54	99.66	101.36	99.96	103.25
Dai	102.08	100.95	106.97	100.22	101.49	98.89	102.38
Daur	102.47	100.94	108.17	99.61	101.32	99.57	102.50
Deang	102.07	100.95	107.00	100.22	101.49	98.90	102.38
Derung	102.31	100.82	106.67	100.13	101.46	99.03	102.46
Dong	103.82	100.55	105.48	99.76	101.05	99.48	103.08
Dongxiang	102.38	101.60	104.99	100.33	102.01	100.46	102.36
Ewenki	102.14	99.60	109.40	99.66	101.12	99.19	102.37
Gaoshan	103.38	100.70	105.39	100.12	101.62	99.99	102.83
Gelao	104.48	100.06	105.53	99.64	101.36	99.98	103.26
Han	103.48	100.68	105.20	99.95	101.29	99.54	102.83
Hani	102.08	100.95	106.99	100.22	101.49	98.90	102.38
Hezhe	103.04	103.54	105.57	99.57	101.62	100.20	102.74
Hui	103.17	101.11	105.95	99.90	101.58	99.80	102.58
Jing	103.85	100.74	105.55	100.14	101.86	99.92	102.71
Jingpo	102.09	100.95	106.98	100.22	101.49	98.90	102.38
Jino	102.08	100.94	106.99	100.22	101.49	98.89	102.38
Kazak	104.13	101.69	106.46	99.46	102.26	100.73	102.94
Kirgiz	104.12	101.71	106.45	99.46	102.26	100.72	102.94
Korean	103.03	100.52	106.81	100.02	101.56	99.62	102.73
Lahu	102.08	100.95	106.98	100.22	101.49	98.90	102.38

Lhoba	100.79	101.46	104.01	101.09	103.13	101.27	102.94
Li	104.48	101.49	103.49	101.45	103.58	102.86	102.38
Lisu	102.11	100.94	106.90	100.22	101.49	98.87	102.39
Manchu	103.68	101.06	105.64	100.02	101.62	100.22	102.86
Maonan	104.07	100.55	105.54	100.00	101.73	99.95	102.86
Miao	103.66	100.47	105.50	99.74	101.14	99.36	102.99
Monba	100.61	101.47	104.02	101.18	103.22	101.30	102.92
Mongol	102.43	99.62	108.65	99.76	101.22	99.36	102.46
Mulao	103.97	100.65	105.52	100.07	101.78	99.91	102.77
Naxi	102.10	100.94	106.90	100.22	101.50	98.87	102.39
Nu	102.08	100.95	106.91	100.23	101.51	98.94	102.40
Oroqen	102.60	101.62	107.47	99.62	101.38	99.72	102.56
Pumi	102.09	100.95	106.97	100.22	101.49	98.90	102.39
Qiang	102.97	100.55	104.24	100.28	101.61	97.70	102.60
Russian	103.35	100.77	107.55	99.56	101.78	100.06	102.72
Salar	101.11	98.21	105.20	99.49	100.93	99.00	102.31
She	103.73	99.71	102.75	99.92	101.45	100.11	102.87
Shui	104.41	100.11	105.57	99.68	101.38	99.96	103.23
Tajik	104.10	101.65	106.40	99.47	102.23	100.69	102.93
Tatar	104.02	101.64	106.35	99.51	102.21	100.65	102.91
Tibetan	101.34	100.50	104.40	100.53	102.22	99.84	102.66
Tu	101.23	98.35	105.16	99.53	100.93	99.01	102.32
Tujia	103.33	100.41	105.46	99.53	100.68	99.10	102.86
Uygur	104.13	101.69	106.46	99.46	102.26	100.72	102.94
Uzbek	104.12	101.67	106.43	99.47	102.25	100.71	102.93
Va	102.11	100.95	106.92	100.21	101.49	98.90	102.40
Xibe	103.67	100.75	105.24	99.91	101.70	100.32	102.82
Yao	103.36	100.90	105.50	100.02	101.31	99.32	102.73
Yi	102.59	100.74	106.07	100.17	101.51	98.69	102.54
Yugur	102.22	101.55	104.88	100.40	101.97	100.40	102.31
Zhuang	103.75	100.75	105.61	100.14	101.82	99.83	102.67

Table 4.17 Consumer price indices by category (preceding year = 100) (VII)

Ethnic group	Fees for vehicles use and maintenance	Incity traffic fare	Intercity traffic fare	Communication	Communication facility	Communication services	Recreation, education and culture
National average	104.51	101.41	101.63	97.99	87.76	99.92	100.51
Achang	105.22	103.55	103.50	98.53	89.25	100.25	101.22
Bai	104.77	103.10	102.98	98.51	89.36	100.25	101.21
Baonan	104.28	101.01	103.31	98.80	93.50	99.82	100.95
Blang	105.21	103.53	103.50	98.53	89.25	100.25	101.22
Buyi	103.16	101.55	100.85	97.81	85.59	100.42	101.22
Dai	105.22	103.55	103.50	98.53	89.23	100.26	101.22
Daur	103.68	101.76	102.75	97.18	90.51	98.82	100.45
Deang	105.23	103.55	103.51	98.53	89.26	100.26	101.23
Derung	104.96	103.15	103.21	98.40	89.05	100.15	101.13
Dong	102.68	101.17	101.00	98.33	89.44	100.21	101.20
Dongxiang	104.44	101.01	103.43	98.67	92.68	99.84	100.88
Ewenki	104.25	102.21	102.47	97.18	93.02	98.36	100.70
Gaoshan	104.24	102.33	102.43	98.15	88.21	99.95	100.74
Gelao	103.11	101.51	100.81	97.79	85.49	100.43	101.23
Han	103.85	101.66	101.90	98.18	88.59	99.95	100.58
Hani	105.22	103.55	103.50	98.53	89.26	100.26	101.22
Hezhe	102.35	100.96	102.96	97.29	85.96	99.74	100.03
Hui	104.21	102.62	101.99	97.75	87.63	99.99	100.36
Jing	102.34	101.64	104.01	98.23	90.41	100.10	101.40
Jingpo	105.21	103.54	103.50	98.53	89.25	100.25	101.22
Jino	105.23	103.55	103.50	98.53	89.23	100.25	101.22
Kazak	106.47	100.57	103.90	96.72	81.32	100.20	100.07
Kirgiz	106.43	100.57	103.89	96.72	81.34	100.19	100.07
Korean	106.13	101.55	101.99	97.74	87.66	100.01	100.73

Lahu	105.21	103.55	103.51	98.53	89.27	100.25	101.22
Lhoba	102.34	107.94	100.53	98.29	95.38	99.36	100.36
Li	109.81	106.75	101.68	97.43	82.60	99.06	102.09
Lisu	105.22	103.53	103.49	98.52	89.15	100.26	101.17
Manchu	105.19	101.74	101.37	98.14	86.64	100.08	100.85
Maonan	102.42	101.56	103.17	98.11	89.15	100.20	101.37
Miao	103.08	101.51	101.37	98.16	88.64	100.17	101.16
Monba	102.41	108.28	100.44	98.32	95.75	99.32	100.32
Mongol	104.68	102.17	102.25	97.43	91.83	98.76	100.78
Mulao	102.27	101.57	103.64	98.18	89.92	100.14	101.39
Naxi	105.21	103.55	103.46	98.52	89.15	100.25	101.17
Nu	105.16	103.59	103.44	98.53	89.34	100.24	101.20
Oroqen	103.25	101.57	102.76	97.25	89.53	99.05	100.35
Pumi	105.21	103.53	103.49	98.53	89.25	100.25	101.21
Qiang	105.14	103.07	103.02	98.19	85.31	100.31	99.56
Russian	105.67	101.26	103.09	96.94	85.82	99.51	100.36
Salar	104.28	100.36	101.24	97.92	89.57	100.07	100.79
She	102.95	101.37	102.45	98.08	84.93	99.89	99.42
Shui	103.15	101.55	100.98	97.83	85.79	100.42	101.23
Tajik	106.37	100.60	103.84	96.76	81.54	100.19	100.10
Tatar	106.32	100.63	103.74	96.83	81.95	100.17	100.14
Tibetan	103.54	104.82	101.45	98.26	91.90	99.76	100.32
Tu	104.15	100.46	101.28	97.97	89.72	100.05	100.80
Tujia	102.64	100.87	100.51	98.27	90.85	99.93	100.95
Uygur	106.46	100.57	103.89	96.72	81.32	100.20	100.07
Uzbek	106.43	100.60	103.85	96.74	81.41	100.19	100.09
Va	105.17	103.50	103.51	98.52	89.27	100.25	101.21
Xibe	105.35	101.46	101.70	98.07	85.28	100.30	100.84
Yao	102.29	101.37	102.88	98.51	91.84	99.99	101.30
Yi	104.97	103.19	103.07	98.36	87.75	100.29	100.76
Yugur	104.25	101.05	103.33	98.83	93.64	99.81	100.97
Zhuang	102.35	101.72	104.05	98.24	90.48	100.09	101.40

Table 4.18 Consumer price indices by category (preceding year = 100) (VIII)

Ethnic group	Durable consumer goods and service for recreational use	Education	Teaching materials and reference books	Educational services	Recreational articles	Cultural articles	Newspapers and magazines
National average	94.48	101.72	101.71	101.72	101.28	100.38	101.37
Achang	95.49	102.08	100.90	102.28	100.38	98.32	100.83
Bai	95.75	102.13	100.88	102.32	100.53	98.72	101.00
Baonan	97.48	101.26	100.41	101.33	102.45	100.35	100.11
Blang	95.48	102.08	100.91	102.28	100.38	98.33	100.84
Buyi	96.67	102.64	100.72	102.90	101.47	100.30	102.09
Dai	95.47	102.08	100.91	102.28	100.38	98.32	100.84
Daur	94.57	101.44	101.66	101.42	101.12	99.93	100.30
Deang	95.48	102.09	100.91	102.29	100.37	98.31	100.83
Derung	95.44	102.02	101.12	102.17	100.55	98.73	100.93
Dong	96.74	102.43	100.74	102.63	101.50	100.48	101.63
Dongxiang	97.14	101.37	100.71	101.40	102.46	100.26	100.06
Ewenki	96.02	101.22	101.40	101.21	101.54	100.17	100.48
Gaoshan	94.91	101.78	101.57	101.82	101.58	100.40	101.99
Gelao	96.71	102.66	100.70	102.93	101.48	100.33	102.12
Han	94.86	101.70	101.72	101.71	101.24	100.40	101.47
Hani	95.48	102.08	100.91	102.28	100.37	98.31	100.83
Hezhe	91.76	101.88	101.87	101.89	100.22	99.63	100.02
Hui	93.81	102.02	102.76	101.86	101.21	100.13	101.43
Jing	94.65	102.99	100.45	103.34	103.39	100.06	100.33
Jingpo	95.49	102.09	100.91	102.29	100.38	98.32	100.84
Jino	95.48	102.09	100.90	102.29	100.37	98.31	100.84
Kazak	92.96	102.34	103.46	102.16	101.18	99.05	100.52
Kirgiz	92.93	102.34	103.46	102.16	101.17	99.06	100.51
Korean	94.38	102.15	100.84	102.44	100.70	100.69	100.88

Lahu	95.49	102.08	100.91	102.28	100.38	98.32	100.84
Lhoba	98.49	101.03	99.75	101.69	101.20	100.58	101.62
Li	99.83	101.78	99.52	102.24	101.94	100.86	100.41
Lisu	95.38	102.06	100.90	102.26	100.41	98.35	100.85
Manchu	93.90	102.18	101.69	102.25	100.94	100.91	100.89
Maonan	95.19	102.95	100.48	103.29	102.97	100.15	100.79
Miao	96.51	102.36	100.80	102.55	101.29	100.21	101.65
Monba	98.54	100.98	99.65	101.68	101.21	100.59	101.60
Mongol	95.82	101.43	101.44	101.44	101.47	100.33	100.72
Mulao	94.85	103.01	100.45	103.36	103.25	100.12	100.51
Naxi	95.39	102.06	100.90	102.26	100.41	98.36	100.86
Nu	95.52	102.06	100.90	102.26	100.40	98.37	100.85
Oroqen	93.85	101.54	101.67	101.52	100.87	99.89	100.23
Pumi	95.47	102.08	100.91	102.28	100.38	98.33	100.84
Qiang	92.14	101.39	100.67	101.50	101.63	99.54	101.56
Russian	94.18	101.93	102.57	101.83	101.36	99.58	100.63
Salar	96.41	100.92	99.38	101.17	99.53	100.00	102.23
She	94.19	99.37	102.47	99.10	101.18	99.44	102.23
Shui	96.60	102.65	100.71	102.91	101.52	100.27	102.03
Tajik	93.03	102.33	103.41	102.16	101.19	99.10	100.55
Tatar	93.19	102.30	103.26	102.14	101.24	99.16	100.55
Tibetan	96.55	101.08	99.83	101.50	100.96	100.16	101.64
Tu	96.44	100.96	99.45	101.21	99.66	100.03	102.15
Tujia	96.42	101.96	101.56	101.97	101.05	100.62	101.89
Uygur	92.96	102.34	103.46	102.17	101.18	99.06	100.52
Uzbek	93.00	102.34	103.42	102.17	101.19	99.08	100.53
Va	95.49	102.07	100.91	102.27	100.39	98.36	100.85
Xibe	93.62	102.36	102.31	102.35	100.96	100.66	100.94
Yao	95.59	102.67	100.54	102.94	102.40	100.23	100.57
Yi	94.69	101.96	100.82	102.14	100.85	98.88	101.18
Yugur	97.49	101.29	100.43	101.35	102.56	100.38	100.05
Zhuang	94.64	103.00	100.44	103.35	103.29	99.97	100.28

Table 4.19 Consumer price indices by category (preceding year = 100) (IX)

Ethnic group	Expenditure on culture and recreation	Touring and outing	Residence	Building and decoration materials	Renting	Private housing	Water, electricity and fuels
National average	101.86	101.71	102.14	101.04	102.73	102.30	102.45
Achang	102.41	106.18	102.15	101.85	104.06	102.51	101.22
Bai	102.23	105.47	102.05	101.79	103.77	102.22	101.41
Baonan	103.88	102.49	102.00	101.12	100.91	102.10	102.56
Blang	102.40	106.16	102.15	101.85	104.06	102.51	101.22
Buyi	101.88	101.57	101.43	100.88	103.20	101.01	101.91
Dai	102.42	106.15	102.15	101.83	104.06	102.50	101.23
Daur	102.07	101.64	102.92	100.58	103.97	103.78	102.65
Deang	102.41	106.20	102.16	101.85	104.07	102.52	101.22
Derung	102.30	105.44	102.17	101.64	103.89	102.53	101.43
Dong	102.17	102.23	101.76	101.46	102.60	101.04	102.82
Dongxiang	104.07	102.16	101.95	100.90	100.89	102.11	102.44
Ewenki	102.57	102.30	102.55	100.65	104.32	103.42	101.82
Gaoshan	102.42	102.36	102.30	100.98	102.88	102.31	103.03
Gelao	101.86	101.51	101.41	100.87	103.20	100.97	101.91
Han	101.85	101.93	102.07	100.87	102.78	102.21	102.47
Hani	102.41	106.19	102.15	101.85	104.07	102.51	101.21
Hezhe	100.79	100.35	103.65	100.91	103.34	104.33	104.43
Hui	102.00	102.45	102.12	99.74	104.36	102.71	102.51
Jing	107.90	102.80	103.52	101.41	103.05	102.14	107.51
Jingpo	102.41	106.17	102.15	101.85	104.06	102.51	101.22
Jino	102.41	106.18	102.15	101.85	104.07	102.51	101.22
Kazak	103.63	101.15	102.76	97.47	102.72	104.22	102.17
Kirgiz	103.60	101.14	102.77	97.50	102.73	104.23	102.20
Korean	100.68	101.30	102.38	102.11	104.02	102.14	102.50
Lahu	102.41	106.17	102.15	101.85	104.06	102.51	101.22
Lhoba	101.62	100.63	101.42	102.21	100.46	101.30	102.98

Li	104.72	106.68	101.74	98.83	102.33	103.10	102.37
Lisu	102.44	105.95	102.11	101.74	104.01	102.47	101.26
Manchu	100.98	102.88	102.58	101.72	103.49	102.81	102.28
Maonan	106.47	102.39	102.99	101.27	103.08	101.78	106.20
Miao	101.97	102.61	101.77	101.45	102.92	101.31	102.32
Monba	101.66	100.52	101.39	102.30	100.32	101.27	103.01
Mongol	102.30	102.63	102.49	100.77	104.19	103.23	101.78
Mulao	107.36	102.56	103.31	101.36	103.04	101.96	107.05
Naxi	102.44	105.93	102.11	101.75	104.00	102.46	101.27
Nu	102.40	106.05	102.14	101.84	103.99	102.49	101.26
Oroqen	101.67	101.33	103.11	100.78	103.82	103.89	103.14
Pumi	102.41	106.13	102.15	101.83	104.05	102.51	101.23
Qiang	103.69	98.29	100.81	98.09	102.07	100.81	102.72
Russian	103.16	101.71	102.64	98.84	103.34	103.81	102.00
Salar	98.54	108.22	104.55	98.96	105.69	106.11	104.73
She	101.84	101.83	101.76	100.43	101.44	101.69	102.82
Shui	102.09	101.68	101.51	100.91	103.22	101.06	102.09
Tajik	103.59	101.19	102.74	97.59	102.73	104.16	102.20
Tatar	103.58	101.26	102.71	97.74	102.66	104.08	102.20
Tibetan	101.51	102.05	102.03	100.50	102.08	102.34	103.31
Tu	98.76	107.84	104.35	99.20	105.46	105.76	104.57
Tujia	100.95	102.66	101.97	101.91	102.84	101.75	102.05
Uygur	103.63	101.15	102.76	97.48	102.72	104.22	102.17
Uzbek	103.63	101.18	102.75	97.53	102.72	104.19	102.20
Va	102.40	106.08	102.15	101.82	104.03	102.51	101.24
Xibe	101.30	103.25	102.80	101.27	103.45	103.43	101.98
Yao	105.28	103.05	102.87	101.81	102.56	101.67	105.66
Yi	102.70	103.48	101.70	100.70	103.42	101.87	101.71
Yugur	104.07	102.31	101.91	101.22	100.78	101.95	102.50
Zhuang	107.79	102.96	103.50	101.47	103.08	102.14	107.38

Table 4.20 Ownership of major durable consumer goods per 100 urban households at year-end (I)

Ethnic group	Motorcycle (unit)	Hand car (unit)	Automobile (unit)	Washing machine (set)	Refrigerator (set)
National average	20.27	34.47	21.54	98.02	98.48
Achang	31.58	23.80	28.97	98.04	87.46
Bai	28.22	20.70	26.38	98.07	89.23
Baonan	11.06	13.05	9.97	98.77	90.72
Blang	31.49	23.81	28.91	98.07	87.52
Buyi	6.85	3.46	13.98	99.75	97.51
Dai	31.48	23.68	28.90	98.07	87.49
Daur	16.81	19.82	17.78	96.18	95.97
Deang	31.57	23.64	28.96	98.07	87.40
Derung	28.92	24.43	26.90	97.98	89.54
Dong	16.11	12.45	15.47	98.31	97.68
Dongxiang	11.53	13.65	10.44	98.72	91.04
Ewenki	20.49	26.39	22.17	97.02	98.64
Gaoshan	22.62	39.18	19.31	97.95	97.76
Gelao	6.38	2.61	13.68	99.81	97.65
Han	20.98	35.72	20.48	98.05	98.05
Hani	31.56	23.75	28.97	98.07	87.45
Hezhe	9.57	6.50	9.18	94.30	90.32
Hui	17.11	28.92	17.74	97.72	95.15
Jing	44.49	59.21	22.09	98.19	99.77
Jingpo	31.53	23.69	28.94	98.07	87.49
Jino	31.52	23.58	28.93	98.07	87.44
Kazak	14.21	15.77	15.58	97.63	96.97
Kirgiz	14.19	15.71	15.53	97.59	96.92
Korean	10.20	7.90	13.23	96.14	94.32
Lahu	31.53	23.88	28.94	98.08	87.48
Lhoba	16.02	10.89	26.17	89.11	86.83
Li	32.70	35.82	16.00	73.54	82.35
Lisu	30.92	23.58	28.56	98.08	87.77
Manchu	10.08	18.50	17.64	95.47	97.19
Maonan	34.67	44.58	19.77	98.77	99.51
Miao	16.27	11.56	16.49	98.16	96.41
Monba	15.91	10.67	26.68	88.69	86.32
Mongol	18.43	25.37	21.36	97.02	98.73
Mulao	40.83	53.33	21.36	98.51	99.90
Naxi	30.83	23.40	28.55	98.04	87.76
Nu	31.27	23.81	28.90	97.93	87.57
Oroqen	15.05	16.70	15.57	95.66	94.52
Pumi	31.40	23.80	28.86	98.07	87.55

(*continued*)

Table 4.20 Continued

Ethnic group	Motorcycle (unit)	Hand car (unit)	Automobile (unit)	Washing machine (set)	Refrigerator (set)
Qiang	9.70	14.05	14.42	98.44	98.18
Russian	16.53	20.79	18.69	97.52	97.87
Salar	5.62	4.11	8.69	97.72	95.02
She	33.50	42.00	22.74	99.22	103.21
Shui	8.26	5.52	14.32	99.73	97.47
Tajik	14.48	16.33	15.68	97.62	97.00
Tatar	14.20	16.16	15.67	97.65	96.77
Tibetan	12.15	10.08	18.79	93.68	91.13
Tu	7.04	5.47	9.63	97.79	95.01
Tujia	17.92	11.44	14.15	97.49	98.28
Uygur	14.25	15.86	15.61	97.63	96.99
Uzbek	14.52	16.17	15.76	97.59	96.99
Va	31.32	24.24	28.80	98.08	87.76
Xibe	7.79	11.28	15.56	95.14	97.78
Yao	38.31	41.89	21.89	97.47	98.15
Yi	22.68	18.73	23.21	98.37	91.55
Yugur	11.40	13.71	10.17	98.82	90.61
Zhuang	45.46	58.43	23.18	98.24	99.30

Table 4.21 Ownership of major durable consumer goods per 100 urban households at year-end (II)

Ethnic group	Color TV set (set)	Computer (set)	Hi-Fi stereo component system (set)	Video camera (set)	Camera (set)
National average	136.07	87.03	23.63	10.00	46.42
Achang	121.22	70.06	36.18	8.54	41.32
Bai	121.03	70.74	34.07	8.20	39.55
Baonan	108.21	63.09	20.19	5.77	27.60
Blang	121.33	70.12	36.12	8.55	41.33
Buyi	117.05	72.20	28.26	6.57	30.91
Dai	121.31	70.07	36.15	8.54	41.31
Daur	107.23	63.17	11.72	8.52	31.97
Deang	121.10	69.92	36.21	8.53	41.26
Derung	121.94	71.76	33.02	8.65	40.97
Dong	121.54	76.55	26.38	6.74	33.60
Dongxiang	108.08	63.49	20.14	6.01	28.14
Ewenki	106.79	63.87	13.22	8.99	33.74
Gaoshan	132.90	83.92	22.78	8.72	42.69
Gelao	116.62	72.11	28.27	6.53	30.67

(*continued*)

Table 4.21 Continued

Ethnic group	Color TV set (set)	Computer (set)	Hi-Fi stereo component system (set)	Video camera (set)	Camera (set)
Han	134.57	84.81	23.08	9.27	44.22
Hani	121.25	70.04	36.20	8.55	41.33
Hezhe	110.55	63.90	9.33	7.79	29.62
Hui	116.42	72.19	18.23	7.97	35.56
Jing	136.12	96.52	35.48	7.56	49.73
Jingpo	121.17	70.08	36.17	8.55	41.32
Jino	121.21	70.01	36.19	8.54	41.30
Kazak	106.76	65.78	16.01	8.52	33.80
Kirgiz	106.80	65.75	15.93	8.51	33.76
Korean	114.44	73.37	13.03	9.48	36.22
Lahu	121.26	70.06	36.13	8.54	41.33
Lhoba	128.82	64.77	29.26	10.57	47.00
Li	113.83	66.31	20.19	4.34	20.50
Lisu	121.67	70.14	35.73	8.50	41.17
Manchu	114.92	75.63	16.36	10.99	38.93
Maonan	130.65	90.56	33.83	7.26	44.86
Miao	121.85	74.98	27.06	6.95	33.81
Monba	129.63	64.64	29.75	10.76	47.98
Mongol	108.99	66.55	14.45	9.32	34.97
Mulao	134.00	94.85	35.12	7.52	48.24
Naxi	121.79	70.17	35.74	8.51	41.21
Nu	121.62	70.17	35.98	8.59	41.49
Oroqen	108.60	63.78	11.14	8.38	31.58
Pumi	121.35	70.12	36.03	8.55	41.32
Qiang	137.77	74.36	21.66	6.68	35.85
Russian	108.50	66.73	15.55	8.99	35.22
Salar	106.49	57.47	12.30	4.62	24.27
She	169.53	102.41	28.59	8.98	50.00
Shui	117.52	72.82	28.59	6.60	31.51
Tajik	107.59	66.37	16.25	8.52	34.07
Tatar	107.74	66.47	16.43	8.53	34.15
Tibetan	124.45	64.67	23.41	7.99	38.10
Tu	108.43	59.51	13.79	4.87	25.61
Tujia	127.32	77.95	23.98	7.33	34.73
Uygur	106.88	65.87	16.03	8.53	33.86
Uzbek	107.31	66.29	16.26	8.55	34.12
Va	121.37	70.35	35.83	8.58	41.46
Xibe	113.34	74.85	17.14	11.50	38.82
Yao	131.77	90.64	32.07	7.72	45.57
Yi	125.29	71.43	31.25	7.80	38.59
Yugur	108.57	63.68	20.55	5.87	28.02
Zhuang	135.61	96.66	36.41	7.79	50.53

Table 4.22 Ownership of major durable consumer goods per 100 urban households at year-end (III)

Ethnic group	Piano (set)	Other medium and high grade musical instrument (unit)	Microwave oven (unit)	Air conditioner (unit)	Water heater for shower (unit)
National average	2.81	4.64	62.24	126.81	91.02
Achang	2.58	8.15	57.79	5.28	92.15
Bai	2.50	7.23	56.10	17.46	90.71
Baonan	2.17	6.06	39.45	7.32	66.42
Blang	2.58	8.13	57.87	5.99	92.16
Buyi	2.67	3.76	48.60	27.07	79.70
Dai	2.58	8.13	57.82	5.61	92.18
Daur	1.69	3.32	41.69	17.52	59.07
Deang	2.58	8.16	57.75	4.44	92.08
Derung	2.54	7.34	57.34	22.02	90.36
Dong	2.13	3.50	51.04	75.42	86.62
Dongxiang	2.23	6.17	39.27	7.71	67.88
Ewenki	1.81	3.37	42.73	20.61	62.99
Gaoshan	2.38	4.48	58.46	118.62	89.77
Gelao	2.67	3.69	48.35	26.38	79.41
Han	2.61	4.55	60.15	124.60	90.89
Hani	2.58	8.16	57.84	5.09	92.15
Hezhe	1.46	3.03	41.69	20.29	51.07
Hui	2.12	4.79	50.44	56.37	80.44
Jing	1.38	6.38	70.90	133.38	108.75
Jingpo	2.59	8.14	57.76	5.29	92.11
Jino	2.58	8.15	57.83	5.00	92.13
Kazak	2.63	6.21	41.61	13.86	79.48
Kirgiz	2.62	6.17	41.61	13.95	79.20
Korean	2.10	4.30	52.98	23.92	63.87
Lahu	2.58	8.15	57.80	5.56	92.13
Lhoba	1.13	1.81	40.86	21.87	37.69
Li	0.69	1.70	32.95	82.61	87.48
Lisu	2.55	8.00	57.76	8.39	92.22
Manchu	2.40	3.36	55.99	46.67	74.67
Maonan	1.70	5.67	65.15	105.63	101.24
Miao	2.19	3.91	52.16	68.66	87.03
Monba	1.09	1.73	40.53	20.67	35.60
Mongol	1.99	3.54	45.97	26.85	67.13
Mulao	1.53	6.09	68.90	124.87	106.13
Naxi	2.55	7.97	57.72	8.53	92.00
Nu	2.56	8.03	57.64	6.75	91.37

(*continued*)

Table 4.22 Continued

Ethnic group	Piano (set)	Other medium and high grade musical instrument (unit)	Microwave oven (unit)	Air conditioner (unit)	Water heater for shower (unit)
Oroqen	1.63	3.17	42.14	20.08	56.88
Pumi	2.58	8.11	57.82	6.07	92.08
Qiang	1.58	2.78	56.15	120.36	95.53
Russian	2.38	5.13	43.75	23.13	74.38
Salar	1.46	3.58	48.07	5.40	56.53
She	3.68	4.87	73.10	181.48	106.54
Shui	2.62	3.90	49.44	29.13	80.66
Tajik	2.61	6.14	42.22	17.59	79.86
Tatar	2.61	6.14	42.39	17.66	79.36
Tibetan	1.33	2.72	45.82	37.42	56.42
Tu	1.57	3.69	48.96	12.88	58.97
Tujia	2.05	2.97	56.76	125.27	91.92
Uygur	2.63	6.20	41.69	14.40	79.56
Uzbek	2.63	6.18	42.03	16.40	79.86
Va	2.59	8.09	57.77	8.04	92.13
Xibe	2.78	4.02	55.57	28.40	75.22
Yao	1.59	5.30	63.76	132.72	103.44
Yi	2.31	6.17	56.29	39.28	91.63
Yugur	2.20	6.14	39.51	8.95	67.03
Zhuang	1.46	6.59	71.17	131.91	109.23

Table 4.23 Ownership of major durable consumer goods per 100 urban households at year-end (IV)

Ethnic group	Disinfection cupboard (unit)	Dishwasher (unit)	Health equipment (set)	Telephone (unit)	Mobile telephone (unit)
National average	19.51	0.88	4.27	68.41	212.64
Achang	14.31	1.10	3.95	51.00	220.97
Bai	16.78	1.04	3.87	52.79	218.74
Baonan	1.93	0.52	3.16	55.24	196.71
Blang	14.24	1.10	3.95	51.06	220.93
Buyi	29.56	0.54	4.09	62.35	215.11
Dai	14.27	1.10	3.94	51.03	220.96
Daur	4.26	0.32	2.44	51.08	201.18
Deang	14.16	1.10	3.94	50.89	220.94

(continued)

Table 4.23 Continued

Ethnic group	Disinfection cupboard (unit)	Dishwasher (unit)	Health equipment (set)	Telephone (unit)	Mobile telephone (unit)
Derung	14.36	1.03	3.87	53.76	218.13
Dong	33.52	0.75	3.76	61.04	212.60
Dongxiang	2.18	0.51	3.05	56.18	196.76
Ewenki	4.86	0.32	2.77	47.33	205.34
Gaoshan	23.14	0.80	3.84	63.93	212.63
Gelao	30.02	0.54	4.09	62.45	215.16
Han	19.05	0.85	4.07	66.49	211.86
Hani	14.21	1.10	3.95	50.96	220.98
Hezhe	5.12	0.39	2.07	57.72	195.48
Hui	7.08	0.57	2.97	62.26	203.68
Jing	67.31	0.72	4.55	58.97	235.01
Jingpo	14.37	1.10	3.95	51.01	220.98
Jino	14.21	1.10	3.94	50.96	220.99
Kazak	5.42	0.33	1.37	78.26	192.26
Kirgiz	5.43	0.33	1.37	78.07	192.28
Korean	7.61	0.54	2.65	60.14	212.33
Lahu	14.18	1.10	3.95	50.97	220.92
Lhoba	7.67	1.33	3.19	67.39	189.03
Li	51.45	0.83	2.09	79.71	201.69
Lisu	14.09	1.08	3.90	51.43	220.61
Manchu	6.19	0.74	3.05	64.39	197.23
Maonan	59.07	0.66	4.46	59.79	230.41
Miao	28.36	0.81	3.68	60.51	212.96
Monba	6.86	1.35	3.21	67.59	188.22
Mongol	5.30	0.41	2.85	51.68	204.04
Mulao	65.33	0.70	4.56	59.59	233.68
Naxi	14.13	1.08	3.90	51.53	220.50
Nu	14.23	1.10	3.94	51.40	220.43
Oroqen	4.77	0.35	2.41	52.36	200.13
Pumi	14.19	1.09	3.94	51.12	220.84
Qiang	13.23	0.34	2.42	67.73	210.28
Russian	5.52	0.36	2.11	66.59	198.53
Salar	2.13	0.16	2.32	76.19	186.56
She	39.72	1.07	5.51	76.49	229.06
Shui	30.56	0.55	4.10	62.01	215.85
Tajik	6.01	0.35	1.45	77.85	192.90
Tatar	5.73	0.36	1.55	77.05	193.21
Tibetan	6.94	0.80	2.81	68.27	193.70
Tu	4.52	0.23	2.51	75.10	189.12
Tujia	22.42	0.98	3.45	61.17	206.76
Uygur	5.50	0.33	1.38	78.25	192.33

(continued)

Table 4.23 Continued

Ethnic group	Disinfection cupboard (unit)	Dishwasher (unit)	Health equipment (set)	Telephone (unit)	Mobile telephone (unit)
Uzbek	6.14	0.34	1.43	78.14	192.82
Va	14.19	1.10	3.96	51.21	220.79
Xibe	6.75	0.73	2.85	69.80	192.65
Yao	55.47	0.95	4.10	59.76	225.38
Yi	15.64	0.82	3.53	56.86	217.33
Yugur	2.19	0.53	3.24	54.38	197.48
Zhuang	67.47	0.77	4.59	58.83	235.75

Table 4.24 Per capita net income of rural households (yuan)

Ethnic group	1990	1995	2000	2005	2010	2011	2012
National average	686.31	1577.74	2253.42	3254.93	5919.01	6977.29	7916.58
Achang	543.08	1020.14	1492.68	2063.04	3985.32	4761.08	5460.00
Bai	543.34	1064.01	1543.03	2137.30	4079.75	4862.03	5568.00
Baonan	446.68	899.57	1443.12	2013.02	3502.27	4012.33	4630.80
Blang	542.15	1018.97	1495.98	2068.78	3995.13	4773.00	5473.28
Buyi	452.75	1123.81	1438.81	1973.10	3634.74	4334.23	4963.41
Dai	542.78	1019.07	1492.20	2062.84	3985.04	4760.82	5459.75
Daur	671.72	1423.80	2092.15	3101.75	5814.46	7011.71	8004.18
Deang	541.69	1014.43	1484.52	2051.15	3966.72	4739.01	5435.63
Derung	560.89	1098.75	1641.15	2301.74	4367.80	5214.96	5967.31
Dong	547.06	1282.23	1760.53	2435.63	4433.43	5226.00	5958.06
Dongxiang	460.46	911.59	1453.33	2041.48	3572.22	4095.29	4733.68
Ewenki	634.05	1300.62	2092.32	3074.01	5693.86	6841.02	7824.48
Gaoshan	682.40	1603.12	2372.79	3414.65	6171.88	7306.48	8299.37
Gelao	447.60	1115.97	1423.84	1947.22	3588.35	4280.37	4903.18
Han	709.39	1673.09	2491.84	3590.78	6439.14	7636.87	8657.82
Hani	542.78	1018.77	1491.26	2061.27	3983.14	4758.37	5456.90
Hezhe	767.38	1771.46	2211.18	3325.73	6348.72	7707.04	8736.72
Hui	620.96	1299.25	1980.70	2887.72	5285.15	6222.49	7110.66
Jing	640.02	1453.05	1892.74	2545.06	4628.90	5351.26	6137.48
Jingpo	543.00	1020.46	1491.98	2061.56	3982.42	4757.41	5455.83
Jino	542.13	1016.32	1489.06	2058.35	3978.60	4753.31	5451.40
Kazak	683.04	1136.98	1619.29	2483.31	4643.78	5443.11	6393.96
Kirgiz	684.42	1144.25	1626.22	2493.52	4664.73	5471.01	6423.52
Korean	801.36	1688.86	2161.66	3393.99	6435.69	7750.06	8831.03
Lahu	542.43	1018.82	1492.91	2064.02	3988.05	4764.43	5463.72
Lhoba	648.41	1224.60	1410.87	2178.88	4284.66	5077.31	5904.29
Li	686.71	1508.48	2156.90	2968.81	5220.90	6370.28	7317.97

(*continued*)

Table 4.24 Continued

Ethnic group	1990	1995	2000	2005	2010	2011	2012
Lisu	543.11	1023.23	1503.77	2083.93	4016.42	4799.80	5503.63
Manchu	778.64	1729.24	2368.50	3609.25	6651.98	7966.53	9029.71
Maonan	585.85	1359.79	1751.15	2355.57	4295.67	4994.32	5729.14
Miao	509.28	1166.55	1720.67	2395.71	4399.04	5217.26	5952.41
Monba	662.05	1241.20	1411.82	2189.68	4309.75	5101.39	5932.04
Mongol	650.38	1334.44	2096.86	3108.52	5749.22	6891.96	7877.74
Mulao	623.79	1434.90	1857.68	2494.13	4529.87	5245.38	6014.09
Naxi	544.38	1025.90	1505.54	2088.13	4024.66	4808.12	5513.01
Nu	546.99	1031.59	1503.47	2084.04	4020.09	4800.46	5505.05
Oroqen	699.66	1535.56	2149.65	3195.36	6015.18	7270.46	8276.03
Pumi	544.05	1023.29	1497.79	2072.17	4000.85	4779.27	5480.47
Qiang	558.89	1163.28	1908.06	2807.84	5095.44	6136.66	7010.06
Russian	675.96	1246.10	1872.39	2817.37	5224.94	6178.10	7155.14
Salar	554.33	1032.27	1510.58	2179.16	3905.82	4631.66	5383.33
She	824.94	2172.95	3244.15	4670.63	7935.46	9318.52	10,509.90
Shui	456.85	1125.26	1439.90	1970.89	3635.28	4330.27	4961.21
Tajik	681.22	1147.60	1643.32	2512.33	4690.93	5502.08	6453.91
Tatar	679.10	1157.47	1658.25	2529.81	4710.34	5517.46	6463.28
Tibetan	590.87	1131.76	1522.63	2272.21	4271.37	5079.77	5878.63
Tu	560.46	1074.86	1571.75	2249.37	4016.55	4763.20	5520.00
Tujia	518.66	1173.95	2063.06	2902.13	5335.20	6330.84	7197.42
Uygur	683.86	1140.14	1623.91	2489.83	4655.39	5457.25	6409.30
Uzbek	685.98	1152.77	1641.33	2511.06	4688.36	5495.42	6448.96
Va	543.21	1026.46	1510.96	2092.58	4033.96	4819.33	5524.90
Xibe	800.79	1640.99	2220.49	3452.70	6459.58	7728.56	8788.38
Yao	667.82	1502.80	2062.16	2799.48	5049.32	5877.84	6704.44
Yi	536.40	1068.62	1597.36	2253.08	4244.00	5083.16	5821.40
Yugur	445.72	907.47	1458.91	2033.33	3533.85	4042.21	4659.18
Zhuang	647.55	1462.66	1908.62	2555.24	4644.72	5373.48	6161.13

Table 4.25 Per capita annual net income of rural households by sources (yuan)

Ethnic group	Net income	Income from wages and salaries	Income from household operations	Income from properties	Income from transfers
National average	7916.58	3447.46	3533.37	249.05	686.70
Achang	5460.00	1471.72	3331.57	234.90	421.81
Bai	5568.00	1721.57	3193.79	211.87	440.76
Baonan	4630.80	1779.29	2203.32	115.07	533.11

(*continued*)

Table 4.25 Continued

Ethnic group	Net income	Income from wages and salaries	Income from household operations	Income from properties	Income from transfers
Blang	5473.28	1483.60	3330.94	234.88	423.85
Buyi	4963.41	2087.87	2323.94	85.92	465.68
Dai	5459.75	1474.36	3327.13	234.72	423.54
Daur	8004.18	1722.51	4862.86	410.68	1008.12
Deang	5435.63	1452.13	3328.19	234.38	420.94
Derung	5967.31	1845.12	3389.45	239.59	493.15
Dong	5958.06	2730.42	2624.06	98.31	505.26
Dongxiang	4733.68	1712.43	2353.78	119.04	548.43
Ewenki	7824.48	1682.69	4687.81	354.93	1099.05
Gaoshan	8299.37	3655.87	3697.67	262.44	683.39
Gelao	4903.18	2071.58	2286.88	81.71	463.00
Han	8657.82	4077.71	3567.62	290.96	721.53
Hani	5456.90	1469.37	3330.03	235.08	422.41
Hezhe	8736.72	2155.85	5202.93	564.23	813.71
Hui	7110.66	2895.12	3287.17	225.14	703.23
Jing	6137.48	2354.37	3226.08	74.02	483.01
Jingpo	5455.83	1472.50	3326.94	234.67	421.71
Jino	5451.40	1464.76	3328.13	235.30	423.21
Kazak	6393.96	1016.52	4231.20	171.20	975.04
Kirgiz	6423.52	1025.76	4248.27	175.38	974.11
Korean	8831.03	2296.08	5303.05	425.11	806.79
Lahu	5463.72	1474.65	3332.47	234.59	422.02
Lhoba	5904.29	1401.59	3647.74	140.00	714.96
Li	7317.97	2490.54	4082.80	171.89	572.74
Lisu	5503.63	1516.54	3323.16	232.86	431.07
Manchu	9029.71	3442.36	4484.64	327.51	775.20
Maonan	5729.14	2243.94	2944.53	67.98	472.68
Miao	5952.41	2596.00	2719.47	120.34	516.59
Monba	5932.04	1404.84	3632.69	147.05	747.45
Mongol	7877.74	1998.58	4538.00	314.46	1026.70
Mulao	6014.09	2365.60	3092.70	74.21	481.57
Naxi	5513.01	1522.22	3322.55	233.93	434.30
Nu	5505.05	1499.95	3341.05	234.33	429.72
Oroqen	8276.03	1904.67	4963.98	456.69	950.68
Pumi	5480.47	1487.23	3332.29	235.26	425.68
Qiang	7010.06	3094.58	3006.49	168.25	740.74
Russian	7155.14	1547.33	4304.36	261.17	1042.28
Salar	5383.33	1987.76	2296.02	108.11	991.44
She	10,509.90	5075.42	4402.90	356.34	675.24
Shui	4961.21	2060.30	2352.53	84.34	464.04

(continued)

Table 4.25 Continued

Ethnic group	Net income	Income from wages and salaries	Income from household operations	Income from properties	Income from transfers
Tajik	6453.91	1108.68	4204.49	174.15	966.59
Tatar	6463.28	1201.27	4117.28	183.34	961.39
Tibetan	5878.63	1890.10	3089.64	134.32	764.57
Tu	5520.00	2135.85	2312.49	118.40	953.26
Tujia	7197.42	3340.31	3154.39	119.83	582.89
Uygur	6409.30	1029.13	4233.03	171.93	975.21
Uzbek	6448.96	1085.59	4214.70	175.81	972.86
Va	5524.90	1524.34	3339.21	234.53	426.82
Xibe	8788.38	3071.92	4654.97	265.04	796.44
Yao	6704.44	2978.87	3090.22	124.25	511.11
Yi	5821.40	1981.63	3125.86	199.11	514.80
Yugur	4659.18	1829.82	2186.48	122.02	520.85
Zhuang	6161.13	2373.39	3221.60	87.77	478.36

Table 4.26 Per capita consumption expenditure of rural households (yuan) (I)

Ethnic group	Consumption expenditure	Food	Clothing	Residence	Household facilities and articles
National average	5908.02	2323.89	396.39	1086.35	341.71
Achang	4585.60	2086.85	243.04	809.23	248.59
Bai	4629.41	2093.29	248.70	827.20	255.25
Baonan	4243.89	1670.26	312.41	725.74	250.16
Blang	4592.37	2088.17	244.06	809.52	249.49
Buyi	4043.38	1794.15	234.85	780.76	219.68
Dai	4585.51	2088.17	243.21	808.15	248.82
Daur	6149.78	2298.54	502.61	989.62	259.75
Deang	4572.26	2082.44	242.34	806.85	247.78
Derung	4854.38	2134.91	279.48	856.62	263.92
Dong	4763.44	2086.48	256.16	929.82	276.75
Dongxiang	4287.93	1679.23	318.37	754.46	247.54
Ewenki	6357.35	2379.54	487.41	1059.18	271.67
Gaoshan	5979.57	2349.46	404.32	1113.94	349.45
Gelao	3999.81	1780.92	231.54	773.67	217.14
Han	6322.79	2466.76	418.29	1150.14	368.56
Hani	4584.77	2086.46	243.12	808.63	248.63
Hezhe	5893.70	2220.85	539.00	820.63	250.17
Hui	5567.47	2047.84	422.30	1080.47	315.08

(continued)

Table 4.26 Continued

Ethnic group	Consumption expenditure	Food	Clothing	Residence	Household facilities and articles
Jing	4984.01	2115.20	172.22	1176.13	276.91
Jingpo	4582.69	2085.81	242.96	809.08	248.39
Jino	4580.49	2086.30	242.95	806.85	248.39
Kazak	5301.30	1891.73	429.74	1296.99	219.51
Kirgiz	5310.53	1896.07	431.20	1293.25	219.73
Korean	6165.19	2288.65	500.76	878.45	260.96
Lahu	4586.92	2085.63	243.68	809.53	249.07
Lhoba	3228.30	1660.68	374.53	326.25	187.36
Li	4769.19	2388.08	184.06	831.70	210.27
Lisu	4607.45	2096.84	246.24	808.79	251.13
Manchu	6024.56	2231.55	498.55	1015.31	285.46
Maonan	4682.21	2009.51	182.05	1072.17	258.67
Miao	4722.29	2082.89	264.61	877.58	278.62
Monba	3182.80	1661.10	377.50	298.89	185.53
Mongol	6227.40	2326.58	478.08	1066.06	274.46
Mulao	4894.22	2088.51	176.04	1142.18	271.27
Naxi	4607.46	2097.87	247.23	807.54	251.18
Nu	4588.98	2086.56	247.28	806.59	249.21
Oroqen	6111.38	2293.28	513.56	937.10	259.75
Pumi	4597.23	2089.14	244.78	810.57	249.47
Qiang	5372.08	2510.52	338.98	791.84	333.03
Russian	5828.91	2122.85	457.16	1218.60	253.12
Salar	5232.01	1851.31	395.70	1153.69	258.26
She	7701.94	3296.02	493.66	1316.43	437.26
Shui	4054.37	1795.28	230.91	790.62	220.34
Tajik	5322.52	1908.69	428.33	1288.97	223.90
Tatar	5331.12	1915.20	428.07	1273.42	228.17
Tibetan	4180.11	1888.33	362.98	628.66	237.90
Tu	5261.35	1900.58	388.49	1134.02	263.59
Tujia	5406.12	2278.51	318.24	976.41	360.19
Uygur	5308.59	1895.16	429.98	1297.63	220.13
Uzbek	5328.76	1909.00	428.92	1296.52	222.42
Va	4617.32	2090.90	247.07	815.92	251.69
Xibe	5917.33	2233.23	502.50	1041.11	251.23
Yao	5347.81	2336.02	221.69	1134.05	306.74
Yi	4734.77	2168.29	268.40	799.65	268.32
Yugur	4244.29	1675.42	311.08	714.96	252.99
Zhuang	5012.58	2146.30	171.67	1170.86	277.30

Table 4.27 Per capita consumption expenditure of rural households (yuan) (II)

Ethnic group	Transport and communications	Education, culture and recreation	Health care and medical services	Others
National average	652.79	445.49	513.81	147.58
Achang	473.86	291.96	364.73	67.34
Bai	466.73	295.14	368.05	75.05
Baonan	454.35	323.99	405.03	101.95
Blang	474.88	293.08	365.66	67.52
Buyi	391.42	240.44	294.25	87.84
Dai	473.08	291.69	365.10	67.29
Daur	798.16	508.97	631.82	160.31
Deang	471.79	290.42	363.87	66.77
Derung	513.96	326.06	396.23	83.18
Dong	435.07	298.95	371.45	108.77
Dongxiang	461.56	320.47	404.29	102.02
Ewenki	880.16	517.19	602.13	160.06
Gaoshan	652.74	450.13	503.88	155.64
Gelao	384.16	235.34	289.82	87.22
Han	710.12	498.94	551.11	158.88
Hani	473.81	292.10	364.85	67.17
Hezhe	642.00	529.25	720.90	170.90
Hui	641.31	403.66	513.24	143.56
Jing	464.89	281.63	386.30	110.72
Jingpo	473.15	291.38	364.52	67.39
Jino	472.61	291.40	364.88	67.10
Kazak	646.16	262.44	444.42	110.30
Kirgiz	646.81	265.20	447.32	110.96
Korean	694.55	582.56	767.37	191.89
Lahu	474.13	292.27	365.25	67.35
Lhoba	388.94	76.42	119.08	95.04
Li	437.60	256.50	308.57	152.41
Lisu	474.00	293.23	369.01	68.23
Manchu	683.26	526.95	607.26	176.21
Maonan	436.51	262.65	356.91	103.75
Miao	440.87	301.38	374.49	101.86
Monba	388.71	66.68	110.01	94.39
Mongol	833.63	504.35	585.11	159.14
Mulao	456.41	274.64	375.54	109.62
Naxi	474.12	292.83	368.09	68.59
Nu	476.45	291.42	362.85	68.61
Oroqen	759.35	522.87	660.39	165.07
Pumi	475.20	293.53	366.60	67.92
Qiang	466.70	330.85	497.67	102.49

(continued)

Table 4.27 Continued

Ethnic group	Transport and communications	Education, culture and recreation	Health care and medical services	Others
Russian	749.64	378.81	515.18	133.55
Salar	655.92	292.35	504.83	119.95
She	901.94	596.08	468.87	191.68
Shui	391.88	241.71	296.15	87.48
Tajik	645.73	268.59	446.83	111.47
Tatar	645.34	277.63	450.45	112.84
Tibetan	464.24	191.69	305.76	100.55
Tu	651.18	302.37	499.36	121.76
Tujia	484.63	374.06	483.90	130.18
Uygur	646.83	263.33	444.98	110.55
Uzbek	647.75	266.65	445.90	111.60
Va	478.99	295.09	369.10	68.56
Xibe	673.06	503.35	548.21	164.64
Yao	486.67	322.73	417.06	122.85
Yi	461.32	296.31	393.33	79.15
Yugur	450.99	330.57	405.60	102.70
Zhuang	468.21	281.18	386.15	110.90

Table 4.28 Per capita cash consumption expenditure of rural households (yuan) (I)

Ethnic group	Cash consumption expenditure	Food	Clothing	Residence	Household facilities and articles
National average	5414.47	1863.11	396.14	1054.17	341.42
Achang	3764.03	1341.19	243.04	733.73	248.58
Bai	3816.45	1349.33	248.68	758.59	255.21
Baonan	3779.61	1224.22	312.22	707.87	249.99
Blang	3771.61	1342.98	244.06	734.35	249.48
Buyi	3307.54	1108.08	234.82	731.03	219.66
Dai	3762.39	1340.79	243.21	732.80	248.82
Daur	5646.62	1873.77	502.44	912.47	258.69
Deang	3748.55	1334.80	242.34	731.19	247.78
Derung	4101.22	1450.08	279.44	788.74	263.84
Dong	4000.78	1365.52	256.07	888.38	276.58
Dongxiang	3823.45	1233.11	317.97	736.94	247.09
Ewenki	5755.00	1855.16	487.35	982.15	270.80
Gaoshan	5529.63	1936.24	404.21	1077.59	349.25
Gelao	3260.97	1091.85	231.51	723.94	217.12

(*continued*)

Table 4.28 Continued

Ethnic group	Cash consumption expenditure	Food	Clothing	Residence	Household facilities and articles
Han	5864.23	2041.42	418.10	1117.39	368.32
Hani	3762.33	1339.97	243.12	733.08	248.63
Hezhe	5605.96	2017.78	538.94	737.05	249.17
Hui	5133.31	1636.87	421.89	1058.24	314.62
Jing	4229.08	1416.36	172.21	1120.09	276.90
Jingpo	3761.05	1340.08	242.96	733.59	248.39
Jino	3757.06	1338.87	242.95	731.26	248.39
Kazak	4785.00	1392.07	426.41	1287.70	215.50
Kirgiz	4796.44	1399.38	427.89	1283.16	215.74
Korean	5760.18	1965.69	500.40	797.03	260.71
Lahu	3766.10	1340.54	243.68	734.20	249.06
Lhoba	2576.33	1014.01	374.41	321.14	187.29
Li	4406.90	2078.66	184.05	778.83	210.26
Lisu	3784.94	1348.51	246.24	735.00	251.13
Manchu	5702.96	1962.39	498.47	963.19	285.28
Maonan	3926.50	1308.45	182.04	1017.54	258.66
Miao	3963.25	1367.30	264.53	834.40	278.48
Monba	2526.46	1008.19	377.41	295.58	185.51
Mongol	5658.94	1826.65	477.92	998.45	273.70
Mulao	4139.30	1389.40	176.03	1086.41	271.26
Naxi	3785.57	1349.95	247.23	733.97	251.17
Nu	3772.97	1344.90	247.27	732.65	249.20
Oroqen	5669.49	1932.78	513.52	856.70	258.81
Pumi	3777.23	1344.64	244.78	735.47	249.47
Qiang	4498.61	1655.65	338.98	773.26	333.02
Russian	5288.74	1621.46	455.21	1184.41	250.50
Salar	4682.03	1310.64	394.79	1146.09	257.48
She	7294.63	2917.86	493.42	1288.20	436.63
Shui	3314.24	1105.53	230.89	740.29	220.32
Tajik	4806.62	1410.02	425.11	1278.86	220.02
Tatar	4821.20	1422.64	424.98	1262.88	224.46
Tibetan	3501.25	1220.02	362.75	618.52	237.73
Tu	4708.06	1359.87	387.71	1122.89	262.93
Tujia	4678.98	1579.31	317.85	949.15	359.92
Uygur	4792.29	1395.55	426.65	1288.26	216.13
Uzbek	4812.76	1410.16	425.65	1286.58	218.48
Va	3804.05	1352.13	247.06	741.82	251.68
Xibe	5547.80	1910.61	501.87	995.65	250.42
Yao	4572.00	1610.54	221.65	1083.95	306.58
Yi	3907.66	1398.33	268.40	742.75	268.31
Yugur	3785.65	1235.61	310.96	696.36	252.88
Zhuang	4251.16	1443.68	171.66	1112.13	277.30

Table 4.29 Per capita cash consumption expenditure of rural households (yuan) (II)

Ethnic group	Transport and communications	Education, culture and recreation	Health care and medical services	Others
National average	652.79	445.49	513.81	147.54
Achang	473.86	291.96	364.73	66.94
Bai	466.73	295.14	368.05	74.72
Baonan	454.35	323.99	405.03	101.94
Blang	474.88	293.08	365.66	67.12
Buyi	391.42	240.44	294.25	87.83
Dai	473.08	291.69	365.10	66.89
Daur	798.16	508.97	631.82	160.30
Deang	471.79	290.42	363.87	66.37
Derung	513.96	326.06	396.23	82.86
Dong	435.07	298.95	371.45	108.76
Dongxiang	461.56	320.47	404.29	102.01
Ewenki	880.16	517.19	602.13	160.05
Gaoshan	652.74	450.13	503.88	155.58
Gelao	384.16	235.34	289.82	87.22
Han	710.12	498.94	551.11	158.84
Hani	473.81	292.10	364.85	66.77
Hezhe	642.00	529.25	720.90	170.86
Hui	641.31	403.66	513.24	143.49
Jing	464.89	281.63	386.30	110.70
Jingpo	473.15	291.38	364.52	66.99
Jino	472.61	291.40	364.88	66.70
Kazak	646.16	262.44	444.42	110.30
Kirgiz	646.81	265.20	447.32	110.96
Korean	694.55	582.56	767.37	191.88
Lahu	474.13	292.27	365.25	66.95
Lhoba	388.94	76.42	119.08	95.03
Li	437.60	256.50	308.57	152.40
Lisu	474.00	293.23	369.01	67.84
Manchu	683.26	526.95	607.26	176.16
Maonan	436.51	262.65	356.91	103.73
Miao	440.87	301.38	374.49	101.80
Monba	388.71	66.68	110.01	94.39
Mongol	833.63	504.35	585.11	159.13
Mulao	456.41	274.64	375.54	109.60
Naxi	474.12	292.83	368.09	68.20
Nu	476.45	291.42	362.85	68.22
Oroqen	759.35	522.87	660.39	165.06
Pumi	475.20	293.53	366.60	67.53

(*continued*)

Table 4.29 Continued

Ethnic group	Transport and communications	Education, culture and recreation	Health care and medical services	Others
Qiang	466.70	330.85	497.67	102.48
Russian	749.64	378.81	515.18	133.53
Salar	655.92	292.35	504.83	119.94
She	901.94	596.08	468.87	191.63
Shui	391.88	241.71	296.15	87.47
Tajik	645.73	268.59	446.83	111.46
Tatar	645.34	277.63	450.45	112.83
Tibetan	464.24	191.69	305.76	100.54
Tu	651.18	302.37	499.36	121.75
Tujia	484.63	374.06	483.90	130.15
Uygur	646.83	263.33	444.98	110.55
Uzbek	647.75	266.65	445.90	111.59
Va	478.99	295.09	369.10	68.17
Xibe	673.06	503.35	548.21	164.62
Yao	486.67	322.73	417.06	122.81
Yi	461.32	296.31	393.33	78.90
Yugur	450.99	330.57	405.60	102.69
Zhuang	468.21	281.18	386.15	110.86

Table 4.30 Per capita consumption of major foods by rural households (kg) (I)

Ethnic group	Grain	Vegetables	Edible oil	Pork, beef and mutton	Poultry
National average	164.26	84.72	7.83	16.36	4.49
Achang	178.64	96.80	5.04	26.99	5.59
Bai	176.53	98.65	5.28	25.75	5.27
Baonan	188.53	45.66	6.54	12.81	1.55
Blang	178.61	96.87	5.05	26.96	5.58
Buyi	147.72	97.04	4.91	21.20	2.34
Dai	178.65	96.97	5.04	27.02	5.59
Daur	167.71	69.74	7.91	20.29	3.47
Deang	178.90	96.85	5.03	27.04	5.58
Derung	175.62	94.67	5.58	25.04	5.27
Dong	164.51	103.48	6.13	19.76	4.38
Dongxiang	191.98	48.18	7.10	12.79	1.68
Ewenki	176.16	69.78	5.97	24.37	3.61
Gaoshan	156.75	85.79	7.51	15.35	4.84
Gelao	147.31	97.30	4.88	21.20	2.28
Han	157.45	87.94	7.95	15.94	4.85
Hani	178.73	96.88	5.04	27.01	5.58

(continued)

Table 4.30 Continued

Ethnic group	Grain	Vegetables	Edible oil	Pork, beef and mutton	Poultry
Hezhe	141.50	72.08	11.41	11.80	3.52
Hui	170.93	71.84	7.85	14.77	3.58
Jing	170.68	87.33	5.69	16.72	10.17
Jingpo	178.66	96.83	5.04	26.98	5.58
Jino	178.77	97.00	5.04	27.04	5.58
Kazak	227.28	77.08	12.82	17.40	3.00
Kirgiz	226.46	77.07	12.82	17.36	3.01
Korean	161.47	108.95	9.62	13.69	3.79
Lahu	178.64	96.81	5.04	26.95	5.57
Lhoba	266.02	21.19	7.74	20.71	0.40
Li	117.41	62.82	6.03	18.50	13.40
Lisu	178.15	97.32	5.10	26.95	5.58
Manchu	158.17	93.18	9.21	14.58	2.14
Maonan	164.43	89.74	5.40	17.79	8.16
Miao	163.86	103.85	6.05	21.04	4.24
Monba	270.62	17.77	7.74	20.93	0.31
Mongol	175.73	75.77	6.39	22.81	3.26
Mulao	168.23	88.31	5.57	17.15	9.48
Naxi	178.48	97.03	5.11	26.95	5.56
Nu	179.89	95.54	5.11	26.81	5.51
Oroqen	158.66	70.64	8.72	17.96	3.52
Pumi	178.57	96.80	5.06	26.93	5.58
Qiang	160.14	115.98	6.94	26.00	5.85
Russian	204.32	75.00	9.97	20.03	3.26
Salar	174.31	43.37	4.50	21.70	1.50
She	151.35	84.21	7.81	18.64	6.78
Shui	148.77	96.79	4.91	21.12	2.60
Tajik	225.05	77.54	12.66	17.37	3.08
Tatar	222.85	76.30	12.41	17.23	3.03
Tibetan	217.12	48.66	6.59	22.00	1.97
Tu	172.70	46.08	4.50	21.61	1.84
Tujia	167.06	116.03	8.09	19.74	4.19
Uygur	227.11	77.22	12.82	17.40	3.01
Uzbek	226.00	77.29	12.73	17.42	3.10
Va	178.23	96.62	5.10	26.71	5.55
Xibe	171.68	95.83	9.95	16.05	2.02
Yao	179.00	97.76	6.41	18.39	9.12
Yi	170.07	102.19	5.55	26.07	5.28
Yugur	187.79	45.89	6.56	12.46	1.60
Zhuang	172.14	87.61	5.63	17.36	10.36

Table 4.31 Per capita consumption of major foods by rural households (kg) (II)

Ethnic group	Eggs and processed products	Aquatic products	Sugar	Liquor
National average	5.87	5.36	1.19	10.04
Achang	2.86	1.97	0.92	8.21
Bai	2.98	2.17	0.91	8.05
Baonan	3.84	0.57	1.10	8.43
Blang	2.88	1.97	0.92	8.23
Buyi	2.46	0.92	0.72	7.89
Dai	2.86	1.95	0.92	8.22
Daur	6.39	2.79	0.94	16.71
Deang	2.84	1.91	0.92	8.20
Derung	3.59	2.54	0.99	8.79
Dong	3.23	3.17	0.85	7.54
Dongxiang	3.89	0.56	1.05	8.06
Ewenki	6.48	2.53	0.94	14.64
Gaoshan	6.47	5.91	1.06	10.49
Gelao	2.41	0.83	0.72	7.81
Han	6.56	6.34	1.19	10.68
Hani	2.86	1.94	0.92	8.22
Hezhe	6.53	4.11	1.00	22.47
Hui	5.64	2.56	1.08	7.82
Jing	2.38	4.06	0.95	8.97
Jingpo	2.86	1.95	0.92	8.21
Jino	2.85	1.93	0.92	8.23
Kazak	3.63	0.59	0.53	1.94
Kirgiz	3.66	0.64	0.53	2.15
Korean	7.71	4.35	0.81	19.17
Lahu	2.88	1.94	0.92	8.22
Lhoba	0.98	0.48	2.38	4.01
Li	2.46	19.83	0.87	7.42
Lisu	2.94	1.95	0.92	8.27
Manchu	8.51	4.46	0.83	15.60
Maonan	2.31	3.05	0.88	8.59
Miao	3.31	3.02	0.91	7.98
Monba	0.84	0.39	2.45	3.83
Mongol	6.70	2.69	0.90	13.62
Mulao	2.34	3.74	0.92	8.75
Naxi	2.91	1.96	0.93	8.25
Nu	2.87	1.98	0.94	8.19
Oroqen	6.55	3.30	0.97	18.67
Pumi	2.89	1.96	0.92	8.24
Qiang	4.87	2.59	1.17	9.50
Russian	4.93	1.60	0.71	7.01
Salar	2.00	0.65	1.19	4.41

(*continued*)

Table 4.31 Continued

Ethnic group	Eggs and processed products	Aquatic products	Sugar	Liquor
She	5.01	14.44	1.41	15.15
Shui	2.44	0.93	0.73	7.88
Tajik	3.71	0.78	0.55	2.23
Tatar	3.77	0.83	0.58	2.56
Tibetan	2.17	0.87	1.77	5.56
Tu	2.14	1.15	1.19	4.83
Tujia	4.54	5.62	1.04	9.11
Uygur	3.64	0.62	0.53	1.96
Uzbek	3.65	0.77	0.54	2.07
Va	3.00	2.00	0.92	8.27
Xibe	7.43	4.24	0.68	13.18
Yao	3.10	5.27	1.00	7.75
Yi	3.37	1.99	0.97	8.54
Yugur	3.95	0.62	1.10	8.71
Zhuang	2.35	4.19	0.96	8.76

Table 4.32 Ownership of durable consumer goods per 100 rural households at year-end (I)

Ethnic group	Washing machine (set)	Refrigerator (set)	Air conditioner (set)	Exhaust fan (set)	Bicycle (unit)	Motorcycle (unit)
National average	67.22	67.32	25.36	14.69	78.97	62.20
Achang	58.18	35.33	0.95	5.37	24.35	64.72
Bai	59.78	39.68	3.02	5.24	23.16	62.09
Baonan	79.82	36.14	0.52	5.10	71.71	72.51
Blang	58.28	35.56	1.13	5.41	24.52	64.59
Buyi	69.38	46.21	2.67	2.08	8.88	40.73
Dai	58.25	35.44	0.95	5.35	24.20	64.58
Daur	81.00	80.84	2.45	9.02	49.07	68.35
Deang	58.18	35.16	0.70	5.27	23.97	64.70
Derung	61.43	42.97	5.01	6.71	33.46	64.13
Dong	63.87	57.99	11.54	4.55	20.90	53.85
Dongxiang	79.47	37.23	0.48	5.05	72.96	72.85
Ewenki	79.93	83.22	2.88	8.68	48.64	73.13
Gaoshan	73.71	72.99	31.67	14.30	84.13	63.86
Gelao	69.44	45.98	2.18	1.76	7.64	40.32
Han	74.21	74.41	35.12	16.94	86.90	61.75
Hani	58.22	35.32	0.94	5.37	24.27	64.63
Hezhe	83.15	76.65	4.88	11.23	50.29	56.82

(*continued*)

Table 4.32 Continued

Ethnic group	Washing machine (set)	Refrigerator (set)	Air conditioner (set)	Exhaust fan (set)	Bicycle (unit)	Motorcycle (unit)
Hui	82.99	65.67	17.13	11.37	89.31	67.41
Jing	38.50	60.65	11.53	4.84	50.63	86.72
Jingpo	58.24	35.37	0.90	5.35	24.31	64.68
Jino	58.21	35.31	0.84	5.32	23.98	64.61
Kazak	77.37	68.70	1.42	5.77	66.22	79.80
Kirgiz	77.41	68.87	1.45	5.83	66.03	79.59
Korean	86.21	78.93	4.51	8.52	53.67	63.87
Lahu	58.32	35.44	1.03	5.37	24.59	64.60
Lhoba	32.03	36.12	2.51	1.28	13.12	77.82
Li	20.61	35.47	12.74	2.43	35.41	103.36
Lisu	58.75	36.42	1.32	5.37	24.77	64.07
Manchu	84.66	81.50	13.44	12.68	92.07	62.17
Maonan	46.44	56.65	8.42	3.66	38.63	74.66
Miao	64.17	55.86	10.92	4.63	19.71	52.70
Monba	30.29	34.95	2.66	1.25	12.52	78.49
Mongol	80.50	82.02	4.75	8.86	56.57	71.56
Mulao	41.74	59.37	10.81	4.62	46.36	82.33
Naxi	58.57	36.39	1.44	5.42	24.47	64.08
Nu	57.92	35.77	1.40	5.51	24.82	64.85
Oroqen	81.68	80.17	3.58	9.84	50.02	64.98
Pumi	58.39	35.69	1.14	5.42	24.69	64.58
Qiang	73.18	71.24	14.02	5.10	29.83	45.44
Russian	78.74	74.77	5.14	8.26	62.66	75.64
Salar	86.41	73.00	2.28	7.91	33.98	79.31
She	65.32	86.64	57.80	35.59	66.06	71.11
Shui	68.29	46.27	2.58	1.97	10.00	42.30
Tajik	77.02	68.84	2.34	6.01	66.40	79.24
Tatar	77.43	67.80	3.04	6.47	67.41	78.56
Tibetan	56.02	51.53	4.11	3.51	23.68	70.76
Tu	84.99	71.52	4.14	8.47	35.75	78.66
Tujia	64.07	72.54	24.69	8.97	28.80	58.58
Uygur	77.34	68.81	1.58	5.82	66.29	79.74
Uzbek	77.00	68.74	2.15	6.05	66.44	79.73
Va	58.71	36.32	1.55	5.53	26.11	64.47
Xibe	80.48	79.16	3.70	10.65	77.05	66.33
Yao	46.84	63.77	16.92	6.87	45.19	81.41
Yi	63.63	46.46	4.65	4.86	23.95	56.59
Yugur	79.65	35.08	1.07	5.31	73.65	71.98
Zhuang	38.66	59.49	11.57	5.17	50.72	87.93

Table 4.33 Ownership of durable consumer goods per 100 rural households at year-end (II)

Ethnic group	Telephone (unit)	Mobile telephone (unit)	Black and white TV set (set)	Color TV set (set)	Camera (set)	Computer (set)
National average	42.23	197.80	1.44	116.90	5.18	21.36
Achang	12.32	205.09	0.47	102.02	3.45	6.39
Bai	14.21	201.09	0.55	102.28	3.29	6.84
Baonan	29.86	192.23	1.56	106.04	2.86	11.37
Blang	12.48	205.00	0.48	102.10	3.46	6.46
Buyi	16.92	175.37	0.36	97.31	1.83	5.81
Dai	12.36	204.96	0.48	102.03	3.44	6.37
Daur	25.20	194.11	1.11	106.96	3.49	14.80
Deang	12.13	205.04	0.47	101.91	3.43	6.28
Derung	18.55	202.13	0.63	104.13	3.69	9.02
Dong	23.13	186.13	0.86	103.52	2.42	9.05
Dongxiang	29.21	188.14	1.79	105.35	2.78	11.53
Ewenki	20.19	200.34	1.15	106.59	3.40	12.89
Gaoshan	41.77	201.28	1.09	116.93	5.35	22.04
Gelao	16.64	174.80	0.34	96.83	1.75	5.55
Han	45.29	201.00	1.43	119.01	5.72	23.76
Hani	12.29	205.05	0.47	102.04	3.45	6.38
Hezhe	37.79	188.68	0.63	110.30	4.13	20.36
Hui	36.26	203.14	1.50	113.48	4.87	18.17
Jing	30.16	213.85	1.19	109.94	2.40	12.09
Jingpo	12.33	205.04	0.47	101.99	3.44	6.39
Jino	12.26	205.06	0.47	101.99	3.45	6.33
Kazak	29.90	147.52	4.18	96.96	3.43	12.47
Kirgiz	29.97	147.85	4.15	97.09	3.44	12.55
Korean	42.95	200.22	0.39	115.05	3.55	21.24
Lahu	12.35	205.02	0.47	102.06	3.45	6.42
Lhoba	50.01	137.46	1.59	107.01	1.91	2.24
Li	24.53	208.48	0.89	98.89	1.90	8.53
Lisu	12.90	204.27	0.52	102.19	3.43	6.52
Manchu	60.77	179.83	0.47	114.60	5.60	22.99
Maonan	26.43	203.39	0.95	106.11	2.12	10.12
Miao	22.63	187.04	0.80	103.15	2.63	8.86
Monba	51.12	135.42	1.63	107.62	1.92	1.82
Mongol	28.22	195.29	1.11	107.72	3.74	14.15
Mulao	29.31	210.11	1.08	108.55	2.34	11.56
Naxi	13.10	204.03	0.52	102.27	3.45	6.52
Nu	13.26	204.01	0.50	102.38	3.47	6.54

(*continued*)

Table 4.33 Continued

Ethnic group	Telephone (unit)	Mobile telephone (unit)	Black and white TV set (set)	Color TV set (set)	Camera (set)	Computer (set)
Oroqen	29.20	194.12	0.88	108.44	3.69	16.61
Pumi	12.59	204.90	0.48	102.14	3.46	6.49
Qiang	32.42	178.24	2.18	106.76	2.62	10.09
Russian	27.96	170.44	2.89	102.26	4.00	13.80
Salar	45.41	214.50	0.92	106.84	5.95	9.51
She	60.16	224.02	1.22	140.36	8.91	34.08
Shui	16.98	176.68	0.39	97.52	1.83	5.85
Tajik	30.34	149.18	4.09	97.55	3.48	12.74
Tatar	30.68	151.38	3.96	98.19	3.69	13.05
Tibetan	43.33	168.09	1.53	106.65	2.96	5.69
Tu	45.09	215.25	0.86	107.60	5.86	10.17
Tujia	33.19	195.46	1.22	109.99	3.45	14.11
Uygur	29.97	147.63	4.17	97.04	3.44	12.52
Uzbek	30.21	148.76	4.13	97.36	3.52	12.71
Va	12.92	204.81	0.49	102.26	3.47	6.76
Xibe	66.55	160.92	1.05	109.58	5.52	19.11
Yao	31.20	210.09	1.23	110.19	3.00	12.91
Yi	18.33	194.22	0.93	102.76	3.02	7.29
Yugur	29.56	192.53	1.54	106.38	2.87	11.73
Zhuang	30.27	215.45	1.14	109.72	2.51	12.17

Table 4.34 Housing conditions of rural households

Ethnic group	Per capita floor space of houses (sq.m/person)	Value of houses (yuan/sq.m)	House structures (sq.m/person)	
			Reinforced concrete structure	Brick and wood structure
National average	37.09	681.90	17.12	16.35
Achang	31.81	591.27	10.12	8.54
Bai	32.70	577.66	11.01	10.42
Baonan	24.48	545.02	4.35	10.06
Blang	31.88	590.80	10.18	8.59
Buyi	30.15	543.96	11.02	15.95
Dai	31.83	590.87	10.15	8.54
Daur	25.44	652.09	1.74	18.45

(*continued*)

Table 4.34 Continued

Ethnic group	Per capita floor space of houses (sq.m/person)	Value of houses (yuan/sq.m)	House structures (sq.m/person)	
			Reinforced concrete structure	Brick and wood structure
Deang	31.76	590.11	10.05	8.49
Derung	32.28	605.47	10.76	10.34
Dong	35.86	513.66	16.13	17.21
Dongxiang	24.49	541.31	4.21	10.24
Ewenki	25.44	579.18	1.97	17.77
Gaoshan	37.65	713.42	19.21	16.24
Gelao	29.94	540.59	10.89	16.01
Han	38.58	716.68	18.86	17.00
Hani	31.83	591.18	10.12	8.54
Hezhe	25.98	855.39	2.25	20.36
Hui	31.21	659.51	9.09	16.47
Jing	35.91	491.68	27.14	6.84
Jingpo	31.79	590.97	10.11	8.55
Jino	31.80	591.32	10.09	8.52
Kazak	27.19	487.76	2.83	14.19
Kirgiz	27.19	491.09	2.82	14.26
Korean	26.20	717.25	2.09	22.27
Lahu	31.85	590.41	10.15	8.57
Lhoba	29.44	353.11	2.13	16.74
Li	25.64	849.75	12.73	12.68
Lisu	31.99	588.51	10.27	8.76
Manchu	29.80	816.41	5.91	22.50
Maonan	34.13	497.26	22.91	9.18
Miao	35.33	526.13	15.09	16.27
Monba	29.40	354.51	1.65	16.84
Mongol	26.75	596.24	3.31	18.33
Mulao	35.17	496.58	25.58	7.75
Naxi	32.00	590.36	10.28	8.77
Nu	31.90	589.09	10.14	8.73
Oroqen	25.73	712.50	2.10	19.14
Pumi	31.86	591.71	10.16	8.61
Qiang	37.86	510.30	16.28	15.32
Russian	27.26	567.81	3.26	15.90
Salar	29.11	522.71	4.54	13.77
She	50.85	878.13	36.79	11.78
Shui	30.26	539.58	11.41	15.59
Tajik	27.53	493.91	3.35	14.26
Tatar	27.44	515.39	3.33	14.23
Tibetan	30.87	430.59	5.83	15.12

(continued)

Table 4.34 Continued

Ethnic group	Per capita floor space of houses (sq.m/person)	Value of houses (yuan/sq.m)	House structures (sq.m/person)	
			Reinforced concrete structure	Brick and wood structure
Tu	29.52	532.96	5.61	13.55
Tujia	41.85	508.17	20.66	18.06
Uygur	27.25	488.68	2.90	14.22
Uzbek	27.38	496.40	3.17	14.19
Va	31.98	590.11	10.26	8.81
Xibe	28.82	768.06	5.26	21.02
Yao	38.07	504.99	24.21	11.30
Yi	33.28	562.80	11.90	11.25
Yugur	24.44	557.48	4.52	9.99
Zhuang	35.54	498.37	26.62	6.46

Table 4.35 Electricity consumption (100 million kWh)

Ethnic group	2000	2005	2010	2011	2012
Achang	0.22	0.45	0.81	0.97	1.06
Bai	12.52	24.57	43.83	51.90	56.60
Baonan	0.20	0.33	0.57	0.66	0.72
Blang	0.60	1.22	2.19	2.63	2.87
Buyi	24.62	42.15	72.29	81.68	90.21
Dai	7.54	15.33	27.58	33.02	36.07
Daur	1.53	3.13	6.44	7.66	8.29
Deang	0.12	0.24	0.43	0.51	0.56
Derung	0.06	0.11	0.20	0.23	0.25
Dong	23.16	39.30	68.05	76.19	82.26
Dongxiang	5.99	10.00	16.97	19.78	21.85
Ewenki	0.34	0.83	1.85	2.23	2.41
Gaoshan	0.05	0.09	0.15	0.17	0.18
Gelao	4.80	8.18	14.00	15.81	17.48
Han	12,595.97	22,976.44	38,702.90	43,178.69	45,394.31
Hani	9.37	19.06	34.31	41.09	44.88
Hezhe	0.06	0.08	0.11	0.12	0.12
Hui	143.54	275.68	503.14	612.70	650.33
Jing	0.17	0.27	0.52	0.59	0.61
Jingpo	0.86	1.75	3.15	3.77	4.12
Jino	0.14	0.28	0.50	0.60	0.65
Kazak	12.42	21.04	44.86	56.84	73.83
Kirgiz	1.60	2.70	5.75	7.28	9.45

(continued)

Table 4.35 Continued

Ethnic group	2000	2005	2010	2011	2012
Korean	23.76	32.64	49.62	54.09	55.33
Lahu	2.95	6.01	10.81	12.95	14.14
Lhoba	0.00	0.01	0.03	0.03	0.04
Li	6.65	13.89	26.75	31.08	34.82
Lisu	4.13	8.39	15.07	18.02	19.67
Manchu	163.42	255.12	413.65	454.96	469.20
Maonan	0.82	1.35	2.51	2.82	2.98
Miao	69.86	118.36	205.59	232.62	251.30
Monba	0.01	0.01	0.09	0.10	0.11
Mongol	69.56	155.46	332.10	396.51	427.32
Mulao	1.58	2.61	4.91	5.49	5.75
Naxi	2.01	4.07	7.32	8.75	9.55
Nu	0.19	0.38	0.68	0.82	0.89
Oroqen	0.10	0.18	0.34	0.40	0.43
Pumi	0.22	0.45	0.80	0.96	1.05
Qiang	1.96	3.55	5.84	6.60	6.91
Russian	0.17	0.34	0.72	0.88	1.04
Salar	2.17	4.06	8.98	10.80	11.64
She	8.51	16.94	29.12	32.98	34.32
Shui	3.33	5.71	9.84	11.12	12.28
Tajik	0.41	0.69	1.46	1.85	2.39
Tatar	0.05	0.08	0.18	0.22	0.28
Tibetan	39.43	72.76	167.16	197.90	213.98
Tu	4.86	9.11	19.89	23.86	25.65
Tujia	66.35	102.74	176.57	196.36	206.03
Uygur	83.38	141.34	301.15	381.44	495.33
Uzbek	0.12	0.21	0.44	0.56	0.73
Va	2.61	5.29	9.51	11.37	12.40
Xibe	3.00	4.56	7.43	8.32	8.95
Yao	20.10	34.59	62.43	69.71	72.89
Yi	51.79	99.82	174.81	205.22	222.33
Yugur	0.16	0.27	0.45	0.52	0.57
Zhuang	120.79	202.97	384.30	431.51	450.01

5

Agricultural Production and Other Rural Activity

The data in this chapter show the basic conditions of agricultural production and rural economy, including mainly cultivated land, quantity of agricultural machinery, output of agriculture, forestry, animal husbandry and fishery, output of major products, facilities of water conservancy and efforts to eliminate water-logging and combat alkalinity, productive fixed assets owned by rural households, basic conditions of State-owned farms. Statistics on agriculture cover all agricultural production activities except horse raising for military purpose and agricultural production activities undertaken by agriculture research institutions. In other words, included in agriculture statistics are production activities in agriculture, forestry, animal husbandry and fishery undertaken by rural economic units of various types and by rural households; production activities of farms specializing in agriculture, forestry, animal husbandry and fishery; production activities in agriculture undertaken by government agencies, institutions, schools and military units; production activities in agriculture undertaken by collective farms run by townships and villages; and production activities in agriculture, forestry, animal husbandry and fishery undertaken by manufacturing and mining enterprises.

R. Guo, *China Ethnic Statistical Yearbook 2016*,
DOI 10.1007/978-3-319-49199-8_5

Data on agricultural production are provided by the Department of Rural Social and Economic Survey of the NBS using data from *The Statistical Survey System on Agriculture, Forestry, Animal Husbandry and Fishery; The Statistical Reporting System on Agricultural Output and Price* and *The Statistical Reporting System on the Basic Condition of Social and Economic Activities of Counties.*

The Statistical Survey System on Agriculture, Forestry, Animal Husbandry and Fishery is composed of three parts: (i) the sample survey conducted by the nation taking the province as the population on major farm crops such as grain and cotton, on animal husbandry such as hog, cattle, sheep and poultry, and a sample survey on 362 pig output counties taking the county as the population; (ii) the comprehensive reporting system, statistical reporting forms are used on agricultural production conditions, tropical farm crops, garden crops, agricultural facilities and other poultry; and (iii) the statistical reporting forms of forestry and fishery industries from forestry department and fishery department. *The Statistical Reporting System on the Basic Condition of Social and Economic Activities of Counties* is a special survey designed by the NBS to understand the basic conditions of social and economic activities at county, township and rural level and the energy consumption of the units engaged in agriculture, forestry, animal husbandry and fishery. Under this survey system, a complete enumeration is conducted every three years to collect information on the basic conditions of all towns, townships and villages, and a complete enumeration is conducted every year in counties administratively designated towns.

Data on fixed assets, sales of farm products of rural households are collected and compiled by the Office of Household Surveys of the NBS through the *System of Rural Household Survey.*

Table 5.1 Gross output value of agriculture, forestry, animal husbandry and fishery (100 million yuan)

Ethnic groups	Total	Farming	Forestry	Animal husbandry	Fishery
National total	89,453.05	46,940.46	3447.08	27,189.39	8706.01
Achang	2.15	1.12	0.18	0.73	0.05
Bai	115.32	60.93	8.92	38.46	3.27
Baonan	0.93	0.67	0.01	0.18	0.00
Blang	5.82	3.04	0.49	1.98	0.15
Buyi	125.67	74.52	5.00	36.89	3.51
Dai	73.42	38.29	6.13	25.00	1.81
Daur	13.97	7.37	0.51	5.62	0.23
Deang	1.14	0.59	0.10	0.39	0.03
Derung	0.49	0.25	0.04	0.16	0.02
Dong	168.57	93.63	8.13	50.06	9.37
Dongxiang	31.69	22.97	0.50	5.78	0.09
Ewenki	3.16	1.55	0.12	1.39	0.05
Gaoshan	0.34	0.17	0.02	0.10	0.03
Gelao	24.10	14.37	0.93	7.05	0.62
Han	81,384.41	42,526.42	3079.75	24,618.79	8249.57
Hani	91.20	47.57	7.63	31.01	2.25
Hezhe	0.48	0.28	0.02	0.17	0.01
Hui	713.74	419.45	20.83	213.95	32.00
Jing	1.75	0.87	0.12	0.53	0.17
Jingpo	8.37	4.37	0.70	2.84	0.21
Jino	1.32	0.69	0.11	0.45	0.03
Kazak	153.79	113.16	2.91	32.82	1.04
Kirgiz	19.78	14.52	0.38	4.25	0.14
Korean	182.99	88.79	6.76	75.51	6.82
Lahu	28.76	15.01	2.40	9.78	0.71
Lhoba	0.14	0.07	0.00	0.07	0.00
Li	171.41	73.47	21.53	34.25	36.86
Lisu	40.31	21.01	3.30	13.80	1.01
Manchu	984.28	448.96	30.42	378.99	91.75
Maonan	7.28	3.73	0.47	2.21	0.61
Miao	504.04	279.26	25.97	152.99	25.57
Monba	0.41	0.19	0.01	0.20	0.00
Mongol	579.08	279.67	21.67	249.08	17.38
Mulao	15.25	7.66	1.02	4.65	1.40
Naxi	19.55	10.19	1.60	6.70	0.48
Nu	1.82	0.95	0.15	0.62	0.05
Oroqen	0.86	0.45	0.03	0.34	0.02
Pumi	2.13	1.11	0.18	0.73	0.05
Qiang	20.17	10.28	0.57	8.38	0.62

(continued)

Table 5.1 Continued

Ethnic groups	Total	Farming	Forestry	Animal husbandry	Fishery
Russian	1.75	1.12	0.05	0.51	0.02
Salar	5.98	2.97	0.11	2.72	0.02
She	51.87	22.72	3.97	9.96	13.56
Shui	17.74	10.43	0.75	5.23	0.54
Tajik	4.97	3.64	0.10	1.07	0.04
Tatar	0.58	0.42	0.01	0.12	0.01
Tibetan	289.57	142.63	6.95	128.79	3.46
Tu	13.53	6.65	0.28	6.06	0.17
Tujia	524.82	287.78	19.84	155.25	41.61
Uygur	1032.53	759.20	19.61	220.60	7.21
Uzbek	1.51	1.11	0.03	0.32	0.01
Va	25.24	13.17	2.07	8.56	0.68
Xibe	19.10	9.08	0.56	6.77	2.05
Yao	198.84	101.09	12.91	60.44	17.10
Yi	478.67	250.64	30.56	171.90	12.66
Yugur	0.77	0.55	0.01	0.14	0.00
Zhuang	1254.99	621.48	88.49	385.06	118.14

Table 5.2 Indices of gross output value of agriculture, forestry, animal husbandry and fishery (preceding year = 100)

Ethnic group	Total	Farming	Forestry	Animal husbandry	Fishery
National average	104.91	104.40	106.68	105.22	105.15
Achang	107.01	105.38	109.96	107.79	113.98
Bai	106.94	105.74	109.40	107.28	114.27
Baonan	106.34	106.89	103.61	104.43	108.96
Blang	107.00	105.37	109.94	107.78	114.01
Buyi	109.10	111.55	107.14	105.26	122.36
Dai	107.00	105.38	109.98	107.78	113.97
Daur	106.06	105.74	106.56	106.51	105.10
Deang	107.02	105.39	110.00	107.81	114.10
Derung	106.66	105.37	109.25	107.23	112.81
Dong	106.86	107.79	106.70	105.00	115.33
Dongxiang	106.46	106.94	103.69	104.82	103.21
Ewenki	105.75	105.71	105.86	105.82	104.10
Gaoshan	104.92	104.59	108.82	104.59	107.30
Gelao	109.18	111.73	107.16	105.23	122.68
Han	104.75	104.19	107.22	104.86	106.99
Hani	107.01	105.38	109.96	107.80	114.00

(*continued*)

Table 5.2 Continued

Ethnic group	Total	Farming	Forestry	Animal husbandry	Fishery
Hezhe	106.44	105.48	109.04	107.32	107.85
Hui	105.60	105.14	109.15	105.34	121.00
Jing	105.79	106.04	108.73	104.55	106.21
Jingpo	107.01	105.40	109.97	107.79	114.00
Jino	107.01	105.38	110.00	107.79	114.03
Kazak	107.44	106.77	107.68	109.79	104.14
Kirgiz	107.43	106.76	107.67	109.78	104.13
Korean	105.80	104.96	105.76	106.53	104.98
Lahu	107.00	105.37	109.94	107.79	113.97
Lhoba	103.84	103.34	103.02	104.53	99.02
Li	106.38	105.40	106.81	106.81	107.47
Lisu	106.94	105.36	109.90	107.68	113.78
Manchu	104.99	105.40	108.54	104.26	104.77
Maonan	106.75	107.71	108.27	104.67	110.68
Miao	106.92	107.57	107.28	105.28	115.93
Monba	103.63	103.07	102.92	104.38	98.11
Mongol	105.60	105.73	106.08	105.46	106.76
Mulao	106.14	106.72	108.55	104.51	107.92
Naxi	106.92	105.35	109.97	107.66	113.73
Nu	106.93	105.33	109.81	107.71	113.68
Oroqen	106.09	105.62	107.14	106.59	105.68
Pumi	106.99	105.37	109.97	107.77	113.96
Qiang	104.57	104.73	108.37	103.82	106.94
Russian	106.61	106.12	108.53	107.86	104.63
Salar	105.59	105.78	109.29	104.88	249.70
She	104.06	103.60	103.13	104.28	105.90
Shui	109.02	111.38	107.23	105.30	121.88
Tajik	107.35	106.69	107.66	109.62	104.27
Tatar	107.28	106.62	108.24	109.35	104.50
Tibetan	104.52	104.35	105.57	104.43	136.99
Tu	105.57	105.78	108.73	104.77	240.42
Tujia	105.24	104.58	107.25	105.31	112.12
Uygur	107.43	106.75	107.68	109.78	104.11
Uzbek	107.38	106.70	107.87	109.68	104.12
Va	106.95	105.34	109.85	107.74	113.82
Xibe	105.46	106.47	106.88	104.64	104.69
Yao	104.99	104.60	107.67	104.59	106.36
Yi	106.58	105.91	109.20	106.41	112.99
Yugur	106.34	106.88	103.89	104.32	104.02
Zhuang	105.75	105.88	108.79	104.62	106.12

Table 5.3 Major agricultural machinery at year-end

Ethnic group	Total power of agricultural machinery (10,000 kw)	Large and medium-sized agricultural tractors: Number (unit)	Large and medium-sized agricultural tractors: Towing farm machinery (unit)	Small tractors: Number (unit)	Small tractors: Towing farm machinery (unit)	Diesel engines: Number (unit)
National total	102,558.96	4,852,400	7,635,200	17,972,300	30,806,220	9,823,100
Achang	2.05	10	16	139	151	76
Bai	100.51	1915	2777	7305	8761	4746
Baonan	1.93	38	49	239	278	266
Blang	5.42	28	43	363	392	193
Buyi	49.56	3586	1685	5323	5832	15,087
Dai	67.92	316	478	4498	4817	2401
Daur	28.29	895	1669	7695	13,513	1376
Deang	1.06	5	8	70	75	37
Derung	0.50	8	12	52	73	24
Dong	94.17	10,191	13,656	10,047	16,172	14,701
Dongxiang	55.16	1286	846	7246	7876	8168
Ewenki	5.73	163	292	1398	2289	270
Gaoshan	0.38	17	27	67	112	31
Gelao	8.74	680	278	920	944	2939
Han	90,934.09	4,076,392	6,596,113	16,278,643	28,329,558	9,055,881
Hani	84.53	395	598	5595	5995	2974
Hezhe	1.24	40	91	392	748	64
Hui	1136.73	50,540	61,756	230,771	293,284	65,126
Jing	1.25	27	22	75	79	121
Jingpo	7.78	38	57	518	557	279
Jino	1.23	6	9	81	86	43
Kazak	194.56	18,074	3093	25,123	21,752	13,858
Kirgiz	25.24	2319	427	3350	3055	1786
Korean	240.39	12,510	20,515	54,185	97,479	16,880

Lahu	26.56	126	192	1764	1900	934
Lhoba	2.05	354	619	348	658	16
Li	1638.39	33,238	63,606	22,7036	303,385	163,652
Lisu	36.32	183	273	2398	2569	1279
Manchu	779.09	51,412	80,846	184,566	322,304	40,451
Maonan	4.15	108	46	194	130	513
Miao	383.90	26,025	35,286	41,246	60,212	48,730
Monba	6.42	1112	1950	1091	2065	46
Mongol	893.74	29,847	47,270	199,827	317,333	41,799
Mulao	9.18	208	103	409	277	985
Naxi	18.57	247	411	1326	1553	634
Nu	1.97	62	107	164	220	62
Oroqen	1.85	57	120	536	975	91
Pumi	1.99	12	19	136	150	71
Qiang	2.52	75	106	144	226	183
Russian	2.52	165	84	439	571	154
Salar	44.49	1799	3049	3615	5479	1225
She	37.37	2176	4457	7749	15,767	1851
Shui	7.16	468	194	697	710	2042
Tajik	6.32	579	108	823	735	452
Tatar	0.75	66	13	98	89	55
Tibetan	2422.54	340,098	595,782	360,003	662,314	33,548
Tu	96.52	3818	6578	7885	11,982	2777
Tujia	428.73	30,315	42,248	36,673	53,893	70,192
Uygur	1304.42	121,337	21,044	168,643	146,431	92,788
Uzbek	1.94	177	33	251	222	139
Va	23.02	119	182	1561	1713	822

(continued)

Table 5.3 Continued

Ethnic group	Total power of agricultural machinery (10,000 kw)	Large and medium-sized agricultural tractors		Small tractors		Diesel engines
		Number (unit)	Towing farm machinery (unit)	Number (unit)	Towing farm machinery (unit)	Number (unit)
Xibe	11.96	768	603	2391	3408	639
Yao	137.69	8211	11,620	10,712	15,327	11,839
Yi	309.88	2880	3201	21,098	23,367	15,475
Yugur	1.44	20	25	189	216	223
Zhuang	853.08	15,502	9288	42,535	34,035	78,375

Table 5.4 Original value of productive fixed assets of rural households at year-end (yuan/household)

Ethnic group	Total original value	Agriculture	Industry	Construction	Transport, postal and tele-communication services
National average	16,974.09	11,406.20	1109.48	361.18	2283.42
Achang	18,968.58	14,341.50	239.36	79.83	3732.60
Bai	17,532.01	13,021.22	245.05	106.75	3471.18
Baonan	20,156.81	13,816.39	137.90	83.68	2571.77
Blang	18,955.75	14,326.74	243.53	81.55	3724.88
Buyi	12,198.27	8080.81	189.92	196.35	2512.25
Dai	18,948.38	14,332.02	234.49	79.48	3726.35
Daur	29,797.02	26,089.63	193.09	244.60	1884.01
Deang	19,009.96	14,391.55	227.92	79.20	3743.63
Derung	18,794.01	14,100.77	339.63	133.84	3426.43
Dong	11,099.50	7207.24	283.48	227.77	2223.66
Dongxiang	21,207.58	14,882.41	226.59	179.87	2529.07
Ewenki	28,897.84	25,257.07	148.35	245.05	1995.36
Gaoshan	15,213.18	10,188.29	887.42	291.49	2170.96
Gelao	12,015.33	7964.03	153.41	195.44	2492.87
Han	15,284.69	9757.43	1235.37	329.64	2103.70
Hani	18,978.98	14,351.97	237.64	79.72	3737.21
Hezhe	29,766.14	26,065.97	234.40	116.01	1593.40
Hui	20,570.22	14,263.88	755.76	379.53	3066.78
Jing	12,054.17	9016.06	297.71	242.25	1686.18
Jingpo	18,949.75	14,329.73	234.18	80.20	3730.46
Jino	18,974.43	14,361.59	229.60	79.11	3734.68
Kazak	34,996.79	29,010.99	1284.99	1428.67	2311.99
Kirgiz	34,983.75	29,022.81	1277.61	1417.68	2303.50
Korean	25,661.57	21,680.38	309.03	376.08	1738.25
Lahu	18,965.95	14,337.88	240.06	80.17	3730.91
Lhoba	49,576.46	40,738.28	113.49	1497.99	5966.87
Li	11,446.22	8778.72	396.07	49.14	827.23
Lisu	18,851.42	14,242.07	245.27	80.98	3671.75
Manchu	23,797.48	17,197.08	1065.16	479.76	3005.35
Maonan	11,894.02	8641.35	237.62	230.16	1874.70
Miao	12,211.38	8265.02	278.44	216.85	2352.91
Monba	50,972.68	41,985.74	76.70	1540.55	6117.72
Mongol	27,342.91	23,027.85	337.66	330.18	2266.86
Mulao	11,863.13	8732.49	288.54	242.83	1738.98
Naxi	18,973.55	14,342.99	246.30	87.65	3684.51
Nu	19,438.67	14,715.06	259.23	105.39	3757.74

(continued)

Table 5.4 Continued

Ethnic group	Total original value	Agriculture	Industry	Construction	Transport, postal and tele-communication services
Oroqen	29,427.69	25,751.61	184.23	178.17	1806.42
Pumi	18,976.33	14,345.51	242.42	82.15	3720.45
Qiang	13,785.68	10,218.05	316.79	109.56	1428.95
Russian	31,530.89	26,329.19	891.31	938.31	2233.27
Salar	22,049.75	15,788.92	148.51	262.50	3358.22
She	14,154.91	6816.54	2291.67	330.82	2475.17
Shui	12,245.79	8183.86	177.33	195.19	2502.69
Tajik	34,308.67	28,374.43	1268.24	1391.02	2295.86
Tatar	33,695.13	27,695.98	1246.23	1334.58	2320.56
Tibetan	33,579.04	26,670.59	130.78	801.91	4202.10
Tu	21,124.12	14,945.22	179.31	233.33	3290.05
Tujia	10,810.17	7198.59	373.03	294.98	1888.85
Uygur	34,942.32	28,961.69	1286.68	1427.09	2309.87
Uzbek	34,588.71	28,624.59	1282.68	1408.94	2303.32
Va	18,901.42	14,263.82	259.19	84.26	3689.14
Xibe	26,849.13	20,043.89	1015.46	714.58	3309.34
Yao	11,354.99	7993.84	344.46	251.91	1855.90
Yi	16,774.15	12,506.83	247.91	100.39	2959.19
Yugur	19,818.11	13,478.50	137.35	63.39	2546.32
Zhuang	12,281.22	9209.56	292.51	239.24	1756.36

Table 5.5 Original value of productive fixed assets of rural households at year-end (yuan/household)

Ethnic group	Wholesale and retail trades and catering services	Social services	Education, culture, and health care	Others
National average	1279.80	261.14	121.18	151.69
Achang	413.96	16.29	60.63	84.41
Bai	479.61	40.88	79.72	87.59
Baonan	2834.27	259.41	166.34	287.04
Blang	416.64	16.89	60.83	84.69
Buyi	831.67	62.80	214.99	109.48
Dai	414.84	17.01	60.58	83.61
Daur	962.27	121.35	107.33	194.74
Deang	408.65	14.84	60.19	83.99

(continued)

Table 5.5 Continued

Ethnic group	Wholesale and retail trades and catering services	Social services	Education, culture, and health care	Others
Derung	563.71	60.48	71.81	97.33
Dong	748.09	133.39	161.74	114.12
Dongxiang	2711.10	253.60	170.27	254.67
Ewenki	868.85	92.48	83.91	206.77
Gaoshan	1191.07	235.18	129.05	119.72
Gelao	824.66	58.98	216.81	109.12
Han	1310.62	279.65	121.48	146.80
Hani	412.05	15.83	60.49	84.08
Hezhe	1239.43	194.02	148.77	174.15
Hui	1599.01	208.55	106.32	190.39
Jing	476.39	85.73	64.24	185.62
Jingpo	413.38	16.43	60.90	84.47
Jino	410.28	15.50	60.26	83.42
Kazak	606.53	122.85	163.60	67.17
Kirgiz	607.60	123.27	163.49	67.79
Korean	1179.39	180.83	119.62	77.99
Lahu	414.86	16.59	60.89	84.60
Lhoba	1037.36	79.21	13.18	130.08
Li	1221.68	86.49	63.66	23.24
Lisu	440.44	25.44	62.16	83.30
Manchu	1490.18	342.18	128.80	88.98
Maonan	559.26	76.22	106.10	168.61
Miao	730.63	112.83	151.13	103.57
Monba	1041.20	76.36	4.41	129.99
Mongol	968.85	135.74	91.13	184.64
Mulao	513.11	85.76	81.67	179.75
Naxi	441.90	25.58	62.06	82.55
Nu	433.78	20.63	60.90	85.94
Oroqen	1054.95	144.59	116.40	191.31
Pumi	421.91	18.54	60.85	84.50
Qiang	1261.51	310.48	106.62	33.71
Russian	763.39	123.86	129.32	122.25
Salar	1625.06	129.84	55.79	680.92
She	1560.59	387.66	187.77	104.69
Shui	808.03	59.09	207.92	111.68
Tajik	621.78	126.17	161.62	69.54
Tatar	725.12	134.11	161.15	77.40
Tibetan	1326.21	150.68	48.65	248.13
Tu	1631.13	138.21	59.77	647.10
Tujia	704.63	165.18	105.98	78.93

(continued)

Table 5.5 Continued

Ethnic group	Wholesale and retail trades and catering services	Social services	Education, culture, and health care	Others
Uygur	603.65	123.17	163.38	66.80
Uzbek	614.40	125.06	162.05	67.66
Va	432.85	21.22	62.47	88.47
Xibe	1286.32	299.66	122.11	57.77
Yao	542.99	144.84	70.66	150.40
Yi	693.99	102.40	90.68	72.76
Yugur	2883.62	266.20	168.82	273.91
Zhuang	458.66	84.62	58.45	181.82

Table 5.6 Number of major productive fixed assets per 100 rural households at year-end

Ethnic group	Motor vehicles (set)	Large and medium tractors (set)	Mini and walking tractors (set)	Motorized threshing machines (set)	Carts with rubber tires (set)	Pumps (unit)	Draught animals (unit)	Commodity animals (unit)
National average	4.04	4.40	20.49	11.49	4.31	25.46	26.36	86.13
Achang	4.36	3.20	14.49	18.08	1.89	20.42	56.29	78.88
Bai	4.20	2.81	12.46	17.92	1.75	20.08	52.49	71.84
Baonan	3.79	5.32	32.48	14.75	11.27	15.51	47.11	91.85
Blang	4.36	3.20	14.50	18.09	1.89	20.45	56.19	78.76
Buyi	3.83	1.32	2.13	16.84	0.63	11.35	50.88	49.41
Dai	4.36	3.19	14.44	18.17	1.88	20.47	56.25	78.68
Daur	4.32	15.77	48.20	6.71	9.08	33.17	28.82	211.60
Deang	4.37	3.22	14.55	18.12	1.91	20.37	56.56	79.29
Derung	4.31	3.65	15.81	16.58	2.72	21.68	49.83	83.71
Dong	3.29	1.17	4.79	17.93	1.37	18.91	36.64	39.66
Dongxiang	3.75	5.95	32.14	13.95	13.10	15.45	48.33	118.17
Ewenki	4.82	12.59	48.23	8.42	10.73	36.54	36.38	252.11
Gaoshan	3.73	3.99	20.05	11.94	3.90	27.92	18.84	64.53
Gelao	3.81	1.27	1.77	16.90	0.58	11.05	51.19	48.59
Han	3.74	3.89	18.44	11.44	3.73	26.83	15.37	56.03
Hani	4.37	3.20	14.50	18.10	1.89	20.41	56.36	78.79
Hezhe	3.17	21.77	47.16	3.92	2.32	27.78	7.84	79.97
Hui	4.80	6.47	30.20	8.77	6.21	22.89	27.71	113.24
Jing	2.07	2.15	19.04	26.95	3.90	30.43	38.25	42.07
Jingpo	4.36	3.20	14.49	18.08	1.90	20.39	56.29	78.77

(*continued*)

Table 5.6 Continued

Ethnic group	Motor vehicles (set)	Large and medium tractors (set)	Mini and walking tractors (set)	Motorized threshing machines (set)	Carts with rubber tires (set)	Pumps (unit)	Draught animals (unit)	Commodity animals (unit)
Jino	4.37	3.21	14.49	18.14	1.88	20.39	56.40	78.85
Kazak	4.61	13.12	36.60	2.50	31.76	10.22	62.60	483.12
Kirgiz	4.60	13.24	36.73	2.48	31.50	10.41	62.05	479.83
Korean	4.07	14.66	43.88	6.26	5.81	31.42	18.31	120.99
Lahu	4.37	3.21	14.55	18.08	1.89	20.49	56.21	78.69
Lhoba	11.71	6.94	53.79	13.00	7.40	1.69	351.70	738.44
Li	0.69	0.40	3.47	4.20	1.10	23.52	22.24	155.82
Lisu	4.34	3.15	14.23	18.40	1.87	20.90	55.38	78.21
Manchu	5.16	9.01	25.28	4.90	8.73	31.57	19.09	99.62
Maonan	2.50	1.87	14.50	24.64	3.05	25.34	42.16	42.77
Miao	3.47	1.36	5.19	17.79	1.27	18.72	38.91	46.71
Monba	12.04	6.99	55.52	13.18	7.35	1.00	366.37	766.19
Mongol	4.97	10.76	42.33	8.32	11.11	35.11	35.52	230.83
Mulao	2.22	1.99	17.13	26.09	3.59	28.31	39.56	41.30
Naxi	4.37	3.16	14.34	18.38	1.89	20.72	56.72	81.03
Nu	4.48	3.26	15.13	17.96	2.00	20.15	60.57	89.07
Oroqen	4.00	17.30	47.77	6.09	6.54	32.44	21.78	164.96
Pumi	4.36	3.22	14.58	18.09	1.91	20.52	56.15	79.10
Qiang	3.02	0.91	2.97	29.90	0.95	36.59	24.66	54.25
Russian	4.73	12.09	39.44	5.02	22.49	20.42	50.88	375.21
Salar	6.45	4.68	49.27	9.95	4.17	6.56	36.71	170.85
She	3.81	1.42	4.63	10.69	1.49	13.05	11.43	62.91
Shui	3.78	1.37	2.83	17.22	0.74	12.00	50.86	49.40
Tajik	4.57	12.81	35.94	2.87	30.81	10.78	61.12	468.90
Tatar	4.56	12.47	35.68	3.22	29.86	10.92	60.14	451.70
Tibetan	8.14	4.85	40.33	16.69	5.04	11.68	190.22	415.69
Tu	6.22	4.33	46.55	10.53	3.61	7.53	35.57	153.56
Tujia	3.04	1.17	6.96	14.97	1.75	24.45	22.20	35.62
Uygur	4.61	13.10	36.52	2.51	31.69	10.29	62.44	482.20
Uzbek	4.58	12.92	36.14	2.69	31.24	10.45	61.80	475.52
Va	4.36	3.22	14.62	17.96	1.94	20.81	55.29	78.24
Xibe	5.01	9.19	20.55	4.71	15.71	30.99	30.91	168.14
Yao	2.39	1.65	14.03	23.42	3.25	28.55	30.81	37.15
Yi	3.93	2.36	9.93	21.24	1.48	23.88	47.00	68.66
Yugur	3.68	5.25	31.64	14.97	11.14	15.98	46.38	82.86
Zhuang	2.12	2.17	19.14	26.83	3.94	30.19	38.91	42.91

Table 5.7 Output of major farm products per hectare (kg/hectare) (I)

Ethnic group	Cereals	Cotton	Peanuts	Rapeseeds	Sesame
National average	5823.69	1458.15	3598.46	1884.77	1463.16
Achang	4550.33	1641.94	1557.20	1900.90	894.57
Bai	4680.98	1527.27	1672.11	1840.11	970.43
Baonan	4320.26	1622.78	3975.10	1944.13	33.28
Blang	4558.55	1639.74	1562.15	1904.34	896.13
Buyi	4541.55	730.79	1950.43	1580.52	1185.25
Dai	4553.54	1641.12	1556.84	1903.70	894.92
Daur	5647.12	1017.46	2405.21	1651.17	1081.08
Deang	4543.27	1647.29	1548.93	1902.78	889.91
Derung	4775.34	1542.17	1829.55	1872.44	976.25
Dong	5185.22	957.38	2233.39	1498.83	1303.98
Dongxiang	4467.49	1704.86	4168.62	1933.62	86.76
Ewenki	5449.97	1340.37	2062.25	1273.18	958.00
Gaoshan	5786.09	1079.88	3214.51	1671.20	1373.22
Gelao	4524.88	710.29	1940.51	1570.98	1185.63
Han	5835.92	1072.54	3198.27	1842.64	1389.86
Hani	4550.12	1645.27	1554.32	1903.56	893.95
Hezhe	6086.15	223.28	2888.83	2347.26	1416.77
Hui	5392.28	993.20	3009.18	1966.97	918.31
Jing	5245.65	1008.62	2678.95	1060.22	1270.42
Jingpo	4550.21	1640.45	1558.23	1899.67	894.85
Jino	4549.87	1644.95	1549.36	1900.13	892.73
Kazak	6063.80	2053.76	4887.88	1876.71	737.54
Kirgiz	6067.72	2035.22	4868.07	1882.11	746.55
Korean	7107.65	1458.71	3192.86	878.57	1797.73
Lahu	4555.08	1642.98	1563.53	1905.66	895.95
Lhoba	5623.85	96.88	2098.47	2552.02	115.20
Li	4751.71	44.88	2645.04	93.95	1159.51
Lisu	4584.62	1624.00	1585.21	1914.73	905.90
Manchu	6296.56	1435.98	3209.78	1665.01	1823.57
Maonan	5037.96	910.61	2485.94	1176.97	1252.45
Miao	5131.56	998.56	2121.19	1589.51	1241.66
Monba	5638.08	59.56	2055.55	2599.60	58.82
Mongol	5602.97	1454.71	2316.77	1321.83	1108.24
Mulao	5171.15	948.47	2611.15	1096.41	1268.79
Naxi	4588.40	1618.01	1582.59	1913.97	901.37
Nu	4580.16	1616.05	1578.94	1912.60	886.19
Oroqen	5770.66	776.76	2482.40	1836.89	1198.06
Pumi	4562.47	1638.62	1569.31	1904.53	897.41
Qiang	5739.51	914.37	2475.89	2252.22	1288.17
Russian	5816.93	1762.95	3738.15	1616.84	847.50
Salar	3960.01	280.97	691.42	2110.72	46.84
She	6036.92	973.83	2668.89	1529.49	1307.34

(continued)

Table 5.7 Continued

Ethnic group	Cereals	Cotton	Peanuts	Rapeseeds	Sesame
Shui	4552.02	751.67	1964.45	1569.15	1183.73
Tajik	6053.37	2017.12	4823.73	1870.88	757.29
Tatar	5985.51	1997.41	4780.14	1863.38	731.30
Tibetan	5151.10	403.20	1894.86	2368.21	338.31
Tu	4015.38	310.43	790.53	2081.74	111.19
Tujia	5924.29	1062.55	2482.09	1701.47	1414.51
Uygur	6068.07	2050.95	4883.13	1875.89	742.37
Uzbek	6056.80	2031.33	4851.07	1862.50	747.90
Va	4585.69	1628.60	1604.19	1910.64	907.83
Xibe	6461.68	1762.87	3499.23	1902.75	1871.06
Yao	5511.04	1091.15	2570.19	1224.27	1305.44
Yi	4876.64	1339.59	1853.91	1963.11	1035.79
Yugur	4328.99	1654.56	4061.75	1930.06	42.32
Zhuang	5220.11	1017.24	2636.86	1077.58	1251.11

Table 5.8 Output of major farm products per hectare (kg/hectare) (II)

Ethnic group	Jute and ambary hemp	Sugarcane	Beetroots	Flue-cured tobacco
National average	3898.72	68,600.30	49,792.75	2111.65
Achang	1956.16	61,430.43	16,459.08	2109.59
Bai	1904.93	60,270.62	14,035.16	2058.64
Baonan	7.92	182.82	47,584.35	3098.48
Blang	1951.23	61,301.16	16,417.73	2109.61
Buyi	853.29	58,787.40	4534.68	1589.33
Dai	1952.47	61,395.15	16,485.94	2110.82
Daur	48.07	690.94	38,727.39	3630.92
Deang	1948.15	61,409.64	16,556.10	2111.46
Derung	1829.49	54,158.56	17,857.99	2200.51
Dong	1668.65	57,596.16	2538.45	1797.14
Dongxiang	4.29	131.23	50,885.34	3131.67
Ewenki	73.07	1553.90	37,317.51	4151.82
Gaoshan	2652.88	44,535.85	11,861.69	2137.76
Gelao	820.57	59,001.19	4223.54	1583.67
Han	2133.63	38,592.82	14,044.72	2148.88
Hani	1949.26	61,435.17	16,478.40	2110.67
Hezhe	127.11	2158.37	35,542.29	2545.76
Hui	1184.44	17,319.86	28,799.29	2661.08
Jing	2322.09	68,122.25	792.52	1831.81
Jingpo	1949.38	61,389.22	16,461.45	2111.47

(*continued*)

Table 5.8 Continued

Ethnic group	Jute and ambary hemp	Sugarcane	Beetroots	Flue-cured tobacco
Jino	1946.67	61,395.81	16,491.19	2110.62
Kazak	1.94	52.02	69,687.75	2084.88
Kirgiz	4.26	92.36	69,382.07	2089.44
Korean	104.03	1607.05	34,078.76	2631.99
Lahu	1958.62	61,384.77	16,446.96	2112.44
Lhoba	131.96	3608.92	1440.19	172.67
Li	6451.51	66,172.90	293.43	853.97
Lisu	1957.19	60,658.83	16,700.81	2113.24
Manchu	512.62	1254.14	43,415.19	2555.64
Maonan	1875.50	66,223.83	1361.38	1756.90
Miao	1671.13	56,145.29	4535.30	1828.72
Monba	68.06	2023.27	704.96	83.78
Mongol	236.02	3260.22	37,909.78	3778.05
Mulao	2119.92	67,879.09	760.18	1797.31
Naxi	1949.65	60,575.41	16,524.77	2099.55
Nu	1924.01	60,321.59	16,235.68	2076.90
Oroqen	92.46	1468.20	36,850.40	3372.46
Pumi	1947.53	61,107.60	16,525.92	2111.38
Qiang	2233.51	41,408.61	20,320.38	2177.97
Russian	99.00	2093.60	54,423.23	2814.02
Salar	29.05	573.03	8153.93	469.77
She	3175.78	60,286.77	406.27	1588.42
Shui	885.72	59,231.45	4544.04	1603.14
Tajik	73.50	1340.98	67,755.57	2088.19
Tatar	65.08	1247.49	66,609.26	2109.49
Tibetan	591.88	11,549.46	9396.04	853.39
Tu	165.77	4784.84	7651.24	603.13
Tujia	2235.85	47,096.41	1560.65	1956.20
Uygur	12.39	233.85	69,486.81	2083.11
Uzbek	53.33	1092.08	68,466.99	2077.82
Va	1965.72	60,623.28	16,443.03	2118.75
Xibe	46.03	827.87	52,689.57	2662.88
Yao	2469.82	65,035.72	1354.52	1982.55
Yi	1903.49	55,563.51	16,214.06	2072.10
Yugur	23.57	570.99	48,248.96	3193.39
Zhuang	2313.32	69,159.42	1322.01	1860.28

Table 5.9 Per capita output of major farm products (kg)

Ethnic group	Grain	Cotton	Oil-bearing crops	Pork, beef and mutton	Total aquatic products	Milk
National average	436.50	5.06	25.44	47.43	43.74	27.72
Achang	376.52	0.04	13.66	66.40	9.38	11.65
Bai	374.70	0.35	16.22	64.66	10.73	9.95
Baonan	427.41	8.42	27.44	33.25	0.86	18.03
Blang	376.83	0.06	13.73	66.34	9.28	11.61
Buyi	311.54	0.10	24.59	49.70	6.42	2.09
Dai	376.64	0.03	13.74	66.44	9.09	11.59
Daur	1130.74	6.81	38.02	69.83	9.30	265.41
Deang	377.03	0.14	13.65	66.51	8.81	11.69
Derung	404.48	1.45	16.44	63.64	15.29	22.64
Dong	351.82	1.38	25.76	55.51	22.73	1.83
Dongxiang	446.35	20.10	26.29	33.94	1.22	20.52
Ewenki	1025.34	0.53	51.62	80.24	8.41	328.69
Gaoshan	450.08	3.33	29.43	52.20	49.22	32.52
Gelao	309.25	0.05	24.74	49.48	5.79	1.66
Han	448.09	3.72	26.61	47.74	44.31	26.71
Hani	376.82	0.04	13.65	66.42	9.07	11.61
Hezhe	1363.09	0.97	9.09	47.83	14.88	131.01
Hui	483.82	15.52	31.28	46.42	20.65	63.78
Jing	321.69	0.19	12.54	57.06	62.57	2.89
Jingpo	376.57	0.06	13.70	66.35	9.20	11.67
Jino	377.18	0.01	13.64	66.47	8.88	11.59
Kazak	572.44	158.70	26.58	51.42	5.50	59.37
Kirgiz	581.55	157.36	26.41	51.45	5.65	60.52
Korean	1118.34	0.52	24.09	60.33	22.92	49.64
Lahu	377.36	0.05	13.79	66.40	9.14	11.67
Lhoba	319.26	1.88	20.97	78.81	3.55	77.81
Li	231.13	0.03	12.43	57.94	185.13	0.56
Lisu	378.14	0.06	14.31	66.46	9.27	11.74
Manchu	648.57	1.96	24.85	58.35	61.45	62.10
Maonan	314.18	0.04	15.67	54.94	47.33	2.06
Miao	355.68	1.20	24.41	56.51	19.65	3.23
Monba	311.65	0.24	20.78	79.96	1.51	80.72
Mongol	884.39	4.53	48.59	76.52	19.29	264.49
Mulao	313.65	0.07	13.63	55.77	56.79	2.24
Naxi	376.99	0.07	14.27	66.45	9.19	11.90
Nu	375.53	0.15	13.83	66.40	9.58	12.78
Oroqen	1199.67	0.48	30.30	64.16	12.43	231.19
Pumi	378.14	0.09	13.84	66.33	9.28	11.85
Qiang	410.30	0.33	35.46	67.83	15.01	9.11

(*continued*)

Table 5.9 Continued

Ethnic group	Grain	Cotton	Oil-bearing crops	Pork, beef and mutton	Total aquatic products	Milk
Russian	712.04	91.43	35.95	61.56	8.19	156.84
Salar	223.30	6.12	55.69	49.20	1.46	44.61
She	210.33	0.61	11.01	40.15	122.52	3.70
Shui	313.27	0.16	24.08	50.19	7.72	2.09
Tajik	568.43	153.50	26.47	51.36	6.77	58.28
Tatar	560.65	146.89	26.38	50.46	6.62	56.98
Tibetan	320.48	0.50	32.75	67.69	4.35	51.19
Tu	226.47	2.36	53.23	48.61	4.55	41.75
Tujia	399.44	4.15	33.52	58.99	35.02	2.44
Uygur	572.34	158.38	26.58	51.46	5.68	59.34
Uzbek	567.44	155.88	26.38	51.32	6.70	58.72
Va	378.95	0.15	14.19	66.13	10.03	12.01
Xibe	554.08	29.27	26.57	60.38	79.27	45.02
Yao	344.64	1.07	17.18	58.76	52.58	2.60
Yi	379.36	0.10	20.96	64.96	10.29	9.90
Yugur	433.51	6.51	26.27	32.50	1.23	17.62
Zhuang	316.39	0.08	11.88	57.21	61.56	2.90

Table 5.10 Per capita major farm products sold by rural households (kg)

Ethnic group	Grain	Cotton	Oil-bearing crops	Tobacco	Vegetables	Fruits
National average	529.75	22.98	18.52	4.80	164.13	71.04
Achang	107.93	0.19	6.02	35.93	275.59	42.05
Bai	110.89	2.27	6.76	31.50	237.49	40.63
Baonan	305.49	29.97	26.25	0.08	190.50	67.51
Blang	108.85	0.25	6.05	35.82	274.99	41.93
Buyi	59.59	0.37	8.24	14.22	71.18	8.46
Dai	107.15	0.14	6.07	35.88	274.70	41.94
Daur	1873.60	16.29	73.97	0.90	202.45	12.37
Deang	107.65	0.38	6.04	36.09	275.65	41.91
Derung	221.18	4.53	10.50	29.59	259.90	47.65
Dong	118.55	9.66	9.36	10.72	75.74	34.06
Dongxiang	364.57	56.83	28.56	0.07	203.38	76.27
Ewenki	1305.95	1.55	103.05	0.45	227.98	6.32
Gaoshan	546.02	11.70	18.31	5.70	171.44	69.14
Gelao	53.83	0.21	8.21	14.05	67.39	7.17

(continued)

Table 5.10 Continued

Ethnic group	Grain	Cotton	Oil-bearing crops	Tobacco	Vegetables	Fruits
Han	556.04	17.57	17.03	4.43	171.97	72.61
Hani	108.12	0.17	6.00	36.01	275.43	41.88
Hezhe	3096.50	2.99	8.48	2.05	131.11	10.76
Hui	558.83	42.19	24.37	4.02	217.95	62.39
Jing	147.54	0.71	3.85	4.36	149.27	56.68
Jingpo	108.62	0.25	6.05	35.89	275.03	42.01
Jino	108.83	0.09	6.03	36.01	275.07	41.82
Kazak	1007.05	371.20	66.02	0.01	297.09	154.29
Kirgiz	1030.94	368.04	65.55	0.03	295.69	152.95
Korean	2607.62	1.86	36.10	1.03	154.19	24.27
Lahu	109.33	0.23	6.07	35.91	275.39	41.92
Lhoba	110.69	4.81	5.72	0.69	15.49	8.58
Li	55.91	0.14	9.14	0.73	266.37	102.45
Lisu	109.11	0.27	6.49	35.13	271.87	42.34
Manchu	1444.07	9.21	24.53	2.17	265.79	101.25
Maonan	112.45	0.20	4.80	6.52	124.66	42.29
Miao	115.20	8.13	9.49	13.84	104.84	33.58
Monba	84.42	0.67	5.10	0.21	7.90	5.39
Mongol	1162.13	11.53	89.56	1.10	238.47	29.74
Mulao	126.93	0.37	4.08	4.83	137.72	50.53
Naxi	107.74	0.24	6.43	35.00	269.86	42.18
Nu	110.23	0.52	6.07	35.12	270.62	41.89
Oroqen	2216.32	1.65	55.48	1.26	181.73	9.52
Pumi	113.23	0.34	6.19	35.67	274.20	42.03
Qiang	101.24	0.50	21.61	7.13	131.73	50.39
Russian	1046.06	214.47	77.38	0.34	265.28	96.24
Salar	143.79	15.69	44.71	0.08	85.64	14.35
She	145.21	2.35	3.62	8.78	158.44	136.89
Shui	62.10	0.44	8.03	14.26	75.23	9.49
Tajik	991.14	359.28	64.28	0.16	292.73	151.26
Tatar	962.91	344.33	62.49	0.19	288.14	147.21
Tibetan	105.77	2.07	18.91	2.56	67.93	20.32
Tu	132.70	7.30	41.55	0.86	88.78	15.39
Tujia	237.15	34.66	22.45	8.09	106.15	61.90
Uygur	1006.77	370.47	65.89	0.03	296.73	154.12
Uzbek	993.13	364.67	64.99	0.08	294.66	152.88
Va	116.87	0.71	6.39	35.25	275.79	42.49
Xibe	1330.73	68.80	32.77	2.70	315.99	135.33
Yao	147.02	6.98	5.50	7.08	132.86	59.05
Yi	101.85	0.22	10.60	25.55	212.31	40.38
Yugur	307.69	25.81	24.92	0.11	192.82	68.58
Zhuang	134.71	0.33	3.59	5.64	158.59	56.36

Table 5.11 Sales of livestock, poultry, small animals and fishery per capita rural household (kg)

Ethnic group	Pork	Mutton	Beef	Poultry	Poultry eggs	Milk	Aquatic products
National average	30.74	3.32	3.34	8.09	10.13	9.32	9.71
Achang	37.40	0.57	1.78	2.37	2.68	17.62	2.06
Bai	35.70	0.56	1.70	2.38	2.47	14.49	2.46
Baonan	9.94	5.22	5.69	1.23	5.93	2.20	0.05
Blang	37.40	0.57	1.78	2.39	2.76	17.52	2.06
Buyi	22.85	0.62	1.83	2.74	0.94	0.44	0.99
Dai	37.47	0.56	1.78	2.32	2.66	17.56	2.04
Daur	18.02	28.21	13.95	3.15	4.60	99.33	1.23
Deang	37.35	0.58	1.80	2.26	2.64	17.70	1.94
Derung	36.20	2.05	2.48	3.97	4.78	18.89	3.09
Dong	26.98	0.51	1.33	3.22	1.55	0.11	5.01
Dongxiang	9.75	6.38	6.41	1.48	6.36	2.93	0.04
Ewenki	15.04	39.40	16.03	2.68	5.45	131.73	0.93
Gaoshan	37.34	2.95	3.14	8.54	10.38	8.08	10.42
Gelao	22.41	0.60	1.82	2.67	0.78	0.13	0.90
Han	34.07	2.23	2.41	9.96	11.60	6.88	11.41
Hani	37.40	0.56	1.78	2.34	2.69	17.63	2.00
Hezhe	28.16	2.58	8.23	4.88	3.13	31.78	3.09
Hui	22.93	7.19	7.31	6.54	8.56	26.32	3.60
Jing	26.59	0.52	1.37	7.55	2.12	0.60	8.81
Jingpo	37.35	0.57	1.78	2.36	2.66	17.60	2.02
Jino	37.44	0.56	1.79	2.29	2.67	17.64	1.98
Kazak	4.81	22.46	16.75	4.27	9.32	10.94	0.01
Kirgiz	5.05	22.32	16.69	4.28	9.26	11.30	0.05
Korean	52.37	3.04	8.54	11.72	18.12	10.75	1.98
Lahu	37.44	0.57	1.77	2.37	2.72	17.58	2.01
Lhoba	3.59	5.11	11.34	0.73	1.05	5.63	0.80
Li	32.91	0.49	1.29	15.92	0.38	0.09	42.42
Lisu	37.79	0.58	1.81	2.41	2.73	17.17	2.17
Manchu	54.42	4.88	8.46	17.44	28.30	13.97	3.72
Maonan	25.04	0.52	1.49	6.26	1.50	0.08	6.45
Miao	28.95	0.59	1.48	3.37	2.98	2.19	4.96
Monba	2.39	5.13	11.62	0.56	0.60	5.83	0.47
Mongol	23.50	32.65	14.51	5.89	10.61	104.83	1.42
Mulao	25.91	0.50	1.40	7.13	1.75	0.11	8.01
Naxi	37.66	0.59	1.85	2.35	2.69	17.11	2.18
Nu	36.87	0.66	1.93	2.39	2.74	17.34	2.09
Oroqen	21.74	20.99	12.16	3.91	4.49	82.06	1.97
Pumi	37.40	0.59	1.80	2.39	2.75	17.54	2.07
Qiang	51.54	0.62	2.59	4.01	2.38	0.27	8.63

(continued)

Table 5.11 Continued

Ethnic group	Pork	Mutton	Beef	Poultry	Poultry eggs	Milk	Aquatic products
Russian	10.04	27.77	15.73	4.24	8.42	55.60	0.72
Salar	3.65	10.27	9.75	0.52	1.18	7.94	0.16
She	44.71	0.52	0.57	6.40	4.52	0.82	25.04
Shui	22.82	0.61	1.81	2.81	1.03	0.61	1.15
Tajik	5.72	21.79	16.27	4.46	9.37	10.83	0.36
Tatar	6.04	21.04	15.81	4.43	9.26	10.66	0.38
Tibetan	15.14	5.06	8.58	1.24	1.35	5.02	2.18
Tu	5.84	9.30	8.95	0.85	1.33	7.75	1.19
Tujia	30.98	0.63	1.04	3.84	8.70	0.15	16.37
Uygur	4.94	22.41	16.72	4.30	9.34	10.95	0.06
Uzbek	5.31	22.10	16.48	4.38	9.25	10.90	0.33
Va	37.45	0.61	1.78	2.74	2.91	17.30	2.11
Xibe	61.28	6.72	11.09	21.73	31.99	6.51	4.64
Yao	30.14	0.42	1.07	6.03	1.71	1.34	9.51
Yi	39.66	0.59	2.01	2.82	2.39	10.90	3.69
Yugur	10.37	4.86	5.39	1.35	6.12	2.46	0.13
Zhuang	27.26	0.48	1.35	7.50	1.87	1.33	9.01

Table 5.12 Price indices for means of agricultural production by category (preceding year = 100) (I)

Ethnic group	General index	Farm handtools	Forage	Commodity animals	Semi-mechanized farm tools	Mechanized farm machinery
National average	105.56	104.38	105.66	104.58	102.07	102.07
Achang	104.58	101.66	105.01	106.25	101.21	101.06
Bai	104.07	102.75	103.87	105.19	100.79	100.80
Baonan	105.27	102.84	103.92	134.93	100.88	100.39
Blang	104.32	101.40	104.74	105.98	100.94	100.80
Buyi	100.76	113.32	98.07	94.04	97.09	99.41
Dai	104.54	101.63	104.95	106.21	101.15	101.01
Daur	104.84	100.15	103.18	112.26	100.96	101.24
Deang	104.59	101.64	105.01	106.31	101.20	101.05
Derung	102.32	99.89	102.57	104.01	98.97	98.90
Dong	102.25	108.40	100.32	98.99	99.31	100.18
Dongxiang	105.27	102.96	104.21	133.27	100.86	100.54
Ewenki	104.14	99.64	102.79	112.53	101.53	101.52
Gaoshan	99.24	98.86	99.97	97.16	97.04	96.07
Gelao	100.52	113.44	97.75	93.66	96.84	99.23

(*continued*)

Table 5.12 Continued

Ethnic group	General index	Farm handtools	Forage	Commodity animals	Semi-mechanized farm tools	Mechanized farm machinery
Han	99.14	98.08	99.03	99.25	96.24	95.97
Hani	104.53	101.61	104.95	106.21	101.15	101.00
Hezhe	104.86	100.11	102.37	109.96	98.43	99.35
Hui	101.08	98.57	101.03	107.99	97.34	97.38
Jing	103.68	103.70	110.14	92.32	100.90	101.15
Jingpo	104.58	101.70	105.00	106.24	101.20	101.06
Jino	104.40	101.48	104.82	106.09	101.02	100.88
Kazak	106.15	101.49	107.68	109.57	101.18	101.55
Kirgiz	106.16	101.50	107.66	109.54	101.18	101.55
Korean	104.85	102.34	104.78	105.86	98.43	100.23
Lahu	104.52	101.59	104.95	106.19	101.15	100.99
Lhoba	100.78	101.15	98.05	101.94	100.41	102.21
Li	104.05	101.90	103.53	102.51	102.44	101.02
Lisu	104.60	101.78	104.96	106.28	101.19	101.06
Manchu	103.90	102.33	103.07	104.14	99.40	99.90
Maonan	102.92	106.61	107.10	92.32	99.87	100.74
Miao	96.77	101.94	94.95	94.39	93.87	94.65
Monba	100.39	100.53	97.56	101.88	100.17	102.02
Mongol	104.30	100.59	103.27	110.92	101.40	101.39
Mulao	103.31	104.85	108.92	92.07	100.42	100.92
Naxi	104.44	101.65	104.79	106.09	101.05	100.92
Nu	104.52	101.66	104.90	106.13	101.19	101.07
Oroqen	104.96	100.33	103.02	111.65	100.42	100.88
Pumi	104.55	101.64	104.97	106.23	101.17	101.02
Qiang	104.44	105.39	102.89	105.70	100.07	100.30
Russian	103.31	98.97	103.71	108.41	99.43	99.61
Salar	107.67	97.99	104.76	127.70	102.55	99.55
She	103.55	106.72	105.81	94.02	103.11	101.40
Shui	100.95	113.03	98.58	94.13	97.29	99.54
Tajik	105.51	100.98	107.00	108.82	100.62	100.97
Tatar	105.01	100.55	106.36	109.35	100.16	100.47
Tibetan	104.02	101.82	101.55	111.52	101.41	101.59
Tu	107.44	98.52	104.65	126.56	102.48	99.67
Tujia	85.87	86.38	83.60	88.13	83.60	83.05
Uygur	106.10	101.45	107.63	109.45	101.15	101.51
Uzbek	105.86	101.27	107.39	109.14	100.96	101.30
Va	104.23	101.31	104.64	105.87	100.85	100.70
Xibe	105.57	104.24	105.38	104.81	100.20	100.80
Yao	104.06	102.72	107.18	98.77	101.58	101.31
Yi	104.11	104.02	103.63	104.72	100.42	100.66
Yugur	104.78	102.65	103.49	134.64	100.45	100.05
Zhuang	103.89	103.40	110.35	93.00	101.09	101.27

Table 5.13 Price indices for means of agricultural production by category (preceding year = 100) (II)

Ethnic group	Chemical fertilizer	Pesticide and its appliances	Oil for farm machinery	Other means of agricultural production	Service for agricultural production
National average	106.64	102.43	104.17	105.93	108.28
Achang	106.40	101.74	103.72	102.69	106.02
Bai	106.19	102.01	103.45	102.35	105.50
Baonan	103.40	105.96	101.90	102.86	101.58
Blang	106.12	101.47	103.45	102.42	105.75
Buyi	105.46	105.93	100.84	98.10	103.15
Dai	106.34	101.69	103.67	102.64	106.00
Daur	105.61	106.08	101.22	106.45	104.53
Deang	106.40	101.73	103.71	102.68	106.01
Derung	103.97	99.78	101.35	100.91	103.73
Dong	105.68	104.03	102.85	101.39	103.87
Dongxiang	103.61	105.81	101.90	103.37	101.45
Ewenki	104.99	109.05	100.88	104.08	102.22
Gaoshan	100.30	97.30	98.30	100.12	101.84
Gelao	105.31	105.89	100.62	97.82	102.89
Han	99.96	96.43	98.07	99.38	101.91
Hani	106.34	101.68	103.66	102.63	105.96
Hezhe	105.41	98.94	100.58	109.63	108.54
Hui	101.22	98.29	99.13	100.26	101.90
Jing	104.63	103.25	105.69	105.20	106.58
Jingpo	106.40	101.75	103.71	102.69	106.01
Jino	106.21	101.56	103.53	102.50	105.85
Kazak	107.54	100.65	103.19	107.97	105.33
Kirgiz	107.56	100.66	103.19	108.03	105.40
Korean	105.69	103.56	101.46	103.57	111.70
Lahu	106.33	101.67	103.66	102.63	105.95
Lhoba	99.90	99.17	104.50	98.60	100.27
Li	105.40	103.07	102.45	104.63	109.53
Lisu	106.36	101.76	103.77	102.71	106.21
Manchu	104.96	101.36	101.29	106.91	105.35
Maonan	104.95	104.24	104.55	103.35	105.58
Miao	99.90	98.07	97.06	95.64	98.42
Monba	99.30	98.72	104.34	98.11	99.80
Mongol	105.24	107.78	101.37	104.35	103.08
Mulao	104.71	103.64	105.21	104.43	106.04
Naxi	106.18	101.61	103.62	102.55	106.03
Nu	106.27	101.69	103.73	102.63	105.95
Oroqen	105.66	104.40	101.18	107.45	105.78

(*continued*)

Table 5.13 Continued

Ethnic group	Chemical fertilizer	Pesticide and its appliances	Oil for farm machinery	Other means of agricultural production	Service for agricultural production
Pumi	106.35	101.70	103.69	102.67	106.02
Qiang	104.57	101.95	104.86	102.91	111.94
Russian	104.46	101.98	100.40	104.23	102.18
Salar	107.00	99.93	104.86	100.54	112.95
She	104.83	101.49	102.40	102.52	110.02
Shui	105.53	105.91	101.10	98.42	103.31
Tajik	106.89	100.12	102.63	107.30	104.80
Tatar	106.25	99.88	102.11	106.62	104.18
Tibetan	103.28	100.84	105.12	100.70	106.54
Tu	106.86	100.26	104.73	100.64	112.47
Tujia	88.07	84.02	85.96	85.61	86.30
Uygur	107.50	100.61	103.15	107.93	105.30
Uzbek	107.25	100.44	102.95	107.67	105.11
Va	106.03	101.38	103.38	102.37	105.66
Xibe	107.02	101.48	102.91	109.39	105.57
Yao	105.38	102.49	105.49	105.46	105.94
Yi	105.78	102.27	103.70	102.23	107.33
Yugur	102.86	105.81	101.41	102.55	100.80
Zhuang	104.83	103.23	105.83	105.38	106.60

Table 5.14 Producer price indices for farm products

Ethnic group	General index	Planting products	Forestry products	Animal husbandry	Fishery products
National average	102.74	104.80	101.23	99.73	106.18
Achang	110.64	113.55	92.27	104.61	100.78
Bai	109.18	111.97	94.32	103.76	101.81
Baonan	105.77	106.41	3.99	106.23	103.98
Blang	110.60	113.50	92.29	104.58	100.77
Buyi	104.31	106.23	103.42	102.65	107.97
Dai	110.63	113.54	92.33	104.61	100.79
Daur	105.02	105.75	93.67	103.20	104.69
Deang	110.68	113.58	92.15	104.65	100.70
Derung	109.19	111.86	93.61	103.72	101.74
Dong	102.56	105.32	103.39	99.55	106.05
Dongxiang	105.62	106.13	11.09	106.09	107.23
Ewenki	104.78	105.56	93.29	104.22	106.61
Gaoshan	103.16	105.46	101.03	98.97	105.82

(*continued*)

Table 5.14 Continued

Ethnic group	General index	Planting products	Forestry products	Animal husbandry	Fishery products
Gelao	104.25	106.15	103.61	102.68	108.10
Han	103.35	105.33	100.71	98.98	106.30
Hani	110.66	113.56	92.28	104.63	100.78
Hezhe	105.65	106.90	94.29	100.36	101.11
Hui	104.39	104.97	61.12	102.55	99.00
Jing	99.98	107.21	99.43	93.33	98.57
Jingpo	110.63	113.53	92.31	104.61	100.80
Jino	110.67	113.57	92.26	104.64	100.76
Kazak	103.21	100.29	99.06	105.05	101.17
Kirgiz	103.23	100.34	99.26	105.00	101.18
Korean	105.28	107.53	104.52	98.83	108.45
Lahu	110.63	113.53	92.32	104.61	100.79
Lhoba	9.59	9.71	9.28	9.31	9.67
Li	103.30	108.88	79.87	99.27	107.27
Lisu	110.46	113.38	92.62	104.52	100.90
Manchu	104.95	107.38	107.29	100.86	109.64
Maonan	100.89	106.84	100.57	95.62	100.89
Miao	103.85	106.37	102.11	100.76	105.93
Monba	5.13	5.23	4.81	4.93	5.12
Mongol	104.79	105.75	95.26	103.84	106.07
Mulao	100.20	106.98	100.06	94.12	99.41
Naxi	110.03	112.94	92.27	104.12	100.51
Nu	109.00	111.86	91.06	103.07	99.38
Oroqen	105.21	106.23	94.20	102.27	104.05
Pumi	110.55	113.44	92.29	104.54	100.75
Qiang	104.02	107.57	104.32	101.14	105.23
Russian	103.68	102.41	96.46	104.36	103.29
Salar	107.48	104.32	5.19	110.47	17.62
She	103.29	105.39	105.37	96.54	106.83
Shui	104.26	106.37	103.17	102.40	107.60
Tajik	103.19	100.45	99.10	104.82	101.29
Tatar	103.35	100.77	95.13	104.90	101.42
Tibetan	58.56	58.79	27.80	58.43	37.14
Tu	107.42	104.72	9.50	109.85	23.65
Tujia	102.69	104.43	104.77	99.33	107.36
Uygur	103.19	100.28	99.31	105.00	101.19
Uzbek	103.18	100.39	99.11	104.89	101.24
Va	110.47	113.35	92.50	104.49	100.90
Xibe	105.75	107.39	108.77	102.82	110.35
Yao	100.83	106.50	100.33	94.91	100.50
Yi	108.10	111.08	96.87	103.44	102.83
Yugur	105.82	106.68	4.19	106.10	107.24
Zhuang	100.37	107.59	98.93	93.62	98.25

6

Education, Science and Technological Progress

Data in this chapter show the development of China's education and the basic conditions on China's scientific and technological development.

Data on education cover the situations on education funded by government and non-government agencies, and the education with and without academic credentials including higher education (education of postgraduates, general higher education and adult education), secondary education (senior and junior high schools), elementary education (primary schools), preschool education, special education (schools for the blind, deaf-mutes and mentally retarded) and their expenditure. The main indicators include the number of schools, the number of students enrolled, the number of new students enrolled, the number of graduates, the number of staff and workers, the number of full-time teachers, sources and outlay of education funding, and education expenditure from the State budget.

The Ministry of Education provides statistical data on education undertakings and education funding. Data on technical training schools are provided by Ministry of Human Resources and Social Security. Detailed information can be found in "Statistical Yearbook on China's Education" compiled by Department of Planning and Development, Ministry of

R. Guo, *China Ethnic Statistical Yearbook 2016*,
DOI 10.1007/978-3-319-49199-8_6

Education; and the "Statistical Yearbook on National Education Funding" compiled by the Department of Finance, Ministry of Education.

Data on technology mainly include: data on scientific and technological activities (R&D) all over the country, including industrial enterprises, scientific and technological institutions under the government and institutions of higher education, data on domestic and foreign patents application accepted and granted, data on production, research and development activities of high-tech enterprises, data on scientific and technological papers; data on import and export trade of high-technological products; data on technological markets; main economic indicators of high and new-tech industrial enterprises in development zones; data on the scientific and technological activities in the system of associations for science and technology; data on operation institutions and activities of the polytechnic departments of meteorology, earthquake, surveying and mapping, product quality supervision, inspection and quarantine.

Data on research and development (R&D) activities of enterprises and institutions all over the country mainly include industrial enterprises above designated size, scientific research and technological development institutions and scientific and technological information and literature institutions of prefecture level and above cities under the government with independent accounting, full-time universities and colleges, affiliated hospitals and relatively R&D-intensive industries (such as agriculture, forestry, animal husbandry, fishery, construction, transport, storage and post, information transmission, software and information technology service, financial intermediation, leasing and business services, scientific research and technical services, management of water conservancy, environment and public facilities, health and social service, culture, sports and entertainment).

Data on the general national information and R&D activities of enterprises and institutions are from National Bureau of Statistics; data on scientific and technological institutions under the government are from Ministry of Science and Technology, and State Administration of Science, Technology and Industry for National Defense; data on R&D of scientific research and technical service enterprises and institutions, scientific and technological papers, technological markets information and high and new-tech industrial enterprises in development zones are from Ministry of Science and Technology; data on scientific and technological activities in institutions of higher education are from Ministry of Education; data on import and export trade of high-technological products are from General Administration of Customs; The China Association for Science and Technology provides data on the scientific and technological activities of associations for science and technology. Data on the development of surveying and mapping, meteorology, earthquake, product quality supervision and inspection and quarantine are provided separately by the State Bureau of Surveying, Mapping and Geoinformation, China Meteorological Administration, China Earthquake Administration, General Administration of Quality Supervision, Inspection and Quarantine, and State Intellectual Property Office.

Data on the Internet development come from China Telecom, China Mobile, and China Unicom.

Table 6.1 Number of students in undergraduate or specialized courses in institutions of higher education

Ethnic group	Entrants	Enrollment	Anticipated graduates for next year	Graduates with degrees or diplomas
National total	6,888,336	23,913,155	6,517,623	6,247,338
Achang	115	413	105	96
Bai	6589	23,196	5926	5496
Baonan	84	277	71	66
Blang	313	1121	285	261
Buyi	10,768	33,365	8279	7504
Dai	3935	14,106	3579	3282
Daur	652	2374	656	651
Deang	61	218	55	51
Derung	28	100	26	24
Dong	12,407	40,447	10,628	10,158
Dongxiang	2597	8655	2225	2068
Ewenki	144	530	149	143
Gaoshan	24	84	23	22
Gelao	2092	6454	1597	1445
Han	6,404,929	22,260,407	6,078,518	5,834,703
Hani	4882	17,511	4443	4076
Hezhe	26	92	25	26
Hui	51,528	175,941	46,426	43,723

(continued)

Table 6.1 Continued

Ethnic group	Entrants	Enrollment	Anticipated graduates for next year	Graduates with degrees or diplomas
Jing	100	328	91	84
Jingpo	449	1608	408	374
Jino	71	254	64	59
Kazak	5141	18,228	4863	4382
Kirgiz	663	2352	628	567
Korean	11,599	41,295	10,732	10,755
Lahu	1541	5525	1403	1287
Lhoba	12	39	10	10
Li	8001	27,071	7170	6570
Lisu	2172	7774	1977	1811
Manchu	63,702	227,189	61,062	59,032
Maonan	447	1442	391	359
Miao	37,635	123,589	32,044	30,258
Monba	35	118	29	30
Mongol	28,332	103,150	28,766	27,275
Mulao	898	2923	804	742
Naxi	1060	3790	963	883
Nu	98	352	89	82
Oroqen	42	152	42	42
Pumi	115	411	104	96
Qiang	1358	4561	1218	1070
Russian	71	254	69	64
Salar	353	1180	310	284
She	4074	14,116	3867	3645
Shui	1475	4588	1144	1037
Tajik	171	605	161	146
Tatar	21	73	20	18
Tibetan	21,311	71,302	18,242	17,518
Tu	844	2816	740	679
Tujia	43,840	147,592	38,756	37,397
Uygur	34,577	122,603	32,721	29,495
Uzbek	51	182	49	44
Va	1363	4881	1242	1142
Xibe	1110	3929	1044	995
Yao	12,055	40,327	11,093	10,597
Yi	28,763	99,421	25,592	23,118
Yugur	71	235	60	56
Zhuang	70,902	233,462	64,623	59,715

Table 6.2 Situations on teachers and staff in regular schools (institutions) of higher education

Ethnic group	Full-time teachers	Senior	Sub-senior	Middle	Junior	No rank
National total	1,440,292	169,423	412,692	576,013	209,811	72,353
Achang	25	3	7	10	4	2
Bai	1409	147	392	549	223	98
Baonan	15	2	4	6	2	1
Blang	69	7	19	27	11	5
Buyi	1982	190	607	752	283	150
Dai	863	90	236	336	141	60
Daur	152	18	47	59	21	8
Deang	13	1	4	5	2	1
Derung	6	1	2	2	1	0
Dong	2360	239	696	919	332	175
Dongxiang	477	48	137	192	73	27
Ewenki	34	4	10	13	5	2
Gaoshan	5	1	1	2	1	0
Gelao	383	37	118	145	55	29
Han	1,339,254	158,243	383,444	536,353	195,280	65,934
Hani	1071	112	293	417	174	75
Hezhe	6	1	2	2	1	0
Hui	11,286	1461	3328	4276	1629	591
Jing	18	2	5	7	3	2
Jingpo	98	10	27	38	16	7
Jino	16	2	4	6	3	1
Kazak	1192	84	352	525	146	86
Kirgiz	154	11	45	68	19	11
Korean	2675	393	823	1041	357	60
Lahu	338	35	92	132	55	24
Lhoba	3	0	1	1	0	0
Li	1344	140	319	488	264	132
Lisu	475	50	129	185	78	33
Manchu	14,720	2094	4542	5808	1812	464
Maonan	82	8	22	31	12	8
Miao	7247	740	2113	2831	1048	515
Monba	8	1	2	3	1	1
Mongol	6561	721	2004	2489	991	357
Mulao	164	16	44	63	24	16
Naxi	232	24	63	91	38	16
Nu	22	2	6	8	4	2
Oroqen	10	1	3	4	1	0
Pumi	25	3	7	10	4	2
Qiang	273	28	71	110	49	15

(*continued*)

Table 6.2 Continued

Ethnic group	Full-time teachers	Senior	Sub-senior	Middle	Junior	No rank
Russian	17	2	5	7	2	1
Salar	85	16	29	26	11	3
She	826	95	234	330	122	45
Shui	272	26	83	103	39	21
Tajik	39	3	12	17	5	3
Tatar	5	0	1	2	1	0
Tibetan	4750	481	1354	1843	793	279
Tu	197	35	66	61	26	8
Tujia	8579	955	2514	3371	1222	517
Uygur	8016	564	2367	3531	979	575
Uzbek	12	1	4	5	1	1
Va	298	31	81	116	49	21
Xibe	257	33	80	104	31	9
Yao	2282	235	618	896	331	202
Yi	6020	619	1635	2366	1001	398
Yugur	13	1	4	5	2	1
Zhuang	13,076	1310	3436	5040	1967	1323

Table 6.3 Situations on students in secondary vocational schools (institutions) (person)

Ethnic group	New enrollment	Total enrollment	Graduates	With professional qualification certificates	Graduates for next year
National total	5,970,785	16,898,820	5,543,840	3,483,872	5,663,952
Achang	147	455	131	77	176
Bai	8000	24,209	6994	4214	9078
Baonan	78	217	67	37	64
Blang	398	1232	354	209	475
Buyi	12,846	32,996	8720	5922	10,164
Dai	5029	15,555	4461	2636	6007
Daur	489	1409	558	269	485
Deang	78	240	69	41	93
Derung	33	99	29	17	37
Dong	13,277	35,839	10,325	6720	11,168
Dongxiang	2415	6707	2070	1138	1986
Ewenki	123	353	139	65	124
Gaoshan	23	64	21	12	22
Gelao	2501	6399	1683	1145	1960
Han	5,465,621	15,481,495	5,113,109	3,233,888	5,195,552

(continued)

Table 6.3 Continued

Ethnic group	New enrollment	Total enrollment	Graduates	With professional qualification certificates	Graduates for next year
Hani	6230	19,297	5536	3262	7455
Hezhe	14	40	16	8	13
Hui	50,899	143,520	46,501	26,184	47,109
Jing	155	428	108	60	131
Jingpo	573	1772	508	300	684
Jino	90	280	80	47	108
Kazak	5877	15,941	4831	2748	5251
Kirgiz	753	2043	621	353	673
Korean	5539	17,097	6593	2891	5945
Lahu	1966	6085	1747	1030	2350
Lhoba	9	22	11	6	8
Li	8260	22,912	6697	2496	6863
Lisu	2779	8546	2453	1469	3292
Manchu	35,879	110,472	41,368	19,921	39,258
Maonan	671	1824	461	264	555
Miao	39,469	107,880	31,231	20,286	34,433
Monba	28	65	32	17	23
Mongol	23,418	67,603	25,821	12,416	23,697
Mulao	1381	3792	956	536	1156
Naxi	1350	4148	1192	714	1598
Nu	124	383	111	65	148
Oroqen	29	83	33	16	28
Pumi	146	451	129	76	174
Qiang	1855	4680	1333	1191	1648
Russian	70	193	65	34	65
Salar	626	1613	497	301	457
She	4206	10,913	3380	2719	3415
Shui	1790	4622	1216	815	1426
Tajik	193	525	159	91	173
Tatar	23	63	19	11	21
Tibetan	24,769	62,082	22,095	14,177	20,391
Tu	1427	3706	1141	693	1061
Tujia	30,232	87,387	31,253	20,318	28,120
Uygur	39,470	107,080	32,463	18,474	35,285
Uzbek	58	158	48	27	52
Va	1723	5321	1531	905	2049
Xibe	625	1874	636	328	651
Yao	15,629	44,058	11,979	6972	13,856
Yi	37,322	106,080	30,142	20,840	39,098
Yugur	65	180	56	31	53
Zhuang	110,851	308,274	77,937	42,943	95,316

Table 6.4 Basic statistics on regular senior secondary schools (person)

Ethnic group	Schools (unit)	New enrollment	Total enrollment	Graduates	Teachers and staff	Full-time teachers
National total	13,509	8,446,071	24,671,712	7,915,046	2,462,575	1,595,035
Achang	0	210	567	158	59	36
Bai	20	11,974	32,026	8888	3238	2014
Baonan	0	147	432	139	40	27
Blang	1	568	1536	428	160	98
Buyi	37	26,415	64,682	16,570	5326	3516
Dai	12	7158	19,364	5393	2014	1240
Daur	2	895	2633	858	271	175
Deang	0	111	299	83	31	19
Derung	0	47	130	37	13	8
Dong	34	22,917	58,757	16,128	5172	3379
Dongxiang	9	4587	13,434	4296	1287	835
Ewenki	0	219	639	207	65	42
Gaoshan	0	30	88	28	9	6
Gelao	7	5191	12,679	3236	1039	686
Han	12,241	7,701,301	22,602,866	7,289,606	2,255,052	1,464,385
Hani	15	8887	24,036	6690	2500	1541
Hezhe	0	26	80	27	8	6
Hui	132	76,083	219,567	69,441	21,857	14,309
Jing	0	152	414	123	36	23
Jingpo	1	818	2211	615	230	142
Jino	0	129	349	97	36	22
Kazak	25	10,516	29,850	9151	4145	2192
Kirgiz	3	1348	3827	1174	531	281
Korean	19	11,297	33,778	11,073	3138	2122
Lahu	5	2802	7581	2112	788	486
Lhoba	0	20	55	15	5	4
Li	17	10,412	28,861	8600	3648	1782
Lisu	7	3921	10,631	2973	1104	679
Manchu	108	61,074	184,864	62,881	18,047	12,596
Maonan	1	792	2075	589	175	115
Miao	100	68,041	176,496	48,795	15,941	10,222
Monba	0	60	163	46	15	12
Mongol	68	40,818	119,317	38,695	12,063	7782
Mulao	2	1461	3911	1141	334	219
Naxi	3	1909	5175	1447	538	331
Nu	0	178	482	134	50	31
Oroqen	0	52	156	51	16	10
Pumi	0	208	562	157	58	36
Qiang	3	1946	5649	1779	560	323
Russian	0	122	351	110	44	25

(continued)

Table 6.4 Continued

Ethnic group	Schools (unit)	New enrollment	Total enrollment	Graduates	Teachers and staff	Full-time teachers
Salar	2	839	2350	785	275	167
She	10	4771	14,425	4588	1730	1021
Shui	5	3579	8781	2257	724	478
Tajik	1	343	974	299	134	71
Tatar	0	41	116	36	16	8
Tibetan	74	38,126	106,756	32,527	10,753	7392
Tu	5	1932	5417	1799	622	380
Tujia	80	53,466	152,105	47,941	14,242	9301
Uygur	166	70,555	200,281	61,402	27,805	14,705
Uzbek	0	104	294	90	41	22
Va	4	2455	6651	1857	690	426
Xibe	2	1148	3430	1138	354	238
Yao	27	17,523	48,132	14,339	4472	2867
Yi	80	50,708	137,835	39,390	13,724	8369
Yugur	0	122	360	115	33	22
Zhuang	168	108,938	297,180	88,423	25,999	16,941

Table 6.5 Basic statistics on regular junior secondary schools (person)

Ethnic group	Schools (unit)	New enrollment	Total enrollment	Graduates	Full-time teachers
National total	53,216	15,707,700	47,630,607	16,607,751	3,504,363
Achang	1	539	1563	533	97
Bai	80	29,802	86,258	29,108	5351
Baonan	1	248	774	288	56
Blang	4	1457	4226	1443	262
Buyi	183	60,526	173,994	55,161	9596
Dai	46	18,395	53,342	18,208	3303
Daur	5	1377	4398	1508	368
Deang	1	285	827	282	51
Derung	0	113	330	113	21
Dong	166	50,529	145,576	46,725	8901
Dongxiang	32	7810	24,363	9020	1797
Ewenki	1	317	987	345	82
Gaoshan	0	61	179	61	13
Gelao	36	11,894	34,184	10,822	1878
Han	48,292	14,169,946	43,081,580	15,072,826	3,187,125
Hani	57	22,864	66,287	22,623	4105

(continued)

Table 6.5 Continued

Ethnic group	Schools (unit)	New enrollment	Total enrollment	Graduates	Full-time teachers
Hezhe	0	45	154	51	13
Hui	467	143,800	428,041	145,733	31,194
Jing	1	345	1016	334	61
Jingpo	5	2101	6092	2079	377
Jino	1	332	962	328	60
Kazak	77	21,281	63,846	21,633	5812
Kirgiz	10	2725	8182	2771	745
Korean	84	17,191	54,335	19,416	4920
Lahu	18	7204	20,887	7128	1294
Lhoba	0	49	146	52	10
Li	64	19,954	60,715	22,270	4127
Lisu	25	10,007	29,051	9926	1803
Manchu	417	103,215	313,493	109,131	26,798
Maonan	5	1805	5266	1706	306
Miao	476	149,549	433,164	141,068	26,589
Monba	0	146	438	156	30
Mongol	210	62,138	190,080	66,602	15,709
Mulao	9	3310	9709	3171	574
Naxi	12	4871	14,141	4833	878
Nu	1	456	1323	452	82
Oroqen	0	82	267	91	22
Pumi	1	532	1544	527	96
Qiang	15	3690	11,348	4075	761
Russian	1	223	673	230	59
Salar	6	1589	4583	1534	330
She	29	8898	26,184	9147	2012
Shui	25	8222	23,641	7502	1306
Tajik	2	692	2078	705	188
Tatar	0	82	246	84	22
Tibetan	240	81,517	243,905	86,176	16,859
Tu	13	3656	10,587	3560	752
Tujia	362	100,080	296,631	100,823	21,572
Uygur	514	142,803	428,407	145,135	38,996
Uzbek	1	210	629	213	57
Va	16	6269	18,197	6209	1131
Xibe	8	1981	6069	2141	540
Yao	118	38,294	112,349	37,280	7255
Yi	345	119,030	349,200	119,349	21,677
Yugur	1	205	642	240	46
Zhuang	683	247,847	730,106	241,082	43,909

Table 6.6 Basic statistics on regular primary schools (person)

Ethnic group	Schools (unit)	New enrollment	Total enrollment	Graduates	Teachers and staff	Full-time teachers
National total	228,585	17,146,640	96,958,985	16,415,565	5,538,481	5,585,476
Achang	10	499	3252	578	187	187
Bai	550	27,549	177,031	31,745	10,014	10,014
Baonan	7	229	1381	263	93	93
Blang	28	1349	8791	1561	505	505
Buyi	952	49,450	316,668	62,898	16,550	16,550
Dai	354	17,019	110,919	19,706	6372	6372
Daur	16	1341	7741	1384	614	614
Deang	6	264	1720	306	99	99
Derung	2	106	677	120	40	40
Dong	786	46,648	281,726	52,422	14,699	14,699
Dongxiang	198	7244	43,488	8248	2968	2968
Ewenki	3	308	1791	319	145	145
Gaoshan	1	68	384	63	21	21
Gelao	187	9679	62,025	12,356	3236	3236
Han	203,565	15,589,026	87,746,225	14,817,056	5,043,219	5,043,219
Hani	440	21,146	137,897	24,498	7924	7924
Hezhe	1	44	250	45	19	19
Hui	2561	152,807	890,846	152,374	52,623	52,623
Jing	7	378	2182	355	112	112
Jingpo	40	1943	12,667	2251	728	728
Jino	6	307	2001	356	115	115
Kazak	240	22,448	128,643	21,732	9209	9209
Kirgiz	31	2874	16,466	2782	1179	1179
Korean	322	17,796	103,550	17,449	8133	8133
Lahu	139	6669	43,465	7719	2496	2496
Lhoba	1	57	324	53	21	21
Li	338	20,231	124,335	21,376	8352	8352
Lisu	190	9282	60,300	10,710	3462	3462
Manchu	1512	111,135	635,185	104,568	42,560	42,560
Maonan	33	1805	10,727	1861	551	551
Miao	2354	137,168	836,340	155,468	44,550	44,550
Monba	3	173	977	159	63	63
Mongol	727	61,809	359,903	62,829	27,387	27,387
Mulao	63	3491	20,365	3409	1044	1044
Naxi	93	4522	29,361	5214	1686	1686
Nu	9	424	2756	489	159	159
Oroqen	1	80	459	82	36	36
Pumi	10	493	3211	570	185	185

(*continued*)

Table 6.6 Continued

Ethnic group	Schools (unit)	New enrollment	Total enrollment	Graduates	Teachers and staff	Full-time teachers
Qiang	33	3766	20,947	3742	1140	1140
Russian	3	231	1325	227	97	97
Salar	32	1754	10,505	1739	574	574
She	116	10,334	57,441	9206	3203	3203
Shui	131	6769	43,258	8543	2261	2261
Tajik	8	731	4186	707	298	298
Tatar	1	86	494	84	35	35
Tibetan	1481	90,883	523,270	87,830	31,545	31,545
Tu	73	3999	23,955	3996	1305	1305
Tujia	1409	105,645	591,485	102,545	32,321	32,321
Uygur	1608	150,713	863,494	145,828	61,783	61,783
Uzbek	2	221	1269	214	91	91
Va	120	5819	37,827	6713	2172	2172
Xibe	25	1968	11,601	2003	807	807
Yao	677	42,045	240,072	39,698	12,483	12,483
Yi	1960	110,614	694,311	125,473	38,964	38,964
Yugur	5	188	1135	217	77	77
Zhuang	4880	270,718	1,567,524	255,723	80,847	80,847

Table 6.7 Student-teacher ratio by level of regular schools (number of teachers = 1)

Ethnic group	Primary school	Junior secondary school	Regular senior secondary school	Vocational senior secondary school	Regular institution of higher education
National average	17.36	13.59	15.47	24.19	17.52
Achang	17.40	16.15	15.60	26.63	18.49
Bai	17.70	16.07	15.87	26.79	18.46
Baonan	14.86	13.89	16.22	22.14	18.74
Blang	17.40	16.14	15.60	26.62	18.48
Buyi	19.13	18.10	18.41	29.18	18.18
Dai	17.41	16.15	15.61	26.66	18.49
Daur	12.62	11.98	15.00	17.30	17.09
Deang	17.40	16.16	15.60	26.62	18.49
Derung	17.12	15.55	15.60	25.88	18.33
Dong	19.14	16.12	17.36	28.95	18.26
Dongxiang	14.67	13.67	16.11	21.67	18.73
Ewenki	12.38	12.05	15.36	16.90	17.47

(continued)

Table 6.7 Continued

Ethnic group	Primary school	Junior secondary school	Regular senior secondary school	Vocational senior secondary school	Regular institution of higher education
Gaoshan	17.98	14.01	15.88	26.21	17.62
Gelao	19.17	18.19	18.49	29.30	18.18
Han	17.31	13.41	15.52	24.58	17.65
Hani	17.40	16.15	15.60	26.62	18.49
Hezhe	13.24	12.03	14.47	18.81	16.37
Hui	16.90	13.72	15.41	23.76	17.48
Jing	19.49	16.63	17.71	38.28	17.83
Jingpo	17.40	16.16	15.61	26.64	18.49
Jino	17.40	16.15	15.60	26.63	18.49
Kazak	13.97	10.99	13.62	16.30	16.88
Kirgiz	13.96	11.00	13.62	16.31	16.87
Korean	12.79	11.00	16.03	14.58	17.01
Lahu	17.41	16.15	15.60	26.61	18.49
Lhoba	15.64	14.45	13.31	28.59	16.30
Li	14.94	14.71	16.22	31.13	19.27
Lisu	17.43	16.11	15.65	26.70	18.48
Manchu	14.84	11.66	14.74	17.54	17.20
Maonan	19.47	17.15	18.02	36.31	17.92
Miao	18.75	16.07	17.23	28.22	18.25
Monba	15.55	14.44	13.14	28.75	16.24
Mongol	13.16	12.08	15.36	17.24	17.45
Mulao	19.52	16.87	17.85	37.70	17.87
Naxi	17.42	16.10	15.64	26.72	18.47
Nu	17.38	16.10	15.55	26.64	18.44
Oroqen	12.81	12.02	14.90	17.84	16.90
Pumi	17.40	16.12	15.60	26.61	18.48
Qiang	18.37	14.92	17.51	30.29	18.35
Russian	13.53	11.46	14.28	16.91	17.13
Salar	18.38	13.92	14.10	23.30	15.35
She	17.91	12.91	14.26	29.76	17.32
Shui	19.12	18.06	18.37	29.47	18.16
Tajik	14.08	11.08	13.70	16.62	16.90
Tatar	14.09	11.17	13.75	16.82	16.97
Tibetan	16.89	14.49	14.62	27.56	16.70
Tu	18.38	14.08	14.29	23.79	15.58
Tujia	18.17	13.50	16.34	25.12	18.09
Uygur	13.98	10.99	13.62	16.32	16.88
Uzbek	14.03	11.05	13.65	16.55	16.90

(continued)

Table 6.7 Continued

Ethnic group	Primary school	Junior secondary school	Regular senior secondary school	Vocational senior secondary school	Regular institution of higher education
Va	17.41	16.09	15.61	26.57	18.47
Xibe	14.47	11.26	14.52	16.94	17.09
Yao	19.25	15.47	16.85	34.14	18.16
Yi	17.87	16.03	16.45	27.93	18.42
Yugur	14.77	13.91	16.30	22.25	18.86
Zhuang	19.41	16.64	17.60	38.23	17.89

Table 6.8 Number of students per 100,000 population by level (person)

Ethnic group	Kindergartens	Primary education	Junior secondary	Senior secondary	Higher education
National average	2736.00	7196.00	3535.00	3411.00	2335.00
Achang	2429.53	8765.59	4213.34	2981.51	1574.31
Bai	2488.67	8849.71	4318.07	3029.76	1603.76
Baonan	1952.58	8090.73	4548.42	4179.26	2088.17
Blang	2431.29	8755.41	4209.18	2983.60	1578.37
Buyi	2835.08	10,771.60	5922.73	3439.74	1428.57
Dai	2429.75	8759.42	4212.22	2982.77	1575.42
Daur	1888.50	5445.18	3098.85	3124.18	2197.94
Deang	2426.40	8774.09	4216.11	2978.43	1570.37
Derung	2455.65	8383.28	4085.22	3071.60	1718.70
Dong	2860.74	9424.77	4883.05	3340.73	1709.80
Dongxiang	2019.99	8118.61	4560.33	4135.68	2080.49
Ewenki	1968.57	5495.10	3029.28	3186.23	2114.66
Gaoshan	2926.14	8096.64	3768.83	3468.52	2258.73
Gelao	2839.91	10,840.17	5976.81	3450.17	1418.61
Han	2752.27	7187.46	3529.97	3450.04	2364.87
Hani	2427.59	8763.71	4212.28	2978.88	1573.81
Hezhe	1613.96	5054.20	3110.86	2982.53	2498.76
Hui	2558.51	8210.89	3954.91	3605.08	2141.32
Jing	3494.80	9137.48	4256.21	3753.28	1843.97
Jingpo	2429.91	8771.65	4218.45	2983.05	1573.90
Jino	2426.42	8761.07	4211.86	2979.40	1575.18
Kazak	3138.61	8601.53	4269.05	3294.98	1599.35
Kirgiz	3125.47	8564.06	4255.88	3289.79	1607.04

(*continued*)

Table 6.8 Continued

Ethnic group	Kindergartens	Primary education	Junior secondary	Senior secondary	Higher education
Korean	1675.34	5151.96	2702.21	2804.60	2785.38
Lahu	2430.51	8767.17	4212.59	2982.17	1575.34
Lhoba	2102.26	9475.56	4274.79	2291.20	1565.30
Li	3060.89	8662.16	4235.12	3936.81	2180.87
Lisu	2435.95	8710.50	4197.38	2996.19	1587.30
Manchu	2050.94	5571.79	2757.54	2844.60	2649.43
Maonan	3343.06	9659.58	4755.01	3691.13	1713.93
Miao	2797.97	9223.16	4791.31	3334.82	1746.13
Monba	2055.53	9463.24	4243.12	2227.24	1560.30
Mongol	2074.80	5785.34	3058.96	3148.62	2170.33
Mulao	3445.79	9344.98	4461.50	3744.03	1790.83
Naxi	2435.11	8715.23	4198.48	2992.20	1589.86
Nu	2429.11	8759.51	4205.07	2972.75	1579.70
Oroqen	1789.04	5252.81	3061.89	3082.05	2303.11
Pumi	2429.15	8745.60	4205.15	2983.60	1580.66
Qiang	2724.98	6988.46	3786.98	3581.95	2038.29
Russian	2673.63	7333.70	3733.81	3237.59	1877.19
Salar	2617.02	8655.05	3793.05	3641.82	1295.52
She	3541.68	7293.74	3331.49	3583.99	2236.56
Shui	2850.31	10,723.10	5866.34	3441.39	1437.20
Tajik	3126.97	8555.60	4247.91	3303.23	1624.41
Tatar	3065.00	8495.17	4235.14	3321.73	1666.36
Tibetan	2330.63	8655.76	4064.19	2994.08	1621.30
Tu	2610.40	8609.57	3825.80	3660.97	1348.23
Tujia	2700.73	7348.59	3694.42	3265.91	2355.06
Uygur	3139.57	8596.15	4264.63	3292.93	1601.82
Uzbek	3136.18	8580.78	4256.21	3298.94	1615.63
Va	2437.73	8734.56	4201.58	2994.01	1589.56
Xibe	2167.06	5617.32	2946.26	2829.46	2572.10
Yao	3197.86	8516.35	3977.98	3545.44	1900.17
Yi	2555.27	8502.83	4290.11	3198.34	1685.40
Yugur	1923.94	8040.38	4557.86	4197.99	2137.70
Zhuang	3464.11	9081.22	4225.92	3747.80	1830.04

Table 6.9 Basic statistics on educational funds (10,000 yuan)

Ethnic group	Government appropriation for education	Budgetary (public expenditure on education)	Funds from private schools	Donations and fund-raising for running schools	Income from teaching research and other auxiliary activity	Tuition and miscellaneous fees	Other educational funds
Achang	4531.90	4195.47	14.88	19.25	621.25	489.25	97.19
Bai	238,860.47	221,353.97	889.63	961.06	35,002.16	27,385.86	5520.12
Baonan	2236.80	2101.42	3.06	5.24	281.55	234.15	27.18
Blang	12,268.18	11,357.12	40.14	52.30	1685.88	1326.99	264.43
Buyi	332,116.54	310,086.88	1641.26	801.67	46,791.31	35,077.45	8306.06
Dai	154,568.22	143,105.12	508.83	655.19	21,205.06	16,680.51	3309.66
Daur	21,873.88	19,898.15	42.17	19.70	3137.51	2516.73	271.21
Deang	2396.19	2219.15	7.74	10.09	326.22	256.88	51.18
Derung	1010.39	931.28	3.87	4.14	150.59	118.70	22.26
Dong	315,503.45	294,335.46	1988.04	847.70	61,897.99	47,469.71	9476.33
Dongxiang	70,401.47	65,970.01	90.18	156.82	8794.79	7281.52	1007.88
Ewenki	5611.13	5078.51	13.44	5.58	707.16	555.97	66.89
Gaoshan	615.42	558.72	4.85	2.44	128.82	104.13	16.11
Gelao	64,397.18	60,200.14	319.99	146.80	9003.79	6735.52	1599.69
Han	154,863,929.71	139,369,551.27	1,054,735.65	810,544.92	35,827,202.88	28,409,034.14	4,652,709.83
Hani	192,213.72	177,945.08	623.47	814.37	26,313.14	20,718.42	4127.03
Hezhe	553.53	509.29	0.68	0.62	124.84	104.17	6.92
Hui	1,722,284.93	1,589,948.36	5733.19	4415.21	230,958.66	184,088.94	42,911.59
Jing	2574.17	2422.45	17.34	5.18	490.17	387.77	40.02
Jingpo	17,637.16	16,330.21	57.70	74.34	2417.12	1903.48	377.22
Jino	2791.57	2584.78	9.07	11.80	381.82	300.53	59.81
Kazak	283,074.00	262,521.86	110.62	467.33	20,466.65	15,435.42	7600.03
Kirgiz	36,247.81	33,612.95	14.38	59.72	2650.41	2002.15	971.14
Korean	260,124.89	240,513.97	589.13	295.55	53,299.72	44,648.36	3485.76
Lahu	60,513.68	56,024.62	197.68	256.18	8299.69	6536.51	1299.81

Lhoba	872.17	861.01	0.42	0.88	25.52	20.46	1.35
Li	221,605.14	200,814.08	5194.35	2371.97	44,998.53	37,445.04	5434.87
Lisu	84,073.45	77,822.74	291.90	359.36	11,686.27	9150.50	1789.83
Manchu	1,553,573.73	1,397,962.53	5590.60	2140.71	311,136.56	260,539.42	26,964.46
Maonan	12,038.83	11,328.26	73.43	22.06	2119.43	1656.01	209.72
Miao	995,078.97	926,715.04	6029.46	3621.84	187,448.06	143,094.35	30,152.79
Monba	2701.37	2667.69	1.04	2.56	72.99	58.71	3.04
Mongol	1,049,303.83	951,061.34	2837.47	1188.23	137,789.26	109,489.74	14,102.70
Mulao	23,549.52	22,153.39	151.36	45.68	4415.54	3477.62	384.58
Naxi	41,232.88	38,185.40	141.54	175.97	5692.54	4457.68	876.02
Nu	3915.52	3631.06	12.48	16.33	525.81	414.04	81.87
Oroqen	1229.25	1119.64	2.38	1.14	204.21	166.07	14.50
Pumi	4488.59	4155.26	14.75	19.02	616.68	485.25	96.18
Qiang	30,083.05	27,733.57	430.36	192.20	7203.23	4784.51	484.39
Russian	3310.28	3037.99	3.90	5.44	314.50	241.94	74.11
Salar	29,272.44	27,792.67	28.03	77.57	1482.00	1141.01	301.05
She	106,896.86	92,606.79	1229.94	1074.30	28,437.03	22,301.99	3544.19
Shui	45,476.91	42,493.86	222.78	107.30	6396.95	4802.51	1119.49
Tajik	9163.34	8494.66	4.94	15.71	690.82	522.41	246.43
Tatar	1085.11	1005.33	0.58	1.94	84.03	63.77	28.92
Tibetan	1,286,372.00	1,248,323.12	2472.98	2554.49	72,499.39	53,745.81	6484.33
Tu	64,615.10	61,268.68	79.15	179.68	3728.66	2891.75	684.56
Tujia	814,649.19	758,896.23	5297.21	4404.58	221,058.15	166,980.91	34,891.73
Uygur	1,899,826.58	1,761,715.95	773.54	3147.19	138,057.34	104,144.79	51,073.17
Uzbek	2789.43	2585.73	1.41	4.78	207.48	156.80	75.01
Va	52,817.94	48,877.46	176.34	223.16	7329.65	5768.92	1135.12
Xibe	31,318.92	28,296.93	107.72	39.51	5423.39	4493.51	639.40
Yao	296,505.99	277,231.65	2226.58	841.13	67,040.36	52,945.79	6942.92
Yi	940,614.34	870,914.24	5557.10	4239.22	150,590.71	111,817.09	19,343.46
Yugur	1789.36	1678.15	2.61	4.28	239.78	199.66	22.33
Zhuang	1,871,919.90	1,760,303.42	12,309.37	3986.79	359,650.99	285,022.99	28,777.79

Table 6.10 Number of patents application accepted (piece)

Ethnic group	Total	Inventions	Utility models	Designs
National total	1,912,151	535,313	734,437	642,401
Achang	8	3	4	1
Bai	541	178	244	120
Baonan	5	2	2	1
Blang	23	8	11	4
Buyi	1194	314	440	440
Dai	277	97	131	49
Daur	67	20	31	17
Deang	4	1	2	1
Derung	3	1	1	1
Dong	1507	423	597	487
Dongxiang	173	65	80	29
Ewenki	11	4	5	2
Gaoshan	5	2	2	1
Gelao	220	60	81	80
Han	1,828,021	502,939	699,368	625,715
Hani	345	121	163	62
Hezhe	5	1	2	1
Hui	8169	2996	3508	1664
Jing	9	4	3	2
Jingpo	31	11	15	5
Jino	5	2	2	1
Kazak	481	116	230	135
Kirgiz	63	15	30	18
Korean	1308	500	566	242
Lahu	109	38	52	20
Lhoba	1	0	0	0
Li	341	150	137	54
Lisu	161	55	75	31
Manchu	9684	4279	4169	1236
Maonan	38	15	14	9
Miao	4686	1317	1953	1416
Monba	2	1	1	0
Mongol	2489	933	1142	414
Mulao	84	34	31	19
Naxi	80	27	38	15
Nu	7	3	3	1
Oroqen	5	2	2	1
Pumi	8	3	4	2
Qiang	249	62	100	87
Russian	8	3	4	2
Salar	25	9	9	7

(*continued*)

Table 6.10 Continued

Ethnic group	Total	Inventions	Utility models	Designs
She	1534	255	698	581
Shui	160	44	57	60
Tajik	17	4	8	5
Tatar	2	1	1	1
Tibetan	1650	498	653	498
Tu	77	25	28	24
Tujia	6615	1846	3012	1757
Uygur	3273	791	1560	922
Uzbek	5	1	2	1
Va	103	35	49	18
Xibe	171	76	73	22
Yao	1497	505	577	415
Yi	3189	915	1352	922
Yugur	5	2	2	1
Zhuang	6546	2704	2414	1428

Table 6.11 Number of patents application granted (piece)

Ethnic group	Total	Inventions	Utility models	Designs
National total	1,163,226	143,847	566,750	452,629
Achang	5	1	3	1
Bai	336	63	189	84
Baonan	2	0	2	0
Blang	14	3	8	3
Buyi	680	71	339	270
Dai	175	37	101	37
Daur	43	7	23	13
Deang	3	1	2	1
Derung	2	0	1	0
Dong	895	112	467	316
Dongxiang	78	14	50	13
Ewenki	7	1	4	2
Gaoshan	3	0	2	1
Gelao	123	13	62	48
Han	1,111,057	131,872	538,412	440,773
Hani	217	46	126	46
Hezhe	3	0	1	1
Hui	4475	829	2579	1066
Jing	4	1	2	1

(continued)

Table 6.11 Continued

Ethnic group	Total	Inventions	Utility models	Designs
Jingpo	20	4	11	4
Jino	3	1	2	1
Kazak	235	32	162	41
Kirgiz	31	4	21	6
Korean	793	163	445	184
Lahu	69	14	40	14
Lhoba	0	0	0	0
Li	205	66	94	45
Lisu	102	20	58	23
Manchu	5361	1132	3358	872
Maonan	19	3	10	6
Miao	2757	353	1490	915
Monba	1	0	0	0
Mongol	1469	279	882	308
Mulao	42	6	22	14
Naxi	51	10	29	12
Nu	5	1	3	1
Oroqen	3	1	2	1
Pumi	5	1	3	1
Qiang	158	17	74	68
Russian	4	1	3	1
Salar	14	3	7	5
She	1123	88	552	483
Shui	89	9	44	36
Tajik	8	1	6	2
Tatar	1	0	1	0
Tibetan	1037	172	473	393
Tu	47	8	21	17
Tujia	3712	504	2180	1027
Uygur	1606	216	1103	287
Uzbek	3	0	2	0
Va	64	13	38	13
Xibe	90	17	60	13
Yao	881	131	451	299
Yi	1995	288	1018	689
Yugur	2	0	1	0
Zhuang	3317	506	1750	1061

Table 6.12 Transaction value in technical markets (10,000 yuan)

Ethnic group	2005	2006	2007	2008	2009	2010	2011	2012
National total	15,513,694	18,181,813	22,265,261	26,652,288	30,390,024	39,065,753	47,635,589	64,370,683
Achang	131	71	84	48	90	98	108	379
Bai	7464	5032	5847	4568	6594	7598	8638	21,490
Baonan	112	139	173	198	234	286	353	483
Blang	357	194	227	133	244	269	292	1020
Buyi	2426	2045	2463	3971	3962	9409	14,751	13,043
Dai	4516	2496	2949	1753	3205	3494	3828	13,119
Daur	955	1098	1471	1602	2001	2702	2901	6543
Deang	69	38	44	25	48	52	57	201
Derung	39	31	36	33	43	52	59	124
Dong	9333	9214	9935	11,814	11,439	15,107	18,643	19,932
Dongxiang	3406	4165	5038	5709	6599	8085	9867	13,633
Ewenki	216	240	284	294	388	578	582	1631
Gaoshan	69	85	103	120	140	176	211	276
Gelao	452	410	492	810	795	1890	2947	2542
Han	14,785,404	16,659,829	20,278,701	24,171,461	27,430,833	34,792,745	42,830,708	55,837,372
Hani	5586	3031	3573	2054	3834	4165	4540	16,029
Hezhe	53	68	101	118	140	167	199	281
Hui	145,861	181,060	228,915	267,075	314,660	396,087	497,046	648,207
Jing	63	26	31	44	43	67	84	89
Jingpo	515	283	336	200	365	400	439	1499
Jino	82	46	55	33	60	65	71	240
Kazak	5583	5386	5159	5362	1262	3612	3636	4523
Kirgiz	715	689	666	693	172	472	477	607

(continued)

Table 6.12 Continued

Ethnic group	2005	2006	2007	2008	2009	2010	2011	2012
Korean	21,167	25,525	32,415	37,000	42,594	49,007	60,490	78,718
Lahu	1744	931	1097	618	1170	1271	1384	4982
Lhoba	4	5	6	8	9	11	13	17
Li	1872	1676	1569	6081	1459	5924	6462	2200
Lisu	2407	1314	1552	923	1706	1840	2023	7029
Manchu	221,929	256,385	314,376	353,603	422,959	506,260	612,042	845,671
Maonan	205	63	75	132	116	229	325	272
Miao	32,390	34,081	33,938	41,635	38,563	55,437	63,790	74,181
Monba	21	28	33	37	43	49	57	69
Mongol	51,954	56,986	66,508	70,551	89,135	123,587	132,868	307,285
Mulao	544	242	291	435	413	647	831	827
Naxi	1254	768	913	635	1049	1169	1311	3831
Nu	112	62	73	44	80	88	97	324
Oroqen	69	83	116	130	160	205	229	435
Pumi	134	76	90	57	100	111	123	394
Qiang	795	1074	1265	1773	2204	2274	2807	4488
Russian	163	197	231	257	277	379	430	721
Salar	471	786	1377	1874	2097	2771	3897	4619
She	4354	3827	4603	5783	6340	8580	9517	12,280
Shui	332	233	280	459	462	1196	1902	1681
Tajik	193	190	186	197	69	151	158	197
Tatar	34	38	41	46	36	53	61	79
Tibetan	10,862	15,823	24,298	32,698	37,897	46,785	63,767	82,324
Tu	990	1597	2841	3914	4348	5746	8136	9644
Tujia	59,835	69,642	67,333	85,518	79,040	107,782	119,161	145,865

Uygur	37,917	36,679	35,244	36,711	9307	25,217	25,543	31,779
Uzbek	63	64	65	70	33	61	67	85
Va	1578	867	1020	636	1110	1231	1347	4461
Xibe	3567	3618	4269	4682	5472	6304	7638	10,791
Yao	11,842	9146	10,098	12,478	11,443	13,808	15,180	19,064
Yi	24,422	17,866	21,076	20,012	28,912	31,958	38,463	87,518
Yugur	111	141	174	199	237	291	355	486
Zhuang	46,525	17,902	21,443	31,578	29,050	43,784	53,920	62,727

Table 6.13 Main indicators on Internet development (year-end)

Ethnic group	Broad band subscribers port of Internet (10,000 ports)	Dial-up subscribers of Internet (10,000 subscribers)	Broadband subscribers of Internet (10,000 subscribers)
National total	32,108.45	569.80	17,518.30
Achang	0.54	0.06	0.30
Bai	29.32	2.96	16.47
Baonan	0.29	0.01	0.11
Blang	1.46	0.17	0.82
Buyi	41.69	0.60	21.91
Dai	18.30	2.21	10.35
Daur	3.13	0.03	1.62
Deang	0.28	0.03	0.16
Derung	0.13	0.01	0.07
Dong	47.26	0.42	26.05
Dongxiang	9.55	0.22	3.78
Ewenki	0.73	0.00	0.37
Gaoshan	0.12	0.00	0.06
Gelao	8.02	0.10	4.21
Han	29,892.81	519.09	16,322.68
Hani	22.74	2.76	12.86
Hezhe	0.11	0.00	0.06
Hui	235.77	5.63	118.78
Jing	0.44	0.01	0.26
Jingpo	2.09	0.25	1.18
Jino	0.33	0.04	0.19
Kazak	37.10	0.44	17.26
Kirgiz	4.76	0.06	2.22
Korean	48.16	0.71	27.04
Lahu	7.16	0.87	4.05
Lhoba	0.05	0.00	0.02
Li	27.54	0.02	15.54
Lisu	10.04	1.18	5.69
Manchu	307.01	4.75	167.96
Maonan	1.92	0.02	1.11
Miao	143.95	3.05	79.90
Monba	0.15	0.00	0.06
Mongol	143.66	0.90	73.87
Mulao	3.97	0.05	2.34
Naxi	4.90	0.57	2.77
Nu	0.46	0.05	0.26
Oroqen	0.19	0.00	0.10

(*continued*)

Table 6.13 Continued

Ethnic group	Broad band subscribers port of Internet (10,000 ports)	Dial-up subscribers of Internet (10,000 subscribers)	Broadband subscribers of Internet (10,000 subscribers)
Pumi	0.53	0.06	0.30
Qiang	4.94	0.06	3.07
Russian	0.44	0.00	0.21
Salar	2.29	0.02	1.06
She	27.59	0.36	14.24
Shui	5.73	0.09	3.02
Tajik	1.21	0.01	0.57
Tatar	0.14	0.00	0.07
Tibetan	93.64	0.83	44.75
Tu	5.27	0.05	2.48
Tujia	144.36	0.87	86.21
Uygur	249.32	2.99	116.09
Uzbek	0.37	0.00	0.17
Va	6.32	0.75	3.58
Xibe	5.64	0.10	3.03
Yao	52.20	0.85	30.65
Yi	121.48	9.64	70.18
Yugur	0.24	0.01	0.10
Zhuang	320.53	5.64	190.68

7

Health Care and Social Security

Data on public health are mainly from the Information Center under the Ministry of Health. Data on civil affairs are from the Ministry of Civil Affairs based on statistical reporting form scheme. Data on disabled persons are from the China Disabled Persons Federation. For detailed information please refer to *Annual Statistical Yearbook on National Health Care* (Ministry of Health of the People's Republic of China), *Statistical Yearbook on Civil Affairs of China* (Department of Financial and Planning, Ministry of Civil Affairs) and *China Statistical Yearbook on the Work for Persons with Disabilities* (China Disabled Persons Federation).

Data on labor and social security mainly include revenue and expenses of social insurance fund, urban employee basic pension insurance, urban basic medical care insurance, unemployment insurance, etc. Data are from the Ministry of Human Resources and Social Security.

R. Guo, *China Ethnic Statistical Yearbook 2016*,
DOI 10.1007/978-3-319-49199-8_7

Table 7.1 Medical technical personnel in health care institutions per 1000 persons (person)

Ethnic group	Medical technical personnel			Licensed (assistant) doctors			Registered nurses		
	Total	City	County	Total	City	County	Total	City	County
National total	4.93	8.55	3.41	1.94	3.19	1.40	1.85	3.65	1.09
Achang	3.60	8.97	2.83	1.48	3.78	1.15	1.31	3.51	0.99
Bai	3.69	8.84	2.81	1.49	3.64	1.14	1.35	3.56	0.97
Baonan	4.43	6.50	3.19	1.71	2.58	1.20	1.49	2.62	0.89
Blang	3.60	8.95	2.83	1.48	3.77	1.15	1.31	3.51	0.99
Buyi	3.78	8.00	2.37	1.43	3.02	0.91	1.42	3.56	0.78
Dai	3.60	8.96	2.83	1.48	3.77	1.15	1.31	3.51	0.99
Daur	5.52	10.19	3.88	2.27	3.91	1.71	1.89	4.13	1.08
Deang	3.59	8.97	2.83	1.47	3.78	1.15	1.31	3.51	0.99
Derung	3.88	8.90	2.98	1.58	3.68	1.22	1.42	3.55	1.01
Dong	4.12	8.11	2.69	1.57	2.98	1.06	1.56	3.67	0.89
Dongxiang	4.53	7.37	3.31	1.74	2.90	1.24	1.55	3.00	0.95
Ewenki	5.58	10.63	3.92	2.35	4.14	1.78	1.89	4.27	1.08
Gaoshan	4.86	8.68	3.40	1.90	3.22	1.42	1.83	3.78	1.09
Gelao	3.76	7.98	2.34	1.43	3.00	0.89	1.41	3.56	0.77
Han	4.93	8.42	3.58	1.94	3.15	1.50	1.84	3.62	1.14
Hani	3.59	8.96	2.83	1.47	3.78	1.15	1.31	3.51	0.99
Hezhe	5.31	8.47	3.70	2.09	3.14	1.57	1.87	3.48	1.02
Hui	5.03	8.34	3.49	1.97	3.15	1.45	1.83	3.49	1.07
Jing	4.67	7.12	3.11	1.66	2.54	1.11	1.81	3.11	1.08
Jingpo	3.60	8.97	2.83	1.48	3.78	1.15	1.31	3.51	0.99
Jino	3.59	8.96	2.83	1.48	3.77	1.15	1.31	3.51	0.99
Kazak	6.12	15.30	4.81	2.26	5.79	1.76	2.35	6.48	1.76
Kirgiz	6.11	15.25	4.80	2.26	5.77	1.76	2.34	6.46	1.75
Korean	5.33	7.92	4.11	2.21	3.23	1.75	1.92	3.23	1.27
Lahu	3.60	8.96	2.83	1.48	3.77	1.15	1.31	3.51	0.99
Lhoba	3.20	10.27	2.61	1.36	4.51	1.11	0.68	3.23	0.45
Li	5.02	9.13	3.59	1.74	3.04	1.28	2.15	4.25	1.44
Lisu	3.63	8.91	2.85	1.49	3.74	1.16	1.32	3.50	0.99
Manchu	5.36	9.01	3.60	2.22	3.56	1.62	2.00	3.82	1.08
Maonan	4.43	7.29	2.89	1.60	2.64	1.04	1.70	3.21	0.99
Miao	4.07	8.02	2.74	1.57	3.01	1.09	1.53	3.55	0.91
Monba	3.15	10.32	2.61	1.35	4.56	1.13	0.64	3.19	0.43
Mongol	5.52	10.26	3.85	2.31	4.01	1.73	1.91	4.18	1.10
Mulao	4.59	7.20	3.02	1.64	2.58	1.09	1.77	3.16	1.04
Naxi	3.63	8.92	2.85	1.49	3.75	1.16	1.32	3.50	0.99
Nu	3.60	8.98	2.84	1.48	3.78	1.15	1.31	3.51	0.99
Oroqen	5.44	9.55	3.79	2.21	3.64	1.67	1.88	3.88	1.04
Pumi	3.61	8.95	2.84	1.48	3.77	1.15	1.32	3.51	0.99

(continued)

Table 7.1 Continued

Ethnic group	Medical technical personnel			Licensed (assistant) doctors			Registered nurses		
	Total	City	County	Total	City	County	Total	City	County
Qiang	4.82	6.98	3.31	2.01	2.64	1.48	1.73	3.01	1.01
Russian	5.91	13.26	4.48	2.30	5.06	1.79	2.17	5.53	1.49
Salar	5.07	1.46	3.22	2.04	0.57	1.39	1.74	0.60	0.90
She	4.89	9.34	3.68	1.87	3.47	1.46	1.91	4.02	1.30
Shui	3.79	7.96	2.38	1.44	3.00	0.91	1.42	3.54	0.79
Tajik	6.07	15.05	4.77	2.25	5.69	1.75	2.33	6.38	1.73
Tatar	6.03	14.72	4.73	2.24	5.58	1.74	2.30	6.23	1.71
Tibetan	4.02	7.14	2.90	1.67	3.03	1.25	1.18	2.46	0.69
Tu	4.99	1.76	3.17	2.01	0.68	1.37	1.72	0.73	0.89
Tujia	4.51	7.63	3.10	1.74	2.78	1.27	1.74	3.46	1.02
Uygur	6.12	15.29	4.81	2.26	5.78	1.76	2.35	6.48	1.76
Uzbek	6.10	15.19	4.79	2.26	5.75	1.76	2.34	6.44	1.75
Va	3.63	8.93	2.85	1.49	3.75	1.16	1.32	3.50	1.00
Xibe	5.70	9.97	3.76	2.28	3.85	1.61	2.22	4.29	1.22
Yao	4.57	7.84	3.09	1.69	2.84	1.17	1.75	3.47	1.04
Yi	3.95	8.30	2.91	1.62	3.37	1.21	1.44	3.38	0.97
Yugur	4.41	6.62	3.19	1.70	2.62	1.20	1.48	2.67	0.88
Zhuang	4.64	7.23	3.10	1.66	2.61	1.12	1.79	3.14	1.08

Table 7.2 Village clinics

Ethnic group	Village clinics (unit)						Villages with clinics as % of total
	Total	Run by village	Township hospitals	Jointly run	Run by private	Others	
National total	653,419	370,099	58,317	32,278	167,025	25,700	93.25
Achang	11	7	1	1	0	1	99.88
Bai	695	454	78	40	84	39	99.85
Baonan	11	6	1	1	3	0	99.98
Blang	29	20	4	2	1	2	99.86
Buyi	1775	729	163	44	697	142	99.56
Dai	368	255	48	26	18	21	99.92
Daur	67	35	9	2	20	2	99.56
Deang	6	4	1	0	0	0	99.97
Derung	3	2	0	0	0	0	99.35
Dong	1816	958	120	48	589	100	99.57
Dongxiang	336	161	41	24	99	11	99.98

(*continued*)

Table 7.2 Continued

Ethnic group	Village clinics (unit)						Villages with clinics as % of total
	Total	Run by village	Township hospitals	Jointly run	Run by private	Others	
Ewenki	17	8	2	0	6	0	99.59
Gaoshan	2	1	0	0	1	0	97.37
Gelao	349	142	32	8	138	28	99.77
Han	593,521	342,934	49,060	29,130	150,164	22,233	94.58
Hani	455	316	60	33	20	26	99.90
Hezhe	2	1	0	0	0	0	99.01
Hui	5502	2651	683	396	1550	221	96.97
Jing	12	4	0	0	6	1	99.83
Jingpo	42	29	6	3	2	2	99.90
Jino	7	5	1	0	0	0	99.94
Kazak	711	120	382	86	41	83	99.99
Kirgiz	91	16	49	11	5	11	99.97
Korean	817	388	59	68	273	29	98.98
Lahu	144	100	19	10	7	8	99.87
Lhoba	6	2	3	0	0	1	99.64
Li	469	132	18	5	245	70	99.91
Lisu	208	141	26	15	14	12	99.87
Manchu	6118	3020	221	235	2528	114	99.06
Maonan	59	22	3	2	28	3	99.87
Miao	5037	2693	376	153	1520	295	99.56
Monba	17	6	9	1	0	2	99.64
Mongol	3409	1599	393	120	1206	92	99.58
Mulao	111	42	5	4	55	5	99.73
Naxi	103	69	14	7	6	6	99.85
Nu	10	7	2	1	0	1	99.75
Oroqen	4	2	0	0	1	0	99.45
Pumi	11	7	1	1	1	1	99.88
Qiang	202	98	7	11	74	12	99.94
Russian	9	3	3	1	2	1	99.21
Salar	89	42	10	14	19	3	99.86
She	370	226	12	8	101	23	86.79
Shui	241	98	22	6	95	19	99.79
Tajik	23	4	12	3	1	3	99.88
Tatar	3	1	1	0	0	0	99.64
Tibetan	7054	2683	2686	390	621	674	99.90
Tu	199	97	21	30	44	7	99.66
Tujia	4282	2735	340	184	849	175	98.92
Uygur	4776	811	2559	574	278	554	99.97
Uzbek	7	1	4	1	0	1	99.88

(*continued*)

Table 7.2 Continued

Ethnic group	Village clinics (unit) Total	Run by village	Township hospitals	Jointly run	Run by private	Others	Villages with clinics as % of total
Va	128	88	17	9	7	7	99.61
Xibe	96	42	12	6	33	3	99.63
Yao	1444	772	55	47	520	50	99.93
Yi	3444	1946	292	195	799	212	99.92
Yugur	9	5	1	1	3	0	99.88
Zhuang	8245	3178	328	311	4071	357	99.90

Table 7.3 Number of beds in health institutions per 1000 population (bed)

Ethnic group	Beds of medical institutions per 1000 population Total	Urban	Rural	Hospitals and health centers per 1000 population	Beds of township health centers per 1000 rural population
National average	4.23	6.88	3.11	3.50	1.16
Achang	4.18	8.66	3.57	3.93	1.05
Bai	4.17	8.42	3.45	3.92	1.06
Baonan	4.41	6.43	3.19	3.93	1.15
Blang	4.18	8.65	3.57	3.94	1.05
Buyi	4.00	6.97	2.76	3.73	0.94
Dai	4.18	8.65	3.57	3.94	1.05
Daur	4.58	8.48	3.14	4.15	1.16
Deang	4.18	8.68	3.57	3.94	1.05
Derung	4.23	8.37	3.50	3.96	1.09
Dong	4.05	7.00	2.84	3.77	1.11
Dongxiang	4.52	7.10	3.34	4.05	1.20
Ewenki	4.46	8.50	3.11	4.03	1.18
Gaoshan	4.17	7.12	2.98	3.85	1.14
Gelao	3.99	6.95	2.75	3.73	0.94
Han	4.25	6.97	3.14	3.91	1.24
Hani	4.18	8.67	3.57	3.94	1.05
Hezhe	4.64	7.77	2.99	4.22	1.05
Hui	4.46	7.06	3.16	4.15	1.10
Jing	3.64	5.01	2.62	3.38	1.13
Jingpo	4.18	8.66	3.56	3.93	1.05
Jino	4.18	8.66	3.57	3.94	1.05
Kazak	5.88	12.45	4.96	5.59	1.74

(continued)

Table 7.3 Continued

Ethnic group	Beds of medical institutions per 1000 population			Hospitals and health centers per 1000 population	Beds of township health centers per 1000 rural population
	Total	Urban	Rural		
Kirgiz	5.87	12.42	4.94	5.58	1.74
Korean	4.70	7.46	3.38	4.33	1.23
Lahu	4.18	8.66	3.57	3.94	1.05
Lhoba	2.87	6.48	2.53	2.72	1.05
Li	3.45	5.90	2.58	3.23	0.97
Lisu	4.20	8.60	3.57	3.95	1.07
Manchu	4.79	7.94	3.24	4.42	1.24
Maonan	3.72	5.43	2.63	3.46	1.08
Miao	4.11	7.07	2.98	3.83	1.13
Monba	2.80	6.42	2.50	2.66	1.03
Mongol	4.56	8.35	3.20	4.15	1.22
Mulao	3.66	5.14	2.61	3.40	1.11
Naxi	4.19	8.59	3.56	3.95	1.06
Nu	4.16	8.61	3.55	3.92	1.05
Oroqen	4.55	8.15	3.05	4.13	1.12
Pumi	4.18	8.65	3.56	3.94	1.05
Qiang	4.82	6.19	3.59	4.56	1.68
Russian	5.28	10.68	4.19	4.93	1.49
Salar	4.56	1.31	2.97	4.30	1.12
She	3.76	6.76	2.94	3.46	0.98
Shui	3.99	6.93	2.77	3.72	0.95
Tajik	5.83	12.25	4.90	5.54	1.73
Tatar	5.77	12.01	4.82	5.47	1.69
Tibetan	3.76	5.13	2.89	3.55	1.21
Tu	4.48	1.57	2.93	4.22	1.11
Tujia	4.28	6.78	3.08	3.96	1.35
Uygur	5.88	12.45	4.95	5.59	1.74
Uzbek	5.85	12.35	4.92	5.56	1.73
Va	4.19	8.61	3.57	3.94	1.06
Xibe	5.29	8.75	3.64	4.93	1.39
Yao	3.83	6.09	2.78	3.56	1.21
Yi	4.34	7.79	3.48	4.08	1.21
Yugur	4.39	6.55	3.18	3.90	1.14
Zhuang	3.64	5.13	2.64	3.38	1.13

Table 7.4 Hospitalization services in health institutions

Ethnic group	Number of inpatients (10,000 persons)	Patients discharged (10,000 persons)	Surgical operation of hospitalized (10,000 person-times)	Inpatients per 100 outpatient and emergency visits (person)
National total	17,857.10	17,840.33	3690.25	4.23
Achang	0.50	0.50	0.09	5.30
Bai	27.74	27.67	4.88	5.93
Baonan	0.20	0.20	0.03	4.98
Blang	1.35	1.34	0.24	5.30
Buyi	47.24	47.14	7.05	9.29
Dai	17.01	16.97	3.09	5.30
Daur	1.58	1.58	0.34	5.10
Deang	0.26	0.26	0.05	5.31
Derung	0.11	0.11	0.02	5.31
Dong	47.55	47.40	7.29	8.43
Dongxiang	6.71	6.67	1.07	5.14
Ewenki	0.35	0.34	0.07	4.68
Gaoshan	0.06	0.06	0.01	5.25
Gelao	9.23	9.21	1.37	9.40
Han	16,226.75	16,215.31	3410.12	4.99
Hani	21.11	21.06	3.83	5.30
Hezhe	0.06	0.06	0.01	5.64
Hui	146.25	145.66	28.28	5.07
Jing	0.36	0.36	0.05	5.30
Jingpo	1.94	1.93	0.35	5.31
Jino	0.31	0.31	0.06	5.30
Kazak	30.27	30.18	4.86	7.27
Kirgiz	3.88	3.86	0.62	7.26
Korean	22.74	22.70	4.97	5.32
Lahu	6.65	6.64	1.21	5.30
Lhoba	0.02	0.02	0.00	2.73
Li	14.23	14.19	2.26	3.32
Lisu	9.35	9.32	1.69	5.32
Manchu	137.32	137.17	28.40	5.21
Maonan	1.71	1.70	0.26	6.44
Miao	141.16	140.75	22.22	7.96
Monba	0.05	0.05	0.01	2.46
Mongol	70.28	69.91	13.96	4.87
Mulao	3.29	3.28	0.51	5.73
Naxi	4.54	4.52	0.82	5.30

(*continued*)

Table 7.4 Continued

Ethnic group	Number of inpatients (10,000 persons)	Patients discharged (10,000 persons)	Surgical operation of hospitalized (10,000 person-times)	Inpatients per 100 outpatient and emergency visits (person)
Nu	0.42	0.42	0.08	5.25
Oroqen	0.10	0.09	0.02	5.18
Pumi	0.49	0.49	0.09	5.30
Qiang	5.13	5.11	0.86	5.77
Russian	0.30	0.29	0.05	6.11
Salar	1.63	1.60	0.25	5.50
She	10.52	10.53	2.37	4.22
Shui	6.47	6.45	0.96	9.16
Tajik	0.98	0.98	0.16	7.20
Tatar	0.11	0.11	0.02	7.07
Tibetan	59.91	59.28	9.73	4.10
Tu	3.67	3.61	0.59	5.42
Tujia	124.64	124.49	20.92	6.96
Uygur	203.21	202.62	32.64	7.27
Uzbek	0.30	0.30	0.05	7.21
Va	5.82	5.81	1.06	5.31
Xibe	2.85	2.85	0.54	5.50
Yao	41.92	41.77	6.94	5.91
Yi	119.42	119.04	20.73	5.89
Yugur	0.17	0.16	0.03	4.92
Zhuang	255.21	254.21	40.36	5.12

Table 7.5 Conditions of new cooperative medical system

Ethnic group	Number of enrollees (10,000 persons)	Per capita premiums(yuan)	Premiums this year (100 million yuan)	Number of beneficiaries from reimbursement (10,000 person-times)
National total	80,530.86	308.50	2484.70	174,507.30
Achang	2.77	296.05	0.08	7.34
Bai	151.32	295.94	4.47	369.71
Baonan	1.25	298.19	0.04	2.46
Blang	7.50	296.16	0.22	19.84
Buyi	258.38	293.39	7.56	414.99
Dai	94.63	296.19	2.80	250.42

(*continued*)

Table 7.5 Continued

Ethnic group	Number of enrollees (10,000 persons)	Per capita premiums(yuan)	Premiums this year (100 million yuan)	Number of beneficiaries from reimbursement (10,000 person-times)
Daur	6.46	306.97	0.20	6.14
Deang	1.47	295.98	0.04	3.88
Derung	0.58	298.89	0.02	1.44
Dong	241.93	293.57	7.09	362.93
Dongxiang	38.24	296.12	1.13	75.06
Ewenki	1.57	309.26	0.05	1.22
Gaoshan	0.31	317.79	0.01	0.58
Gelao	50.45	292.65	1.47	79.83
Han	72,882.94	320.63	2253.47	161,321.94
Hani	117.59	296.25	3.48	311.49
Hezhe	0.19	306.26	0.01	0.28
Hui	671.17	334.17	21.94	1397.38
Jing	1.99	293.91	0.06	2.71
Jingpo	10.78	295.97	0.32	28.51
Jino	1.71	296.23	0.05	4.51
Kazak	73.10	315.22	2.30	94.47
Kirgiz	9.37	315.04	0.30	12.10
Korean	91.04	298.14	2.69	92.93
Lahu	37.07	296.08	1.10	98.19
Lhoba	0.26	323.71	0.01	0.52
Li	80.56	299.96	2.42	137.97
Lisu	51.77	296.08	1.53	136.78
Manchu	558.11	304.76	16.73	845.45
Maonan	9.50	292.70	0.28	13.24
Miao	724.13	294.39	21.26	1208.80
Monba	0.79	332.85	0.03	1.60
Mongol	313.62	309.60	9.66	302.50
Mulao	18.20	293.65	0.53	24.77
Naxi	25.17	296.81	0.75	66.38
Nu	2.35	296.95	0.07	6.19
Oroqen	0.38	306.82	0.01	0.41
Pumi	2.74	296.33	0.08	7.25
Qiang	23.10	296.43	0.68	53.55
Russian	0.87	320.85	0.03	1.02
Salar	7.60	391.67	0.30	8.39
She	48.79	341.98	1.65	66.99
Shui	35.52	292.86	1.04	57.01
Tajik	2.41	314.98	0.08	3.16
Tatar	0.29	316.58	0.01	0.39

(*continued*)

Table 7.5 Continued

Ethnic group	Number of enrollees (10,000 persons)	Per capita premiums(yuan)	Premiums this year (100 million yuan)	Number of beneficiaries from reimbursement (10,000 person-times)
Tibetan	443.83	331.27	14.64	844.98
Tu	17.38	384.93	0.67	20.41
Tujia	578.35	296.28	17.09	1118.98
Uygur	490.82	315.31	15.48	634.96
Uzbek	0.72	315.73	0.02	0.94
Va	32.30	296.27	0.96	85.53
Xibe	9.25	303.26	0.28	10.92
Yao	206.85	291.68	6.06	288.62
Yi	625.73	295.78	18.49	1522.71
Yugur	1.04	296.68	0.03	2.08
Zhuang	1400.37	292.85	41.07	1972.03

Table 7.6 Beds of social welfare institutions with residential accommodations (10,000 beds)

Ethnic group	Number of beds	Aged and disable	Mental retardation and mental diseases	Child	Social relief and other	Beds of social services per 1000 population (bed)
National total	449.30	416.50	6.70	8.70	17.40	3.32
Achang	0.01	0.01	0.00	0.00	0.00	0.00
Bai	0.34	0.29	0.01	0.01	0.02	0.07
Baonan	0.00	0.00	0.00	0.00	0.00	0.00
Blang	0.02	0.01	0.00	0.00	0.00	0.00
Buyi	0.52	0.44	0.02	0.02	0.03	0.14
Dai	0.20	0.17	0.00	0.01	0.01	0.04
Daur	0.04	0.04	0.00	0.00	0.00	0.02
Deang	0.00	0.00	0.00	0.00	0.00	0.00
Derung	0.00	0.00	0.00	0.00	0.00	0.00
Dong	0.62	0.55	0.02	0.02	0.03	0.14
Dongxiang	0.12	0.10	0.00	0.01	0.00	0.05
Ewenki	0.01	0.01	0.00	0.00	0.00	0.00
Gaoshan	0.00	0.00	0.00	0.00	0.00	0.00
Gelao	0.10	0.08	0.00	0.00	0.01	0.03

(*continued*)

Table 7.6 Continued

Ethnic group	Number of beds	Aged and disable	Mental retardation and mental diseases	Child	Social relief and other	Beds of social services per 1000 population (bed)
Han	422.06	392.44	6.10	7.64	15.88	86.38
Hani	0.25	0.21	0.00	0.01	0.02	0.05
Hezhe	0.00	0.00	0.00	0.00	0.00	0.00
Hui	2.89	2.58	0.04	0.14	0.12	1.48
Jing	0.00	0.00	0.00	0.00	0.00	0.00
Jingpo	0.02	0.02	0.00	0.00	0.00	0.00
Jino	0.00	0.00	0.00	0.00	0.00	0.00
Kazak	0.38	0.28	0.02	0.05	0.03	0.17
Kirgiz	0.05	0.04	0.00	0.01	0.00	0.02
Korean	0.68	0.61	0.02	0.01	0.04	0.22
Lahu	0.08	0.07	0.00	0.00	0.01	0.02
Lhoba	0.00	0.00	0.00	0.00	0.00	0.00
Li	0.23	0.23	0.00	0.00	0.00	0.26
Lisu	0.11	0.10	0.00	0.00	0.01	0.02
Manchu	4.27	3.92	0.05	0.07	0.23	1.07
Maonan	0.02	0.01	0.00	0.00	0.00	0.00
Miao	1.99	1.77	0.07	0.06	0.10	0.47
Monba	0.00	0.00	0.00	0.00	0.00	0.01
Mongol	2.00	1.83	0.03	0.05	0.09	0.73
Mulao	0.03	0.03	0.00	0.00	0.00	0.01
Naxi	0.06	0.05	0.00	0.00	0.00	0.01
Nu	0.01	0.00	0.00	0.00	0.00	0.00
Oroqen	0.00	0.00	0.00	0.00	0.00	0.00
Pumi	0.01	0.01	0.00	0.00	0.00	0.00
Qiang	0.14	0.13	0.00	0.00	0.01	0.02
Russian	0.01	0.00	0.00	0.00	0.00	0.00
Salar	0.02	0.02	0.00	0.00	0.00	0.04
She	0.23	0.21	0.01	0.00	0.01	0.05
Shui	0.07	0.06	0.00	0.00	0.00	0.02
Tajik	0.01	0.01	0.00	0.00	0.00	0.01
Tatar	0.00	0.00	0.00	0.00	0.00	0.00
Tibetan	1.80	1.48	0.01	0.15	0.15	3.44
Tu	0.06	0.04	0.00	0.01	0.00	0.08
Tujia	2.63	2.43	0.06	0.07	0.07	0.57
Uygur	2.55	1.92	0.14	0.32	0.18	1.12
Uzbek	0.00	0.00	0.00	0.00	0.00	0.00
Va	0.07	0.06	0.00	0.00	0.00	0.01

(*continued*)

Table 7.6 Continued

Ethnic group	Number of beds	Aged and disable	Mental retardation and mental diseases	Child	Social relief and other	Beds of social services per 1000 population (bed)
Xibe	0.08	0.07	0.00	0.00	0.00	0.02
Yao	0.49	0.44	0.02	0.01	0.03	0.09
Yi	1.92	1.72	0.04	0.05	0.12	0.34
Yugur	0.00	0.00	0.00	0.00	0.00	0.00
Zhuang	2.37	2.06	0.10	0.05	0.16	0.50

Table 7.7 Statistics on social relief (10,000 persons)

Ethnic group	Number of urban residents receiving minimum living allowance	Number of rural residents with minimum living allowance	Rural households with centralized livelihood guaranteed in five aspects	Rural households with decentralized livelihood guaranteed in five aspects	Number of persons receiving traditional relief in rural areas
National total	2143.50	5344.50	185.30	360.30	79.60
Achang	0.07	0.35	0.00	0.01	0.00
Bai	3.96	18.97	0.16	0.80	0.19
Baonan	0.06	0.22	0.00	0.01	0.00
Blang	0.20	0.94	0.01	0.04	0.01
Buyi	4.46	41.71	0.17	0.93	0.15
Dai	2.55	11.87	0.10	0.50	0.12
Daur	0.49	0.61	0.02	0.03	0.01
Deang	0.04	0.18	0.00	0.01	0.00
Derung	0.02	0.07	0.00	0.00	0.00
Dong	4.99	30.25	0.27	1.29	0.30
Dongxiang	1.90	6.64	0.03	0.23	0.04
Ewenki	0.10	0.15	0.00	0.01	0.00
Gaoshan	0.01	0.02	0.00	0.00	0.00
Gelao	0.86	8.23	0.03	0.18	0.03
Han	1891.88	4556.84	175.02	316.87	70.24
Hani	3.17	14.77	0.12	0.62	0.15
Hezhe	0.02	0.02	0.00	0.00	0.00
Hui	27.00	64.49	1.06	3.03	0.36
Jing	0.03	0.17	0.00	0.01	0.01
Jingpo	0.29	1.36	0.01	0.06	0.01

(*continued*)

Table 7.7 Continued

Ethnic group	Number of urban residents receiving minimum living allowance	Number of rural residents with minimum living allowance	Rural households with centralized livelihood guaranteed in five aspects	Rural households with decentralized livelihood guaranteed in five aspects	Number of persons receiving traditional relief in rural areas
Jino	0.05	0.21	0.00	0.01	0.00
Kazak	6.46	9.21	0.11	0.60	0.01
Kirgiz	0.83	1.18	0.01	0.08	0.00
Korean	6.35	5.58	0.26	0.57	0.03
Lahu	1.00	4.64	0.04	0.20	0.05
Lhoba	0.01	0.04	0.00	0.00	0.00
Li	2.54	4.72	0.04	0.50	0.00
Lisu	1.40	6.42	0.06	0.27	0.07
Manchu	26.65	29.46	1.20	2.63	0.26
Maonan	0.14	1.02	0.01	0.06	0.02
Miao	15.74	88.99	0.87	3.68	0.81
Monba	0.02	0.11	0.00	0.00	0.00
Mongol	18.80	28.29	0.62	1.64	0.59
Mulao	0.25	1.73	0.01	0.12	0.04
Naxi	0.68	3.13	0.03	0.13	0.03
Nu	0.06	0.29	0.00	0.01	0.00
Oroqen	0.03	0.03	0.00	0.00	0.00
Pumi	0.07	0.34	0.00	0.01	0.00
Qiang	0.69	1.63	0.09	0.09	0.02
Russian	0.07	0.10	0.00	0.01	0.00
Salar	0.48	0.92	0.01	0.04	0.00
She	0.51	2.07	0.05	0.14	0.02
Shui	0.61	5.65	0.02	0.13	0.02
Tajik	0.21	0.30	0.00	0.02	0.00
Tatar	0.02	0.04	0.00	0.00	0.00
Tibetan	14.47	53.87	0.78	2.32	0.15
Tu	1.04	2.11	0.02	0.10	0.00
Tujia	15.75	45.32	1.26	3.27	0.82
Uygur	43.27	61.63	0.73	4.00	0.05
Uzbek	0.06	0.09	0.00	0.01	0.00
Va	0.86	4.00	0.03	0.17	0.04
Xibe	0.59	0.63	0.02	0.05	0.00
Yao	3.97	17.37	0.22	1.56	0.50
Yi	16.60	72.41	1.11	2.99	0.70
Yugur	0.05	0.18	0.00	0.01	0.00
Zhuang	19.89	122.24	0.86	9.92	3.67

Table 7.8 Medical aid of civil affairs offices (10,000 persons or person-times)

	Medical aid in urban areas		Medical aid in rural areas			
Ethnic group	Medical aid	Aid for medical insurance	Medical aid	Aid for cooperative medical care	Expenses of urban medical aid	Expense of rural medical aid
National total	689.90	1387.10	1483.80	4490.40	708,801.60	1,329,104.80
Achang	0.01	0.08	0.06	0.39	17.59	61.77
Bai	0.75	4.04	2.89	20.70	946.47	3288.99
Baonan	0.02	0.02	0.04	0.07	16.57	42.04
Blang	0.04	0.22	0.15	1.06	47.69	167.04
Buyi	0.52	4.10	3.29	41.01	1069.89	5534.32
Dai	0.48	2.74	1.89	13.36	601.37	2109.69
Daur	0.13	0.46	0.13	0.64	170.80	179.59
Deang	0.01	0.04	0.03	0.21	9.34	32.76
Derung	0.00	0.02	0.01	0.07	4.09	12.46
Dong	0.91	3.62	3.44	27.99	1261.28	4541.64
Dongxiang	0.46	0.69	1.16	2.13	540.40	1252.64
Ewenki	0.02	0.10	0.03	0.16	32.45	40.26
Gaoshan	0.00	0.00	0.00	0.02	2.12	4.41
Gelao	0.10	0.80	0.64	8.08	206.30	1083.00
Han	614.75	1190.43	1314.05	3791.88	631,051.17	1,166,855.88
Hani	0.59	3.41	2.34	16.63	746.11	2621.97
Hezhe	0.01	0.02	0.00	0.02	7.45	6.25
Hui	12.47	19.53	24.84	47.78	9385.31	16,735.77
Jing	0.00	0.01	0.02	0.12	6.31	28.77
Jingpo	0.05	0.31	0.21	1.53	68.38	240.37
Jino	0.01	0.05	0.03	0.24	10.87	38.09
Kazak	2.27	6.55	3.14	10.23	2716.85	2277.78
Kirgiz	0.29	0.84	0.40	1.31	348.83	291.77
Korean	1.96	4.40	1.55	4.53	2233.48	1966.30
Lahu	0.19	1.07	0.74	5.23	234.71	824.68
Lhoba	0.00	0.00	0.00	0.00	0.86	11.85
Li	0.87	2.44	1.63	5.66	1275.72	2305.36
Lisu	0.27	1.48	1.06	7.20	331.77	1149.57
Manchu	5.04	12.02	6.17	21.57	6353.02	6999.63
Maonan	0.02	0.08	0.11	0.83	30.12	153.50
Miao	3.79	13.05	12.06	86.35	4190.71	14,140.97
Monba	0.00	0.00	0.01	0.00	2.42	36.73
Mongol	4.27	16.47	6.29	28.13	5551.07	7213.10
Mulao	0.04	0.13	0.22	1.31	55.34	273.66
Naxi	0.13	0.72	0.51	3.49	161.29	562.51
Nu	0.01	0.07	0.05	0.32	14.80	53.14

(*continued*)

Table 7.8 Continued

Ethnic group	Medical aid in urban areas: Medical aid	Medical aid in urban areas: Aid for medical insurance	Medical aid in rural areas: Medical aid	Medical aid in rural areas: Aid for cooperative medical care	Expenses of urban medical aid	Expense of rural medical aid
Oroqen	0.01	0.03	0.01	0.03	10.89	10.81
Pumi	0.01	0.08	0.05	0.39	17.49	61.06
Qiang	0.29	0.35	0.92	1.51	211.32	462.05
Russian	0.02	0.07	0.03	0.11	25.90	24.80
Salar	0.46	0.41	0.88	0.82	223.91	410.07
She	0.24	0.31	0.68	2.11	239.38	639.59
Shui	0.07	0.56	0.45	5.54	145.92	752.99
Tajik	0.07	0.21	0.10	0.33	87.03	73.70
Tatar	0.01	0.02	0.01	0.04	10.12	8.89
Tibetan	7.41	6.93	18.72	19.40	4531.17	18,319.01
Tu	0.99	0.88	1.90	1.84	482.61	905.23
Tujia	5.64	13.16	12.11	44.27	4603.87	9592.44
Uygur	15.22	43.91	21.04	68.62	18,210.53	15,249.70
Uzbek	0.02	0.06	0.03	0.10	26.50	22.33
Va	0.16	0.93	0.64	4.50	204.64	713.31
Xibe	0.12	0.31	0.16	0.50	147.41	138.25
Yao	0.89	2.22	3.00	13.11	990.98	3160.58
Yi	4.13	14.92	15.14	77.47	4255.38	13,510.54
Yugur	0.01	0.01	0.03	0.05	12.96	34.04
Zhuang	3.49	10.69	17.57	89.23	4398.42	20,484.47

Table 7.9 Statistics on urban employee basic pension insurance

Ethnic group	Urban employee basic pension insurance contributors at year-end (10,000 persons)	Number of staff and workers	Number of retirees	Revenue and expenses (100 million yuan): Revenue	Expenses	Balance at year-end
National total	30,426.80	22,981.12	7445.68	20,001.00	15,561.79	23,941.31
Achang	0.30	0.21	0.09	0.24	0.17	0.34
Bai	17.87	12.66	5.20	13.72	9.87	18.97

(*continued*)

Table 7.9 Continued

Ethnic group	Urban employee basic pension insurance contributors at year-end (10,000 persons)	Number of staff and workers	Number of retirees	Revenue and expenses (100 million yuan)		
				Revenue	Expenses	Balance at year-end
Baonan	0.20	0.13	0.07	0.17	0.14	0.20
Blang	0.82	0.57	0.25	0.66	0.47	0.93
Buyi	28.71	21.70	7.01	19.71	13.90	27.01
Dai	10.25	7.16	3.09	8.32	5.91	11.76
Daur	3.15	2.06	1.09	2.50	2.23	2.26
Deang	0.16	0.11	0.05	0.13	0.09	0.18
Derung	0.09	0.06	0.03	0.07	0.05	0.09
Dong	37.88	28.03	9.85	23.73	18.16	30.85
Dongxiang	6.51	4.36	2.14	5.52	4.53	6.97
Ewenki	0.67	0.45	0.22	0.55	0.47	0.54
Gaoshan	0.10	0.08	0.03	0.07	0.05	0.07
Gelao	5.52	4.18	1.34	3.78	2.66	5.20
Han	28,520.30	21,635.96	6884.34	18,620.10	14,427.77	22,295.36
Hani	12.66	8.85	3.82	10.30	7.31	14.56
Hezhe	0.13	0.08	0.05	0.10	0.09	0.07
Hui	211.76	152.49	59.27	158.46	132.28	195.95
Jing	0.28	0.20	0.09	0.18	0.16	0.24
Jingpo	1.17	0.82	0.35	0.95	0.67	1.34
Jino	0.18	0.13	0.06	0.15	0.11	0.21
Kazak	31.06	21.65	9.40	27.16	21.68	37.00
Kirgiz	4.00	2.79	1.22	3.49	2.80	4.74
Korean	52.55	34.06	18.48	35.47	32.92	33.08
Lahu	4.00	2.79	1.20	3.25	2.30	4.59
Lhoba	0.02	0.01	0.01	0.02	0.02	0.03
Li	34.33	25.95	8.38	19.76	18.21	15.61
Lisu	5.78	4.02	1.75	4.66	3.34	6.55
Manchu	337.95	232.24	105.72	250.89	218.28	227.44
Maonan	1.22	0.87	0.36	0.78	0.66	1.08
Miao	116.18	84.58	31.60	76.51	58.03	95.60
Monba	0.06	0.04	0.02	0.07	0.05	0.09
Mongol	133.91	91.53	42.38	108.77	92.37	108.16
Mulao	2.59	1.84	0.75	1.62	1.39	2.27
Naxi	2.83	1.98	0.86	2.29	1.63	3.21
Nu	0.26	0.18	0.08	0.21	0.15	0.29
Oroqen	0.21	0.13	0.07	0.16	0.14	0.13

(continued)

Table 7.9 Continued

Ethnic group	Urban employee basic pension insurance contributors at year-end (10,000 persons)	Number of staff and workers	Number of retirees	Revenue and expenses (100 million yuan)		
				Revenue	Expenses	Balance at year-end
Pumi	0.30	0.21	0.09	0.24	0.17	0.34
Qiang	6.02	4.01	2.01	4.22	3.45	5.45
Russian	0.38	0.27	0.12	0.33	0.27	0.40
Salar	1.84	1.28	0.56	1.54	1.36	1.73
She	19.88	16.52	3.36	9.94	7.19	12.35
Shui	3.86	2.89	0.97	2.67	1.91	3.64
Tajik	1.02	0.71	0.31	0.88	0.71	1.20
Tatar	0.12	0.08	0.04	0.10	0.08	0.14
Tibetan	64.46	44.60	19.86	56.82	45.13	70.99
Tu	4.29	3.03	1.25	3.45	3.03	3.97
Tujia	146.29	103.40	42.89	94.67	75.17	101.68
Uygur	208.90	145.70	63.20	182.49	145.69	248.47
Uzbek	0.31	0.22	0.09	0.27	0.21	0.37
Va	3.61	2.53	1.08	2.90	2.07	4.07
Xibe	6.61	4.53	2.08	5.07	4.35	4.82
Yao	41.24	30.70	10.54	23.84	19.26	34.51
Yi	92.03	63.35	28.69	69.15	52.27	93.79
Yugur	0.16	0.11	0.05	0.14	0.11	0.17
Zhuang	209.29	149.16	60.14	129.23	111.35	185.48

Table 7.10 Statistics of unemployment insurance

Ethnic group	Unemployment insurance contributors at year-end (10,000 persons)	Beneficiaries of unemployment insurance fund (10,000 persons)	Revenue and expenses (100 million yuan)		
			Revenue	Expenses	Balance at year-end
National total	15,224.71	204.03	1138.92	450.58	2929.04
Achang	0.18	0.00	0.02	0.00	0.05
Bai	10.41	0.16	0.90	0.19	2.89
Baonan	0.11	0.00	0.01	0.00	0.03

(continued)

Table 7.10 Continued

Ethnic group	Unemployment insurance contributors at year-end (10,000 persons)	Beneficiaries of unemployment insurance fund (10,000 persons)	Revenue and expenses (100 million yuan)		
			Revenue	Expenses	Balance at year-end
Blang	0.50	0.01	0.05	0.01	0.15
Buyi	15.90	0.11	1.34	0.57	4.41
Dai	6.26	0.11	0.58	0.10	1.85
Daur	1.56	0.02	0.12	0.03	0.33
Deang	0.10	0.00	0.01	0.00	0.03
Derung	0.05	0.00	0.00	0.00	0.01
Dong	18.69	0.19	1.32	0.52	4.13
Dongxiang	3.84	0.04	0.32	0.11	0.82
Ewenki	0.33	0.00	0.03	0.01	0.07
Gaoshan	0.05	0.00	0.00	0.00	0.01
Gelao	3.06	0.02	0.26	0.11	0.85
Han	14,267.87	190.56	1057.15	420.21	2707.94
Hani	7.76	0.13	0.71	0.12	2.30
Hezhe	0.07	0.00	0.00	0.00	0.01
Hui	116.95	1.50	9.54	3.76	24.77
Jing	0.14	0.00	0.01	0.00	0.04
Jingpo	0.71	0.01	0.07	0.01	0.21
Jino	0.11	0.00	0.01	0.00	0.03
Kazak	18.53	0.28	1.86	1.21	3.97
Kirgiz	2.38	0.04	0.24	0.15	0.51
Korean	22.95	0.35	1.81	0.53	4.86
Lahu	2.45	0.04	0.22	0.04	0.72
Lhoba	0.01	0.00	0.00	0.00	0.01
Li	22.23	0.29	1.37	0.41	4.18
Lisu	3.45	0.06	0.32	0.06	1.02
Manchu	152.86	1.75	13.26	3.94	30.84
Maonan	0.61	0.01	0.05	0.02	0.17
Miao	58.23	0.63	4.25	1.51	13.09
Monba	0.04	0.00	0.01	0.00	0.02
Mongol	64.83	0.74	5.53	1.52	14.25
Mulao	1.26	0.02	0.10	0.03	0.34
Naxi	1.70	0.03	0.16	0.03	0.50
Nu	0.16	0.00	0.01	0.00	0.05
Oroqen	0.10	0.00	0.01	0.00	0.02
Pumi	0.18	0.00	0.02	0.00	0.05
Qiang	2.20	0.09	0.27	0.09	0.60
Russian	0.22	0.00	0.02	0.01	0.05

(*continued*)

Table 7.10 Continued

Ethnic group	Unemployment insurance contributors at year-end (10,000 persons)	Beneficiaries of unemployment insurance fund (10,000 persons)	Revenue and expenses (100 million yuan)		
			Revenue	Expenses	Balance at year-end
Salar	0.86	0.01	0.09	0.03	0.32
She	10.61	0.09	0.64	0.25	2.05
Shui	2.14	0.02	0.18	0.08	0.60
Tajik	0.60	0.01	0.06	0.04	0.13
Tatar	0.07	0.00	0.01	0.00	0.02
Tibetan	31.96	0.58	4.07	1.08	13.65
Tu	2.00	0.03	0.21	0.07	0.71
Tujia	66.57	0.66	4.12	1.28	11.62
Uygur	124.57	1.91	12.46	8.09	26.69
Uzbek	0.18	0.00	0.02	0.01	0.04
Va	2.18	0.04	0.20	0.04	0.64
Xibe	2.96	0.04	0.29	0.10	0.63
Yao	19.61	0.30	1.33	0.40	4.21
Yi	45.50	1.10	4.60	1.22	13.07
Yugur	0.10	0.00	0.01	0.00	0.02
Zhuang	101.95	2.00	8.37	2.40	27.37

Table 7.11 Persons covered of urban basic medical care insurance (10,000 persons)

Ethnic group	Persons covered at year-end	Urban workers	Staff and workers	Retirees	Urban non-employment
National total	53,641.27	26,485.56	19,861.32	6624.24	27,155.70
Achang	0.72	0.37	0.26	0.10	0.35
Bai	41.47	20.43	14.60	5.83	21.04
Baonan	0.43	0.21	0.14	0.06	0.22
Blang	1.96	1.00	0.71	0.28	0.97
Buyi	58.95	29.80	21.39	8.41	29.16
Dai	24.50	12.55	8.97	3.58	11.96
Daur	5.70	2.91	2.01	0.91	2.79
Deang	0.38	0.19	0.14	0.06	0.18
Derung	0.19	0.10	0.07	0.03	0.10
Dong	79.09	34.05	24.43	9.63	45.04

(*continued*)

Table 7.11 Continued

Ethnic group	Persons covered at year-end	Urban workers	Staff and workers	Retirees	Urban non-employment
Dongxiang	14.04	6.81	4.81	2.00	7.23
Ewenki	1.30	0.63	0.45	0.19	0.67
Gaoshan	0.17	0.09	0.07	0.02	0.08
Gelao	11.46	5.74	4.12	1.62	5.72
Han	49,921.54	24,696.01	18,584.93	6111.08	25,225.53
Hani	30.40	15.56	11.12	4.44	14.84
Hezhe	0.21	0.12	0.08	0.04	0.09
Hui	480.64	196.82	143.07	53.75	283.82
Jing	0.56	0.25	0.18	0.07	0.30
Jingpo	2.80	1.43	1.02	0.41	1.36
Jino	0.44	0.23	0.16	0.06	0.22
Kazak	57.66	31.75	22.98	8.77	25.91
Kirgiz	7.42	4.09	2.95	1.13	3.33
Korean	96.92	47.92	32.09	15.83	49.00
Lahu	9.59	4.90	3.50	1.40	4.69
Lhoba	0.06	0.03	0.03	0.01	0.03
Li	60.88	32.88	25.26	7.62	28.00
Lisu	13.51	6.93	4.95	1.98	6.58
Manchu	505.17	321.73	219.93	101.80	183.43
Maonan	2.45	1.13	0.81	0.32	1.31
Miao	270.31	105.53	75.56	29.97	164.78
Monba	0.19	0.10	0.08	0.03	0.08
Mongol	249.60	128.50	90.30	38.20	121.11
Mulao	5.11	2.33	1.69	0.64	2.78
Naxi	6.61	3.40	2.43	0.97	3.21
Nu	0.61	0.31	0.23	0.09	0.30
Oroqen	0.36	0.19	0.13	0.06	0.17
Pumi	0.71	0.37	0.26	0.10	0.35
Qiang	8.94	4.64	3.22	1.42	4.30
Russian	0.71	0.38	0.28	0.11	0.33
Salar	3.68	1.85	1.29	0.56	1.82
She	31.27	16.45	13.31	3.14	14.82
Shui	7.96	4.03	2.88	1.15	3.94
Tajik	1.90	1.04	0.75	0.29	0.86
Tatar	0.22	0.12	0.09	0.03	0.10
Tibetan	138.89	72.30	51.46	20.85	66.59
Tu	8.59	4.26	2.99	1.26	4.34
Tujia	369.90	115.18	82.29	32.89	254.72
Uygur	387.71	213.43	154.51	58.92	174.28
Uzbek	0.57	0.32	0.23	0.09	0.26

(*continued*)

Table 7.11 Continued

Ethnic group	Persons covered at year-end	Urban workers	Staff and workers	Retirees	Urban non-employment
Va	8.59	4.35	3.12	1.23	4.24
Xibe	9.80	6.50	4.42	2.08	3.30
Yao	86.01	35.34	26.36	8.98	50.67
Yi	179.47	92.28	65.24	27.04	87.19
Yugur	0.36	0.17	0.12	0.05	0.18
Zhuang	418.48	188.39	137.75	50.63	230.10

Table 7.12 Revenue and expenses of urban basic medical care insurance (100 million yuan)

Ethnic group	Revenue			Expenses		
	Total	Workers	Non-employment	Total	Workers	Non-employment
National total	6938.68	6061.92	876.76	5543.62	4868.49	675.13
Achang	0.11	0.10	0.01	0.09	0.09	0.01
Bai	5.92	5.38	0.54	5.04	4.52	0.52
Baonan	0.05	0.05	0.01	0.05	0.04	0.01
Blang	0.30	0.28	0.02	0.26	0.23	0.03
Buyi	6.78	6.09	0.70	5.97	5.47	0.50
Dai	3.80	3.50	0.30	3.22	2.91	0.32
Daur	0.75	0.67	0.09	0.64	0.58	0.06
Deang	0.06	0.05	0.00	0.05	0.04	0.00
Derung	0.03	0.03	0.00	0.02	0.02	0.00
Dong	7.86	6.69	1.18	6.74	5.88	0.86
Dongxiang	1.79	1.60	0.19	1.58	1.41	0.16
Ewenki	0.17	0.15	0.02	0.15	0.13	0.01
Gaoshan	0.02	0.02	0.00	0.02	0.02	0.00
Gelao	1.30	1.16	0.14	1.14	1.05	0.10
Han	6456.83	5638.78	818.05	5142.48	4512.48	630.00
Hani	4.72	4.34	0.38	4.00	3.61	0.39
Hezhe	0.03	0.02	0.00	0.02	0.02	0.00
Hui	61.75	51.27	10.48	50.98	43.35	7.63
Jing	0.06	0.06	0.01	0.05	0.05	0.00
Jingpo	0.43	0.40	0.03	0.37	0.33	0.04
Jino	0.07	0.06	0.01	0.06	0.05	0.01
Kazak	9.98	9.17	0.82	8.16	7.47	0.69
Kirgiz	1.28	1.18	0.11	1.05	0.96	0.09
Korean	10.21	8.80	1.41	8.37	7.51	0.86

(continued)

Table 7.12 Continued

Ethnic group	Revenue			Expenses		
	Total	Workers	Non-employment	Total	Workers	Non-employment
Lahu	1.48	1.36	0.12	1.26	1.13	0.12
Lhoba	0.02	0.01	0.00	0.01	0.01	0.00
Li	6.63	5.66	0.96	5.43	4.74	0.68
Lisu	2.09	1.92	0.17	1.77	1.59	0.18
Manchu	70.58	65.56	5.02	62.14	58.52	3.62
Maonan	0.28	0.24	0.03	0.23	0.21	0.02
Miao	26.59	22.08	4.51	22.56	18.97	3.59
Monba	0.05	0.04	0.00	0.03	0.03	0.00
Mongol	33.48	29.86	3.62	28.49	25.81	2.68
Mulao	0.58	0.51	0.07	0.47	0.43	0.04
Naxi	1.03	0.95	0.08	0.87	0.79	0.09
Nu	0.10	0.09	0.01	0.08	0.07	0.01
Oroqen	0.05	0.04	0.01	0.04	0.04	0.00
Pumi	0.11	0.10	0.01	0.09	0.08	0.01
Qiang	1.26	1.04	0.22	1.04	0.84	0.20
Russian	0.12	0.11	0.01	0.10	0.09	0.01
Salar	0.73	0.66	0.08	0.60	0.53	0.07
She	4.39	3.90	0.48	3.24	2.83	0.41
Shui	0.92	0.83	0.09	0.81	0.75	0.07
Tajik	0.32	0.30	0.03	0.26	0.24	0.02
Tatar	0.04	0.04	0.00	0.03	0.03	0.00
Tibetan	27.49	24.81	2.68	20.97	18.39	2.58
Tu	1.63	1.45	0.17	1.33	1.17	0.16
Tujia	30.31	23.01	7.30	25.37	19.46	5.91
Uygur	67.09	61.58	5.51	54.84	50.18	4.66
Uzbek	0.10	0.09	0.01	0.08	0.07	0.01
Va	1.31	1.20	0.11	1.11	1.00	0.11
Xibe	1.40	1.31	0.09	1.23	1.16	0.07
Yao	8.58	7.16	1.41	6.91	5.94	0.97
Yi	26.28	23.30	2.99	22.14	19.33	2.81
Yugur	0.04	0.04	0.00	0.04	0.04	0.00
Zhuang	47.68	41.39	6.29	38.12	34.48	3.64

8

Entertainment and Other Cultural Activity

Data on culture are estimated based on the data provided by the Ministry of Culture. Data on radio broadcasting, films and television are from State Administration of Radio, Film and Television. Data on number of books published for children and textbooks are from General Administration of Press and Publication. Data on sports are from General Administration of Sport.

For detailed information please refer to *Collection of China News and Publication Statistical Information* (Department of Publication Industrial Development, General Administration of Press and Publication), *Statistics on National Development Indicators of Radio, Film and Television* (Department of Arrangement and Finance, State Administration of Radio, Film and Television), and *Statistical Yearbook of Sports* (Finance Department, General Administration of Sport).

R. Guo, *China Ethnic Statistical Yearbook 2016*,
DOI 10.1007/978-3-319-49199-8_8

Table 8.1 Population coverage of radio and TV programs, and radio and TV programs produced and broadcasted by region (2012)

Region	Population coverage rate of radio programs (%)	Population coverage rate of TV programs (%)	Number of public radio programs (set)	Number of TV programs (set)	Number of TV plays broadcasted (set)	Number of cartoons broadcasted (hour)
National total	**97.51**	**98.20**	**2627**	**3273**	**242,298**	**304,877**
Achang	96.04	97.05	0	0	8	7
Bai	95.11	96.67	2	7	397	396
Baonan	96.73	97.45	0	0	5	7
Blang	96.06	97.06	0	0	22	20
Buyi	88.99	93.29	3	9	240	242
Dai	96.05	97.05	1	4	272	255
Daur	98.05	97.51	1	1	53	54
Deang	96.04	97.05	0	0	4	4
Derung	96.26	97.20	0	0	2	2
Dong	91.17	95.04	4	8	340	495
Dongxiang	96.70	97.35	2	3	188	258
Ewenki	97.99	97.10	0	0	15	16
Gaoshan	97.27	97.98	0	0	1	1
Gelao	88.79	93.19	1	2	45	45
Han	97.73	98.34	2323	2840	210,252	266,649
Hani	96.04	97.05	2	5	338	317
Hezhe	98.51	98.72	0	0	1	0
Hui	96.65	97.84	31	39	3037	4169
Jing	95.95	97.63	0	0	3	4
Jingpo	96.03	97.04	0	0	31	29
Jino	96.05	97.05	0	0	5	5
Kazak	95.35	95.63	11	13	1326	1261
Kirgiz	95.38	95.66	1	2	169	161
Korean	98.56	98.69	5	6	455	182

Lahu	96.05	97.06	1	2	106	100
Lhoba	93.54	94.72	0	0	1	1
Li	96.14	95.39	4	3	125	388
Lisu	96.08	97.08	1	2	149	139
Manchu	98.68	98.73	29	31	2459	1799
Maonan	93.90	96.38	0	0	13	15
Miao	92.03	95.36	12	24	1169	1539
Monba	93.60	94.70	0	0	2	2
Mongol	97.86	97.25	26	27	2631	2706
Mulao	95.12	97.14	0	1	28	33
Naxi	96.06	97.06	0	1	72	68
Nu	96.03	97.03	0	0	7	6
Oroqen	98.28	97.93	0	0	2	2
Pumi	96.06	97.06	0	0	8	7
Qiang	96.75	97.73	0	1	67	62
Russian	96.47	96.33	0	0	12	12
Salar	94.54	96.47	0	0	29	35
She	97.75	98.48	2	2	98	201
Shui	89.22	93.43	0	1	34	34
Tajik	95.41	95.72	0	0	42	40
Tatar	95.50	95.81	0	0	5	5
Tibetan	94.73	95.99	13	18	1238	1365
Tu	94.69	96.58	1	1	60	77
Tujia	94.89	97.21	11	17	1342	1768
Uygur	95.35	95.64	72	90	8890	8455
Uzbek	95.39	95.68	0	0	13	12
Va	96.09	97.08	0	1	93	87
Xibe	97.97	98.10	1	1	72	62

(continued)

Table 8.1 Continued

Region	Population coverage rate of radio programs (%)	Population coverage rate of TV programs (%)	Number of public radio programs (set)	Number of TV programs (set)	Number of TV plays broadcasted (set)	Number of cartoons broadcasted (hour)
Yao	95.37	97.59	4	7	401	597
Yi	95.44	96.81	10	26	1654	1544
Yugur	96.84	97.53	0	0	4	6
Zhuang	96.16	97.74	23	44	2415	2868

Table 8.2 Transmission trunk and users of cable radios and TVs by region (2012)

Region	Total length of transmission trunk for cable radios and TVs (10,000 km)	Users of cable radios and TVs (10,000 households)	Users of digital TV	Pay TV	Popularization rate of cable TV programs (%)
National total	**376.12**	**21,508.97**	**14,303.07**	**2501.12**	**51.50**
Achang	0.01	0.44	0.33	0.20	43.27
Bai	0.39	23.99	17.99	9.90	42.03
Baonan	0.00	0.14	0.11	0.02	27.05
Blang	0.02	1.21	0.88	0.55	43.32
Buyi	0.47	34.61	30.64	8.54	34.28
Dai	0.25	15.19	11.09	6.95	43.27
Daur	0.04	1.99	1.34	0.18	43.05
Deang	0.00	0.23	0.17	0.11	43.15
Derung	0.00	0.10	0.07	0.04	44.05
Dong	0.51	36.45	29.80	6.70	37.43
Dongxiang	0.10	4.36	3.60	0.51	27.32
Ewenki	0.01	0.44	0.30	0.03	40.54
Gaoshan	0.00	0.07	0.04	0.01	47.58
Gelao	0.09	6.69	5.96	1.64	33.92
Han	346.42	19,964.55	13,242.91	2284.99	52.44
Hani	0.31	18.86	13.80	8.65	43.28
Hezhe	0.00	0.08	0.05	0.01	51.01
Hui	2.39	140.64	107.59	12.30	41.73
Jing	0.00	0.32	0.19	0.04	46.04
Jingpo	0.03	1.73	1.27	0.79	43.24
Jino	0.00	0.27	0.20	0.13	43.25
Kazak	0.24	14.70	13.56	0.15	35.80
Kirgiz	0.03	1.90	1.75	0.02	35.98
Korean	0.72	36.93	26.59	4.77	54.09
Lahu	0.10	5.94	4.34	2.72	43.24
Lhoba	0.00	0.02	0.01	0.00	28.60
Li	0.15	15.76	12.61	1.48	36.83
Lisu	0.14	8.38	6.05	3.75	43.34
Manchu	3.48	203.30	130.03	8.96	53.77
Maonan	0.02	1.45	0.94	0.20	42.52
Miao	1.77	113.21	89.90	24.19	38.26
Monba	0.00	0.07	0.03	0.00	28.56
Mongol	1.20	87.38	59.92	4.67	42.35
Mulao	0.04	2.92	1.79	0.36	44.97
Naxi	0.07	4.08	2.95	1.82	43.32

(*continued*)

Table 8.2 Continued

Region	Total length of transmission trunk for cable radios and TVs (10,000 km)	Users of cable radios and TVs (10,000 households)	Users of digital TV	Pay TV	Popularization rate of cable TV programs (%)
Nu	0.01	0.38	0.27	0.17	43.21
Oroqen	0.00	0.13	0.08	0.01	45.73
Pumi	0.01	0.44	0.32	0.20	43.32
Qiang	0.11	5.17	2.47	0.86	46.15
Russian	0.00	0.21	0.17	0.01	39.25
Salar	0.01	1.28	1.22	0.19	37.45
She	0.30	14.71	10.32	1.93	65.27
Shui	0.06	4.76	4.15	1.17	34.61
Tajik	0.01	0.49	0.44	0.01	36.24
Tatar	0.00	0.06	0.05	0.00	36.39
Tibetan	1.06	58.78	34.77	7.68	34.27
Tu	0.03	3.01	2.80	0.46	38.40
Tujia	2.34	117.21	89.07	15.48	42.96
Uygur	1.62	98.97	91.19	1.03	35.89
Uzbek	0.00	0.15	0.13	0.00	36.22
Va	0.09	5.23	3.80	2.34	43.40
Xibe	0.06	3.72	2.35	0.09	55.77
Yao	0.49	37.18	24.35	4.95	45.45
Yi	1.95	108.39	71.64	36.96	42.98
Yugur	0.00	0.12	0.09	0.02	27.11
Zhuang	2.94	233.69	137.05	30.12	46.70

Note: Total length of transmission trunk for cable radios include 41,900 km directly under the State Administration of Radio, Film and Television

Table 8.3 Number of books published for children and textbooks

Ethnic group	Number of publications (kind)		Printed copies (10,000 copies)		Printed sheets (1000 sheets)	
	Books for children	Textbooks	Books for children	Textbooks	Books for children	Textbooks
National total	30,965	81,271	47,702.00	347,458.00	2,853,998.00	27,078,790.00
Achang	0	0	0.19	6.17	5.15	420.52
Bai	7	11	13.88	340.34	533.93	22,917.36
Baonan	0	0	0.18	2.62	7.90	200.11
Blang	0	1	0.50	16.72	13.74	1140.30
Buyi	12	11	30.55	488.25	1198.74	34,012.81
Dai	3	6	6.24	210.39	170.20	14,362.94
Daur	2	4	2.16	21.81	129.61	1538.84
Deang	0	0	0.09	3.26	2.44	222.23
Derung	0	0	0.07	1.36	3.24	92.90
Dong	33	25	54.39	556.29	2807.61	35,928.30
Dongxiang	4	9	5.89	87.95	277.25	6594.60
Ewenki	1	1	0.50	5.70	29.87	407.82
Gaoshan	0	0	0.14	0.81	8.34	56.04
Gelao	2	2	5.73	94.75	214.17	6606.08
Han	22,864	29,732	36,491.24	227,135.94	2,184,911.13	15,718,858.71
Hani	3	8	7.76	261.95	210.89	17,868.34
Hezhe	0	0	0.11	0.47	6.67	32.40
Hui	165	265	203.98	1857.94	12,406.60	130,600.59
Jing	0	0	0.93	4.46	45.77	303.76
Jingpo	0	1	0.72	24.01	19.69	1637.25
Jino	0	0	0.11	3.80	3.17	259.29
Kazak	31	148	15.63	423.53	1528.73	28,200.68
Kirgiz	4	19	2.02	54.13	196.27	3603.66

(continued)

Table 8.3 Continued

Ethnic group	Number of publications (kind)		Printed copies (10,000 copies)		Printed sheets (1000 sheets)	
	Books for children	Textbooks	Books for children	Textbooks	Books for children	Textbooks
Korean	190	85	183.92	312.16	11,619.94	24,955.57
Lahu	1	2	2.42	82.51	65.31	5625.50
Lhoba	0	0	0.01	1.17	0.87	84.39
Li	24	3	139.45	174.76	6604.62	11,908.52
Lisu	2	4	3.42	114.43	95.74	7831.38
Manchu	376	443	412.88	1302.63	27,643.98	97,466.61
Maonan	2	1	3.49	20.23	168.24	1386.30
Miao	80	94	139.40	1644.46	6914.76	108,029.95
Monba	0	1	0.05	3.64	2.96	264.77
Mongol	136	232	124.09	1060.33	7796.12	76,355.83
Mulao	4	2	7.80	40.51	383.25	2766.23
Naxi	1	2	1.75	55.96	53.38	3834.73
Nu	0	0	0.16	5.33	5.01	364.45
Oroqen	0	0	0.15	1.16	9.05	82.28
Pumi	0	0	0.19	6.11	5.45	416.82
Qiang	2	6	2.39	38.88	128.85	3124.89
Russian	0	1	0.29	4.34	22.00	296.00
Salar	1	5	0.44	20.09	24.96	1459.79
She	15	11	27.55	123.43	1980.08	8536.77
Shui	2	2	4.43	67.39	173.04	4686.84
Tajik	1	5	0.54	13.70	50.91	912.79
Tatar	0	1	0.07	1.59	6.42	106.59
Tibetan	33	225	25.73	1472.17	1322.37	108,341.26
Tu	1	10	1.18	45.58	60.05	3314.55
Tujia	89	206	138.60	1504.53	8107.91	96,752.43

Uygur	206	995	105.95	2844.12	10,317.70	189,360.75
Uzbek	0	1	0.17	4.16	15.71	277.14
Va	1	2	2.25	72.28	64.87	4920.38
Xibe	6	13	5.90	24.13	417.10	1769.01
Yao	51	29	85.77	549.35	4392.07	35,456.24
Yi	32	72	50.93	1276.58	1921.79	90,637.59
Yugur	0	0	0.17	2.13	7.56	163.63
Zhuang	332	155	632.29	3219.55	30,981.51	219,420.07

Table 8.4 Number of certified athletes at various technical grades (person)

Ethnic group	International master of sports	Female	Master of sports	Female	First grade	Female
National total	167	85	1820	864	9690	3396
Achang	0	0	0	0	0	0
Bai	0	0	0	0	2	1
Baonan	0	0	0	0	0	0
Blang	0	0	0	0	0	0
Buyi	0	0	3	1	16	5
Dai	0	0	0	0	0	0
Daur	0	0	0	0	1	0
Deang	0	0	0	0	0	0
Derung	0	0	0	0	0	0
Dong	0	0	2	1	15	5
Dongxiang	0	0	0	0	3	1
Ewenki	0	0	0	0	0	0
Gaoshan	0	0	0	0	0	0
Gelao	0	0	1	0	3	1
Han	144	74	1586	761	8922	3122
Hani	0	0	0	0	0	0
Hezhe	0	0	0	0	0	0
Hui	2	1	11	5	72	21
Jing	0	0	0	0	0	0
Jingpo	0	0	0	0	0	0
Jino	0	0	0	0	0	0
Kazak	0	0	1	1	5	2
Kirgiz	0	0	0	0	1	0
Korean	0	0	4	2	18	6
Lahu	0	0	0	0	0	0
Lhoba	0	0	0	0	0	0
Li	0	0	1	1	22	7
Lisu	0	0	0	0	0	0
Manchu	1	1	27	14	121	45
Maonan	0	0	0	0	0	0
Miao	1	0	8	3	45	16
Monba	0	0	0	0	1	0
Mongol	1	0	10	4	53	18
Mulao	0	0	0	0	1	0
Naxi	0	0	0	0	0	0
Nu	0	0	0	0	0	0
Oroqen	0	0	0	0	0	0
Pumi	0	0	0	0	0	0
Qiang	0	0	0	0	0	0
Russian	0	0	0	0	0	0

(*continued*)

Table 8.4 Continued

Ethnic group	International master of sports	Female	Master of sports	Female	First grade	Female
Salar	0	0	0	0	0	0
She	0	0	1	1	7	3
Shui	0	0	0	0	2	1
Tajik	0	0	0	0	0	0
Tatar	0	0	0	0	0	0
Tibetan	3	1	11	4	157	60
Tu	0	0	0	0	1	1
Tujia	1	0	9	4	53	21
Uygur	0	0	8	4	36	11
Uzbek	0	0	0	0	0	0
Va	0	0	0	0	0	0
Xibe	0	0	1	0	2	1
Yao	0	0	1	0	12	5
Yi	0	0	1	0	8	3
Yugur	0	0	0	0	0	0
Zhuang	0	0	8	3	66	25

Appendix 1. A Brief Description of China's 56 Ethnic Groups

Throughout history, race, language and religion have divided China as much as physical terrain, political fiat and conquest.[1] However, it is always a politically sensitive issue to identify those non-Han people as different ethnic groups. As a result, the total number of ethnic groups has never been fixed precisely in China. For example, in 1953, only 42 ethnic peoples were identified, while the number increased to 54 in 1964 and 56 in 1982. Of course, this does not include the unknown ethnic groups as well as foreigners with Chinese citizenship.[2]

Specifically, China's current 56 ethnic groups are, in alphabetical order, Achang, Bai, Baonan, Blang, Buyi, Dai, Daur, Deang, Derung, Dong, Dongxiang, Ewenki, Gaoshan, Gelao, Han, Hani, Hezhe, Hui, Jing, Jingpo, Jino, Kazak, Kirgiz, Korean, Lahu, Lhoba, Li, Lisu, Manchu,

[1] The text is prepared by Rongxing Guo based on the following sources: (i) *The Ethnic Minorities in China* (title in Chinese: "zhongguo shaoshu minzu", edited by the State Ethnic Affairs Commission (SEAC) of the People's Republic of China and published in 2010 by the Central Nationality University Press, Beijing) and (ii) the introductory text of China's 56 ethnic groups (in Chinese, available at http://www.seac.gov.cn/col/col107/index.html, accessed on 2016–06–20).

[2] As of 2010, when the Sixth National Population Census of the People's Republic of China was conducted, the populations of the unknown ethnic groups and foreigners with Chinese citizenship were 640,101 and 1448, respectively.

R. Guo, *China Ethnic Statistical Yearbook 2016*,
DOI 10.1007/978-3-319-49199-8

Maonan, Miao, Monba, Mongol, Mulao, Naxi, Nu, Oroqen, Pumi, Qiang, Russian, Salar, She, Shui, Tajik, Tatar, Tibetan, Tu, Tujia, Uygur, Uzbek, Va, Xibe, Yao, Yi, Yugur, and Zhuang. In the following, the general geographical and historical background of and the linguistic and religious features of each of them are briefly reported.

Achang

The Achang ethnic minority lives mainly in the Dehong Dai-Jingpo autonomous prefecture of Yunnan province. They lived in the reaches of Nu river as long ago as the second century, and then migrated southwest to the present Longchuan and Lianghe counties. The Achang are mountain farmers. As one of the earliest people, they have their own language that belongs to the Tibetan-Burman family of the Sino-Tibetan phylum. However, the Achange language has no written form. Over time, they have accepted the language of the Dai ethnic minority as well as the written and spoken Mandarin of the Han people. In the past, some groups of the Achang believe in primitive spirits and practice ancestor worship, the others follow Theravada Buddhism, and they hold different religion festivals and activities to show their piety. Southern Buddhism is another popular religion among Achang people. Nearly in each of the villages, a Buddhist temple stands with various architecture styles. In addition, Taoism is also of great influences since the Ming dynasty (AD 1368–1644), which is reflected by the Imperial Pavilion Taoist Temple established by Achang people in Dehong of Yunnan.

Bai

The Bai people are mainly dominant in the Dali Bai autonomous county of Yunnan province, together with Lijiang, Kunming, Yuanjiang, Guizhou and so on. A Tibetan-Burman people, the Bai were a major ethnic group and cultural elite in the kingdom of Nanzhao (AD 738–937) that dominated the region to China's southwest. The Bai language derives from the Tibetan-Burman family of the Sino-Tibetan phylum. However, as a result of their close cultural ties with the Han people, the Bai have also applied Chinese characters as their written form of language. Although the Bai people believe in Buddhism, they also worship their village god ('Benzhu'), Nature god, the Prince of the Nanzhao regime, or even a hero of folklore.

Baonan

Located in the southwest of Gansu province, the area of Mt. Jishishan is home to the Baonan ethnic minority. It is thought that the Baonan ethnic minority developed over a long period of time formed largely by Mongolians. During the Yuan, the Ming and the Qing dynasties, some people of the Hui, the Tibetan, and the Tu ethnic minorities were assimilated into the group, often through marriage and in this way the groups influenced each other. The Baonan people did, however, retain most of their Moslem traditions and customs. The Baonan are culturally close to the Hui and, like them, are Muslims. They speak a unique Baonan language which is part of the 'Altai' language family descended from Mongolian. Most can also speak and write Mandarin Chinese like the majority Han people. They continue to follow Islam and are part of the Sunni branch.

Blang

The Blang ethnic minority is one of the oldest peoples in Yunnan province, living mainly in the mountain area of Menghai county of Dai autonomous prefecture in Xishuangbanna. Their earliest record can be traced back to the Han dynasty (BC 206–AD 220). The Blang speak a Mon-Khmer language (it belongs to the Austro-Asiatic phylum with an alveolar sound and pronunciation), and their culture is closely related to those of nearby Myanmer and Laos. As the Blang people live dispersedly, they speak different languages in separate regions. Without their own written characters, they use those of the Dai and the Han peoples. Like many other ethnic minorities, the Blang admire totems. However, the totems they admire are not fierce beasts like the tiger or lion, but the bamboo rat and toad. They believe that when they see those small animals, they must keep away from them, or their relatives will pass away. The Blang also believe in Theravada Buddhism, polytheism and ancestor worship.

Bouyei

The Bouyei ethnic minority have mainly inhabited Southwest China's Guizhou province. Their main living areas are now the Bouyei-Miao autonomous prefecture, Anshun and Guiyang cities. The Bouyei's way of life is quite similar to that of the Miao and their language is closely related to those of the Zhuang and the Dai. The Bouyei people speak their own language belonging to the Sino-Tibetan phylum; and some are able to read and write Mandarin and as well. The Bouyei people believe in many gods. There is a God for each Mountain; River, Lake or Pond; for each old and unusual tree, for megalith, caves, paddy field, and for when it rains or thunders, there are various gods. They also worship ancestors' supreme might with each family setting niches in their home.

Dai

The Dai ethnic minority is distributed throughout the Dai autonomous region and the Dehong Dai-Jingpo autonomous prefecture in Xishuangbanna in the southern part of Yunnan province. The Dai have two main branches – the Water Dai, who have a close affinity with the Thais; and the Han Dai, who are more or less identical with the Shan of the Myanmar. The Dai were one of the main ethnic groups dominating the kingdom of Nanzhao (AD 738–937). In the past, they were called 'baiyue', meaning a vast living area. Therefore, they have established a close relationship with ethnic groups like the Zhuang, the Dong, the Shui, the Bouyei and the Li, who are said to be the descendants of the Dai people. The Dai language belongs to the Zhuang-Dai branch of the Zhuang-Dong group of the Sino-Tibetan languages. The written language was derived from Devanagari and differs from region to region. The religion of the Dai people is Buddhism, which was adopted in the sixth to eighth century and had a profound influence on their politics, economy, culture and arts.

Daur

Daur is the title that the people of the Daur ethnic minority named themselves, meaning cultivator. With historical records dating back to the early seventeen century, there are several stories about the origin of this minority. The most accepted is that they were descendants of the brave Khitan tribe (Qidan) in the Liao dynasty AD (916–1125). This minority helped guard the frontier during the Qing dynasty (AD 1644–1911) near Xinjiang. The population of the Daur ethnic minority is considerably smaller than many other minorities. They mainly inhabit Inner Mongolia autonomous region and Heilongjiang province, while some live in the Xinjiang Uyghur autonomous region. The Daur people have their own language, which has a strong affinity with that of the Mongolian dialect, both of which belong to the Altai phylum. As their land bordering upon the places where the Mongol, the Manchu, the Ewenki, the Han, and the Kazak minorities inhabited, they developed their vocabulary, benefiting from others. However, their language has no written form.

Deang

The Deang ethnic minority lives exclusively in Yunnan province and primarily in Luxi and Zhenkang counties, along with the Dai, the Jingpo, and the Va ethnic minorities. Their language belongs to the Mon-Khmer group of the Austro-Asiatic phylum, much close to that of the Va. They have no traditional written language, so some of people use the written Chinese language along with that of the Dai and the Jingpo languages. Influenced by the Dai ethnic minority, the Deang people are faithful to Theravada Buddhism. Boys of less than ten years old are sent to the temples to become monks, learning sutras. Most of them are secularized after several years, with only few promoted as Buddhists who are highly esteemed as both educated and knowledgeable. Meanwhile, they also worship the original gods, such as Dragon King, God of Mountain, God of Land, etc.

Derung

The Derung (also spelt Drung or Dulong) people are located in a canyon surrounded by the Tibetan plateau in the north, the Gaoligong Mountain in the east, and the Dandanglika Mountain in the west. The inhabitant area of the Derung ethnic minority is quite isolated. Their population is mainly found in the Nujiang autonomous prefecture of Yunnan province, in the Dulong valley, while a few others can be found east of the Dulong valley, living in the mountains above the Nujiang river near the village of Binzhongluo in northern Gongshan county. The Derung language, which is closely related to that of Jingpo, belongs to the Sino-Tibetan phylum and is without written form. The traditional religion of the Derung people is nature worship, with beliefs that there are spirits controlling their fortune and the change of nature, so they often worship and charm away those spirits. Recently, there are also some Christians.

Dong

The Dong ethnic minority lives primarily in the border regions between Guizhou, Hunan and Hubei provinces. The Dong people trace their origins back to about the third century BC and, during the Tang dynasty (AD 618–907), they separated from the mixed minority 'Baiyue', naming themselves Dong. The Dong are thought to be the modern-day descendants of the ancient Liao people. Dong legends generally maintain that the ancestors of the Dong migrated from the east. According to the legends of the Southern Dong people, the ancestors of the Southern Dong came from Guangzhou, Guangdong and Wuzhou, Guangxi. The Northern Dong maintain that their ancestors fled Zhejiang and Fujian because of locust swarms. The Dong people speak a Dai language – a branch of the Zhuang-Dong group of the Sino-Tibetan phylum though many of them also speak Chinese. The Dong's beliefs remain original, believing that all things have spirits and gods – of land, water, ox, and the spirit of ancestors, etc.

Dongxiang

The Dongxiang ethnic minority derived their name from their native region – Dongxiang. Today, the Dongxiang people mainly inhabit the Dongxiang autonomous county in Gansu province, with a small number in Xinjiang Uyghur and the Ningxia Hui autonomous regions. Historians are divided in their views about the origin of the Dongxiang ethnic minority. Some hold that they are descendants of Mongolian troops posted in the Hezhou area by Genghis Khan (AD 1162–1227) during his march to the west. Other historians say they are a mixture of many ethnic groups – Hui, Mongolian, Han and Tibetan. The Dongxiang language is similar to Mongolian, both of which belong to a branch of the Mongolian Austronesian of the Altaic phylum. Since the Dongxiang have no written language, literature developed orally. Huaer, a popular form can be sung in both daily life and at festivals, absorbing fully, the essence of their oratory creativity, though most can speak and write in Chinese. The Dongxiang ethnic minority holds firm faith in Islam.

Ewenki

The Ewenki ethnic minority treasures their name of nationality which means 'people living in the mountain forests'. This ethnic minority is distributed across seven banners (counties) in the Inner Mongolia autonomous region and in Nahe county of Heilongjiang province, where they live together with Mongolians, Daurs, Hans, and Oroqens. Nantunzhen, the seat of the banner government, is a rising city on the grassland. A communication hub, it is the political, economic and cultural center of the Ewenki autonomous banner (*Qi*). The Ewenki are a Tungus people and speak a Tungus language which belongs to the Tungus-Manchu branch of the Altaic phylum. Interestingly it has no written characters. In the Qing dynasty (1644–1911), the Ewenki group learned to write in the Manchu form whilst today they can master Mongolian and Chinese languages. Most of the Ewenki people are disciples of shamanism. Meanwhile, they also believe that there are gods controlling their life. The god of mountain, in their eyes, is a long bearded senior man.

Gaoshan

The Taiwanese aborigines in maninland China are collectively known as the "Gaoshan". They now mainly live in Henan, Fujian, Liaoning and Hebei provinces and Guangxi Zhuang autonomous region. It is said these Taiwanese aborigines originated from one branch of the ancient Yue people living along the coast of the mainland China during the Stone Age. They were later joined by immigrants from the Philippines, Borneo and Micronesia. The Gaoshan people do not have their own script, and their spoken language belongs to the Indonesian Austronesian branch of the Malay-Polynesian Phylum. They altogether have more than 20 languages, 13 of which are still in use. As they have lived with Han people for a long time, many of them can speak southern Min language. The Gaoshan people are animists who believe that everything in nature has a soul. They believe in strength of spirit, ancestors and totem. They think that after a person's death, his soul stays to protect his descendants.

Gelao

The Gelao are mountain subsistence farmers and hunters in Guizhou and Yunnan provinces and Guangxi autonomous region. They are an old ethnic minority. Over 2000 years ago, the Gelao people lived in many places in China. At present, some bridges, graves, wells, and even villages in Guizhou province still bear Gelao names. The ethnic minority's name dates back to the Ming dynasty (AD 1368–1644). Before then, they were called the "Liao". The Gelao people have their own language which belongs to the Zhuang-Dong Group of the Sino-Tibetan phylum. But their dialects are quite different from each other. Some cannot communicate with each other, although they live in the same county. Only one fourth Gelao people actually speak the Gelao language, while the other use Chinese language as well as those of the Miao, the Yi and the Bouyei ethnic minorities. They write in Chinese as they don't have their own written form of characters. The Gelao people believe in the blessing of many gods as well as their ancestors.

Han

Members of the ethnic majority in China have traditionally been referred to as the Han race. This may well be because of the relatively long period of social, political, economic, and military consolidation and stability enjoyed by the Chinese nation during the period of the Han dynasty (206 BC–AD 220). The term 'Han', however, does not offer a full account of the cultural and ethnic origins of the Chinese people. It was, instead, an inclusive name for the various tribes that lived together on the Central China Plains well before the time of Christ. The trend over the ages was for many ethnic groups living adjacent to the Hua-Xia people to be assimilated at different times and to different degrees into what the Chinese have ultimately termed the Han culture. The original ethnic stock for this amalgam seems to have primarily included the Hua-Xia, the Eastern Yi, the Chu-Wu, and the Baiyue groups. Other non-Han peoples were assimilated into the Han culture at different points in China's history. They are, for example, the Huns (Xiongnu) and Xianbei between the third and fifth century AD, the Eastern Hu and the Jurchens (ancestors of the Manchus) from the tenth through the early thirteenth century, and the Manchus through their conquest of China in the seventeenth century.

Hani

The Hani people mainly inhabit an area within the reaches of the Yuan and the Lantsang rivers. This is a branch of the ancient Qiang people who had been nomadic on the Tibetan plateau and then emigrated southward. Most of the Hani people live in the valleys between the Yuanjiang and

Lancang (Mekong) rivers – a vast area between the Ailao and the Mengle mountains in southern Yunnan province. They are under the jurisdiction of Honghe Hani-Yi autonomous prefecture, which includes Honghe, Yuanyang, Luchun and Jinping counties. Others dwell in Simao prefecture, Xishuangbanna, etc. The Hani are subsistence farmers who speak a Tibetan-Burman language, which belongs to the Sino-Tibetan phylum. The language has no characters of its own, so in 1957 the Chinese government created a set of spelling characters based on Latin. The Hani people are convinced that everything has soul, so they worship many gods and their ancestors. Since the early twentieth century, Christianity and Buddhism have spread to them, but with little influence on the Hani society.

Hezhen

The Hezhen ethnic minority is one of the smallest minorities of China. From generation to generation, they lived in the reaches of the Amur river (Heilongjiang river), the Songhua river, and the Ussuri river (Wusuli river) and appropriately named themselves 'Hezhen', meaning people of the eastern lower reaches. They are descendants of Heshui Tribe which reigned during the Sui (AD 581–618) and the Tang (AD 618–907) dynasties. Among China's least populous ethnic group, the Hezhen people speak a Manchu-Tungus language. The Hezhen people speak a language that belongs to the Altaic phylum. But they do not have their own characters, so most of them write in Chinese. The Hezhen people are shamanists, believing all have spirits and worship as many gods are there as varieties of animals and plants.

Hui

One of China's largest ethnic minorities, the Hui people can be found in most of the counties and cities throughout China, especially in Ningxia Hui autonomous region and Gansu, Qinghai, Henan, Hebei, Shandong and Yunnan provinces and Xinjiang Uygur autonomous region. The name Hui is an abbreviation for "Huihui," which first appeared in the literature of the

Northern Song dynasty (AD 960–1127). The Hui minority is descended from the Arabic and Persian merchants who came to China during the seventeenth century. During the early years of the thirteenth century when Mongolian troops were making their western expeditions, group after group of Islamic-oriented people from Middle Asia, as well as Persians and Arabs, either were forced to move or voluntarily migrated into China. Chinese is the native language. In addition, they retain some of the Arabic and Persian words. Islamism plays a vital role in the development of the Hui ethnic minority in China. There is typically a mosque in each community. In fact, the religious thought has influenced the Hui people in all walks of life.

Jing

The Jing ethnic minority has a small population. Most live on the three islands of Guangxi Zhuang autonomous region, and the rest live and mingle with the Han, Zhuang and Yao ethnic groups. The Jing cultivate rice and are good fishermen. The ancestors of the Jing emigrated from Vietnam to Southwest China in the early sixteenth century and settled on the uninhabited lands beyond the neighborhood which had been populated by people of the Han and the Zhuang ethnic groups. The Jing's spoken language is similar to Vietnamese while many now speak Cantonese. The Jing are descendants of Vietnamese migrants who arrived in China from the fifteenth century. The word 'jing' is an equivalent of the Vietnamese Kinh, a name given to the majority people of Vietnam. Most of the Jing people believe in Taoism together with some thoughts of Buddhism and wizardry. They believe there are many gods who control their life, which include the god who is said to have made manitou to pacify the sea.

Jingpo

The Jingpo ethnic minority lives mainly in the Dehong and the Dai-Jingpo autonomous prefectures with some in Nujiang Lisu autonomous prefecture of Yunnan province, as well as in Myanmar. According to local legends and historical records, Jingpo ancestors in ancient times inhabited the southern part of the Xikang-Tibetan plateau. They gradually migrated south to the northwestern part of Yunnan, west of the Nujiang river. The local people, together with the newly-arrived Jingpos, were called "Xunchuanman," who lived mainly on hunting. The Jingpo live in the mountain areas along the border with Myanmar and speak a language closely related to that of the Derung, both of which belong to the Tibetan-Burman group of the Sino-Tibetan phylum. They do, however, also use the Chinese language. The main traditional religion is polytheism. The Jingpo people think everything has a soul that can never die, so, if a Jingpo meets with misfortune, she or he will turn to worship the spirits. However, some Jingpo people are Christian as a result of missionaries who first came to these areas in the early twentieth century.

Jino

The Jino ethnic minority, which was not officially recognized as a nationality until 1979, lives mainly in Jino town of Jinghong county, Xishuangbanna Dai autonomous prefecture of Yunnan province. It is said that the Jinos migrated to Jinoluoke from Pu'er and Mojiang or places even farther north. Jinoluoke is a mountainous area stretching for 70 kilometers from east to west and 50 kilometers from north to south. The expression Jino refers to an ethnic group that respects the mother's brother as a prominent person in the family. The Jino people have their own language, which belongs to a Tibetan-Burman branch of the Sino-Tibetan phylum. However, they have no written characters. The Juno's religion is animism. It is said that their ancestors who were part of the troops of Zhuge Lian during the Three Kingdoms Period (AD 220 –280) were dispersed from the main force. Therefore, they regard Zhuge Lian as a distinguished joss (god).

Kazak

The Kazaks (also spelled Kazakhs) are a Turkic people of Eastern Europe and the northern parts of Central Asia (largely Kazakhstan, but also found in parts of Uzbekistan, Russia, Mongolia, and China). Kazakh identity is of medieval origin and was strongly shaped by foundation of the Kazak Khanate in AD 1456–1465. In China, the Kazak ethnic minority is mainly in Ili Kazak autonomous prefecture, Mori and Barkol autonomous counties of Xinjiang Uyghur autonomous region, as well as in Qinghai and Gansu provinces. The Kazaks are Turkic people, speaking a language which belongs to the Turkic group of the Altaic phylum. The Kazak language has two scripts, one based on Arabic, the other on Latin letters. However, many Kazak people can use Chinese, Uyghur and Mongolian languages. In the past, they believed in the shamanism. In about the eleventh century, they began to turn to Islam while some continued to admire nature, soul and fire like the shamanists.

Kirgiz

The Kirgiz ethnic minority is named after a word meaning 40 girls. Its population is mostly distributed throughout the Kirgiz autonomous prefecture, Ili, Dacheng, Aksu, Kashgar, the southwest of Xinjiang autonomous region, as well as in Heilongjiang province. The forefathers of the Kirgiz lived on the upper reaches of the Yenisey river. In the mid-sixth century the Kirgiz tribe was under the rule of the Turkic khanate. After the Tang dynasty (AD 618–907) defeated the Eastern Turkic khanate, the Kirgiz came into contact with the dynasty. Most of them speak the Kirgiz language, which belongs to the Turkic group of Altaic phylum, and has a written form based on Arabic letters. The Kirgiz people have used different spoken languages in Xinjiang. While those living in the south of Xinjiang speak Uyghur language, those in the north of Xinjiang speak Kazak. Most Kirgiz people believe in Islam, but a few of the other follow the Tibetan Buddhism.

Korean

The Korean (also called "Chaoxian" in China) ethnic group is scattered mainly in Heilongjiang, Jilin and Liaoning provinces. Smaller populations of Korean people live in other areas in the Inner Mongolian autonomous region, and Beijing, Xi'an and other cities. Members of this ethnic minority living in Yanbian Korean autonomous prefecture of Jilin province speak and write in Korean while those living in other parts of China usually speak Chinese. The ancestors of the present Korean people were immigrants from the Korea peninsula. When they settled in China they gradually formed unique customs and evolved into a Chinese ethnic group. The Korean ethnic group does not follow one particular religion. While most of them are atheists, some believe in Buddhism, a belief that has influenced Korean life in the past, and others follow Christianity which spread to them from South Korea.

Lahu

Most of the Lahu people are scattered around three autonomous counties of Lancangjiang Lahu, Menglian, and Shuangjiang, with the others living in Simao, Lincang and Xishuangbanna of Yunnan province. The forebears of the Lahu people, who were hunters, began migrating southward to lush grassland which they discovered while pursuing a red deer. In the eighth century, after the rise of the kingdom of Nanzhao in present Yunnan province, the Lahu people were compelled to move south. By no later than the beginning of the eighteenth century they already had settled in their present-day places. The Lahu ethnic minority have their own language, which belong to the Yi branch of the Tibetan-Burman group of the Sino-Tibetan phylum. Most Lahu people also speak Chinese or Dai, as a result of their close relations to the Han and the Dai peoples. Their written characters were not formed until 1957. Lahu, in their language, means to roast the meat of the tiger. It indicates that this ethnic group was quite good at hunting. Some Lahu people practice nature and ancestor worship, but still others believe in Mahayana Buddhism. In addition, a few of them are Christians.

Lhoba

Scattered primarily throughout the Luoyu region of southeast Tibet, the Lhoba is the smallest of China's 56 ethnic groups. The name "Lhoba" is derived from the Tibetan word for southerners. The majority of the

Lhoba ethnic minority have their homes in Mainling, Medog, Lhunze and Nangxian counties in southeastern Tibet. Additionally, a small number of them live in Luoyu in southern Tibet. Living at the foot of Himalayas, almost completely isolated from the outside world, the Lhoba lagged behind the rest of the world. The Lhobas speak a distinctive language belonging to the Tibetan-Myanmese language family, a branch of the Sino-Tibetan phylum. Few of them know the Tibetan language. Having no written script, Lhoba people used to keep records by notching wood or tying knots. The Lhoba's traditional religion is nature worship, not Tibetan Buddhism. They pray to the spirits, seeking blessings, and believe that shamans have the power to control them.

Li

The Li ethnic minority live mainly in Li-Miao autonomous prefecture in the center and south of Hainan province, with a small number of the others being mixed with the Han people. As a branch of the ancient Baiyue groups, the Li people had a close relationship with such present ethnic minorities as the Buyi, the Dong, the Dai, the Shui, and the Zhuang. The name "Li" is derived from their pronunciation of 'mountains'. The Li's language, which has diverse dialects, belongs to the Zhuang-Dong group of the Sino-Tibetan phylum. Because of long association with the Han people, some of the Li can also speak Chinese. In 1957, they created the written form of their language based on Roman script. The Li people believe all things have spirits and in some places, there are still relics of totem adoration. Owing to the spread of Christianity, some of Li have taken to this religion.

Lisu

The Lisu ethnic minority mainly inhabit in Nujiang Lisu autonomous prefecture in Yunnan province, with a few others living in the other cities within Yunnan and Sichuan provinces. They can also be found in the mountain areas of Myanmar, Thailand, and the northeast Indian state of Arunachal Pradesh. According to their clan history, which is passed from one generation to the next in the form of songs, the Lisu originate from eastern Tibet. They had close ties with the Yi and the Naxi ethnic minorities. The Lisu's language belongs to the Tibetan-Burman branch of the Sino-Tibentan phylum. There have been three distinct forms of writing, with the last one, created in 1957 and based on the Latin alphabet, being widely used now. The Lisu people believe the existence of gods and totem; but in the late nineteenth century some of them began to turn to the Christian faiths as a result of the preaching of missionaries in China.

Manchu

Arising from the Jurchen tribes and establishing the Jin dynasty (AD 1115 –1234) and the Qing dynasty (AD 1644–1911), the Manchu people have greatly influenced Chinese history. Today, the Manchu ethnic minority has a population mainly in Heilongjiang, Jilin and Liaoning provinces of northeast China although they can also be found in many other cities as well. In the sixteenth century, the written language of the Manchu people was created from characters based on the Mongolian language. The Manchu language is part of the Tungus-Manchu group, a branch of Altaic phylum. As the Manchu people migrated from the northern to the central China, they learned and adopted the language of the dominant Han Chinese. The ancient Manchu people believed in shamanism. Later, with the influence of Buddhism, Daoism and Confucianism, their beliefs took on a pluralistic quality.

Maonan

The Maonan ethnic minority lives mostly in Huanjiang county of Guangxi Zhuang autonomous region, especially in the three regions of Shangnan, Zhongnan, and Xianan. Interestingly, more than 80 % of the Maonan share the same surname: Tan. Maonan with the surname "Tan" believe that they are descended from the old inhabitants of the province of Hunan that emigrated to Guangxi and married Maonan women. Their language belongs to the Zhuang-Dong group of the Sino-Tibetan phylum; nearly all of the Maonan people can speak Chinese and the Zhuang language. Traditional Maonan religion is both animistic and polytheistic, with heavy Taoist influences. Many deities and rituals are borrowed from Chinese folk religion. They think that there are many gods who can control their life and they must sacrifice during festive days.

Miao

The Miao ethnic minority is one of the largest minority groups in China. They live mainly in Guizhou, Yunnan, Hunan, Hubei, and Hainan provinces and in Guangxi Zhuang autonomous region. As early as the Qin and Han dynasties (2000 years ago), the ancestors of the Miao people lived in the western part of present-day Hunan province and the eastern part of present-day Guizhou province. As a result of large-scale migrations over many centuries the Miao became widely dispersed. The Miao are now divided into several branches, such as Black Hmong, White Hmong, Striped Hmong, etc. The Miao language, which belongs to the Miao-Yao group of the Sino-Tibetan phylum, has developed into three dialects: the dialect of western Hunan province, the one of eastern Guizhou province and the one of the border area of Sichuan, Guizhou and Yunnan provinces. As a result of the long time living with the Han and other people, the Miao can also speak Chinese and the Dong and Zhuang languages. They have been writing their own Miao language based on Latin since 1956. The Miao people believe that everything in nature has a spirit. They worship their ancestors. Some also believe in Catholicism or other forms of Christianity.

Monba

The Monba ethnic minority has a long history. Their name, 'Monba', pronounced 'Menba' in Chinese, derives from Tibetan, referring to the people living in Menyu in the lower reaches of the Yarlung Tsangpo (Brahmaputra) river. The area became the hereditary manor of Tibet during the mid-fourteenth and early fifteenth centuries. In the mid-seventeenth century, the Fifth Dalai Lama sent two of his disciples to Menyu to set up an office there. As a result, the Tibetan rule of religion and politics over the area was integrated. The Monba now occupy Tsona, Metog, and Nyingchi counties in Tibet. Thanks to their proximity to the Zang people (Tibetan people), the Monba's customs, traditions and life styles appear very similar to those of the Tibetans. The Monba language is a member of the Tibetan-Burman group of the Sino-Tibetan phylum. The Monba are sub-divided into six sub-groups because of their variations in their language. There is no written language; instead Tibetan is used. The Monba are generally adherents of the Gelugpa sect of Tibetan Buddhism (Lamaism), which they adopted in the seventeenth century as a result of the evangelical influence of the Bhutanese-educated Mera Lama. In addition, some still follow traditional religions.

Mongol

The Mongol ethnic minority is distributed primarily in the Inner Mongolia autonomous region along with the other areas in Qinghai, Gansu, Liaoning, Jilin, and Heilongjiang provinces. They originated from a tribe in northern China and Mongolia during the seventh century. "Mongolian" originally was the name of one of the Mongolian tribes roaming along the Erguna river. At the beginning of the thirteenth century, a Mongolian tribe headed by Genghis Khan unified all the Mongolian tribes, giving birth to a new people – the Mongolian ethnic minority. In AD 1206, he was elected the Great Khan of all Mongols with the title of Genghis Khan. Kublai Khan, the grandson of Genghis Khan founded the Yuan dynasty (AD 1206–1368) in 1272, and subdued the Southern Song dynasty (AD 1127–1279) in 1279, bringing the whole of China under his centralized rule. The Mongol language belongs to the Mongolian group of the Altaic phylum and has three main dialects. The written form is derived from that of the thirteenth century and experienced many changes. They once believed in shamanism but have turned to Lamaism (Tibetan Buddhism) since the Yuan dynasty.

Mulao

The majority of the Mulao ethnic minority live in Luocheng county of Guangxi Zhuang autonomous region. Others are scattered in other, neighboring counties. In their own language, Mulao means mother. Historical records trace the Mulao ethnic minority back to the period of the Yuan dynasty (AD 1271–1368). The Mulaos lived in Luocheng city of present Guangxi autonomous region and called themselves Lings or Jins, but the neighboring Zhuang people called them Bujins and the Hans called them Mulao. The Mulaos were mostly inhabited by families sharing the same surname. The Mulao language is a member of the Zhuang-Dong branch of the Sino-Tibetan phylum. But because of their extensive contacts with the Han and local Zhuang peoples, many Mulaos speak one or both of these languages in addition to their own. The Mulaos have no written language of their own, and the Chinese characters are commonly used for communication. Although the religion no longer plays a main role in their daily life, traditionally the Mulao have been mostly animists. Some of them also practice Daoism and Buddhism.

Naxi

The Naxi are an ethnic group inhabiting the foothills of the Himalayas in the northwestern part of Yunnan province (mostly living in Naxi autonomous county in Lijiang), as well as the southwestern part of Sichuan province and Tibet autonomous region. The Naxi are thought to have come originally from Northwest China, migrating south toward Tibetan populated regions, and usually inhabiting the most fertile river-side land. According to historical documents, the Naxi's forefathers were closely related to a tribe called "Maoniu Yi" in the Han dynasty (206 BC–AD 220), "Mosha Yi" in the Jin dynasty (AD 265–420) and "Moxie Yi" in the Tang dynasty (AD 618–907). In the name Naxi, Na means 'black' and Xi means people. The Naxi people speak a language belonging to the Yi branch of the Tibetan-Burman group of the Sino-Tibetan phylum. Before 1949, most of the Naxi people were Lamaists, with some also holding the faiths of Dongba (a form of shamanism), believing that all have spirits and those spirits could never die. Although there was Buddhism, Taoism and Christianity being taught there, few Naxi people turned to those religions.

Nu

The Nu people are divided into the Northern, Central and Southern groups. Their homeland is a country of high mountains and deep ravines crossed by the Lancang (Mekong), Dulong and Nujiang rivers. The name "Nu" comes from the fact that they were living near the Nujiang river, and the name of their ethnic group derives from there. There is also a sparse distribution of the Nu in Weixi county in Diqing Tibetan autonomous prefecture of Yunnan province and in Zayu county of Tibet autonomous region, particularly around the border between Yunnan and Tibet. In comparison to the other ethnic groups in China, the Nu population is relatively small. The Nu language belongs to the Tibetan-Burman subgroup of the Sino-Tibetan language family. The dialects within the Nu language, however differ so much that Nu people from different regions cannot communicate with each other. The language has no written characters, so most Nu people use written Chinese. The religious beliefs remain primitive and animistic, believing everything has spirits and admiring the power of nature. Some of them believe in Lamaism (Tibetan Buddhism) and Christianity.

Oroqen

The Oroqen mainly live in the Oroqen autonomous banner (*Qi*) of Hulunbuir League of Inner Mongolia autonomous region and in the Greater and Lesser Xing'an Mountains of Heilongjiang province, an area known for its abundant wild animal resources. A small number of others are scattered in the neighboring provinces. For generations the Oroqens had lived a life of hunting and fishing in the forests. The name Oroqen appeared as early as the Qing dynasty (AD 1644 –1911). The Oroqen people speak a language that belongs to the Tungus-Manchu group of the Altaic phylum. Since there is no written form of the language they usually use Chinese whilst some use Mongolian. The Oroqen hold their faith in the power of nature, ancestors and totems. This is a kind of shamanism. There are many gods such as the god of the sun, moon, fire, wind, mountains, etc. To the Oroqen people, bears and tigers are known as god, lord, and governor.

Pumi

The Pumi ethnic minority is mainly distributed in Lanping, Lijiang, Weixi and Yongsheng counties of Yunnan province, as well as in the Yi autonomous county of Ninglang. Some live in Muli and Yanyuan counties of Sichuan province as well. According to Pumi legends and historical records, ancient Pumis were a nomadic tribe, roaming the Qinghai-Tibet plateau. Their descendents later moved south to warmer, more verdant areas along valleys within the Hengduan mountain range. By the seventh century, the Pumis were living in Sichuan's Yuexi, Mianning, Hanyuan, Jiulong and Shimian areas, constituting one of the major ethnic minorities in the Xichang prefecture. After the thirteenth century, the Pumis gradually settled down in their present places. The Pumi people speak a language that belongs to the Tibetan-Burman group of the Sino-Tibetan phylum. In the past, the Pumi used Tibetan characters, however, today, most write in Chinese. Though a few of the Pumi do follow Lamaism and Taoism, most believe that many gods and their ancestors influence their lives, They are led by wizards in their ceremonies for peace, happiness and harvest.

Qiang

This ethnic minority lives mainly in Aba Tibetan autonomous prefecture of Sichuan province. And Maowen Qiang autonomous county is the largest area that is home to the Qiang. They have a profound history as evidenced by inscriptions on oracle bones. "Qiang" was a name given by ancient Hans to the nomadic people living in western China. The Qiangs were not a single distinctive ethnic group then. According to historical records, a clan group made their homes in what is today's Sichuan province. The Han dynasty (206 BC – AD 220) court in the second century had set up an administrative prefecture for the area. During AD 600–900 when the Tibetans gradually expanded their rule over the region, some Qiangs were assimilated by the Tibetans. Closely related to the Tibetans, the Qiangs speak a similar language that belongs to the Tibetan-Burman group of the Sino-Tibetan phylum. The Qiang language is divided into two dialects. But the Qiangs do not have a written language; instead, most of them can write in Chinese. The Qiangs believe that everything in nature has a spirit. They especially consider white quartz stone as the symbol of rightness having the power of gods, while the black quartz represents evil.

Russian

The Russian ethnic minority descends from Russian immigrants to China in as early as the eighteenth century. The largest Russian population arrived in Northeast China and Xinjiang after the Russian Civil War of 1918–22. Most of the ethnic Russians now live in Ili, Tacheng, Altay and Urumqi of Xinjiang Uyghur autonomous region whilst a few live in the Heilongjiang province and Inner Mongolian autonomous region. These immigrants were called "Guihua people" and their villages "Guihua village". The Russians use their own language (Russian) and written script, which belongs to the Slavic group of the Indo-European language family, when they communicate with each other. They also use the Chinese language and script in their social or official activities. Culturally and linguistically, the Russians are the same as those in Russia. While the Russians speak and write Russian, most of them also use Chinese. The Russians believed in Eastern Orthodox, with fewer people believing in Christianity, but in the recent years, they are more and more tended to hold no religious thoughts.

Salar

The Salar people live mostly in the Qinghai-Gansu border region, on both sides of the Yellow river, namely in Xunhua Salar and Hualong Hui autonomous counties of Qinghai and the adjacent Jishishan Bonan, Dongxiang and Salar autonomous county of Gansu province. There are also Salars in Xinjiang (especially in the Ili Kazakh autonomous prefecture). Having arrived and settled in the Qinghai province 700 years ago, they originally made their living by hunting, forestry and livestock farming. More recently, they thrive on agriculture, handicrafts and horticulture. Living in a semi-desert area, the Salars are Muslims. The Salars' ancestors were migrating Oghuz Turks who intermarried with the Han, the Tibetans, and the Hui Chinese. They have their own Turkic language which is a subfamily of the Altaic language family that includes Turkish. Most Salar people can also speak Chinese and Tibetan and use Chinese script.

She

The She people live primarily in the mountain areas of Fujian and Zhejiang provinces, and to a lesser extent in Jiangxi, Guangdong, and Anhui provinces. They refer to themselves as 'Shanha' where Shan means mountain and Ha means customers, 'customers of the mountain'. Though scholars disagree about the true origins of the She, most believe that the She's ancestors originally lived in the Phoenix mountains in Chaozhou of Guangdong province. They left their native place to escape the oppression of their feudal rulers. That's why they called themselves "guests from the mountains." The only ethnic minority to live in the provinces of Zhejiang and Jiangxi, the She are in many ways quite similar to the Han. Always most She nowadays speak Chinese, some use a language that belongs to the Miao branch of the Miao-Yao group of the Sino-Tibetan phylum. The She language is similar to the Hakka language, one of the seven dialects in China. Because they do not have their own written language, they choose to write in

Chinese. Some She are Buddhists, while others are polytheists or ancestor worshippers.

Shui

Most of the Shui people dwell on the upper reaches of the Longjiang and Duliu rivers that meander across plains and rolling land interspersed with vast expanses of forests in southern Guizhou province. Some Shuis have their homes in the northwestern part of the Guangxi Zhuang autonomous region. The She live in villages of several dozen households or live along with Hans. Most reside in hilly country 500–1500 meters high. Rivers have carved out their valleys. The Shui people have a language that is closely related to that of the Dong, both of which belong to the Zhuang-Dong group of the Sino-Tibetan phylum. As no written form of the Shui language exists, they usually write using Chinese characters. Historically there was a written form of the Shui language whose characters were called 'Shui Shu', but it was used only for religious activities. The Shuis are believers of polytheism. In former days a shaman would be employed to say prayers and animals slaughtered to be offered to evil spirits when someone fell ill or died or when something bad happened. Catholicism that came to the area in the late Qing dynasty (AD 1644–1911) won very few converts.

Tajik

According to folklore, the word Tajik means crown and this is usually how they refer to themselves. The Tajik ethnic minority is mainly distributed across the Tashi Ku'ergan Tajik autonomous county in Xinjiang Uyghur autonomous region. Although the Tajik is among the smaller ethnic groups of China, they boast a rich history. The origin of the Tajik ethnic group can be traced to tribes speaking eastern Iranian who had settled in the eastern part of the Pamirs more than twenty centuries ago. In the eleventh century, the nomadic Turkic tribes called those people "Tajiks" who lived in Central Asia. Of Iranian stock, the Tajiks speak an

Iranian language that belongs to the Iranian group of the Indo-European language family. Some Tajik people can also speak the Uyghur language and most of them write in Uyghur since the Tajik language has no written form. The Tajik follow the faith of Islam but usually only go to mosque during major festivals.

Tatar

The Tatars were a native people of the Volga region of Russia, Tatarstan and Bashkortostan. Most Tatars live in Uzbekistan, Kazakhstan, Ukraine, and Russia. The Tatar ethnic minority live mainly in Yining, Tacheng and Urumqi of Xinjiang Uyghur autonomous region. Historically this minority was known as "Dada" in China. The name Tatar likely originated amongst the nomadic Tatar confederation in the north-eastern Gobi desert in the fifth century. Their history in China dates from the Tang dynasty (AD 618–907), when the Tatar tribe was ruled by the nomadic Turkic khanate in northern China. As this state fell into decline, the Tatars grew in strength, and their name was used to refer to several tribes in the north after the Tang dynasty. Their homeland was later annexed by the Mongols, and when the Mongols pushed west, many Central Asians and Europeans called them Tatars. The Tatars have their own language which is a member of the Turkic subgroup of the Altaic phylum. They also speak and write Uyghur and Kazak as a result of their proximity to these minorities. The Tatars now follow Islam.

Tibetan

The Tibetan ethnic people (also known as Zang in Chinese) mainly live in the Tibetan autonomous region on the Tibetan Plateau, with some groupings in Qinghai, Gansu, Sichuan and Yunnan provinces. According to archeological findings, their ancestors lived in the Yarlung Tsangpo (Brahmaputra) river delta. Historical records suggest that the Tibetans were part of the Xiqiang group during the Han dynasty (206 BC – AD 220). The Tibetans first settled along the middle reaches of the Yarlung Tsangpo river in Tibet. At the beginning of the seventh century, King Songzan Gambo began to rule the whole of Tibet and made Losha (today's Lhasa) the capital. He designated official posts, defined military and administrative areas, created the Tibetan script, formulated laws and unified weights and measures, thus establishing the slavery kingdom known as "Bo," which was called "Tubo" in Chinese historical documents. The Tibetan language that belongs to the Tibetan-Burman group of the Sino-Tibetan language family is divided into three dialects and has both spoken and written forms. The Tibetans believe in the Indian Mahayana form of Buddhism but have gradually developed a distinctive Tibetan Buddhism which is also called Lamaism.

Tu

The Tu (or Monguor) ethnic minority is located mainly in Huzhu, Minhe, and Datong counties of Qinghai province as well as in Gansu province. Chinese term "Tu" was derived from the name of Tuyühu Khan, who was the older son of the King of Murong Xianbei who migrated westward from the northeast in AD 284. The last character of Tuyühu, pronounced as "hun" today, may have been pronounced "hu" in some dialect of ancient Chinese language. The Tu people speak a language belongs to the Mongolian group of the Altaic phylum. However, no written form exists. They can write in Chinese and today they are also using the characters created in recent years. The Tu people practice the faith of animism and some are the followers of Daoism. After the Ming dynasty (AD 1368–1644), many turned to Lamaism. There are over 40 temples of that religion as the center of Buddhist activities where they live. Dignitaries had also edited many Buddhist sutras and spread widely. In most villages, a Buddhist temple and a Taoist shrine coexist. There have also been multiple Catholic churches constructed in the past.

Tujia

The Tujia are an ethnic minority found in the provinces of Hunan, Hubei, Sichuan, and Guizhou. The Tujia people have a long history, dating back more than 2000 years, when the Ba kingdom reached the zenith of its power between 600 and 400 BC but was destroyed by the Qin in 316 BC. Their ancestors first immigrated to the western parts of Hunan and Hubei provinces. After being referred to by a long succession of different names in ancient documents, the Tujia people appear in historical records as their present status from about fourteenth century onwards. The Tujia speak a language that is very similar to the one used in Tibet autonomous region and Myanmar. Because the Tujia language has no written form, many Tujia people use Chinese. The Tujia people believe in the power of ancestors and gods, and hold sacrificial ceremonies during festivals. White tigers are highly revered and are thought to prevent evil.

Uyghur

The Uyghur ethnic minority lives mainly in Xinjiang Uyghur autonomous regions, especially to the south of Mt. Tianshan. The name Uyghur, which they also use to refer to themselves, means alliance or assistance. The Uyghurs have a profound history. Historical records indicate that Uyghur people had strong trade and communication links with a variety of middle Asian countries and other ethnic groups of China. The origin of the ethnic group can be traced back to the Dingling nomads in northern and northwestern China and in areas south of Lake Baikal and between the Irtish river and Lake Balkhash in the third century BC. The Uyghurs have their own language and alphabet which belongs to the Turkic group of the Altaic phylum. Much of the written Uygur literature has been passed down from the eleventh century. Originally the Uyghurs had believed in shamanism, Manicheanism, Jing, Zoroastrianism, and Buddhism. Since the eleventh century the Uyghur people have gradually turned to Islam. This has strongly influenced their way of life and most festivals celebrated today relate to this religion.

Uzbek

The Uzbek people live in Yining, Tacheng, Kashgar, Shache, Yecheng and Urumqi cities of Xinjiang Uyghur autonomous region. The name, Uzbek means 'leader of self'. It originated from the Uzbek Khan, one of the local rulers under the Mongol Empire in the fourteenth century. The ancestors of the Uzbek group moved to China's Xinjiang from Central Asia in ancient times. In the Yuan dynasty (AD 1271–1368), Uzbek merchants often traveled along "the Silk Road" through Xinjiang to do business in inland areas. Their language belongs to Turkic group of the Altaic phylum, and they write in Uyghur character. Living along the famous Silk Road, the Uzbek people were mainly involved in commerce and trade until the Qing dynasty (AD 1644–1911). The Uzbek people are Islamic, and their adherence to Islamic customs is reflected in their food, clothing and culture, which are similar to those of the Uyghur and Tatar people.

Va

The Va (or Wa) live mainly in northern Myanmar, especially in the northern part of Shan state and the eastern part of Kachin state, near and along the Sino-Myanmar border. In China, the Va ethnic minority lives primarily in Ximeng, Cangyuan and Menglian counties of Yunnan province. The Va were known as the "Wild Wa [Va]" by British administrators during Britain's colonial control of Myanmar due to their practice of headhunting. The Va speak a Mon-Khmer language that belongs to the Austro-Asiatic phylum, and the Va people use three different dialects. In 1957 a written formal language was created for the Va, since there were no characters that had been widely used. Traditionally the Va believe in the power of natural things and believe that all things have their spirits, including for example water, mountain, and wood. In recent years, some of the Va have become followers of Buddhism and Christianity.

Xibe

The Xibe ethnic minority mainly inhabits Liaoning and Jilin provinces, and Xinjiang Uyghur autonomous region. The Xibes think they are descendants of the ancient Xianbei people – a branch of the ancient Donghu ethnic group in northern China. Between AD 158 and 167, the Xianbei people formed a powerful tribal alliance and, between the third and sixth centuries, established political regimes in central China, where they mixed with Han people. But a small number of the Xianbei people never strayed very far from their native land. They were probably the ancestors of the Xibe people. They traditionally lived in the northeast of Liaoning with the Manchus, but in AD 1764 many were sent to the west as guards on the border with Russian frontier. At present, the Xibe living in Xinjiang speak the Xibe language, part of the Tungus-Manchu group of the Altaic phylum; whereas those in Northeast China usually speak Chinese and Mongolian. The Xibe people once were animists, shamanists, Lamaists. More recently, as they assimilated other cultures, a few of them also observed Confucianism and Tibetan Buddhism.

Yao

The Yao ethnic minority is a typical nationality living in the mountain regions of the southern China. Their main habitats are Hunan, Yunnan, Guangdong, Guizhou, and Jiangxi provinces together with Guangxi Zhuang autonomous region. They are divided into several branches. Their language belongs to the Miao-Yao sub-group of the Sino-Tibetan language family. While most people speak the Yao language, some speak a language similar to the Miao language, and a few even use the Zhuang and Dong languages. They can also speak Han and Zhuang languages. As to the written characters, Nv Shu – a special written language in South China used only by women – is used. Han characters are widely used among Yao people, but written words were created in 1982. Traditional religions include nature worship, ancestor, and Daoism. However, the Yao people living in different regions have differing beliefs.

Yi

Although different groups of the Yi refer to themselves in different ways (including Nuosu, Nisu, Sani, Axi, Lolo, etc.), they have been grouped into a single ethnicity by the Chinese. The Yi minority lives mainly in the hillside and basin areas in Yunnan, Sichuan, and Guizhou provinces together with the northwestern part of Guangxi Zhuang autonomous region. Nearly all the Yi people live in mountain areas. The altitudinal differences of the Yi areas are the basis of the old saying that "weather is different a few miles away". This is the primary reason why the Yi in various areas are so different from one another in the ways they make a living. Divided into six mutually unintelligible dialects – Northern Yi (Nuosu), Western Yi (Lalo), Central Yi (Lolopo), Southern Yi (Nisu), Southeastern Yi (Sani), and Eastern Yi (Nasu), their language derives from the Tibetan-Burman family of the Sino-Tibetan phylum. With regard to its characters, the Yi ethnic minority created the earliest syllable letters in the thirteenth century. Various beliefs are treasured, such as the belief of the spirit, the worship of their ancestors, and the adoration of nature, along with the cherishing of Catholicism, Christianity, and Buddhism.

Yugur

In Chinese, 'Yugur' means 'wealth and solidity'. Most of the Yugur people live in the four areas of Sunan Yugur autonomous county, and the rest in the Yugur village of Huangnibao area in Jiuquan city (in western Gansu province). Though descended from the Uyghurs of the ninth century and originally speaking a Turkic language, three languages are being used by the Yugurs: the western Yuhur language, a Turkic branch of the Altaic language family, used by the Yugur people who live in the western part of Sunan Yugur autonomous county; the eastern Yuhur language, a Mongolian branch of the Altaic language family, used by the Yugur people living in the eastern part of the autonomous county; and Chinese language. However, they don't have their own written language.

Chinese characters are widely used amongst all the Yugur people. The Yugur people believe in Tibetan Buddhism (Lamaism). Other forms of spirit worship, such as an original belief called the God Khan, are also cherished by them.

Zhuang

The Zhuang ethnic minority is the largest minority group in China. Over 90 % of the population is dominant in Guangxi Zhuang autonomous region. The remaining Zhuang people reside in Yunnan, Guangdong, Guizhou and Hunan provinces. Thousands of years ago, ancestors of the Zhuang settled down in southern China. During the Spring and Autumn Period (770–221 BC), they were one branch of the Baiyue people. "Zhuang" was one of the names the ancestors of this ethnic minority gave to themselves. The Zhuang used to call themselves by at least a dozen other names, too. The Zhuang have a language of their own that belongs to the Zhuang-Dai branch of the Sino-Tibetan phylum. The language is divided into two dialects. Chinese characters were used before 1955 for writing. Since 1957, a writing system – which is based on the Latin alphabet – has been created. Since ancient times, the Zhuang have had numerous kinds of beliefs. They believe in the totem and their ancestors. Other religions include Buddhism, Daoism, and Christianity.

Appendix 2. China's Ethnic Populations by Province

R. Guo, *China Ethnic Statistical Yearbook 2016*,
DOI 10.1007/978-3-319-49199-8

Table A.1 China's total populations reported by the 2000 and 2010 national population censuses

Ethnic group	2000			2010		
	Population	Male	Female	Population	Male	Female
Total	1,242,612,226	640,275,969	602,336,257	1,332,810,869	682,329,104	650,481,765
Achang	33,936	17,189	16,747	39,555	19,751	19,804
Bai	1,858,063	947,019	911,044	1,933,510	978,998	954,512
Baonan	16,505	8416	8089	20,074	10,016	10,058
Blang	91,882	47,534	44,348	119,639	61,230	58,409
Buyi	2,971,460	1,530,887	1,440,573	2,870,034	1,455,720	1,414,314
Dai	1,158,989	578,938	580,051	1,261,311	625,176	636,135
Daur	132,394	65,699	66,695	131,992	64,866	67,126
Deang	17,935	9032	8903	20,556	10,039	10,517
Derung	7426	3649	3777	6930	3349	3581
Dong	2,960,293	1,566,575	1,393,718	2,879,974	1,511,959	1,368,015
Dongxiang	513,805	264,453	249,352	621,500	317,490	304,010
Ewenki	30,505	14,740	15,765	30,875	14,668	16,207
Gaoshan	4461	2418	2043	4009	2029	1980
Gelao	579,357	310,775	268,582	550,746	289,369	261,377
Han	1,137,386,112	586,159,888	551,226,224	1,220,844,520	625,032,848	595,811,672
Hani	1,439,673	751,899	687,774	1,660,932	863,370	797,562
Hezhe	4640	2289	2351	5354	2651	2703
Hui	9,816,805	5,002,072	4,814,733	10,586,087	5,373,741	5,212,346
Jing	22,517	11,328	11,189	28,199	14,416	13,783
Jingpo	132,143	65,291	66,852	147,828	71,318	76,510
Jino	20,899	10,596	10,303	23,143	11,744	11,399
Kazak	1,250,458	633,875	616,583	1,462,588	747,368	715,220
Kirgiz	160,823	81,695	79,128	186,708	94,645	92,063
Korean	1,923,842	956,946	966,896	1,830,929	910,535	920,394
Lahu	453,705	234,144	219,561	485,966	247,667	238,299
Lhoba	2965	1484	1481	3682	1803	1879
Li	1,247,814	647,547	600,267	1,463,064	756,992	706,072

Lisu	634,912	326,274	308,638	702,839	355,374	347,465
Manchu	10,682,262	5,547,750	5,134,512	10,387,958	5,401,812	4,986,146
Maonan	107,166	56,443	50,723	101,192	52,836	48,356
Miao	8,940,116	4,656,974	4,283,142	9,426,007	4,870,328	4,555,679
Monba	8923	4428	4495	10,561	5261	5300
Mongol	5,813,947	2,875,453	2,938,494	5,981,840	2,999,520	2,982,320
Mulao	207,352	107,154	100,198	216,257	110,516	105,741
Naxi	308,839	154,971	153,868	326,295	162,635	163,660
Nu	28,759	14,857	13,902	37,523	18,907	18,616
Oroqen	8196	3872	4324	8659	4033	4626
Pumi	33,600	17,043	16,557	42,861	21,433	21,428
Qiang	306,072	155,981	150,091	309,576	156,539	153,037
Russian	15,609	7365	8244	15,393	7284	8109
Salar	104,503	53,715	50,788	130,607	66,281	64,326
She	709,592	381,038	328,554	708,651	383,213	325,438
Shui	406,902	213,488	193,414	411,847	213,644	198,203
Tajik	41,028	20,954	20,074	51,069	26,112	24,957
Tatar	4890	2550	2340	3556	1899	1657
Tibetan	5,416,021	2,697,807	2,718,214	6,282,187	3,155,625	3,126,562
Tu	241,198	123,571	117,627	289,565	148,055	141,510
Tujia	8,028,133	4,196,469	3,831,664	8,353,912	4,307,260	4,046,652
Uygur	8,399,393	4,272,863	4,126,530	10,069,346	5,097,594	4,971,752
Uzbek	12,370	6498	5872	10,569	5673	4896
Va	396,610	202,626	193,984	429,709	216,439	213,270
Xibe	188,824	98,737	90,087	190,481	99,571	90,910
Yao	2,637,421	1,391,332	1,246,089	2,796,003	1,458,842	1,337,161
Yi	7,762,272	3,989,391	3,772,881	8,714,393	4,456,382	4,258,011
Yugur	13,719	6935	6784	14,378	7325	7053
Zhuang	16,178,811	8,376,754	7,802,057	16,926,381	8,689,488	8,236,893

Note: Total population includes servicemen (while ethnic breakdowns do not include them) as well as unknown ethnic groups and foreigners with Chinese citizenship

Table A.2 Anhui's populations reported by the 2000 and 2010 national population censuses

	2000			2010		
Ethnic group	Population	Male	Female	Population	Male	Female
Total	58,999,948	30,437,820	28,562,128	59,500,468	30,245,513	29,254,955
Achang	5	1	4	25	5	20
Bai	761	117	644	692	284	408
Baonan	1		1	15	5	10
Blang	33	7	26	78	13	65
Buyi	3103	970	2133	3413	845	2568
Dai	373	43	330	831	191	640
Daur	93	42	51	77	29	48
Deang	1		1	18	1	17
Derung	99	41	58	26	2	24
Dong	1917	423	1494	2147	571	1576
Dongxiang	9	3	6	112	83	29
Ewenki	17	4	13	11	5	6
Gaoshan	80	38	42	89	38	51
Gelao	199	73	126	448	196	252
Han	58,602,112	30,247,912	28,354,200	59,104,826	30,054,506	29,050,320
Hani	679	55	624	1138	166	972
Hezhe	8	2	6	23	8	15
Hui	337,521	169,697	167,824	328,062	165,284	162,778
Jing	28	15	13	92	39	53
Jingpo	20	2	18	166	27	139
Jino	3	1	2	8	4	4
Kazak	24	7	17	1203	603	600
Kirgiz	1	1		14	9	5
Korean	2660	1292	1368	1200	570	630
Lahu	219	29	190	347	45	302
Lhoba	8	3	5	2	1	1

Li	225	57	168	1610	672	938
Lisu	102	15	87	589	126	463
Manchu	8688	4204	4484	8516	4373	4143
Maonan	26	9	17	58	17	41
Miao	6995	1758	5237	13,856	4071	9785
Monba	4		4	65	29	36
Mongol	14,354	3730	10,624	2809	1260	1549
Mulao	47	14	33	123	41	82
Naxi	71	14	57	87	19	68
Nu	13	1	12	182	77	105
Oroqen	13	7	6	7	5	2
Pumi	36	8	28	20	8	12
Qiang	87	37	50	183	85	98
Russian	22	11	11	33	19	14
Salar	26	15	11	78	41	37
She	1563	848	715	1682	921	761
Shui	307	47	260	562	201	361
Tajik	98	46	52	3	2	1
Tatar	10	6	4	9	3	6
Tibetan	2263	935	1328	1279	511	768
Tu	223	59	164	493	219	274
Tujia	2196	766	1430	6185	2978	3207
Uygur	1733	912	821	710	409	301
Uzbek	4	2	2	4	3	1
Va	305	86	219	1019	354	665
Xibe	93	52	41	143	72	71
Yao	406	108	298	1171	390	781
Yi	5607	1683	3924	6667	2656	4011
Yugur	2	1	1	43	23	20
Zhuang	4331	1599	2732	6998	2298	4700

Note: Total population includes servicemen (while ethnic breakdowns do not include them) as well as unknown ethnic groups and foreigners with Chinese citizenship

Table A.3 Beijing's populations reported by the 2000 and 2010 national population censuses

Ethnic group	2000			2010		
	Population	Male	Female	Population	Male	Female
Total	13,569,194	7,074,518	6,494,676	19,612,368	10,126,430	9,485,938
Achang	6	4	2	28	14	14
Bai	1554	816	738	3493	1778	1715
Baonan	7	4	3	24	17	7
Blang	8	4	4	68	35	33
Buyi	1035	525	510	2768	1393	1375
Dai	265	105	160	1022	463	559
Daur	853	399	454	2043	868	1175
Deang	4	2	2	19	14	5
Derung	8	5	3	14	9	5
Dong	1616	825	791	3774	1865	1909
Dongxiang	101	65	36	484	345	139
Ewenki	164	74	90	433	182	251
Gaoshan	101	50	51	103	46	57
Gelao	272	169	103	1307	771	536
Han	12,983,696	6,779,560	6,204,136	18,811,154	9,729,984	9,081,170
Hani	164	78	86	680	329	351
Hezhe	84	38	46	201	81	120
Hui	235,837	117,222	118,615	249,223	122,993	126,230
Jing	22	8	14	56	22	34
Jingpo	37	13	24	112	48	64
Jino	6	4	2	20	9	11
Kazak	400	190	210	1602	685	917
Kirgiz	45	23	22	189	71	118
Korean	20,369	9416	10,953	37,380	17,437	19,943
Lahu	28	9	19	202	95	107
Lhoba	6	2	4	11	5	6
Li	343	176	167	1078	501	577
Lisu	48	23	25	264	142	122
Manchu	250,286	128,173	122,113	336,032	167,963	168,069
Maonan	31	20	11	124	51	73
Miao	5291	2835	2456	12957	6698	6259
Monba	19	8	11	31	16	15
Mongol	37,464	18,247	19,217	76,736	36,758	39,978
Mulao	192	102	90	358	162	196
Naxi	246	130	116	554	282	272
Nu	7	5	2	50	22	28
Oroqen	78	33	45	165	77	88
Pumi	14	8	6	46	22	24
Qiang	177	95	82	661	308	353
Russian	216	78	138	343	124	219

(continued)

Table A.3 Continued

Ethnic group	2000			2010		
	Population	Male	Female	Population	Male	Female
Salar	413	305	108	644	399	245
She	629	399	230	1515	842	673
Shui	100	50	50	340	168	172
Tajik	22	13	9	21	12	9
Tatar	29	17	12	23	9	14
Tibetan	2920	1557	1363	5575	2746	2829
Tu	396	225	171	554	285	269
Tujia	8372	4579	3793	23,601	12,088	11,513
Uygur	3129	1798	1331	6975	3430	3545
Uzbek	23	9	14	51	25	26
Va	48	19	29	324	180	144
Xibe	1491	709	782	2569	1201	1368
Yao	1112	623	489	3213	1511	1702
Yi	1919	963	956	5849	3418	2431
Yugur	52	24	28	95	39	56
Zhuang	7322	3630	3692	14,994	7275	7719

Note: Total population includes servicemen (while ethnic breakdowns do not include them) as well as unknown ethnic groups and foreigners with Chinese citizenship

Table A.4 Chongqing's populations reported by the 2000 and 2010 national population censuses

Ethnic group	2000 Population	2000 Male	2000 Female	2010 Population	2010 Male	2010 Female
Total	30,512,763	15,841,429	14,671,334	28,846,170	14,608,870	14,237,300
Achang	12	3	9	19	6	13
Bai	1140	464	676	1569	712	857
Baonan	3	1	2	9	8	1
Blang	261	33	228	288	45	243
Buyi	2401	772	1629	3383	1310	2073
Dai	604	126	478	881	239	642
Daur	47	20	27	118	47	71
Deang	6	1	5	5	1	4
Derung	129	58	71	9	5	4
Dong	2585	1354	1231	3271	1724	1547
Dongxiang	25	13	12	102	56	46
Ewenki	22	9	13	25	12	13
Gaoshan	60	26	34	45	24	21
Gelao	1191	340	851	2808	1298	1510
Han	28,539,156	14,812,506	13,726,650	26,909,061	13,617,247	13,291,814
Hani	959	182	777	1398	365	1033
Hezhe	9	6	3	12	6	6
Hui	10,064	5019	5045	9056	4658	4398
Jing	27	13	14	25	14	11
Jingpo	16	5	11	82	21	61
Jino	31	6	25	27	9	18
Kazak	22	8	14	259	104	155
Kirgiz	2	1	1	28	11	17
Korean	1044	525	519	637	331	306
Lahu	459	51	408	479	82	397
Lhoba	17	6	11	2	2	
Li	228	108	120	587	277	310

Lisu	219	42	177	328	117	211
Manchu	3079	1620	1459	4571	2431	2140
Maonan	15	5	10	63	33	30
Miao	502,421	266,237	236,184	482,714	248,537	234,177
Monba	15	6	9	16	8	8
Mongol	7846	3228	4618	5688	2890	2798
Mulao	111	38	73	208	80	128
Naxi	217	80	137	421	171	250
Nu	10	3	7	28	11	17
Oroqen	5	2	3	3	3	
Pumi	11	3	8	51	28	23
Qiang	365	168	197	675	317	358
Russian	12	4	8	40	15	25
Salar	36	13	23	71	40	31
She	92	56	36	252	146	106
Shui	120	52	68	197	93	104
Tajik	177	121	56	2	1	1
Tatar	6	2	4	1		1
Tibetan	2292	931	1361	3086	1250	1836
Tu	220	81	139	715	351	364
Tujia	1,424,352	742,694	681,658	1,398,707	717,687	681,020
Uygur	1194	572	622	1162	605	557
Uzbek				4	2	2
Va	1445	770	675	577	112	465
Xibe	52	25	27	143	70	73
Yao	474	192	282	1045	455	590
Yi	4531	1397	3134	6336	2598	3738
Yugur	3		3	27	14	13
Zhuang	2764	1380	1384	4634	2066	2568

Note: Total population includes servicemen (while ethnic breakdowns do not include them) as well as unknown ethnic groups and foreigners with Chinese citizenship

Table A.5 Fujian's populations reported by the 2000 and 2010 national population censuses

	2000			2010		
Ethnic group	Population	Male	Female	Population	Male	Female
Total	34,097,947	17,568,535	16,529,412	36,894,217	18,981,054	17,913,163
Achang	3		3	62	29	33
Bai	608	302	306	4008	2127	1881
Baonan	3	2	1	5	2	3
Blang	10	4	6	226	117	109
Buyi	4206	2130	2076	22,172	12,141	10,031
Dai	169	56	113	2401	1230	1171
Daur	24	12	12	96	43	53
Deang	1		1	22	13	9
Derung	47	23	24	11	5	6
Dong	5768	3452	2316	15,608	9111	6497
Dongxiang	15	10	5	339	199	140
Ewenki	12	4	8	16	6	10
Gaoshan	416	218	198	423	224	199
Gelao	618	411	207	3249	1878	1371
Han	33,514,147	17,251,899	16,262,248	36,097,362	18,544,219	17,553,143
Hani	92	24	68	1373	749	624
Hezhe	1		1	43	22	21
Hui	109,880	61,664	48,216	115,978	65,663	50,315
Jing	67	18	49	260	120	140
Jingpo	31	4	27	295	137	158
Jino	4		4	16	5	11
Kazak	6	3	3	1492	709	783
Kirgiz	7	2	5	50	32	18
Korean	1785	895	890	2157	1088	1069
Lahu	26	4	22	375	203	172
Lhoba	26	12	14	16	10	6
Li	524	202	322	3551	1660	1891

Lisu	21	5	16	403	193	210
Manchu	7094	3716	3378	8372	4258	4114
Maonan	86	29	57	372	203	169
Miao	22,065	12,925	9140	88,017	50,024	37,993
Monba	24	10	14	23	9	14
Mongol	6114	2741	3373	5830	2948	2882
Mulao	131	69	62	527	245	282
Naxi	49	22	27	123	53	70
Nu	27	8	19	307	160	147
Oroqen	25	7	18	12	8	4
Pumi	7	2	5	47	28	19
Qiang	99	53	46	458	247	211
Russian	13	4	9	30	13	17
Salar	13	7	6	80	43	37
She	375,193	201,710	173,483	365,514	196,573	168,941
Shui	353	227	126	2433	1301	1132
Tajik	22	14	8	19	13	6
Tatar				17	11	6
Tibetan	1290	526	764	1739	711	1028
Tu	890	515	375	4000	2268	1732
Tujia	29,046	17,638	11,408	89,824	51,104	38,720
Uygur	1080	611	469	1159	632	527
Uzbek	8	3	5	9	4	5
Va	108	49	59	1325	723	602
Xibe	53	20	33	142	51	91
Yao	1226	560	666	5669	3163	2506
Yi	2615	1239	1376	13,536	7630	5906
Yugur	3	1	2	34	15	19
Zhuang	10,818	3909	6909	29,696	15,037	14,659

Note: Total population includes servicemen (while ethnic breakdowns do not include them) as well as unknown ethnic groups and foreigners with Chinese citizenship

Table A.6 Gansu's populations reported by the 2000 and 2010 national population censuses

	2000			2010		
Ethnic group	Population	Male	Female	Population	Male	Female
Total	25,124,282	13,021,654	12,102,628	25,575,263	13,064,193	12,511,070
Achang	1		1	1	1	
Bai	272	158	114	291	181	110
Baonan	15,170	7690	7480	18,170	8908	9262
Blang	9	3	6	12	5	7
Buyi	768	376	392	366	201	165
Dai	13	5	8	89	43	46
Daur	115	57	58	95	45	50
Deang	7	6	1	2	1	1
Derung	37	22	15	8	4	4
Dong	380	208	172	136	77	59
Dongxiang	451,622	231,589	220,033	546,255	276,107	270,148
Ewenki	16	9	7	13	7	6
Gaoshan	55	25	30	27	15	12
Gelao	18	7	11	98	64	34
Han	22,925,063	11,888,144	11,036,919	23,164,817	11,841,566	11,323,251
Hani	40	20	20	88	36	52
Hezhe	21	12	9	42	26	16
Hui	1,184,930	620,249	564,681	1,258,641	642,356	616,285
Jing	7	3	4	109	54	55
Jingpo	11	6	5	19	13	6
Jino	1		1	5	1	4
Kazak	2963	1453	1510	4444	2124	2320
Kirgiz	13	7	6	48	12	36
Korean	1565	804	761	559	273	286
Lahu	10	9	1	14	6	8
Lhoba				1		1
Li	58	32	26	517	250	267

Lisu	115	62	53	28	13	15
Manchu	17,285	8958	8327	14,206	7444	6762
Maonan	77	35	42	12	6	6
Miao	1509	721	788	1212	738	474
Monba	24	12	12	89	41	48
Mongol	15,774	6485	9289	10,935	5351	5584
Mulao	30	20	10	39	24	15
Naxi	28	9	19	53	26	27
Nu	7	4	3	101	44	57
Oroqen	10	7	3	10	5	5
Pumi	11	6	5	8	5	3
Qiang	64	29	35	115	62	53
Russian	55	22	33	48	16	32
Salar	11,784	6195	5589	13,517	6852	6665
She	201	132	69	245	154	91
Shui	88	36	52	50	31	19
Tajik	99	53	46	13	4	9
Tatar	186	90	96	18	10	8
Tibetan	443,228	222,362	220,866	488,359	245,262	243,097
Tu	30,338	15,410	14,928	30,781	15,154	15,627
Tujia	1341	754	587	2092	1269	823
Uygur	2131	987	1144	1937	853	1084
Uzbek	18	7	11	15	7	8
Va	143	75	68	97	50	47
Xibe	312	166	146	299	138	161
Yao	228	121	107	354	181	173
Yi	1722	772	950	870	493	377
Yugur	12,962	6567	6395	13,001	6640	6361
Zhuang	1308	642	666	1647	824	823

Note: Total population includes servicemen (while ethnic breakdowns do not include them) as well as unknown ethnic groups and foreigners with Chinese citizenship

Table A.7 Guangdong's populations reported by the 2000 and 2010 national population censuses

	2000			2010		
Ethnic group	Population	Male	Female	Population	Male	Female
Total	85,225,007	43,381,720	41,843,287	104,320,459	54,400,538	49,919,921
Achang	40	13	27	623	389	234
Bai	5905	2983	2922	16,692	9419	7273
Baonan	5	2	3	25	15	10
Blang	98	35	63	495	258	237
Buyi	23,237	11,089	12,148	64,253	35,809	28,444
Dai	1256	293	963	6675	3554	3121
Daur	158	72	86	411	208	203
Deang	7	1	6	62	38	24
Derung	64	34	30	51	27	24
Dong	55,870	25,767	30,103	83,574	46,825	36,749
Dongxiang	61	34	27	403	309	94
Ewenki	249	82	167	92	49	43
Gaoshan	142	71	71	161	81	80
Gelao	5782	2687	3095	10,897	5910	4987
Han	83,955,870	42,777,757	41,178,113	102,253,138	53,273,872	48,979,266
Hani	1061	425	636	5987	3585	2402
Hezhe	13	7	6	298	150	148
Hui	25,307	12,394	12,913	45,073	24,357	20,716
Jing	285	111	174	484	232	252
Jingpo	261	107	154	677	387	290
Jino	17	3	14	26	7	19
Kazak	46	22	24	4602	2504	2098
Kirgiz	15	7	8	577	314	263
Korean	10,463	5309	5154	17,615	9118	8497
Lahu	350	26	324	1335	723	612
Lhoba	8	4	4	8	5	3
Li	6550	2292	4258	19,579	9950	9629

Lisu	162	56	106	1693	1069	624
Manchu	17,972	9044	8928	29,557	15,200	14,357
Maonan	1263	502	761	5017	2866	2151
Miao	120,606	59,446	61,160	251,970	141,661	110,309
Monba	22	8	14	62	26	36
Mongol	20,669	8215	12,454	14,331	7495	6836
Mulao	4814	2089	2725	10,961	5918	5043
Naxi	144	79	65	499	277	222
Nu	38	15	23	584	277	307
Oroqen	26	12	14	52	24	28
Pumi	32	10	22	121	61	60
Qiang	340	164	176	1886	1058	828
Russian	50	21	29	125	38	87
Salar	89	46	43	823	508	315
She	28,053	15,322	12,731	29,549	16,743	12,806
Shui	1948	1028	920	6525	3675	2850
Tajik	95	41	54	165	98	67
Tatar	10	4	6	55	28	27
Tibetan	7020	2859	4161	5604	2723	2881
Tu	4500	2385	2115	10,161	5629	4532
Tujia	135,431	68,464	66,967	212,513	117,141	95,372
Uygur	3057	1682	1375	6438	2602	3836
Uzbek	42	22	20	73	41	32
Va	655	215	440	4718	2723	1995
Xibe	322	151	171	705	341	364
Yao	202,667	102,744	99,923	276,266	148,395	127,871
Yi	8700	4062	4638	36,264	20,632	15,632
Yugur	9		9	53	32	21
Zhuang	570,200	260,335	309,865	877,509	473,900	403,609

Note: Total population includes servicemen (while ethnic breakdowns do not include them) as well as unknown ethnic groups and foreigners with Chinese citizenship

Table A.8 Guangxi's populations reported by the 2000 and 2010 national population censuses

	2000			2010		
Ethnic group	Population	Male	Female	Population	Male	Female
Total	43,854,538	23,239,376	20,615,162	46,023,761	23,924,704	22,099,057
Achang	19	13	6	26	14	12
Bai	831	392	439	2489	1255	1234
Baonan	2	1	1	1		1
Blang	49	19	30	81	32	49
Buyi	20,826	9484	11,342	20,072	8094	11,978
Dai	847	339	508	796	276	520
Daur	60	23	37	83	37	46
Deang	2	2		7	2	5
Derung	28	15	13	21	9	12
Dong	303,139	156,153	146,986	305,565	153,819	151,746
Dongxiang	98	48	50	17	10	7
Ewenki	35	16	19	46	19	27
Gaoshan	409	228	181	278	159	119
Gelao	3820	1961	1859	3885	2048	1837
Han	27,024,974	14,471,260	12,553,714	28,916,096	15,156,624	13,759,472
Hani	214	90	124	474	222	252
Hezhe	13	10	3	63	34	29
Hui	32,512	16,433	16,079	32,319	16,420	15,899
Jing	20,123	10,256	9867	23,283	12,047	11,236
Jingpo	95	46	49	41	5	36
Jino	5	1	4	4	2	2
Kazak	49	27	22	1884	977	907
Kirgiz	9	5	4	28	16	12
Korean	2008	1055	953	2701	1417	1284
Lahu	65	38	27	111	42	69
Lhoba	1		1	3	3	
Li	2997	1535	1462	4542	2251	2291

Lisu	59	30	29	154	63	91
Manchu	9576	4842	4734	11,159	5695	5464
Maonan	73,578	39,083	34,495	65,587	34,112	31,475
Miao	462,956	237,672	225,284	475,492	241,305	234,187
Monba	3	2	1	77	27	50
Mongol	8651	2872	5779	3017	1485	1532
Mulao	170,225	87,729	82,496	172,305	87,513	84,792
Naxi	52	25	27	149	69	80
Nu	43	21	22	119	65	54
Oroqen	20	10	10	8	4	4
Pumi	21	5	16	25	18	7
Qiang	115	62	53	169	87	82
Russian	13	4	9	8	2	6
Salar	30	17	13	128	59	69
She	418	253	165	829	496	333
Shui	15,476	8332	7144	13,559	7025	6534
Tajik	135	71	64	2		2
Tatar	4	2	2	24	13	11
Tibetan	2194	998	1196	815	393	422
Tu	438	237	201	1501	665	836
Tujia	4630	2586	2044	9155	4830	4325
Uygur	1550	753	797	1795	930	865
Uzbek	47	22	25	13	8	5
Va	248	119	129	662	304	358
Xibe	118	56	62	146	79	67
Yao	1,471,946	775,032	696,914	1,493,530	772,111	721,419
Yi	9712	5033	4679	9700	5045	4655
Yugur	48	21	27	7	2	5
Zhuang	14,207,143	7,403,064	6,804,079	14,448,422	7,406,315	7,042,107

Note: Total population includes servicemen (while ethnic breakdowns do not include them) as well as unknown ethnic groups and foreigners with Chinese citizenship

Table A.9 Guizhou's populations reported by the 2000 and 2010 national population censuses

	2000			2010		
Ethnic group	Population	Male	Female	Population	Male	Female
Total	35,247,695	18,464,477	16,783,218	34,748,556	17,905,471	16,843,085
Achang	28	12	16	26	9	17
Bai	187,362	101,312	86,050	179,510	95,923	83,587
Baonan	3	2	1	8	4	4
Blang	30	14	16	49	16	33
Buyi	2,798,200	1,449,457	1,348,743	2,510,565	1,271,051	1,239,514
Dai	755	281	474	1217	488	729
Daur	120	58	62	32	11	21
Deang	2		2	16	6	10
Derung	82	43	39	87	44	43
Dong	1,628,568	869,205	759,363	1,431,928	750,208	681,720
Dongxiang	412	186	226	958	433	525
Ewenki	46	21	25	1	1	
Gaoshan	228	127	101	191	90	101
Gelao	559,041	300,372	258,669	495,182	258,935	236,247
Han	21,911,687	11,470,182	10,441,505	22,344,156	11,517,873	10,826,283
Hani	891	373	518	1092	403	689
Hezhe	13	3	10	8	4	4
Hui	168,734	87,683	81,051	184,788	95,009	89,779
Jing	641	340	301	1143	620	523
Jingpo	413	222	191	572	282	290
Jino	6	1	5	10	3	7
Kazak	226	98	128	2093	1072	1021
Kirgiz	17	8	9	2	1	1
Korean	1192	610	582	664	318	346
Lahu	82	29	53	182	53	129
Lhoba	70	41	29	85	49	36
Li	56,082	29,735	26,347	135,173	69,980	65,193

Lisu	120	45	75	337	150	187
Manchu	21,932	11,392	10,540	23,086	11,932	11,154
Maonan	31,240	16,426	14,814	27,332	14,243	13,089
Miao	4,299,954	2,247,415	2,052,539	3,968,400	2,040,932	1,927,468
Monba	5	2	3	9	6	3
Mongol	47,531	26,282	21,249	41,561	23,203	18,358
Mulao	28,435	15,500	12,935	24,956	13,293	11,663
Naxi	294	135	159	353	162	191
Nu	21	9	12	28	8	20
Oroqen	8	5	3	24	13	11
Pumi	4		4	16	8	8
Qiang	1431	826	605	1605	899	706
Russian	31	17	14	25	14	11
Salar	87	42	45	99	61	38
She	44,926	24,009	20,917	36,558	19,096	17,462
Shui	369,723	194,337	175,386	348,746	180,317	168,429
Tajik	16	5	11			
Tatar	2	1	1	3	1	2
Tibetan	1787	864	923	1281	585	696
Tu	2942	1531	1411	5154	2755	2399
Tujia	1,430,286	748,222	682,064	1,436,977	736,526	700,451
Uygur	1149	543	606	548	335	213
Uzbek	1	1				
Va	148	58	90	831	345	486
Xibe	171	85	86	185	89	96
Yao	44,392	23,912	20,480	40,879	21,428	19,451
Yi	843,554	441,058	402,496	834,461	429,553	404,908
Yugur	1	1		1	1	
Zhuang	52,065	27,061	25,004	52,577	26,500	26,077

Note: Total population includes servicemen (while ethnic breakdowns do not include them) as well as unknown ethnic groups and foreigners with Chinese citizenship

Table A.10 Hainan's populations reported by the 2000 and 2010 national population censuses

Ethnic group	2000			2010		
	Population	Male	Female	Population	Male	Female
Total	7,559,035	4,002,445	3,556,590	8,671,485	4,592,283	4,079,202
Achang	43	16	27			
Bai	222	101	121	305	150	155
Baonan						
Blang	23	16	7	120	65	55
Buyi	1544	900	644	1789	971	818
Dai	197	73	124	902	417	485
Daur	55	17	38	58	21	37
Deang				1		1
Derung	17	7	10			
Dong	1350	762	588	1819	1096	723
Dongxiang	11	4	7	19	9	10
Ewenki	67	37	30	14	2	12
Gaoshan	80	41	39	111	64	47
Gelao	89	52	37	406	246	160
Han	6,245,329	3,319,929	2,925,400	7,246,067	3,853,244	3,392,823
Hani	93	45	48	154	70	84
Hezhe	9	2	7	13	5	8
Hui	8372	4206	4166	10,670	5405	5265
Jing	123	39	84	189	92	97
Jingpo	37	20	17	15	5	10
Jino				1	1	
Kazak	36	15	21	1553	793	760
Kirgiz	16	8	8	1	1	
Korean	786	422	364	973	456	517
Lahu	3	2	1	48	24	24
Lhoba	1		1			
Li	1,172,181	609,534	562,647	1,262,262	655,504	606,758
Lisu	17	6	11	20	13	7
Manchu	1694	846	848	3750	1853	1897
Maonan	46	27	19	61	40	21
Miao	61,264	30,891	30,373	74,482	37,555	36,927
Monba	1		1	2		2
Mongol	1888	680	1208	3463	1679	1784
Mulao	151	75	76	168	97	71
Naxi	16	9	7	28	11	17
Nu	2	1	1	1385	713	672
Oroqen	1		1	4	1	3
Pumi	4	1	3	3	2	1
Qiang	62	33	29	104	56	48
Russian	14	4	10	17	4	13

(*continued*)

Table A.10 Continued

Ethnic group	2000			2010		
	Population	Male	Female	Population	Male	Female
Salar	49	42	7	21	12	9
She	274	144	130	403	227	176
Shui	72	41	31	130	67	63
Tajik	38	22	16			
Tatar	9	3	6			
Tibetan	450	202	248	248	111	137
Tu	250	157	93	399	220	179
Tujia	3321	1900	1421	4286	2289	1997
Uygur	354	175	179	393	211	182
Uzbek	29	17	12			
Va	37	16	21	154	85	69
Xibe	35	16	19	72	30	42
Yao	6984	3784	3200	7302	3833	3469
Yi	596	316	280	1086	564	522
Yugur	1		1	3	1	2
Zhuang	50,507	26,688	23,819	45,909	23,914	21,995

Note: Total population includes servicemen (while ethnic breakdowns do not include them) as well as unknown ethnic groups and foreigners with Chinese citizenship

Table A.11 Hebei's populations reported by the 2000 and 2010 national population censuses

	2000			2010		
Ethnic group	Population	Male	Female	Population	Male	Female
Total	66,684,419	33,936,333	32,748,086	71,854,210	36,430,286	35,423,924
Achang	8	5	3	15	5	10
Bai	946	197	749	859	380	479
Baonan				7	4	3
Blang	15	4	11	50	14	36
Buyi	4258	1073	3185	3630	1188	2442
Dai	229	49	180	447	134	313
Daur	705	273	432	962	398	564
Deang	6	1	5	7	2	5
Derung	36	15	21	21	7	14
Dong	2317	869	1448	1451	584	867
Dongxiang	37	12	25	78	52	26
Ewenki	127	42	85	172	63	109
Gaoshan	274	147	127	208	107	101
Gelao	161	68	93	425	247	178
Han	63,781,603	32,463,709	31,317,894	68,861,333	34,894,643	33,966,690
Hani	301	81	220	387	109	278
Hezhe	46	19	27	90	45	45
Hui	542,639	271,936	270,703	570,170	286,331	283,839
Jing	29	14	15	77	25	52
Jingpo	36	10	26	70	22	48
Jino	4	1	3	24	12	12
Kazak	29	12	17	320	163	157
Kirgiz	15	5	10	25	14	11
Korean	11,783	5301	6482	11,296	5358	5938
Lahu	89	13	76	175	50	125
Lhoba	5	1	4	6	2	4
Li	238	67	171	861	340	521

Lisu	1355	94	1261	1974	282	1692
Manchu	2,118,711	1,093,798	1,024,913	2,169,311	1,128,634	1,040,677
Maonan	76	20	56	76	23	53
Miao	8088	2756	5332	9703	3726	5977
Monba	10	1	9	17	9	8
Mongol	169,887	83,397	86,490	180,849	92,087	88,762
Mulao	344	102	242	291	90	201
Naxi	299	41	258	259	71	188
Nu	33	3	30	200	73	127
Oroqen	85	32	53	142	67	75
Pumi	15		15	14	4	10
Qiang	122	60	62	407	241	166
Russian	102	50	52	103	50	53
Salar	30	11	19	131	76	55
She	226	135	91	396	230	166
Shui	383	63	320	282	93	189
Tajik	35	14	21	8	6	2
Tatar	6	2	4	17	7	10
Tibetan	3096	1275	1821	1935	869	1066
Tu	341	117	224	598	259	339
Tujia	6354	2900	3454	8061	4071	3990
Uygur	1785	973	812	864	466	398
Uzbek	2	1	1	7	4	3
Va	148	48	100	674	355	319
Xibe	746	351	395	851	421	430
Yao	1491	400	1091	1776	692	1084
Yi	3721	1149	2572	4632	2207	2425
Yugur	13	6	7	33	20	13
Zhuang	20,832	4561	16,271	17,295	4780	12,515

Note: Total population includes servicemen (while ethnic breakdowns do not include them) as well as unknown ethnic groups and foreigners with Chinese citizenship

Table A.12 Heilongjiang's populations reported by the 2000 and 2010 national population censuses

	2000			2010		
Ethnic group	Population	Male	Female	Population	Male	Female
Total	36,237,576	18,520,747	17,716,829	38,313,991	19,426,106	18,887,885
Achang	3	2	1	3		3
Bai	278	142	136	149	83	66
Baonan	7	4	3	3	1	2
Blang	10	6	4	12	4	8
Buyi	856	413	443	425	220	205
Dai	23	15	8	76	29	47
Daur	43,608	21,670	21,938	40,277	19,985	20,292
Deang	3	1	2			
Derung	55	28	27	8	2	6
Dong	940	552	388	217	129	88
Dongxiang	64	42	22	19	11	8
Ewenki	2706	1263	1443	2648	1191	1457
Gaoshan	61	34	27	25	7	18
Gelao	51	31	20	90	54	36
Han	34,465,039	17,588,318	16,876,721	36,939,181	18,696,097	18,243,084
Hani	78	26	52	105	51	54
Hezhe	3910	1957	1953	3613	1803	1810
Hui	124,003	62,634	61,369	101,749	51,338	50,411
Jing	36	20	16	22	11	11
Jingpo	8	3	5	11	2	9
Jino	1		1	1		1
Kazak	48	19	29	165	106	59
Kirgiz	1473	727	746	1431	709	722
Korean	388,458	195,224	193,234	327,806	164,200	163,606
Lahu				11	1	10
Lhoba	7	2	5	4	3	1
Li	83	32	51	477	198	279

Lisu	18	8	10	39	16	23
Manchu	1,037,080	565,269	471,811	748,020	414,472	333,548
Maonan	7	4	3	5	1	4
Miao	3173	1655	1518	2575	1407	1168
Monba				2	1	1
Mongol	141,495	67,960	73,535	125,483	63,393	62,090
Mulao	52	34	18	46	22	24
Naxi	36	17	19	45	27	18
Nu	4	2	2	21	8	13
Oroqen	3871	1851	2020	3943	1872	2071
Pumi	17	10	7	4	2	2
Qiang	25	13	12	34	21	13
Russian	265	121	144	312	158	154
Salar	4	1	3	7	3	4
She	112	73	39	94	61	33
Shui	118	65	53	47	29	18
Tajik	73	40	33	9	5	4
Tatar	11	7	4	3	2	1
Tibetan	1655	766	889	589	312	277
Tu	113	62	51	101	60	41
Tujia	2217	1265	952	2175	1350	825
Uygur	1189	623	566	884	553	331
Uzbek	1	1		5	4	1
Va	73	42	31	64	26	38
Xibe	8886	5053	3833	7608	4294	3314
Yao	358	209	149	437	234	203
Yi	2060	935	1125	730	428	302
Yugur	28	16	12	28	14	14
Zhuang	2700	1432	1268	2070	1060	1010

Note: Total population includes servicemen (while ethnic breakdowns do not include them) as well as unknown ethnic groups and foreigners with Chinese citizenship

Table A.13 Henan's populations reported by the 2000 and 2010 national population censuses

	2000			2010		
Ethnic group	Population	Male	Female	Population	Male	Female
Total	91,236,854	47,046,599	44,190,255	94,029,939	47,493,063	46,536,876
Achang	15	3	12	148	67	81
Bai	946	225	721	581	245	336
Baonan	2		2	4	2	2
Blang	77	10	67	80	18	62
Buyi	2244	904	1340	5958	2604	3354
Dai	500	67	433	511	105	406
Daur	144	68	76	122	42	80
Deang	9	3	6	11		11
Derung	44	17	27	55	27	28
Dong	1314	633	681	558	254	304
Dongxiang	29	13	16	72	47	25
Ewenki	17	7	10	23	7	16
Gaoshan	946	626	320	780	397	383
Gelao	115	64	51	240	119	121
Han	90,093,286	46,468,976	43,624,310	92,908,354	46,924,281	45,984,073
Hani	425	44	381	373	83	290
Hezhe	17	7	10	30	13	17
Hui	953,531	478,488	475,043	957,964	479,252	478,712
Jing	17	7	10	120	51	69
Jingpo	85	6	79	130	12	118
Jino	1		1	7	1	6
Kazak	38	9	29	4805	2330	2475
Kirgiz	15	7	8	37	20	17
Korean	4312	2126	2186	1457	664	793
Lahu	1151	88	1063	700	51	649
Lhoba	8	3	5			
Li	241	79	162	1002	405	597

Lisu	212	28	184	167	25	142
Manchu	61,705	35,649	26,056	55,493	31,697	23,796
Maonan	19	4	15	23	6	17
Miao	5425	2180	3245	4321	1683	2638
Monba	10	4	6	45	16	29
Mongol	82,170	44,437	37,733	63,473	39,117	24,356
Mulao	41	15	26	72	30	42
Naxi	186	40	146	123	35	88
Nu	4	2	2	186	92	94
Oroqen	15	8	7	14	6	8
Pumi	29	8	21	9	2	7
Qiang	75	48	27	216	103	113
Russian	54	24	30	32	12	20
Salar	92	61	31	279	168	111
She	134	70	64	200	104	96
Shui	80	32	48	333	172	161
Tajik	73	32	41	23	8	15
Tatar	8	4	4	4	2	2
Tibetan	3953	1491	2462	1811	598	1213
Tu	419	175	244	576	236	340
Tujia	5122	2516	2606	5287	2642	2645
Uygur	4623	2542	2081	3035	1646	1389
Uzbek	10	2	8	16	13	3
Va	1715	145	1570	1572	337	1235
Xibe	292	142	150	273	123	150
Yao	408	183	225	763	276	487
Yi	5364	2026	3338	1764	672	1092
Yugur	6	3	3	52	21	31
Zhuang	4888	2185	2703	5361	2004	3357

Note: Total population includes servicemen (while ethnic breakdowns do not include them) as well as unknown ethnic groups and foreigners with Chinese citizenship

Table A.14 Hubei's populations reported by the 2000 and 2010 national population censuses

	2000			2010		
Ethnic group	Population	Male	Female	Population	Male	Female
Total	59,508,870	30,982,241	28,526,629	57,237,727	29,391,247	27,846,480
Achang	2	2		12	4	8
Bai	7173	3940	3233	6410	3288	3122
Baonan	3	1	2	6	4	2
Blang	9	4	5	36	10	26
Buyi	1214	683	531	2152	961	1191
Dai	141	62	79	353	162	191
Daur	37	22	15	92	41	51
Deang				20	9	11
Derung	21	7	14	18	8	10
Dong	69,947	38,418	31,529	52,121	27,604	24,517
Dongxiang	78	46	32	67	39	28
Ewenki	24	11	13	24	8	16
Gaoshan	63	38	25	162	88	74
Gelao	385	261	124	585	323	262
Han	56,911,968	29,614,784	27,297,184	54,769,192	28,128,850	26,640,342
Hani	151	63	88	314	117	197
Hezhe	9	3	6	16	10	6
Hui	77,759	40,114	37,645	67,185	34,858	32,327
Jing	42	29	13	93	54	39
Jingpo	15	5	10	38	11	27
Jino	1		1	10	4	6
Kazak	40	18	22	2191	1057	1134
Kirgiz	4	1	3	36	20	16
Korean	2949	1620	1329	1960	1025	935
Lahu	30	8	22	108	46	62
Lhoba	5	2	3	2		2
Li	706	390	316	2709	1327	1382

Lisu	50	26	24	138	59	79
Manchu	14,540	7581	6959	12,899	6762	6137
Maonan	50	30	20	151	62	89
Miao	214,266	117,904	96,362	177,490	94,179	83,311
Monba	4	2	2	25	10	15
Mongol	10,887	4935	5952	10,318	5415	4903
Mulao	177	102	75	276	88	188
Naxi	126	71	55	179	86	93
Nu	4	3	1	156	81	75
Oroqen	7	1	6	11	7	4
Pumi	12	6	6	26	12	14
Qiang	224	153	71	256	146	110
Russian	26	6	20	26	13	13
Salar	58	42	16	135	88	47
She	2523	1571	952	3058	1890	1168
Shui	94	54	40	577	309	268
Tajik	36	20	16	9	6	3
Tatar	2	1	1	10	4	6
Tibetan	1648	803	845	2175	974	1201
Tu	636	390	246	1963	958	1005
Tujia	2,177,409	1,140,541	1,036,868	2,100,052	1,069,839	1,030,213
Uygur	1457	813	644	2577	1457	1120
Uzbek				9	4	5
Va	66	28	38	532	255	277
Xibe	215	104	111	228	109	119
Yao	1569	856	713	2709	1242	1467
Yi	2117	1152	965	2748	1434	1314
Yugur	4	3	1	19	10	9
Zhuang	7824	4480	3344	12,240	5422	6818

Note: Total population includes servicemen (while ethnic breakdowns do not include them) as well as unknown ethnic groups and foreigners with Chinese citizenship

Table A.15 Hunan's populations reported by the 2000 and 2010 national population censuses

	2000			2010		
Ethnic group	Population	Male	Female	Population	Male	Female
Total	63,274,173	32,993,704	30,280,469	65,700,762	33,776,459	31,924,303
Achang	29	1	28	26	8	18
Bai	125,597	65,371	60,226	115,678	59,088	56,590
Baonan	6	4	2	13	7	6
Blang	100	9	91	138	9	129
Buyi	3173	1241	1932	4039	1463	2576
Dai	587	102	485	837	208	629
Daur	116	56	60	39	20	19
Deang	15	6	9	9		9
Derung	66	36	30	36	20	16
Dong	842,123	448,292	393,831	854,960	452,380	402,580
Dongxiang	28	13	15	62	41	21
Ewenki	34	17	17	4	2	2
Gaoshan	189	86	103	128	66	62
Gelao	397	241	156	911	430	481
Han	56,863,479	29,639,115	27,224,364	59,149,353	30,385,867	28,763,486
Hani	1337	285	1052	1055	182	873
Hezhe	5	3	2	36	15	21
Hui	97,368	50,412	46,956	94,705	49,291	45,414
Jing	46	25	21	86	34	52
Jingpo	136	18	118	135	21	114
Jino	13	2	11	17	2	15
Kazak	110	54	56	2775	1409	1366
Kirgiz	10	3	7	62	31	31
Korean	2693	1330	1363	1180	583	597
Lahu	480	27	453	383	38	345
Lhoba	15	9	6	3	2	1
Li	862	430	432	2350	1040	1310

Lisu	145	45	100	199	73	126
Manchu	8206	4112	4094	7566	3944	3622
Maonan	52	20	32	199	74	125
Miao	1,921,495	998,820	922,675	2,060,426	1,061,107	999,319
Monba	7	2	5	60	26	34
Mongol	15,869	5384	10,485	3693	1824	1869
Mulao	719	389	330	906	462	444
Naxi	113	60	53	126	56	70
Nu	29	18	11	210	103	107
Oroqen	8	4	4	5	2	3
Pumi	22	8	14	24	12	12
Qiang	73	34	39	180	88	92
Russian	25	7	18	24	7	17
Salar	272	126	146	79	39	40
She	2891	1736	1155	3059	1735	1324
Shui	270	91	179	598	283	315
Tajik	105	58	47	3	1	2
Tatar	16	8	8	15	8	7
Tibetan	2930	1339	1591	1622	758	864
Tu	1097	570	527	5137	2544	2593
Tujia	2,639,534	1,376,741	1,262,793	2,632,452	1,355,212	1,277,240
Uygur	7939	4148	3791	6716	3696	3020
Uzbek	22	8	14	33	15	18
Va	803	260	543	915	359	556
Xibe	93	44	49	136	71	65
Yao	704,564	378,435	326,129	713,191	377,080	336,111
Yi	4116	1793	2323	3183	1374	1809
Yugur	3	1	2	18	6	12
Zhuang	23,559	12,168	11,391	30,387	12,964	17,423

Note: Total population includes servicemen (while ethnic breakdowns do not include them) as well as unknown ethnic groups and foreigners with Chinese citizenship

Table A.16 Inner Mongolia's populations reported by the 2000 and 2010 national population censuses

	2000			2010		
Ethnic group	Population	Male	Female	Population	Male	Female
Total	23,323,347	12,061,615	11,261,732	24,706,291	12,838,243	11,868,048
Achang	6	2	4	16	11	5
Bai	248	108	140	443	194	249
Baonan	7	4	3	90	73	17
Blang	1		1	15	3	12
Buyi	822	409	413	537	260	277
Dai	96	34	62	179	74	105
Daur	77,188	38,535	38,653	76,255	37,684	38,571
Deang	1		1	5	2	3
Derung	190	91	99	7	3	4
Dong	540	257	283	438	246	192
Dongxiang	118	74	44	574	374	200
Ewenki	26,201	12,851	13,350	26,139	12,578	13,561
Gaoshan	144	69	75	120	62	58
Gelao	20	12	8	249	194	55
Han	18,465,586	9,630,944	8,834,642	19,650,665	10,306,496	9,344,169
Hani	92	30	62	320	106	214
Hezhe	54	24	30	50	23	27
Hui	209,850	106,491	103,359	221,483	113,289	108,194
Jing	13	4	9	25	10	15
Jingpo	28	10	18	39	7	32
Jino	1		1	11	4	7
Kazak	20	10	10	377	206	171
Kirgiz	153	84	69	141	79	62
Korean	21,859	10,726	11,133	18,464	9016	9448
Lahu	35	13	22	347	77	270
Lhoba						
Li	449	176	273	981	444	537

Lisu	145	42	103	443	109	334
Manchu	499,911	254,193	245,718	452,765	233,007	219,758
Maonan	15	6	9	14	9	5
Miao	2159	939	1220	3349	1953	1396
Monba	11	4	7	7	5	2
Mongol	3,995,349	1,994,916	2,000,433	4,226,090	2,108,197	2,117,893
Mulao	30	14	16	37	24	13
Naxi	31	17	14	60	29	31
Nu	9	2	7	18	3	15
Oroqen	3573	1702	1871	3632	1699	1933
Pumi	11	2	9	5	5	
Qiang	109	52	57	144	81	63
Russian	5020	2472	2548	4673	2276	2397
Salar	26	20	6	53	34	19
She	94	53	41	202	127	75
Shui	54	23	31	122	67	55
Tajik	29	11	18	6	3	3
Tatar	6	1	5	6	2	4
Tibetan	2062	906	1156	3259	1821	1438
Tu	437	211	226	557	297	260
Tujia	1678	823	855	3096	1822	1274
Uygur	1259	685	574	658	385	273
Uzbek	8	4	4	6	4	2
Va	206	82	124	519	130	389
Xibe	3023	1549	1474	3000	1555	1445
Yao	231	107	124	318	169	149
Yi	2089	813	1276	2854	1620	1234
Yugur	27	14	13	38	22	16
Zhuang	1895	929	966	2319	1239	1080

Note: Total population includes servicemen (while ethnic breakdowns do not include them) as well as unknown ethnic groups and foreigners with Chinese citizenship

Table A.17 Jiangsu's populations reported by the 2000 and 2010 national population censuses

	2000			2010		
Ethnic group	Population	Male	Female	Population	Male	Female
Total	73,043,577	36,982,038	36,061,539	78,660,941	39,626,707	39,034,234
Achang	42	5	37	98	44	54
Bai	2300	453	1847	4020	1723	2297
Baonan	3	1	2	32	16	16
Blang	180	10	170	265	67	198
Buyi	8229	2062	6167	16,689	7315	9374
Dai	1083	90	993	2189	693	1496
Daur	103	45	58	283	136	147
Deang	9		9	14	5	9
Derung	35	11	24	26	10	16
Dong	9528	2134	7394	12,280	4889	7391
Dongxiang	35	15	20	420	277	143
Ewenki	57	13	44	49	20	29
Gaoshan	120	47	73	120	54	66
Gelao	721	307	414	2488	1291	1197
Han	72,783,674	36,875,556	35,908,118	78,276,015	39,442,857	38,833,158
Hani	2049	123	1926	2916	953	1963
Hezhe	13	1	12	68	36	32
Hui	132,582	66,614	65,968	130,757	67,024	63,733
Jing	90	19	71	218	101	117
Jingpo	60	4	56	298	92	206
Jino	9	1	8	24	5	19
Kazak	73	33	40	2124	985	1139
Kirgiz	30	15	15	61	30	31
Korean	5048	2434	2614	9525	4920	4605
Lahu	610	29	581	1042	187	855
Lhoba	9	1	8	1	1	
Li	738	233	505	2447	974	1473

Lisu	842	53	789	1447	383	1064
Manchu	11,880	5699	6181	18,074	8865	9209
Maonan	54	19	35	184	94	90
Miao	22,246	5123	17,123	49,535	21,979	27,556
Monba	14	5	9	136	65	71
Mongol	14,167	4771	9396	10,691	5160	5531
Mulao	167	41	126	522	223	299
Naxi	256	61	195	329	123	206
Nu	66	5	61	356	158	198
Oroqen	25	9	16	43	16	27
Pumi	66	9	57	38	14	24
Qiang	215	82	133	954	486	468
Russian	67	30	37	109	48	61
Salar	51	18	33	353	187	166
She	742	401	341	1738	958	780
Shui	2775	1369	1406	13,089	7056	6033
Tajik	39	16	23	17	5	12
Tatar	10	5	5	19	11	8
Tibetan	2659	1073	1586	3358	1451	1907
Tu	706	237	469	2263	986	1277
Tujia	16,539	6112	10,427	41,258	20,177	21,081
Uygur	2213	1245	968	4367	2038	2329
Uzbek	5	1	4	15	6	9
Va	378	56	322	1481	701	780
Xibe	207	94	113	433	189	244
Yao	1159	315	844	3575	1644	1931
Yi	8244	1960	6284	18,896	8576	10,320
Yugur	7	2	5	41	25	16
Zhuang	8934	2419	6515	20,880	9272	11,608

Note: Total population includes servicemen (while ethnic breakdowns do not include them) as well as unknown ethnic groups and foreigners with Chinese citizenship

Table A.18 Jiangxi's populations reported by the 2000 and 2010 national population censuses

	2000			2010		
Ethnic group	Population	Male	Female	Population	Male	Female
Total	40,397,598	20,990,240	19,407,358	44,567,797	23,003,521	21,564,276
Achang	1		1	14	4	10
Bai	337	119	218	1621	815	806
Baonan						
Blang	13	6	7	31	16	15
Buyi	1762	680	1082	2156	838	1318
Dai	75	30	45	484	225	259
Daur	52	20	32	57	18	39
Deang	3		3	1		1
Derung	16	4	12	3	2	1
Dong	1564	797	767	2189	1170	1019
Dongxiang	8	3	5	49	31	18
Ewenki	5	2	3	19	6	13
Gaoshan	134	84	50	132	80	52
Gelao	122	52	70	336	156	180
Han	40,271,881	20,924,958	19,346,923	44,415,487	22,919,893	21,495,594
Hani	63	12	51	265	124	141
Hezhe				8	5	3
Hui	9972	5091	4881	8902	4679	4223
Jing	278	153	125	301	170	131
Jingpo	12	8	4	65	23	42
Jino	1	1		5	3	2
Kazak	9	3	6	1718	861	857
Kirgiz	8		8	46	24	22
Korean	1703	873	830	543	226	317
Lahu	12	1	11	140	33	107
Lhoba	1		1	1	1	
Li	301	98	203	1536	699	837

Lisu	21	11	10	96	34	62
Manchu	5075	2684	2391	4942	2638	2304
Maonan	35	17	18	86	41	45
Miao	5414	2533	2881	9125	4369	4756
Monba				78	30	48
Mongol	9010	2811	6199	3479	1770	1709
Mulao	72	35	37	181	81	100
Naxi	31	11	20	89	45	44
Nu	26	13	13	87	44	43
Oroqen	5	3	2	5	2	3
Pumi	5	4	1	6	4	2
Qiang	205	120	85	155	85	70
Russian	4	1	3	7	2	5
Salar	12	7	5	44	26	18
She	77,650	43,457	34,193	91,068	53,907	37,161
Shui	77	33	44	782	374	408
Tajik	57	24	33	33	15	18
Tatar				4	3	1
Tibetan	1649	760	889	1150	595	555
Tu	148	78	70	576	272	304
Tujia	1551	753	798	4815	2372	2443
Uygur	1142	591	551	852	420	432
Uzbek	6	3	3	9	2	7
Va	111	55	56	759	327	432
Xibe	82	42	40	81	35	46
Yao	1198	596	602	2599	1227	1372
Yi	2271	1013	1258	1850	946	904
Yugur	1	1		18	11	7
Zhuang	3046	1375	1671	7979	3363	4616

Note: Total population includes servicemen (while ethnic breakdowns do not include them) as well as unknown ethnic groups and foreigners with Chinese citizenship

Table A.19 Jilin's populations reported by the 2000 and 2010 national population censuses

	2000			2010		
Ethnic group	Population	Male	Female	Population	Male	Female
Total	26,802,191	13,720,747	13,081,444	27,452,815	13,907,218	13,545,597
Achang				22	1	21
Bai	298	161	137	276	148	128
Baonan	8	6	2	6	4	2
Blang				9	4	5
Buyi	1074	584	490	362	191	171
Dai	60	34	26	253	46	207
Daur	490	241	249	587	258	329
Deang				2		2
Derung				1		1
Dong	519	272	247	231	130	101
Dongxiang				32	17	15
Ewenki	75	32	43	104	46	58
Gaoshan	99	53	46	100	49	51
Gelao	90	51	39	71	48	23
Han	24,348,815	12,473,142	11,875,673	25,267,110	12,792,641	12,474,469
Hani	212	78	134	142	40	102
Hezhe	190	107	83	212	106	106
Hui	125,620	63,542	62,078	118,799	59,299	59,500
Jing	1		1	8	5	3
Jingpo	32	10	22	457	50	407
Jino	21	13	8	19	13	6
Kazak	89	46	43	467	209	258
Kirgiz	10	5	5	36	16	20
Korean	1,145,688	571,437	574,251	1,040,167	517,257	522,910
Lahu	12	5	7	33	8	25
Lhoba	5	1	4	3	1	2
Li	157	71	86	545	253	292

Lisu	30	13	17	100	22	78
Manchu	993,112	521,439	471,673	866,365	458,840	407,525
Maonan	3	2	1	6	2	4
Miao	1531	785	746	1446	749	697
Monba	11	6	5	18	8	10
Mongol	172,026	82,524	89,502	145,039	71,851	73,188
Mulao	28	12	16	30	11	19
Naxi	15	11	4	14	8	6
Nu				27	8	19
Oroqen	125	50	75	111	39	72
Pumi	19	7	12	4	2	2
Qiang	26	14	12	238	120	118
Russian	64	37	27	48	21	27
Salar	9	4	5	50	30	20
She	45	24	21	82	34	48
Shui	14	8	6	50	27	23
Tajik	3	2	1	2	1	1
Tatar	2	1	1	5	2	3
Tibetan	1615	721	894	652	264	388
Tu	49	28	21	128	60	68
Tujia	933	517	416	1523	864	659
Uygur	1500	868	632	1127	517	610
Uzbek	1		1	2	2	
Va	5	1	4	132	43	89
Xibe	3168	1649	1519	3113	1622	1491
Yao	220	127	93	308	148	160
Yi	2253	1068	1185	558	326	232
Yugur				8	4	4
Zhuang	1655	864	791	1547	738	809

Note: Total population includes servicemen (while ethnic breakdowns do not include them) as well as unknown ethnic groups and foreigners with Chinese citizenship

Table A.20 Liaoning's populations reported by the 2000 and 2010 national population censuses

	2000			2010		
Ethnic group	Population	Male	Female	Population	Male	Female
Total	41,824,412	21,323,383	20,501,029	43,746,323	22,147,745	21,598,578
Achang	2	1	1	10	7	3
Bai	449	223	226	559	292	267
Baonan				2	1	1
Blang	4	2	2	19	9	10
Buyi	1214	569	645	991	511	480
Dai	104	46	58	231	64	167
Daur	1282	558	724	1858	801	1057
Deang				5	2	3
Derung	169	80	89	6	2	4
Dong	799	430	369	821	454	367
Dongxiang	8	5	3	27	16	11
Ewenki	221	85	136	448	198	250
Gaoshan	305	143	162	211	96	115
Gelao	89	53	36	211	145	66
Han	35,105,991	17,873,551	17,232,440	37,103,174	18,737,977	18,365,197
Hani	157	83	74	304	131	173
Hezhe	82	33	49	154	72	82
Hui	264,407	133,155	131,252	245,798	123,200	122,598
Jing	6	3	3	15	10	5
Jingpo	24	18	6	80	26	54
Jino				10	6	4
Kazak	121	51	70	448	182	266
Kirgiz	45	22	23	125	62	63
Korean	241,052	118,885	122,167	239,537	118,896	120,641
Lahu	14	6	8	48	17	31
Lhoba	9	6	3	11	8	3
Li	615	304	311	1765	846	919

Lisu	152	20	132	646	96	550
Manchu	5,385,287	2,779,918	2,605,369	5,336,895	2,750,732	2,586,163
Maonan	20	8	12	19	12	7
Miao	3009	1626	1383	3952	2342	1610
Monba				9	5	4
Mongol	669,972	335,109	334,863	657,869	330,787	327,082
Mulao	53	34	19	71	28	43
Naxi	86	40	46	125	63	62
Nu	3	1	2	76	20	56
Oroqen	161	63	98	196	72	124
Pumi	16	9	7	14	4	10
Qiang	81	40	41	171	89	82
Russian	150	60	90	185	83	102
Salar	45	29	16	88	59	29
She	200	121	79	257	170	87
Shui	44	21	23	89	51	38
Tajik	46	15	31	10	7	3
Tatar	9	3	6	14	4	10
Tibetan	2017	953	1064	1881	890	991
Tu	171	102	69	264	135	129
Tujia	3757	2327	1430	5190	3185	2005
Uygur	2407	1302	1105	1917	1081	836
Uzbek	1	1		5		5
Va	129	60	69	220	99	121
Xibe	132,615	69,915	62,700	132,431	69,961	62,470
Yao	505	279	226	774	421	353
Yi	2641	1169	1472	1693	1088	605
Yugur	1		1	17	8	9
Zhuang	3576	1812	1764	4285	2160	2125

Note: Total population includes servicemen (while ethnic breakdowns do not include them) as well as unknown ethnic groups and foreigners with Chinese citizenship

Table A.21 Ningxia's populations reported by the 2000 and 2010 national population censuses

Ethnic group	2000			2010		
	Population	Male	Female	Population	Male	Female
Total	5,486,393	2,813,517	2,672,876	6,301,350	3,227,404	3,073,946
Achang				4	1	3
Bai	39	17	22	213	106	107
Baonan	14	10	4	21	12	9
Blang				2		2
Buyi	72	41	31	183	98	85
Dai	11	2	9	44	24	20
Daur	26	10	16	42	17	25
Deang				1		1
Derung				2	1	1
Dong	128	67	61	345	222	123
Dongxiang	2168	1191	977	1261	748	513
Ewenki	4	1	3	7	2	5
Gaoshan	15	10	5	10	8	2
Gelao	9	9		42	31	11
Han	3,590,563	1,850,231	1,740,332	4,086,367	2,103,760	1,982,607
Hani	12	8	4	52	29	23
Hezhe	3	2	1	4	1	3
Hui	1,862,474	947,187	915,287	2,173,820	1,102,835	1,070,985
Jing				5		5
Jingpo	1	1		6	2	4
Jino				2	1	1
Kazak	69	25	44	190	70	120
Kirgiz	5	2	3	12	6	6
Korean	472	227	245	403	207	196
Lahu				13	5	8
Lhoba				1		1
Li	24	13	11	146	69	77
Lisu	1		1	17	8	9
Manchu	21,962	10,723	11,239	24,902	12,287	12,615
Maonan	15	6	9	26	9	17
Miao	407	187	220	1113	732	381
Monba				2		2
Mongol	4898	2054	2844	6661	3174	3487
Mulao	2	2		10	4	6
Naxi	7	3	4	17	8	9
Nu				7	3	4
Oroqen	9	7	2	6	4	2
Pumi				6	3	3
Qiang	28	20	8	89	53	36
Russian	21	9	12	18	6	12

(continued)

Table A.21 Continued

Ethnic group	2000 Population	2000 Male	2000 Female	2010 Population	2010 Male	2010 Female
Salar	38	18	20	72	38	34
She	88	60	28	122	76	46
Shui	3		3	35	15	20
Tajik				1		1
Tatar	2	1	1	2		2
Tibetan	506	255	251	656	316	340
Tu	191	95	96	326	176	150
Tujia	758	362	396	1441	847	594
Uygur	312	165	147	613	272	341
Uzbek	2	1	1	3	2	1
Va				26	14	12
Xibe	216	94	122	184	88	96
Yao	63	38	25	197	108	89
Yi	137	57	80	530	359	171
Yugur	43	23	20	48	24	24
Zhuang	575	283	292	977	495	482

Note: Total population includes servicemen (while ethnic breakdowns do not include them) as well as unknown ethnic groups and foreigners with Chinese citizenship

Table A.22 Qinghai's populations reported by the 2000 and 2010 national population censuses

Ethnic group	2000 Population	2000 Male	2000 Female	2010 Population	2010 Male	2010 Female
Total	4,822,963	2,489,590	2,333,373	5,626,723	2,913,793	2,712,930
Achang	1		1	1		1
Bai	242	149	93	320	174	146
Baonan	635	337	298	904	477	427
Blang	22	6	16	2	2	
Buyi	170	86	84	251	185	66
Dai	4	2	2	31	13	18
Daur	47	17	30	26	15	11
Deang	9	5	4	1	1	
Derung	6	3	3	4	3	1
Dong	148	98	50	161	123	38
Dongxiang	2498	1564	934	6331	3976	2355
Ewenki	12	4	8	5	2	3
Gaoshan	22	9	13	20	8	12
Gelao	17	7	10	69	59	10
Han	2,606,050	1,364,527	1,241,523	2,983,521	1,574,280	1,409,241

(*continued*)

Table A.22 Continued

Ethnic group	2000			2010		
	Population	Male	Female	Population	Male	Female
Hani	3	1	2	17	8	9
Hezhe	15	7	8	11	9	2
Hui	753,378	388,789	364,589	834,298	423,527	410,771
Jing				10	6	4
Jingpo				5	3	2
Jino	3	1	2	1		1
Kazak	407	213	194	680	332	348
Kirgiz	8	3	5	4	1	3
Korean	453	230	223	312	152	160
Lahu	7	5	2	8	4	4
Lhoba	5	3	2			
Li	9	4	5	139	67	72
Lisu	58	39	19	21	13	8
Manchu	7788	4008	3780	8029	4172	3857
Maonan	23	11	12	8	6	2
Miao	436	209	227	911	576	335
Monba	11	6	5	4	1	3
Mongol	86,301	43,562	42,739	99,815	50,744	49,071
Mulao	23	7	16	15	7	8
Naxi	17	8	9	32	16	16
Nu	4	4		5	4	1
Oroqen	1	1		2	1	1
Pumi	12	6	6	3		3
Qiang	86	50	36	104	61	43
Russian	48	26	22	38	19	19
Salar	87,043	44,393	42,650	107,089	53,669	53,420
She	20	8	12	53	32	21
Shui	20	9	11	30	16	14
Tajik	15	7	8	3	1	2
Tatar	12	7	5	2		2
Tibetan	1,086,592	543,708	542,884	1,375,059	693,995	681,064
Tu	187,562	96,038	91,524	204,412	104,572	99,840
Tujia	978	534	444	1537	969	568
Uygur	431	216	215	209	124	85
Uzbek	1	1		2	1	1
Va	6	2	4	20	10	10
Xibe	142	77	65	128	52	76
Yao	105	55	50	209	115	94
Yi	274	133	141	683	550	133
Yugur	140	72	68	163	78	85
Zhuang	618	308	310	980	543	437

Note: Total population includes servicemen (while ethnic breakdowns do not include them) as well as unknown ethnic groups and foreigners with Chinese citizenship

Table A.23 Shaanxi's populations reported by the 2000 and 2010 national population censuses

	2000			2010		
Ethnic group	Population	Male	Female	Population	Male	Female
Total	35,365,072	18,378,759	16,986,313	37,327,379	19,287,575	18,039,804
Achang	4	4		2	1	1
Bai	338	193	145	486	276	210
Baonan	1		1	4	2	2
Blang	2	1	1	6	2	4
Buyi	450	267	183	727	371	356
Dai	68	44	24	117	31	86
Daur	75	28	47	93	42	51
Deang				1	1	
Derung	9	5	4			
Dong	509	310	199	731	413	318
Dongxiang	26	15	11	116	71	45
Ewenki	11	7	4	24	14	10
Gaoshan	27	14	13	15	7	8
Gelao	44	29	15	205	122	83
Han	35,188,651	18,289,425	16,899,226	37,137,743	19,191,534	17,946,209
Hani	40	17	23	99	42	57
Hezhe				4		4
Hui	139,232	70,003	69,229	138,716	69,739	68,977
Jing	9	7	2	28	11	17
Jingpo	19	16	3	22	7	15
Jino	1		1	9	3	6
Kazak	122	61	61	794	407	387
Kirgiz	19	11	8	23	6	17
Korean	1620	820	800	1129	534	595
Lahu	44	1	43	35	14	21

(continued)

Table A.23 Continued

Ethnic group	2000 Population	2000 Male	2000 Female	2010 Population	2010 Male	2010 Female
Lhoba	4	1	3	7	1	6
Li	161	88	73	441	199	242
Lisu	16	12	4	32	15	17
Manchu	15,801	7930	7871	16,291	8442	7849
Maonan	16	8	8	19	8	11
Miao	1388	798	590	2787	1659	1128
Monba	9	3	6	18	9	9
Mongol	6060	2913	3147	6976	3509	3467
Mulao	27	14	13	44	18	26
Naxi	69	34	35	101	48	53
Nu	1		1	31	13	18
Oroqen	6	1	5	8	3	5
Pumi	4	4		4	2	2
Qiang	54	27	27	182	80	102
Russian	69	28	41	73	35	38
Salar	22	15	7	156	95	61
She	104	66	38	212	132	80
Shui	17	10	7	83	50	33
Tajik	7	3	4	3	2	1
Tatar	1	1		1		1
Tibetan	3048	1407	1641	6345	2827	3518
Tu	290	180	110	499	265	234
Tujia	1721	1113	608	3876	2362	1514

Uygur	1187	661	526	1570	725	845
Uzbek	6	5	1	7	2	5
Va	44	22	22	160	86	74
Xibe	446	237	209	416	219	197
Yao	273	179	94	605	313	292
Yi	854	472	382	1644	988	656
Yugur	23	8	15	29	12	17
Zhuang	1987	1220	767	3555	1765	1790

Note: Total population includes servicemen (while ethnic breakdowns do not include them) as well as unknown ethnic groups and foreigners with Chinese citizenship

Table A.24 Shandong's populations reported by the 2000 and 2010 national population censuses

	2000			2010		
Ethnic group	Population	Male	Female	Population	Male	Female
Total	89,971,789	45,542,060	44,429,729	95,792,719	48,446,944	47,345,775
Achang	92	2	90	99	15	84
Bai	2405	220	2185	1247	411	836
Baonan	3		3	7	3	4
Blang	279	13	266	317	99	218
Buyi	2426	860	1566	1839	757	1082
Dai	1797	98	1699	2468	426	2042
Daur	541	224	317	960	432	528
Deang	18		18	50	10	40
Derung	100	30	70	30	5	25
Dong	1245	508	737	867	453	414
Dongxiang	28	10	18	126	77	49
Ewenki	107	34	73	220	95	125
Gaoshan	86	32	54	66	30	36
Gelao	97	52	45	597	364	233
Han	89,339,046	45,245,932	44,093,114	95,066,830	48,090,616	46,976,214
Hani	3041	103	2938	3023	345	2678
Hezhe	33	11	22	68	35	33
Hui	497,597	248,501	249,096	535,679	269,871	265,808
Jing	7		7	80	35	45
Jingpo	343	8	335	608	59	549
Jino	17	4	13	17	7	10
Kazak	49	22	27	1116	459	657
Kirgiz	16	6	10	90	35	55
Korean	27,795	13,032	14,763	61,556	31,229	30,327
Lahu	1403	69	1334	1880	237	1643
Lhoba	7	3	4	2	1	1
Li	297	55	242	1202	466	736

Lisu	1919	91	1828	1841	208	1633
Manchu	33,527	15,658	17,869	46,521	23,274	23,247
Maonan	35	9	26	50	25	25
Miao	6949	1813	5136	8414	3586	4828
Monba	5		5	20	10	10
Mongol	23,743	7104	16,639	17,669	8448	9221
Mulao	130	34	96	126	46	80
Naxi	249	24	225	256	69	187
Nu	97	10	87	373	161	212
Oroqen	60	28	32	98	33	65
Pumi	81	5	76	55	10	45
Qiang	41	13	28	243	121	122
Russian	68	24	44	128	58	70
Salar	21	8	13	609	354	255
She	330	210	120	363	226	137
Shui	95	20	75	191	85	106
Tajik	81	40	41	32	17	15
Tatar	9	4	5	11	4	7
Tibetan	2733	1045	1688	2146	875	1271
Tu	304	80	224	651	270	381
Tujia	2719	1262	1457	5730	3188	2542
Uygur	2386	1294	1092	4635	1551	3084
Uzbek	4	1	3	13	6	7
Va	4693	269	4424	5619	1315	4304
Xibe	356	158	198	661	291	370
Yao	468	109	359	878	353	525
Yi	6208	1366	4842	8298	3422	4876
Yugur	7		7	76	33	43
Zhuang	5444	1520	3924	5822	2273	3549

Note: Total population includes servicemen (while ethnic breakdowns do not include them) as well as unknown ethnic groups and foreigners with Chinese citizenship

Table A.25 Shanghai's populations reported by the 2000 and 2010 national population censuses

	2000			2010		
Ethnic group	Population	Male	Female	Population	Male	Female
Total	16,303,862	8,379,320	7,924,542	23,019,196	11,854,916	11,164,280
Achang	5	2	3	51	28	23
Bai	5296	2942	2354	3893	1979	1914
Baonan	6	3	3	16	11	5
Blang	15	9	6	133	80	53
Buyi	5120	2369	2751	5840	3043	2797
Dai	99	49	50	1289	540	749
Daur	89	36	53	449	186	263
Deang	1		1	15	10	5
Derung	18	6	12	8	5	3
Dong	798	410	388	7787	4156	3631
Dongxiang	77	44	33	362	282	80
Ewenki				63	30	33
Gaoshan	38	8	30	81	36	45
Gelao	212	97	115	2684	1496	1188
Han	6468	2654	3814	22,743,033	11,716,435	11,026,598
Hani	62	33	29	3185	1628	1557
Hezhe	86	40	46	40	20	20
Hui	1642	707	935	78,163	39,480	38,683
Jing	5	2	3	45	20	25
Jingpo	5	1	4	142	68	74
Jino				23	6	17
Kazak	246	73	173	639	274	365
Kirgiz	226	127	99	58	25	33
Korean	9087	4502	4585	22,257	10,292	11,965
Lahu	103	48	55	500	232	268
Lhoba	7	2	5	4	2	2
Li	27	9	18	1725	676	1049

Lisu	87	52	35	580	318	262
Manchu	1970	1011	959	25,165	11,892	13,273
Maonan	215	123	92	160	66	94
Miao	1443	634	809	31,351	16,418	14,933
Monba	4	2	2	3		3
Mongol	57,514	28,491	29,023	11,238	5295	5943
Mulao	54	23	31	441	180	261
Naxi	4	2	2	287	125	162
Nu	5	2	3	65	28	37
Oroqen	14	6	8	55	23	32
Pumi	24	11	13	38	14	24
Qiang	10	6	4	505	246	259
Russian	41	10	31	209	78	131
Salar	14	1	13	941	603	338
She	52	28	24	3020	1538	1482
Shui	20	17	3	745	375	370
Tajik	3	2	1	14	8	6
Tatar	19	11	8	12	4	8
Tibetan	1701	1052	649	2406	1031	1375
Tu	172	78	94	1009	545	464
Tujia	381	124	257	33,584	17,648	15,936
Uygur	4808	2566	2242	5254	2725	2529
Uzbek	76	31	45	14	4	10
Va	859	450	409	1353	807	546
Xibe				696	315	381
Yao	506	244	262	3627	1892	1735
Yi	2923	1138	1785	7113	3497	3616
Yugur	6	3	3	15	10	5
Zhuang	976	517	459	16,219	7894	8325

Note: Total population includes servicemen (while ethnic breakdowns do not include them) as well as unknown ethnic groups and foreigners with Chinese citizenship

Table A.26 Shanxi's populations reported by the 2000 and 2010 national population censuses

	2000			2010		
Ethnic group	Population	Male	Female	Population	Male	Female
Total	32,471,242	16,800,758	15,670,484	35,712,101	18,338,760	17,373,341
Achang	2		2	4		4
Bai	353	120	233	183	96	87
Baonan	2		2			
Blang	6	2	4	22	7	15
Buyi	912	375	537	373	134	239
Dai	68	15	53	187	58	129
Daur	92	39	53	85	43	42
Deang	2		2	6	3	3
Derung	127	67	60	1		1
Dong	632	318	314	280	194	86
Dongxiang	9	5	4	30	21	9
Ewenki	24	8	16	26	11	15
Gaoshan	7	3	4	9	4	5
Gelao	55	33	22	121	78	43
Han	32,368,083	16,751,349	15,616,734	35,618,454	18,290,925	17,327,529
Hani	55	10	45	214	34	180
Hezhe	2	2		12	4	8
Hui	61,690	31,152	30,538	59,709	30,210	29,499
Jing	4	1	3	29	13	16
Jingpo	52	1	51	108	9	99
Jino	4	1	3	1		1
Kazak	23	7	16	277	144	133
Kirgiz	1		1	6	2	4
Korean	1813	867	946	663	316	347
Lahu	35	7	28	136	14	122
Lhoba	2		2			
Li	92	47	45	521	266	255

Lisu	101	9	92	159	23	136
Manchu	13,665	7198	6467	11,741	6314	5427
Maonan	8		8	21	16	5
Miao	2805	1160	1645	2205	1124	1081
Monba	8		8	3	2	1
Mongol	9446	3399	6047	5070	2707	2363
Mulao	35	9	26	28	12	16
Naxi	57	17	40	42	17	25
Nu	9	2	7	88	40	48
Oroqen	1		1	3	2	1
Pumi	11	2	9	3	1	2
Qiang	159	109	50	286	214	72
Russian	8	1	7	5	2	3
Salar	8	4	4	43	26	17
She	251	156	95	171	117	54
Shui	20	2	18	30	15	15
Tajik	94	42	52	1	1	
Tatar				1		1
Tibetan	1544	678	866	1047	494	553
Tu	236	116	120	200	98	102
Tujia	2362	1301	1061	2936	1858	1078
Uygur	1084	566	518	670	414	256
Uzbek	3	1	2	3	1	2
Va	120	43	77	427	117	310
Xibe	152	79	73	158	93	65
Yao	202	88	114	325	164	161
Yi	2473	775	1698	2867	1426	1441
Yugur	8	3	5	7	3	4
Zhuang	2084	534	1550	2007	830	1177

Note: Total population includes servicemen (while ethnic breakdowns do not include them) as well as unknown ethnic groups and foreigners with Chinese citizenship

Table A.27 Sichuan's populations reported by the 2000 and 2010 national population censuses

	2000			2010		
Ethnic group	Population	Male	Female	Population	Male	Female
Total	82,348,296	42,561,620	39,786,676	80,417,528	40,827,834	39,589,694
Achang	26	11	15	54	17	37
Bai	7335	3441	3894	9449	4683	4766
Baonan	16	8	8	43	33	10
Blang	138	22	116	164	46	118
Buyi	8215	4063	4152	8756	4292	4464
Dai	6642	2956	3686	7652	3380	4272
Daur	73	38	35	124	57	67
Deang	11	1	10	24	8	16
Derung	51	22	29	47	20	27
Dong	1940	959	981	2376	1142	1234
Dongxiang	60	40	20	191	135	56
Ewenki	18	10	8	30	15	15
Gaoshan	101	47	54	100	42	58
Gelao	520	273	247	1235	630	605
Han	78,229,697	40,472,128	37,757,569	75,509,724	38,343,974	37,165,750
Hani	1104	290	814	1566	469	1097
Hezhe	14	5	9	84	38	46
Hui	109,960	55,504	54,456	104,544	52,797	51,747
Jing	38	20	18	264	126	138
Jingpo	79	10	69	173	51	122
Jino	48	4	44	54	12	42
Kazak	94	45	49	1882	927	955
Kirgiz	14	5	9	74	41	33
Korean	3137	1555	1582	1548	787	761
Lahu	512	59	453	521	104	417
Lhoba	5	1	4	8	2	6
Li	316	111	205	1688	744	944

Lisu	18,674	9294	9380	21,082	10,381	10,701
Manchu	13,849	7064	6785	15,920	8355	7565
Maonan	36	15	21	88	43	45
Miao	147,526	77,078	70,448	164,642	84,997	79,645
Monba	113	40	73	26	7	19
Mongol	42,316	19,719	22,597	36,646	18,350	18,296
Mulao	116	64	52	225	110	115
Naxi	8725	4448	4277	10,149	5098	5051
Nu	57	19	38	312	113	199
Oroqen	8	4	4	18	9	9
Pumi	166	61	105	137	55	82
Qiang	300,757	153,012	147,745	296,931	149,730	147,201
Russian	48	21	27	57	27	30
Salar	108	68	40	223	122	101
She	232	154	78	447	265	182
Shui	257	121	136	1178	537	641
Tajik	58	31	27	23	4	19
Tatar	7	4	3	15	6	9
Tibetan	1,269,120	631,389	637,731	1,496,524	747,138	749,386
Tu	646	350	296	1333	639	694
Tujia	41,246	22,358	18,888	59,231	31,106	28,125
Uygur	2158	1076	1082	1945	994	951
Uzbek	3		3	17	8	9
Va	1475	170	1305	1334	343	991
Xibe	216	96	120	381	187	194
Yao	742	362	380	1795	770	1025
Yi	2,122,389	1,089,245	1,033,144	2,643,953	1,348,832	1,295,121
Yugur	4	1	3	48	26	22
Zhuang	6905	3671	3234	10,050	4781	5269

Note: Total population includes servicemen (while ethnic breakdowns do not include them) as well as unknown ethnic groups and foreigners with Chinese citizenship

Table A.28 Tianjin's populations reported by the 2000 and 2010 national population censuses

Ethnic group	2000			2010		
	Population	Male	Female	Population	Male	Female
Total	9,848,731	5,016,375	4,832,356	12,938,693	6,907,091	6,031,602
Achang				9	7	2
Bai	184	94	90	686	374	312
Baonan	1	1		10	8	2
Blang	8	5	3	21	18	3
Buyi	507	217	290	839	437	402
Dai	24	8	16	184	100	84
Daur	353	157	196	629	300	329
Deang						
Derung	16	7	9	3	2	1
Dong	521	214	307	912	454	458
Dongxiang	51	29	22	121	95	26
Ewenki	84	35	49	130	59	71
Gaoshan	34	14	20	29	15	14
Gelao	63	36	27	374	260	114
Han	9,581,775	4,885,974	4,695,801	12,607,276	6,739,522	5,867,754
Hani	20	7	13	190	81	109
Hezhe	9	4	5	28	16	12
Hui	172,357	84,999	87,358	177,734	88,336	89,398
Jing	1		1	32	14	18
Jingpo	6	4	2	29	14	15
Jino	4		4	7	1	6
Kazak	34	19	15	476	212	264
Kirgiz	13	6	7	41	17	24
Korean	11,041	5030	6011	18,247	9303	8944
Lahu	7	2	5	44	27	17
Lhoba	4	2	2			
Li	54	25	29	564	304	260
Lisu	10	8	2	63	33	30
Manchu	56,548	28,548	28,000	83,624	43,293	40,331
Maonan	40	7	33	49	14	35
Miao	1582	767	815	3751	2354	1397
Monba				8	6	2
Mongol	11,331	4616	6715	20,328	9817	10,511
Mulao	47	20	27	116	59	57
Naxi	29	16	13	81	45	36
Nu	3	3		41	25	16
Oroqen	10	4	6	38	16	22
Pumi	1		1	16	15	1
Qiang	20	10	10	180	114	66
Russian	60	22	38	119	52	67

(continued)

Table A.28 Continued

Ethnic group	2000			2010		
	Population	Male	Female	Population	Male	Female
Salar	32	25	7	122	85	37
She	78	47	31	263	147	116
Shui	36	15	21	291	166	125
Tajik	30	15	15	11	9	2
Tatar	12	5	7	4	2	2
Tibetan	1271	600	671	1775	911	864
Tu	159	86	73	350	199	151
Tujia	3677	2097	1580	7052	4059	2993
Uygur	974	618	356	2170	970	1200
Uzbek	7	3	4	19	8	11
Va	42	21	21	209	133	76
Xibe	343	169	174	536	282	254
Yao	345	135	210	785	408	377
Yi	780	357	423	1825	1217	608
Yugur				39	20	19
Zhuang	4055	1256	2799	6123	2608	3515

Note: Total population includes servicemen (while ethnic breakdowns do not include them) as well as unknown ethnic groups and foreigners with Chinese citizenship

Table A.29 Tibet's populations reported by the 2000 and 2010 national population censuses

Ethnic group	2000			2010		
	Population	Male	Female	Population	Male	Female
Total	2,616,329	1,325,371	1,290,958	3,002,165	1,542,652	1,459,513
Achang						
Bai	722	505	217	395	247	148
Baonan	24	22	2	15	11	4
Blang	16	7	9	4	1	3
Buyi	437	192	245	81	61	20
Dai	14	10	4	35	17	18
Daur	3	2	1	5	3	2
Deang	1		1			
Derung	6	3	3	37	19	18
Dong	66	34	32	179	100	79
Dongxiang	111	91	20	757	523	234
Ewenki						
Gaoshan				2	1	1
Gelao	32	25	7	27	15	12
Han	158,570	98,589	59,981	245,263	151,158	94,105
Hani	24	19	5	23	16	7
Hezhe	1		1			
Hui	9031	6683	2348	12,630	8263	4367
Jing				5	2	3
Jingpo						
Jino				1	1	
Kazak	8	7	1	2143	1182	961
Kirgiz				2678	1338	1340
Korean	51	22	29	26	18	8
Lahu	19	13	6	4	3	1
Lhoba	2691	1353	1338	3489	1696	1793
Li	3	1	2	26	16	10
Lisu	17	9	8	25	10	15
Manchu	153	88	65	718	391	327
Maonan				1	1	
Miao	389	246	143	416	292	124
Monba	8481	4255	4226	9663	4876	4787
Mongol	690	341	349	307	187	120
Mulao	5	5		2	2	
Naxi	1223	603	620	1133	557	576
Nu	408	209	199	492	242	250
Oroqen						
Pumi	15	10	5	16	11	5
Qiang	20	15	5	94	59	35
Russian	20	9	11	3	1	2

(continued)

Table A.29 Continued

Ethnic group	2000			2010		
	Population	Male	Female	Population	Male	Female
Salar	228	157	71	255	163	92
She	6	2	4	8	8	
Shui				14	8	6
Tajik	4	4				
Tatar						
Tibetan	2,427,168	1,208,765	1,218,403	2,716,388	1,368,355	1,348,033
Tu	335	212	123	1068	634	434
Tujia	303	215	88	451	321	130
Uygur	701	394	307	205	138	67
Uzbek	1	1		4	2	2
Va	7	4	3	43	30	13
Xibe				6	3	3
Yao	26	20	6	137	85	52
Yi	287	199	88	396	293	103
Yugur	3	3		4	2	2
Zhuang	192	106	86	173	128	45

Note: Total population includes servicemen (while ethnic breakdowns do not include them) as well as unknown ethnic groups and foreigners with Chinese citizenship

Table A.30 Xinjiang's populations reported by the 2000 and 2010 national population censuses

	2000			2010		
Ethnic group	Population	Male	Female	Population	Male	Female
Total	18,459,511	9,552,181	8,907,330	21,815,815	11,270,147	10,545,668
Achang	2	1	1	5	3	2
Bai	409	216	193	407	216	191
Baonan	571	311	260	568	342	226
Blang	9	3	6	23	11	12
Buyi	977	555	422	797	516	281
Dai	59	23	36	121	42	79
Daur	5541	2813	2728	5536	2851	2685
Deang	14	9	5	3	1	2
Derung	51	26	25	11	5	6
Dong	946	560	386	753	501	252
Dongxiang	55,841	29,153	26,688	61,613	32,781	28,832
Ewenki	72	37	35	26	11	15
Gaoshan	41	18	23	44	15	29
Gelao	110	70	40	260	166	94
Han	7,489,919	3,972,142	3,517,777	8,829,994	4,674,383	4,155,611
Hani	62	25	37	190	79	111
Hezhe	22	6	16	33	20	13
Hui	839,837	431,196	408,641	983,015	506,076	476,939
Jing	12	4	8	69	40	29
Jingpo	27	15	12	33	13	20
Jino				3	3	
Kazak	1,245,023	631,268	613,755	1,418,278	725,515	692,763
Kirgiz	158,775	80,687	78,088	180,472	91,506	88,966
Korean	1463	745	718	1128	558	570
Lahu	28	13	15	73	41	32
Lhoba	33	20	13	4	2	2
Li	115	64	51	418	233	185

Lisu	34	13	21	104	53	51
Manchu	19,493	9910	9583	18,707	9786	8921
Maonan	9	3	6	28	21	7
Miao	7006	3749	3257	7626	4288	3338
Monba	11	7	4	4	1	3
Mongol	149,857	74,450	75,407	156,280	79,063	77,217
Mulao	29	19	10	77	50	27
Naxi	73	34	39	89	43	46
Nu	18	8	10	58	31	27
Oroqen	14	9	5	12	8	4
Pumi	10	6	4	12	5	7
Qiang	284	162	122	317	162	155
Russian	8935	4206	4729	8489	4067	4422
Salar	3762	1965	1797	3728	1998	1730
She	166	91	75	167	105	62
Shui	301	153	148	90	68	22
Tajik	39,493	20,170	19,323	47,261	24,000	23,261
Tatar	4501	2360	2141	3242	1757	1485
Tibetan	6153	3124	3029	8316	4346	3970
Tu	2837	1525	1312	3455	1777	1678
Tujia	15,787	8495	7292	17,850	9811	8039
Uygur	8,345,622	4,243,646	4,101,976	10,001,302	5,064,182	4,937,120
Uzbek	12,096	6371	5725	10,114	5444	4670
Va	68	32	36	142	60	82
Xibe	34,566	17,416	17,150	34,399	17,416	16,983
Yao	723	369	354	942	534	408
Yi	1593	892	701	2954	1756	1198
Yugur	302	153	149	391	198	193
Zhuang	5642	2780	2862	5646	3113	2533

Note: Total population includes servicemen (while ethnic breakdowns do not include them) as well as unknown ethnic groups and foreigners with Chinese citizenship

Table A.31 Yunnan's populations reported by the 2000 and 2010 national population censuses

	2000			2010		
Ethnic group	Population	Male	Female	Population	Male	Female
Total	42,360,089	22,194,343	20,165,746	45,966,766	23,856,696	22,110,070
Achang	33,519	17,083	16,436	38,059	19,017	19,042
Bai	1,505,644	763,316	742,328	1,564,901	786,370	778,531
Baonan	7	5	2	49	36	13
Blang	90,388	47,279	43,109	116,573	60,117	56,456
Buyi	54,695	29,667	25,028	58,790	31,341	27,449
Dai	1,142,139	573,780	568,359	1,222,836	609,021	613,815
Daur	152	84	68	294	135	159
Deang	17,804	8994	8810	20,186	9889	10,297
Derung	5884	2934	2950	6353	3096	3257
Dong	3498	2169	1329	4389	2505	1884
Dongxiang	179	135	44	181	123	58
Ewenki	16	7	9	23	10	13
Gaoshan	91	48	43	131	66	65
Gelao	2835	1637	1198	3461	2018	1443
Han	28,201,274	14,894,380	13,306,894	30,617,580	16,017,198	14,600,382
Hani	1,424,990	749,084	675,906	1,629,508	851,064	778,444
Hezhe	13	7	6	42	24	18
Hui	643,238	326,023	317,215	698,265	351,169	347,096
Jing	508	196	312	878	351	527
Jingpo	130,212	64,712	65,500	142,956	69,718	73,238
Jino	20,685	10,549	10,136	22,759	11,611	11,148
Kazak	199	91	108	896	456	440
Kirgiz	42	26	16	34	18	16
Korean	1693	884	809	1343	698	645
Lahu	447,631	233,563	214,068	475,011	244,774	230,237
Lhoba	5	4	1	7	5	2
Li	1426	759	667	3231	1622	1609

Lisu	609,768	316,149	293,619	668,336	340,729	327,607
Manchu	12,187	6537	5650	13,490	7161	6329
Maonan	99	57	42	154	93	61
Miao	1,043,535	547,298	496,237	1,202,705	621,721	580,984
Monba	7	2	5	18	3	15
Mongol	28,110	14,549	13,561	22,624	12,104	10,520
Mulao	244	150	94	304	164	140
Naxi	295,464	148,805	146,659	309,858	154,835	155,023
Nu	27,738	14,467	13,271	31,821	16,240	15,581
Oroqen	6	4	2	11	3	8
Pumi	32,923	16,838	16,085	42,043	21,055	20,988
Qiang	506	380	126	552	323	229
Russian	32	10	22	26	8	18
Salar	55	28	27	265	150	115
She	499	290	209	848	552	296
Shui	12,533	6742	5791	8834	4789	4045
Tajik	17	10	7	7	3	4
Tatar	12	8	4	10	6	4
Tibetan	128,432	64,352	64,080	142,257	71,239	71,018
Tu	3157	1712	1445	5632	2988	2644
Tujia	3907	2498	1409	5963	3694	2269
Uygur	1161	815	346	1282	773	509
Uzbek	6	2	4	11	6	5
Va	383,023	199,783	183,240	400,814	204,648	196,166
Xibe	130	65	65	158	69	89
Yao	190,610	100,176	90,434	219,914	113,812	106,102
Yi	4,705,658	2,423,233	2,282,425	5,041,210	2,576,570	2,464,640
Yugur	10	7	3	8	4	4
Zhuang	1,144,021	598,142	545,879	1,215,260	628,603	586,657

Note: Total population includes servicemen (while ethnic breakdowns do not include them) as well as unknown ethnic groups and foreigners with Chinese citizenship

Table A.32 Zhejiang's populations reported by the 2000 and 2010 national population censuses

	2000			2010		
Ethnic group	Population	Male	Female	Population	Male	Female
Total	45,930,651	23,581,512	22,349,139	54,426,891	27,965,641	26,461,250
Achang	25	5	20	93	44	49
Bai	2659	920	1739	11,685	5981	5704
Baonan				17	10	7
Blang	74	4	70	300	107	193
Buyi	21,457	9726	11,731	125,838	67,119	58,719
Dai	540	77	463	5973	2883	3090
Daur	69	21	48	204	93	111
Deang				43	20	23
Derung	14	4	10	26	7	19
Dong	17,906	9524	8382	88,106	48,560	39,546
Dongxiang	55	28	27	322	202	120
Ewenki	21	8	13	40	17	23
Gaoshan	79	44	35	88	50	38
Gelao	2179	1269	910	17,785	9777	8008
Han	45,535,266	23,383,689	22,151,577	53,212,194	27,320,326	25,891,868
Hani	883	94	789	4300	1754	2546
Hezhe	17	5	12	48	20	28
Hui	19,609	10,500	9109	38,192	20,732	17,460
Jing	51	20	31	148	87	61
Jingpo	43	5	38	444	183	261
Jino	5	1	4	21	8	13
Kazak	19	6	13	695	311	384
Kirgiz	37	17	20	279	178	101
Korean	1767	881	886	6496	3288	3208
Lahu	306	17	289	1661	431	1230
Lhoba	4	2	2	1	1	
Li	1640	780	860	9391	4759	4632

Lisu	454	17	437	1514	598	916
Manchu	5089	2447	2642	11,271	5705	5566
Maonan	178	60	118	1199	639	560
Miao	53,418	26,882	26,536	309,064	167,566	141,498
Monba	8	3	5	21	9	12
Mongol	3604	1368	2236	6872	3452	3420
Mulao	786	380	406	2792	1432	1360
Naxi	553	63	490	634	161	473
Nu	75	17	58	109	40	69
Oroqen	2	2		21	9	12
Pumi	20	3	17	47	21	26
Qiang	168	77	91	1482	797	685
Russian	21	5	16	40	16	24
Salar	45	24	21	424	253	171
She	170,993	88,990	82,003	166,276	85,601	80,675
Shui	1421	459	962	11,815	6181	5634
Tajik	7	3	4	3368	1880	1488
Tatar	3	1	2	9		9
Tibetan	1084	456	628	2850	1274	1576
Tu	941	480	461	4709	2539	2170
Tujia	55,310	31,194	24,116	227,012	123,951	103,061
Uygur	785	537	248	5377	2460	2917
Uzbek	8	6	2	86	45	41
Va	274	44	230	2987	1368	1619
Xibe	71	26	45	200	105	95
Yao	1928	808	1120	10,710	5688	5022
Yi	6344	2427	3917	49,243	26,212	23,031
Yugur	2	1	1	14	7	7
Zhuang	18,998	5263	13,735	72,820	35,324	37,496

Note: Total population includes servicemen (while ethnic breakdowns do not include them) as well as unknown ethnic groups and foreigners with Chinese citizenship

Appendix 3. China's Ethnic Minority Autonomous Areas: General Background

R. Guo, *China Ethnic Statistical Yearbook 2016*,
DOI 10.1007/978-3-319-49199-8

Province, municipality, or autonomous region	Number of regions at prefecture level (unit)	Where, cities at prefecture level	Where, autonomous prefecture	Number of regions at county level (unit)	Where, cities at county level	Where, autonomous counties (Qi)	Total population in minority areas (million persons)	Where, ethnic minority population	Ethnic minority population as percentage to total population in minority areas (%)
National Total	**77**	**31**	**30**	**702**	**68**	**120**	**187.62**	**90.03**	**47.99**
Chongqing				4		4	2.08	1.24	71.05
Gansu	2		2	21	2	7	24.90	5.42	58.99
Guangdong				3		3	3.32	1.67	36.82
Guangxi	14	14		109	7	12	3.33	1.14	37.94
Guizhou	3		3	46	4	11	0.25	0.05	58.85
Hainan				6		6	0.17	0.02	51.02
Hebei				6		6	4.64	2.64	59.77
Heilongjiang				1		1	5.21	4.01	20.82
Hubei	1		1	10	2	2	0.50	0.18	56.90
Hunan	1		1	15	1	7	52.40	19.88	77.04
Inner Mongolia	12	9		101	11	3	1.79	0.92	21.78
Jilin	1		1	11	6	3	2.74	1.95	34.27
Liaoning				8		8	7.60	4.60	50.36

Ningxia	5	5		21	2		17.13	10.08	36.32
Qinghai	6		6	35	2	7	22.50	12.73	65.07
Sichuan	3		3	51	1	4	3.08	2.83	60.63
Tibet	7	1		74	1		3.52	2.08	91.83
Xinjiang	14	2	5	101	22	6	3.67	2.38	62.05
Yunnan	8		8	78	7	29	6.47	2.35	56.57
Zhejiang				1		1	22.33	13.85	11.06

Notes: Ethnic minority autonomous areas refer to the areas of 5 ethnic minority autonomous regions, 30 ethnic minority autonomous prefectures and 120 ethnic minority autonomous counties. Data on the administrative divisions of the ethnic minority autonomous areas, shown below, are tabulated and prepared in accordance with *A Concise Book of the Administrative Divisions of the People's Republic of China* (in Chinese) (edited by the Ministry of Civil Affairs (MCA) of the People's Republic of China and published by SinoMaps Press, Beijing, China, 2012)

Appendix 4. China's Ethnic Minority Autonomous Areas: Principal Statistical Indicators

R. Guo, *China Ethnic Statistical Yearbook 2016*,
DOI 10.1007/978-3-319-49199-8

Item	Aggregate data							Average annual growth rate (%)		
	1990	1995	2000	2005	2010	2011	2012	1991–2012	1996–2012	2001–2012
Population and Employment										
Population (million persons)										
Population at Year-end	153.0	160.4	168.2	173.1	185.3	186.6	187.6	0.9	0.9	0.9
Ethnic Minority Population	68.8	72.3	77.7	82.4	88.1	89.1	90.0	1.2	1.3	1.2
Employment										
Persons Employed in Various Units (million persons)	93.9	94.9	95.9	96.9	97.9	98.9	99.9	−0.3	−0.8	−1.5
Macro Economy										
Gross Regional Product (billion yuan)		490.1	748.6	1570.6	3898.9	4791.6	5408.0		11.8	13.0
Primary Industry		162.9	202.2	330.0	619.8	724.3	814.6		5.7	5.7
Secondary Industry		174.7	283.4	641.9	1880.9	2388.5	2655.0		15.2	17.0
Tertiary Industry		152.6	262.9	598.7	1398.2	1678.8	1938.4		11.6	12.2
Per Capita Gross Regional Product (yuan)		3054.7	4451.4	8991.4	22060.0	27400.8	30862.4		14.6	17.5
Fixed Assets (billion yuan)										
Total Investment in Fixed Assets		144.4	247.7	835.8	2987.6	3832.5	4354.9		22.2	27.0

State-owned Units	25.9	98.3	155.3	376.7	1204.6	1243.7	1466.4	20.1	17.2	20.6
Government Finance (billion yuan)										
Revenue of Local Governments	16.7	24.8	47.6	102.6	325.7	427.6	522.0	16.9	19.6	22.1
Expenditure of Local Governments	30.4	59.5	117.3	305.0	1051.2	1358.9	1604.9	19.7	21.4	24.4
Industry										
Agriculture										
Cultivated Area (million hectares)	17.6	15.1	20.9	20.3	23.8	23.8	23.6	1.3	2.7	1.0
Irrigated Areas (million hectares)	7.6	8.4	9.4	10.3	11.6	11.9	12.4	2.2	2.3	2.4
Gross Output Value of Agriculture, Forestry, Animal Husbandry and Fishery (billion yuan)		253.7	320.0	534.9	1037.4	1212.6	1361.3	18.2	6.3	6.6
Output of Major Farm Products										
Grain Output (million tons)	53.7	58.0	63.8	71.9	83.1	86.9	90.4	2.4	2.6	2.9
Cotton Output (million tons)	0.5	0.9	1.5	1.9	2.5	2.9	3.5	9.6	8.1	7.7
Oil-bearing Crops Output (million tons)	2.1	2.6	3.5	3.7	4.2	4.2	4.5	3.6	3.2	2.1

(continued)

Appendix 4 Continued

Item	Aggregate data							Average annual growth rate (%)		
	1990	1995	2000	2005	2010	2011	2012	1991–2012	1996–2012	2001–2012
Number of Large Domestic Animals (year-end) (million heads)	52.9	56.2	55.7	61.5	60.7	60.2	54.9	0.2	−0.1	−0.1
Goats and Sheep (million heads)	113.6	119.1	130.8	163.9	148.9	146.7	151.6	1.3	1.4	1.2
Hogs (year-end) (million heads)	56.7	72.4	82.0	85.3	81.4	81.0	85.0	1.9	0.9	0.3
Industry										
Output of Major Industrial Products										
Cloth (million m)	740.0	690.0	501.0	350.0	363.3	373.6	217.8	-5.4	−6.6	−6.7
Machine-made Paper and Paperboard (million tons)	0.9	1.9	1.8	2.7	3.9	4.4	4.9	7.8	5.6	8.9
Refined Sugar (million tons)	2.2	2.4	5.0	6.8	9.1	9.4	11.0	7.5	9.4	6.8
Coal (billion tons)	0.0	0.0	0.0	0.0	0.1	0.1	0.1	11.6	13.2	20.4
Crude Oil (million tons)	12.7	16.1	22.9	28.3	30.6	31.9	32.3	4.4	4.2	2.9
Amount of Electric Power Generation (billion kwh)	7.4	11.9	17.1	30.5	67.3	71.3	89.9	12.0	12.7	14.8

Crude Steel (million tons)	3.7	7.0	6.5	18.5	40.0	32.4	40.2	11.5	10.8	16.4
Pig Iron (million tons)	4.2	5.5	7.2	20.9	44.5	48.0	51.4	12.1	14.0	17.7
Cement (million tons)	19.6	43.0	57.0	101.6	216.5	232.4	315.9	13.5	12.5	15.3
Construction										
Number of Employed Persons (million persons)			1.3	1.4	1.9	1.9	2.0			3.4
Gross Output Value of Construction (billion yuan)			75.4	165.6	520.3	639.2	680.0			20.1
Floor Space of Buildings under Construction (million sq.m)			92.3	159.6	350.5	427.5	498.4			15.1
Floor Space of Buildings Completed (million sq.m)			53.3	80.7	154.2	174.8	194.5			11.4
Transportation, Postal and Telecommunication Services										
Length of Railways in Operation (000 km)	13.1	17.0	14.3	16.9	21.2	23.0	23.7			4.3

(continued)

Appendix 4 Continued

Item	Aggregate data							Average annual growth rate (%)		
	1990	1995	2000	2005	2010	2011	2012	1991–2012	1996–2012	2001–2012
Highways (000 km)	293.7	332.1	423.6	589.6	911.9	961.4	1024.0	5.8	6.8	7.6
Business Volume of Postal and Telecommunication Services (billion yuan)	0.9	7.8	29.7	89.2	245.6	119.2	133.2			
Total Length of Postal Routes and Rural Delivery Routes (million km)	0.9	1.1	1.1	1.1	1.3	1.4	1.6	2.8	2.5	3.3
Domestic Trade										
Total Retail Sales of Consumer Goods (billion yuan)	68.2	169.2	257.0	487.4	1168.5	1378.1	1591.4	15.4	14.1	16.4
Foreign Trade										
Total Value of Imports and Exports (billion USD)			8.6	22.2	53.3	69.8	83.2			20.9
Exports			5.0	12.6	33.1	42.6	51.4			21.5
Imports			3.6	9.5	20.2	27.3	31.8			19.9
International Tourism										

Number of International Tourists (million person-times)			2.7	4.7	8.2	8.7	9.6			11.2
Foreign Exchange Earnings from International Tourism (billion USD)			0.8	1.3	3.0	3.6	4.6			16.2
Finance										
Deposits of National Banking System (billion yuan)			790.6	1632.4	4662.2	5467.2	6405.2			19.0
Loans of National Banking System (billion yuan)			654.8	1130.0	3057.9	3729.9	4443.1			17.3
Education, Culture and Public Health										
Education										
Number of Students (million persons)										
Regular Institutions of Higher Education	0.1	0.2	0.3	1.0	1.6	1.7	1.7	12.1	13.8	14.2
Regular Secondary Schools	6.1	6.3	8.7	10.8	10.5	10.4	10.2	2.4	2.9	1.3

(*continued*)

Appendix 4 Continued

Item	Aggregate data							Average annual growth rate (%)		
	1990	1995	2000	2005	2010	2011	2012	1991–2012	1996–2012	2001–2012
Regular Primary Schools	18.5	18.9	18.9	16.7	15.4	14.8	14.8	−1.0	−1.4	−2.0
Full-time Teachers (000 persons)										
Regular Institutions of Higher Education	28.0	37.0	36.4	63.0	94.7	96.9	100.6	6.0	6.1	8.8
Regular Secondary Schools	415.0	414.7	478.9	611.0	674.4	698.8	694.5	2.4	3.1	3.1
Regular Primary Schools	848.0	858.0	899.4	881.0	907.3	893.9	889.4	0.2	0.2	-0.1
Culture										
Publications										
Books Published (million copies)	301.7	422.8	423.1	419.6	431.0	493.0	547.9	2.8	1.5	2.2
Number of Magazines Issued (million copies)	78.7	78.8	83.3	102.8	82.8	110.9	121.2	2.0	2.6	3.2
Number of Newspapers (million copies)	791.2	949.8	1232.8	1695.2	1748.5	1718.3	1870.2	4.0	4.1	3.5
Public Health										

Number of Hospitals and Health Centers (000 ports)	10.6	12.3	12.5	11.8	12.0	12.0	12.3	0.7	0.0	-0.2
Number of Beds of Hospitals and Health Centers (000 beds)	332.0	357.0	361.2	384.5	557.3	601.4	658.7	3.2	3.7	5.1
Social Services										
Beds on Social Welfare Institutions (000 beds)					273.1	298.0	339.2			
Number of Urban Community Services Facilities (unit)					6188.0	9798.0	8829.0			
Number of Persons Receiving Minimum Living Allowance in Urban and Rural Areas (millio persons)					19.1	19.6	20.1			

Notes: Data on the social and economic development in ethnic minority autonomous areas, shown below, are collected from the surveys conducted by areas. A statistical reporting form system on the economic and social development in the ethnic minority autonomous areas has been established jointly by the State Ethnic Affairs Commission (SEAC) and the National Bureau of Statistics (NBS) and implemented by the provincial and local ethnic affairs commissions and statistical bureaus. The reporting form system covers all units under the jurisdiction of the 5 ethnic minority autonomous regions, 30 autonomous prefectures and 120 autonomous counties. In addition, data on the public health are provided by the Ministry of Health (MOH)

Notes on the Text

The ethnic groups and their socioeconomic indicators reported in this book are only based on the geographical scope of mainland China. National-level data in this book do not include those of Hong Kong or Macau. The classification of ethnic groups is based on China's official criteria, which sometimes may not satisfy academia. For example, the Pumi are also called Mongolians or Naxi, depending on where they live; and most of the Yao on Hainan island are now classified as Miao.

Unless stated otherwise, all data reported in this book are as of 2012 and indicators in monetary values are measured at current prices, while their time-series indices are calculated at constant prices. The data on a selected set of social and economic indicators of China's 56 ethnic groups for 2005, 2010, and 2011 can be found in *China's Ethnic Minorities – Social and Economic Indicators* (Routledge, London, 2013), *China's Multicultural Economies – Social and Economic Indicators* (Springer, New York, 2013), and *Multicultural China – A Statistical Yearbook* (Springer, Berlin, 2015), respectively. In addition, the following notes are also of usefulness for those who want to apply the data reported in this book:

R. Guo, *China Ethnic Statistical Yearbook 2016*,
DOI 10.1007/978-3-319-49199-8

1. Data have been adjusted for all those Han majority who changed to ethnic minority (shaoshu minzu) status in the 1980s.
2. Unless states otherwise, all data reported in this book are compiled and estimated based on the regional and local data gathered from a variety of sources. (Details about the estimation methodology can be found in *China's Multicultural Economies – Social and Economic Indicators* (Springer, New York, 2013, pp. 165–8); or *China's Ethnic Minorities – Social and Economic Indicators* (Routledge, London, 2013, pp. 208–10).
3. Data may be overestimated if an ethnic group is mainly located in geographically remote and economically poor areas (since geographically remote areas usually have less attractions to statistical officers who either had little professional ethics or wanted to reduce the costs of data collection).
4. Statistical discrepancies due to rounding are not adjusted in the book.
5. Blank space indicates that the figure is not large enough to be measured with the smallest unit in the table, or data are unknown or are not available.
6. Due to reasons that are beyond our control, estimation errors may exist in the indicators reported in the book.

While the definitions of some of the terms and statistical indicators that have been used in this book are consistent with those that have adopted by various international organizations (including the International Monetary Fund and the World Bank), many others are only defined with Chinese characteristics. The explanations of all the terms shown in the following are mainly based on the official definitions provided by the National Bureau of Statistics of China.[3]

Average Real Wage refers to the average wage of employed persons after removing the effects of the price changes.

Average Wage refers to the average per capita wage in money terms during a certain period of time for employed persons. It shows the general level of wage income of staff and worker during a certain period of time, one major indicator to reflect the wage level.

[3] More details are available in Chinese at http://www.stats.gov.cn/tjsj/zbjs/, accessed on 2016–08–18.

Average Wage Index refers to the ratio of average wage of employed persons the reference period to that at the base period, which reflects the relative increasing or decreasing level of real wage of employed persons at the different period.

Birth Rate (or Crude Birth Rate) refers to the ratio of the number of births to the average population (or mid-period population) during a certain period of time (usually a year), expressed in ‰. Birth rate in the chapter refers to annual birth rate. Number of births refers to live births, i.e. when a baby has breathed or showed any vital phenomena regardless of the length of pregnancy. Annual average population is the average of the number of population at the beginning of the year and that at the end of the year. Sometimes it is substituted by the mid-year population.

Budgetary Fund for Education refers to education funding that is planned to be allocated to various schools and education institutions by central and local financial departments at various levels within the reference year, which is within the State budgetary expenditure, including: appropriated funds for education, for science and research, for capital construction and others.

Business Volume of Post and Telecommunications refers to the total amount of postal and telecommunication services, expressed in value terms, provided by the post and telecommunications departments for society. This indicator reflects the overall results of development of postal and telecommunication services. It can be classified as postal services and telecommunication services. Business volume of post and telecommunications is the sum of each service in kind multiplying with its correspondent unit price (constant price).

Cash Income refers to income received by rural households and their members in the form of cash during the reference period. It is classified, by source of income, into income from wages and salaries, cash income from household operations, income from properties and income from transfers.

Certified Grade Athletes refer to those who are awarded the title of athletes through assessment. The titles rank from high to low as: international level athletes, national level athletes, first grade athletes, second grade athletes and third grade athletes.

Children Dependency Ratio also called children dependency coefficient, refers to the ratio of the children population to the working-age population, expressed in %. It describes the number of children population that every 100 people at working ages will take care of.

Consumer Price Index reflect the trend and degree of changes in prices of consumer goods and services purchased by urban and rural households during a given period. China's nation-wide consumer price indices are obtained by combining the consumer price indices of both urban and rural households. The Indices enable the observation and analysis of the degree of impact of the changes in the prices of retailed goods and services on the actual living expenses of urban and rural residents.

Consumption Expenditure of Urban Households in Cash refers to total cash expenditure of households for consumption in daily life, including expenditure on the eight categories of food; clothing; housing; household appliances; transport and communications; education, cultural and recreational activities and medical care.

Cotton Output refers to cotton production in the whole country including cotton planted in spring and in autumn. Output is measured as the weight of ginned cotton. Ceiba is not included.

Currency refers to currency that is in circulation in the market, including local and foreign currencies.

Death Rate (or Crude Death Rate) refers to the ratio of the number of deaths to the average population (or mid-period population) during a certain period of time (usually a year), expressed in ‰. Death rate refers to annual death rate.

Designs refer to the aesthetics and industrially applicable new designs for the shape, pattern and color of the product, or their combinations. This indicator reflects the appearance design achievements with independent intellectual property.

Disposable Income refers to the actual income at the disposal of members of the households which can be used for final consumption, other non-compulsory expenditure and savings. This equals to total income minus income tax, personal contribution to social security and subsidy for keeping diaries in being a sample household.

Electricity Consumption per Unit of GDP refers to the electricity consumption per unit of Gross Domestic Product (GDP) in the same reference period.

Employed Persons refer to persons aged 16 and over who are engaged in gainful employment and thus receive remuneration payment or earn business income. This indicator reflects the actual utilization of total labor force during a certain period of time and is often used for the research on China's economic situation and national power.

Energy Consumption per Unit of GDP refers to the energy consumption per unit of Gross Domestic Product (GDP) in the same reference period.

Energy Consumption per Unit of Industrial Value-added refers to the energy consumption per unit of industrial value-added in a country or region in the same reference period.

Expenditure of basic pension insurance program refer to payment made on pensions and funeral subsidies to those retired and resigned people covered in pension insurance programs according to related national policies on scope and standard of expenditure.

Final Consumption Expenditure refers to the total expenditure of resident units for purchases of goods and services from both the domestic economic territory and abroad to meet the needs of material, cultural and spiritual life. It does not include the expenditure of non-resident units on consumption in the economic territory of the country. The final consumption expenditure is broken down into household consumption expenditure and government consumption expenditure.

Floating population is a terminology used to describe a group of people who reside in a given population for a certain amount of time and for various reasons, but are not generally considered part of the official census count.

Government Appropriation for Education refers to State budgetary fund for education, taxes and fees collected by governments at all levels that are used for education purpose, education fund for enterprise-run schools, income from school-run enterprises, work-study program and social services that are used for education purpose.

Government Consumption Expenditure refers to the consumption expenditure spent for the provision of public services provided by the government to the whole country and the net expenditure on the goods and services provided by the government to households free of charge or at reduced prices. The former equals to the output value of the government services minus the value of operating income obtained by the government departments. The latter equals to the market value of the goods and services provided by the government free of charge or at reduced prices to the households minus the value received by the government from the households.

Government Expenditure refers to the distribution and use of the funds which the government finance has raised, so as to meet the needs of economic construction and various undertakings. Government expenditure is divided into central government expenditure and local government expenditure according to the different functions of the governments played in economic and social activities.

Government Revenue refers to income for the government finance through participating in the distribution of social products. The government revenue includes the following main items: (1) various tax revenues including domestic value added tax (VAT), domestic consumption tax, VAT and consumption tax from imports, VAT and consumption tax rebate for exports, business tax, corporate income tax, individual income tax, resource tax, city maintenance and construction tax, house property tax, stamp tax, urban land use tax, land appreciation tax, tax on vehicles and boat operation, ship tonnage tax, vehicle purchase tax, tariffs, farm land occupation tax, deed tax, and tobacco tax, etc.; and (2) non-tax revenue, including special program receipts, charge of administrative and institutional units, penalty receipts and others non-tax receipts.

Grain Output refers to the total output in the whole country including grains produced by state farms, collective units, rural households, as well as by farms affiliated to industrial and mining enterprises and other production units. Grain includes rice, wheat, corn, sorghum, millet and other miscellaneous grains as well as tubers and beans. Output of beans refers to dry beans without pods. The output of tubers (sweet potatoes and potatoes, not including taros and cassava) are converted into that of grain at the ratio of 5:1. Tubers supplied as vegetables (such as potatoes) in cities and suburbs are calculated as fresh vegetables and their output is not included in the output of grain. Output of all other grains refers to husked grain.

Gross Dependency Ratio refers to the ratio of non-working-age population to the working-age population, expressed in %. Describing in general the number of non-working-age population that every 100 people at working ages will take care of, this indicator reflects the basic relation between population and economic development from the demographic perspective. The gross dependency ratio is the sum of **Children Dependency Ratio** and **Old Dependency Ratio**.

Gross Domestic Product (GDP) refers to the final products at market prices produced by all resident units in a country during a certain period of time. Gross domestic product is expressed in three different perspectives, namely value, income, and products respectively. GDP in its value perspective refers to the balance of total value of all goods and services produced by all resident units during a certain period of time, minus the total value of input of goods and services of the nature of non-fixed assets; in other words, it is the sum of the value-added of all resident units. GDP from the perspective of income includes the primary income created by all resident units and distributed to resident and non-resident units. GDP from the perspective of products refers to the value of all goods and services for final demand by all resident units plus the net exports of goods and services during a given period of time. In the practice of national accounting, gross domestic product is calculated from three approaches, namely production approach, income approach and expenditure approach, which reflect gross domestic product and its composition from different angles.

Gross Output Value of Agriculture, Forestry, Animal Husbandry and Fishery refers to the total value of products of agriculture, forestry, animal husbandry and fishery, and total value of services in support of agriculture, forestry, animal husbandry and fishery activities. It reflects the total scale and results of agricultural production during a given period. The gross output value is obtained by multiplying the output of each product or by-product by its price, resulting in the output value of each single item. For a small number of products, annual output of which is not available or difficult to get due to the long production (growing) process involved, the output value is estimated through an indirect approach. The sum of output values of all products of agriculture, forestry, animal husbandry and fishery and services in support to those industries is then equal to the gross output value of agriculture.

Hospitals include general hospitals, hospitals specialized in traditional Chinese medicine, hospitals of integrated traditional Chinese and western medicine, nationalities hospitals, specialized hospitals and nursing hospitals.

Households refer to resident individuals or groups of resident individuals who share common living facilities, pool together entire or part of their income and properties for their common disposal, and share their housing, food and other consumer goods and services. All households together make up the sector of households.

Household Consumption Expenditure refers to the total expenditure of resident households on the final consumption of goods and services. In addition to the consumption of goods and services bought by the households directly with money, the household consumption expenditure also includes expenditure on goods and services obtained by the households in other ways, i.e. the so-called imputed consumption expenditure, which includes the following: (a) the goods and services provided to households by employers in the form of payment in kind and transfer in kind; (b) goods and services produced and consumed by the households themselves, in which the services refer to the owner-occupied housing and services offered by paid family employees; (c) financial intermediate services provided by financial institution.

Income from Household Operations refers to income by the rural households as units of production and operation. Operations by rural households are classified according to their economic activities namely agriculture, forestry, animal husbandry, fishery, manufacturing, construction, transportation, post and telecommunications, wholesale, retail and catering, social service, culture, education, health, and other household operations.

Income from Properties refers to the income received as returns by owners of financial assets or tangible non-productive assets by providing capitals or tangible non-productive assets to other institutional units.

Income from Transfers refers to the receipt by rural households and their members of goods, services, capital or rights of assets without giving or repaying accordingly, excluding capital provided to them for the formation of fixed assets. In general, it refers to all income received by rural households through redistribution.

Income from Wages and Salaries refers to income from labor earned by the members of rural households employed by other units or individuals.

Internet Users refer to the number of Chinese citizens aged 6 and over who use the Internet in the past six months.

Inventions refer to new technical proposals to the products or methods or their modifications. This is universal core indicator reflecting the technologies with independent intellectual property.

Investment in Fixed Asset refers to the urban investment in fixed assets under the previous statistical coverage plus project investments by rural enterprises and institutions.

Length of Highways refers to the actual length of highways at the end of reference period. It covers public roads running vehicles among cities, city and rural areas, township (villages), highways passing through streets at small cities and towns, length of bridges and tunnels, width of ferry piers. It does not include the length of streets in cities, dead end highways, the length of streets built for agricultural (forest) production and inside factories (mines). It can only be calculated with the actual mileage having been completed, checked and accepted or put into operation. If two or more highways go the same section of the way, the length of the section is only calculated for once.

Length of Railways in Operation refers to the total length of the trunk line for passenger and freight transportation in full operation or temporary operation.

Licensed Assistant Doctors refer to the medical workers who have obtained the licenses of qualified assistant doctors and are employed in medical treatment, disease prevention or healthcare institutions, excluding the licensed assistant doctors engaged in management job. The classification of licensed assistant doctors is clinician, Chinese medicine, dentist and public health.

Licensed Doctors refer to the medical workers who have obtained the licenses of qualified doctors and are employed in medical treatment, disease prevention or healthcare institutions, excluding the licensed doctors engaged in management job. The licensed doctors are divided into 4 categories: clinician, Chinese medicine physicians, dentist and public health physicians.

Life expectancy is the expected (in the statistical sense) number of years of life remaining at a given age. It is important to note that life expectancy is an average. In countries with high infant mortality rates, life expectancy at birth is highly sensitive to the rate of death in the first few years of life. For example, in a hypothetical stationary population in which half the population dies before the age of five, but everybody else dies at exactly 70 years old, the life expectancy at age zero will be about 37 years.

Medical and Health Care Institutions refer to the units which have been qualified the Certification of Health Care Institution by the administration of public health, or qualified the Certification of Corporate Unit by the civil affairs, administration for industry and commerce, commission office for public sector reform, and engaging in medical care, disease prevention and control, health supervision and inspection, medicine research and on-job training, etc., including: hospitals, health care institutions at grass-root level, specialized public health institutions, and other medical and health care institutions.

Natural Growth Rate of Population refers to the ratio of natural increase in population (number of births minus number of deaths) in a certain period of time (usually a year) to the average population (or mid-period population) of the same period, expressed in ‰.

Net Enrolment Ratio of Primary Schools refers to the proportion of school age children enrolled at schools to the total number of school age children both in and outside schools (including retarded children, but excluding blind, deaf and mute children).

Net Income of Rural Households refers to the total income of rural households from all sources minus all corresponding expenses (including household operation expenses, taxes and fees-depreciation of fixed assets for production, and gifts to rural relatives). Net income is mainly used as input for reinvestment in production and as consumption expenditure of the year, and also used for savings and non-compulsory expenses of various forms. "Per capita net income of farmers" is the level of net income averaged by population, reflecting the average income level of rural population in a given area.

New Rural Cooperative Medical System is proposed by the central government to finance farmers who face high medical costs for severe diseases or injuries. It is a multi-channel fundraising system composed by the government, collectives and individuals. Under this system, each farmer pays 20 yuan to join in the fund while the governments contribute 80 yuan (in 2008, this amount has increased to 120 yuan in 2010,

200 yuan in 2011, and 240 yuan in 2012) for each participant. By the end of 2009, about 833 million rural residents had joined in the system, accounting for more than 90 % of the rural population.

Old Dependency Ratio also called old dependency coefficient, refers to the ratio of the elderly population to the working-age population, expressed in %. It describes the number of the elderly population that every 100 people at working ages will take care of. Old dependency ratio is one of the indicators reflecting the social implication of population aging from the economic perspective.

Output of Oil-bearing Crops refers to the total production of oil-bearing crops of various kinds, including peanuts (dry, in shell), rapeseeds, sesame, sunflower seeds, flax seeds, and other oil-bearing crops. Soybeans, oil-bearing woody plants, and wild oil-bearing crops are not included.

Patent is an abbreviation for the patent right and refers to the exclusive right of ownership by the inventors or designers for the creation or inventions, given from the patent offices after due process of assessment and approval in accordance with the Patent Law of the People's Republic of China. This indicator reflects the achievements in science and technology and in design with independent intellectual property. Patents are granted for three types – "**Inventions**", "**Utility Models**" and "**Designs**".

Price Index for Means of Agricultural Production reflects the trend and degree of changes in the prices of the means of agricultural production during a given period. Compilation of these indices helps to understand the price changes of material input in agricultural production and facilitate the compilation of national accounts. Before 1994, price indices for means of agricultural production were a sub-category in the retail price indices for commodities, and it has been compiled separately since 1994.

Primary Industry refers to agriculture, forestry, animal husbandry and fishery industries.

Private Enterprises refer to enterprises which have been registered at the departments of industrial and commercial administration for which the business operation are situated at a county town (i.e. a town where the county government is located), or at urban areas with administrative hierarchy higher than a county town.

Producer Price Index reflects the trend and degree of changes in producers' prices during a given period. These indices depict the change in the level and structure of producer prices for products of the country and meet the needs of national accounts statistics. The producer price index for a given product is calculated as the geometrical mean of individual indices for all surveyed units which sell such product, and the indices for a product category is obtained as the weighted mean of price indices for all products in the category.

Radio Coverage of Population refers to the percentage of population, which can receive central, provincial, city, prefecture, and county radio programs relayed by wireless, cable, satellite and other technical means, in the surveying area, to national total population.

Registered Unemployed Persons in Urban Areas refer to the persons with non-agricultural household registration at certain working ages (16 years old to retirement age), who are capable of working, unemployed and willing to work, and have been registered at the local employment service agencies to apply for a job.

Registered Unemployment Rate in Urban Areas refers to the ratio of the number of the registered unemployed persons to the sum of the number of persons employed in various units (minus the employed rural labor force, re-employed retirees, and Hong Kong, Macau, Taiwan or foreign employees), laid-off staff and workers in urban units, owners of private enterprises in urban areas, owners of self-employed individuals in urban areas, employees of private enterprises in urban areas, employee of self-employed individuals in urban areas, and the registered unemployed persons in urban areas.

Regular Institutions of Higher Education refer to educational establishments set up according to the government evaluation and approval procedures, recruiting graduates from senior secondary schools as the main target by the national matriculation test. They include full-time universities, colleges, institutions of higher professional education, institutions of higher vocational education, institutions of higher vocational education and others (non-university tertiary, branch schools and undergraduate classes).

Retail Price Index reflects the trend and degree of change in retail prices of commodities during a given period. The change in retail prices of commodities is related to government revenue, the equilibrium of market supply and demand, and the ratio of consumption to accumulation. Therefore, the retail price indices are useful from an oblique perspective for observing and analyzing the changes of the above economic activities.

Revenue of the basic pension insurance program refers to payments made by employers and individuals participating in the pension insurance program in accordance with the basis and proportion stipulated in State regulations, and income from other sources that become source of pension insurance fund, including the premium paid by employers and staff and workers, interest income, subsidies from higher level agencies, income as transfer from subordinate agencies, transferred income, government financial subsidies and other income.

Rural Households refer to usual resident households in rural areas. Usual resident households in rural areas are households residing on a long term basis(for more than one year) in the areas under the administration of township governments (not including county towns), and in the areas under the administration of villages in county towns. Households residing in the current addresses for over one year with their household registration in other places are still considered as resident households of the locality. For households with their household registration in one place but all members of the households having moved away to make a living in another place for over one year, they will not be included in the rural households of the area where they are registered, irrespective of whether they still keep their contracted land.

Rural Population refers to population other than **Urban Population.**

Rural Residents Entitled to Minimum Living Allowances refers to those receiving the minimum living allowances from the local government or community in the rural areas where this allowances system is in place as of the end of the reference period.

Secondary Industry refers to mining and quarrying, manufacturing, production and supply of electricity, water and gas, and construction.

Self-Employed Individuals in Urban Areas refer to persons who hold the certificates of residence in urban areas or have resided in the urban areas for a long time and have been registered at the departments of industrial and commercial administration and approved to be engaged in individual industrial or commercial business, including self-employed persons as well as helpers and hired laborers who work in individual households.

Television Coverage of Population refers to the percentage of population, which can receive central, provincial, city, prefecture, and county television programs relayed by wireless, cable, satellite and other technical means, in the surveying area, to national total population.

Tertiary Industry refers to all other economic activities not included in the primary or secondary industries.

Three Strata of Industry Classification of economic activities into three strata of industry is a common practice in the world, although the grouping varies to some extent from country to country. In China economic activities are categorized into the three strata of primary, secondary and tertiary industries. See more details under the separate entries of "**Primary Industry**", "**Secondary Industry**", and "**Tertiary Industry**"

Total Disposable Income Total income from primary distribution is re-distributed through current transfer, resulting in the total disposable income of various institutional sectors. The sum of total disposable income of all institutional sectors makes up the total national disposable income.

Total Expenditure of Urban Households refers to all actual expenditure of households except expenditure on lending. It includes cash expenditure; property expenditure, transfer expenditure, social insurance expenditure and expenditure on house purchasing or house building.

Total Income of Urban Households refers to the sum of wage, net business income, income from properties, and income from transfers of members of the households. Income from selling of properties and income from borrowing are not included.

Total Population refers to the total number of people alive at a certain point of time within a given area. The annual statistics on total population is taken at midnight of 31 December, not including residents in Taiwan, Hong Kong and Macau and Chinese citizens residing abroad.

Total Wage Bill It is revised according to the "Provision of Composition of Total Wages" (Order No.1 by National Bureau of Statistics on January 1, 1990), total wage bill refers to the total remuneration payment to all employed persons in various units during the reporting period (by quarter or by year), including hourly-paid wages, piece-rate wages, bonuses, allowance and subsidies, overtime wages and wages paid under special circumstances. It equals to the sum of total wages of employed staff and workers, dispatch labors and other employed persons. Total wage bill is pre-tax wages, including the room charges, utility bills, housing funds and social insurance paid or withheld by employee's units. Total wage bill, whether or not included in cost, whether or not paid in money or in kind, shall be included in the calculation of total wage.

Urban Population refers to all people residing in cities and towns. Before 2005 urban population does not include **Floating Population**. Since then, part of the latter is also included in urban population. See more details under the entry "**Usual Resident Population**".

Urban Residents Entitled to Minimum Living Allowances refers to those whose average family income is below a minimum local standard by the end of the reporting period, including both the employed and unemployed, laid off and retired, and those jobless people without stable residence or valid IDs.

Usual Resident Population refers to persons staying at home regularly or for over 6 months during a year and integrated with the household economically and in terms of living. Members of the household staying away from the household for over 6 months but keeping a close economic relation with the household by sending the majority of income to the household are regarded as usual resident of the household. Government staff and workers or retirees living as close members of the household are also considered as usual resident. However, servicemen, students of secondary technical schools or schools of higher education and persons with stable jobs and residence outside the household (excluding those visiting relatives or seeking medical service) are not included as resident population of the household.

Utility Models refer to the practical and new technical proposals on the shape and structure of the product or the combination of both. This indicator reflects the condition of technological results with certain technical content.

Index

R. Guo, *China Ethnic Statistical Yearbook 2016*,
DOI 10.1007/978-3-319-49199-8

The manufacturer's authorised representative in the EU is Springer Nature Customer Service Centre GmbH, Europaplatz 3, 69115 Heidelberg, Germany. If you have any concerns regarding our products, please contact ProductSafety@springernature.com

Printed and bound by CPI Group (UK) Ltd, Croydon, CR0 4YY
30/09/2026
02225567-0005